Formal Verification

Formal Verification
An Essential Toolkit for Modern VLSI Design

Erik Seligman

Tom Schubert

M V Achutha Kiran Kumar

AMSTERDAM • BOSTON • HEIDELBERG • LONDON
NEW YORK • OXFORD • PARIS • SAN DIEGO
SAN FRANCISCO • SINGAPORE • SYDNEY • TOKYO

Morgan Kaufmann is an imprint of Elsevier

Acquiring Editor: Todd Green
Editorial Project Manager: Lindsay Lawrence
Project Manager: Priya Kumaraguruparan
Cover Designer: Alan Studholme

Morgan Kaufmann is an imprint of Elsevier
225 Wyman Street, Waltham, MA 02451, USA

ISBN: 978-0-12-800727-3

British Library Cataloguing-in-Publication Data
A catalogue record for this book is available from the British Library

Library of Congress Cataloging-in-Publication Data
A catalog record for this book is available from the Library of Congress

For information on all Morgan Kaufmann publications
visit our website at http://store.elsevier.com/

Working together
to grow libraries in
developing countries

www.elsevier.com • www.bookaid.org

Printed and bound in the United Kingdom

Contents

Foreword for "Formal Verification: An Essential Toolkit for Modern VLSI Design"

Complex VLSI designs pervade almost every aspect of modern life. We take for granted the existence of cell phones, or antilock braking systems, or web servers, without even being aware of the technology under the hood. As users or customers, we also take it for granted that these devices will function correctly. The impact of an undetected functional failure can range from mild annoyance to major catastrophe, and the potential cost—to individuals, to companies, to society as a whole—can be immense. As just one example, the Pentium® "FDIV" bug in 1994 resulted in Intel Corporation taking a $475M charge against earnings to cover the cost associated with replacement of the defective CPUs.

The danger of an undetected functional failure is compounded by the relentless march of semiconductor process technology—"Moore's Law"—that allows us to put ever more complex designs onto a single piece of silicon. With this complexity come an increasing number of bugs, which need to be found and fixed before the design can be qualified for production use. With shorter design cycles and increased competitive pressure to get products to market faster, verification is now the critical path to production. The authors of the 2011 International Technology Roadmap for Semiconductors described verification as "a bottleneck that has now reached crisis proportions."

The traditional "dynamic testing" approach to design verification has been to:

- Create a verification wrapper or "testbench" around all or part of the design
- Write focused tests, or generate directed random tests, in order to stimulate the design
- Run these tests on an executable software model of the design (typically written at the Register Transfer Level, or RTL for short)
- Debug any resulting failures, fix the offending component (either the RTL, the testbench, or the test itself), and re-run tests until the design is "clean"

However, this approach has a number of drawbacks:

- Testbench development can be a lengthy process—typically of the order of months for complex areas of the design
- Testbench development is an error-prone activity, often creating a number of bugs in the testbench equal to or greater than the number that exist in the actual RTL

- Test execution is an expensive business—Intel dedicates tens of thousands of high-performance computer servers to this problem running around the clock, along with dedicated emulation hardware and FPGA-based solutions
- Tests themselves may contain errors that either mask problems in the RTL (false positives) or wrongly indicate errors that do not in fact exist (false negatives)
- Debug of failing tests is a major effort drain—often the largest single component of validation effort—in part because the failure is often detected only long after the point at which it occurred
- It is in general hard to tell how much of the design has been exercised ("covered") by any given set of tests, so even if all tests are passing it still isn't clear that the design is really clean
- Bug detection via dynamic testing is an inherently sequential process, often referred to as "peeling the onion," since bugs can and do hide behind other bugs
- Some bugs—like the Pentium® FDIV bug mentioned earlier—are data-dependent, or involve such a complex set of microarchitectural conditions that it is highly unlikely that they will be hit by random testing on an RTL model

A different approach, formal verification (FV), has gained acceptance in recent years as a shorter-time, lower-effort, and more comprehensive alternative to dynamic testing. The purpose of this book is to explain what FV is, why it offers at least a partial solution to the limitations of dynamic testing, and how, when, and where it should be applied.

FV is a powerful technique that enables a design or validation engineer to directly analyze and mathematically explore the quality or other aspects of an RTL design, providing 100% coverage of large subsets of the design space without needing to create a simulation testbench or test vectors. Its usage and development have been growing at Intel over the last two decades, and it is now increasingly considered a mainstream technique for both design and validation.

The authors of this book start by describing their goal: helping VLSI designers and validators who focus on RTL to do their jobs more effectively and efficiently by leveraging FV techniques. This approach is sometimes referred to at Intel as the democratization of FV, or "FV for All," since the intent is to expand the use of FV beyond the realm of FV experts and enable much wider use of FV tools and techniques. They briefly describe the history of FV: how early artificial intelligence concepts led to formal verification; theoretical objections to formal verification and why they are not true blocking issues; and general techniques for abstracting problems to make them more tractable for formal verification.

Chapter 2 describes basic FV algorithms in enough detail to convince the reader that FV isn't some form of black magic—these techniques really do gain full coverage without requiring exhaustive (and computationally infeasible) simulation cycles. In particular, the Boolean satisfiability (SAT) problem is explained, along with a description of the model-checking algorithms and tools that allow it to be solved for many classes of problem.

Chapter 3 provides an introduction to System Verilog Assertions (SVAs): what they are (and the different types of SVAs such as simple Boolean conditions, temporal assertions, etc.) and how they can be combined into sequences and properties. Chapter 4 builds on this by introducing the concept of Formal Property Verification (FPV): what it is; how it compares with dynamic simulation; and usage models such as design exploration, bug hunting, and bounded- and full-proofs.

The heart of the book lies in Chapters 5 and 6, which explain how to make effective use of FPV for Design Exercise and Verification, respectively. The authors' extensive experience with the application of FPV to real-world problems illuminates almost every page of these two chapters with examples gleaned from current and past Intel development projects, along with many helpful hints that will enable the novice user to make effective use of FPV tools.

Chapter 7 switches gears to describe how FPV can be used to create "Apps" for different design domains such as post-silicon bug reproduction, SoC connectivity checking, standard (non-project-specific) protocol verification, unreachable coverage elimination, and control register access policies. These apps enable design and validation engineers who do not have an FV background to quickly apply formal verification methods to the targeted domains, rather than relying on expensive and time-consuming dynamic simulation.

Chapter 8 discusses Formal Equivalence Verification (FEV), which is one of the most mature FV techniques and one that has been deployed at Intel for many years to ensure that RTL matches schematics, and hence that validation results from RTL simulation or formal verification will be applicable to the functional correctness of actual silicon.

Chapter 9—"FV's Greatest Bloopers: False Positives in Formal Verification" is worth the price of the book all by itself. It discusses some of the limitations of formal methods, in particular, the so-called "vacuity" issue, which is an assumption or set of assumptions that rules out legal data and hence leads to false positives (the absence of counter-examples). The examples given in this chapter, and the tips for avoiding these kinds of real-world problems, are worth their weight in gold!

With all of the benefits that FV can provide, the astute reader may be wondering why the technique is not already used more widely as an integral part of the VLSI design process. The answer is that design complexity, and the capacity needed to handle it, can overwhelm even the best FV tools. Chapter 10 addresses this critical issue, first describing the general concepts of complexity and NP-completeness, and then identifying complexity reduction techniques such as black boxing, case splitting, and property simplification that can be used to make FV a tractable solution. Here again, the authors' experience with complex real-world designs enables them to provide practical advice and solutions to what can appear to be daunting problems.

Chapter 11 wraps things up by describing how the reader can introduce the techniques described in this book into his or her organization, and effectively deploy them to increase design and validation productivity. Once again, the emphasis is on the practical: solving real-life problems, using small experiments to demonstrate the power of FPV techniques, getting measurable results and data that help to convince skeptics.

This book is a valuable addition to the library of both experienced and novice users of formal tools and methods. It has my highest recommendation.

Robert Bentley
Former Director,
Formal Verification Center of Expertise, Intel

Acknowledgments

The contents of this book were inspired by the collective efforts of hundreds of our colleagues, at Intel and in the industry beyond; too numerous to name here. But we must thank all the researchers, mathematicians, designers, and validation engineers, whose hard work over many decades has brought us to a technological state where books like this one, and the methods we describe, are accessible and useful for a general engineering audience.

We would also like to individually thank our colleagues who reviewed and sent notes on various draft sections of this book, making major contributions to the quality of the final version. These include: Dan Benua, Jesse Bingham, Claudia Blank, Shalom Bresticker, Ben Cohen, Craig Deaton, Jim Falkenstrom, Harry Foster, Ziyad Hanna, David Hoenig, Robert Jones, Chris Komar, Joe Leslie-Hurd, Mayank Singhal, Brandon Smith, Noppanunt Utamaphethai, Gordon Vreugdenhil, and Ping Yeung.

Finally, we would like to thank our families, whose patience and support made this book possible.

Formal verification: from dreams to reality

It seems to me now that mathematics is capable of an artistic excellence as great as that of any music, perhaps greater; not because the pleasure it gives (although very pure) is comparable, either in intensity or in the number of people who feel it, to that of music, but because it gives in absolute perfection that combination, characteristic of great art, of godlike freedom, with the sense of inevitable destiny; because, in fact, it constructs an ideal world where everything is perfect and yet true.
—Bertrand Russell

Are you an engineer working on designing complex modern chips or System On Chips (SOCs) at the Register Transfer Level (RTL)? Have you ever been in one of the following frustrating situations?

- Your RTL designs suffered a major (and expensive) bug escape due to insufficient coverage of corner cases during simulation testing.
- You created a new RTL module and want to see its real flows in simulation, but realize this will take another few weeks of testbench development work.
- You tweaked a piece of RTL to aid synthesis or timing and need to spend weeks simulating to make sure you did not actually change its functionality.
- You are in the late stages of validating a design, and the continuing stream of new bugs makes it clear that your randomized simulations are just not providing proper coverage.
- You modified the control register specification for your design and need to spend lots of time simulating to make sure your changes to the RTL correctly implement these registers.

If so, congratulations: you have picked up the right book! Each of these situations can be addressed using formal verification (FV) to significantly increase both your overall productivity and your confidence in your results. You will achieve this by using formal mathematical tools to create orders-of-magnitude increases in efficiency and productivity, as well as introducing mathematical certainty into areas previously dependent on informal testing.

WHAT IS FV?

Let's start with a simple definition:

- FV is the use of tools that mathematically analyze the space of possible behaviors of a design, rather than computing results for particular values.

What does this mean? Essentially, an FV tool will look at the full space of possible simulations, rather than trying specific values. It is not actually running all possible simulations, of course, but it will use clever mathematical techniques to consider all their possible behaviors. Figure 1.1 illustrates the difference between simulation and FV: simulation looks at individual points in the space of possible tests, while FV covers that whole space at once.

From this simple definition, you can probably already sense the amazing power we can gain from using this technique. In many areas, using this powerful method is no longer viewed as optional. You probably heard of the famous Pentium FDIV bug from the early 1990s, where certain rare cases were discovered in which Intel microprocessors could generate incorrect division results. This was a case where simulation-based verification simply failed to "throw the dart" at the right random test cases that would have revealed the issue before the product was on the market. Intel took a USD $475 million charge that year (about USD $755 million in 2014 dollars) to replace the processors; when you account for Intel's growth since then, a similar recall today would have a cost in the billions. Thus, in mission-critical areas, FV is seen as essential for preventing dangerous bug escapes.

FV, however, is no longer just about finding rare bugs. As we will see when we explore the various techniques that are now available, FV should really be thought of as a general-purpose toolkit for interacting with, verifying, and

FIGURE 1.1

Coverage of your design space by simulation and FV. Simulation is like throwing darts at a target, while FV covers your whole target with a paint roller.

understanding our designs. From the start of early development up through the post-silicon debug process, leveraging formal methods appropriately at every design phase can provide increased throughput, increase design confidence, and reduce time to market.

WHY THIS BOOK?

Our goal is to provide useful tools for VLSI design and validation engineers. In the past, there have been numerous publications on FV from an academic standpoint, such as [Mcm93] and [Kro99]. However, these books have generally focused on theoretical foundations, the kind of things you would need to know to implement an advanced FV tool, rather than practical advice for the engineer who wants to *apply* such tools to solve real problems. In some ways, this is understandable, since until sometime during the past decade, FV was very difficult to use, and largely in the domain of researchers who specialized in the area.

On the other hand, in recent years, FV techniques have reached a level of maturity that few believed possible when they were first introduced. These techniques are easily usable by any engineer familiar with RTL design concepts and regularly used at all major companies doing VLSI design. We have used them in a variety of areas on numerous major projects at Intel, and have achieved a solid track record of valuable results: increasing productivity, identifying tricky corner-case bugs, and reducing time to market.

We still see, however, a large number of engineers who are somewhat afraid to tread into the waters of FV. Because formal methods do involve looking at your design in a fundamentally different way from simulation, mathematically examining the space of possible computations instead of trying out individual values, they do require a change of mindset that can be tricky at first. There is also the issue that many engineers still vaguely remember hearing that FV is something that those with PhDs do and are afraid to get started if they don't have that level of qualification.

To those who are afraid to get started with FV, we have a clear message: Dive in! Two of the three authors of this book (Erik and Kiran) have no PhD, but they have successfully done FV on many different projects. The third (Tom) has managed a large and influential FV team whose members came in with a variety of qualifications and experience. Based on these experiences, we believe that FV has reached a level of maturity where an intelligent engineer without specialized training should consider it both highly usable and a regular part of their design and validation toolkit.

We also are focusing on RTL designs. While there are numerous levels of abstraction used in the design process, and constant claims that the industry is moving away from RTL to more abstract methods, we still see the majority of logic design activity occurring at the level of RTL. This is also where the

Electronic Design Automation (EDA) industry currently delivers the most mature tools, due to the inherent compatibility of RTL with Boolean expression and logical analysis and the well-understood relationship between RTL designs and implemented circuits. For a practicing engineer looking to incorporate FV methods for the first time, we consider using mature industry tools on RTL models the best way to start.

Thus, our focus on this book is on practical RTL-related FV techniques that can be used by real engineers using off-the-shelf EDA tools. If you read about some technique in this book, you should be able to go straight to your desk and try it out afterwards.

A MOTIVATING ANECDOTE

Many years ago, one of the authors of this book (Erik) was working in a small team in Intel's Circuit Research Lab, designing and validating test chips to demonstrate new circuit techniques. One day a colleague stopped by his desk, holding a schematic diagram similar to Figure 1.2.

The actual case had many more inputs and outputs, but this should give you the general flavor. Along with this schematic, he also had a specification table, similar to the one in Figure 1.3.

Due to the late arrival of the correct specification table and critical timing requirements in that area, the designer had decided to hand-implement an optimized schematic, a sea of gates that he believed was equivalent to the specified truth table. He had inserted an RTL view of the new version (in other words, a conversion of the schematic into a set of gates in our RTL language) into our full-chip model and verified that our simulation test suite did not generate any failures, but was nervous that our regression would only cover a small subset of the possible behaviors. This was a valid concern: even with this reduced example, you can see that it is very easy for a human

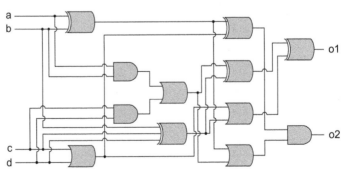

FIGURE 1.2

Example schematic implementing some complex logic.

a	b	c	d	o1	o2
0	0	0	0	0	0
0	0	0	1	0	1
0	0	1	0	0	1
0	0	1	1	0	0
0	1	0	0	0	1
0	1	0	1	1	0
0	1	1	0	1	0
0	1	1	1	1	0
1	0	0	0	0	1
1	0	0	1	0	0
1	0	1	0	0	0
1	0	1	1	0	0
1	1	0	0	1	0
1	1	0	1	1	0
1	1	1	0	0	0
1	1	1	1	1	0

FIGURE 1.3

Specification for Table 3 schematic.

to make a mistake that impacts only a small subset of the possible test cases. Take a close look at the schematic and the table. Can you spot the one case in the Figure 1.3 table that does not logically match the schematic in Figure 1.2? (It is the 1101 entry.)

Due to this risk, the colleague asked Erik if he could set up some kind of standalone validation environment for this recoded block that would quickly simulate all the possible input cases. However, remember that the real example had many more inputs than this reduced version, and with n inputs, it takes 2^n simulation cycles to test all possibilities, assuming the model contains no internal nodes that preserve state. Erik calculated that such a simulation for this particular model would take several weeks based on the number of inputs and the simulation speed of the tools he had at the time—and he only had a few days to verify the fix. However, Erik had recently taken a basic class in FV and decided to try to use this method to tackle the problem. It was fairly easy to set up this test case to run in a formal equivalence verification (FEV) tool, comparing a reference model that directly implemented the table against the rewritten sea of gates. The reference model was just a direct implementation of the specification table in an RTL language. It was actually in an old language called iHDL, but it was similar in concept to the following SystemVerilog fragment:

```
case ({a,b,c,d})
  4'b0000: {o1_next,o2_next} = 2'b00;
  4'b0001: {o1_next,o2_next} = 2'b01;
  4'b0010: {o1_next,o2_next} = 2'b01;
  4'b0011: {o1_next,o2_next} = 2'b00;
  4'b0100: {o1_next,o2_next} = 2'b01;
  4'b0101: {o1_next,o2_next} = 2'b10;
```

```
    4'b0110: {o1_next,o2_next} = 2'b10;
    4'b0111: {o1_next,o2_next} = 2'b10;
    4'b1000: {o1_next,o2_next} = 2'b01;
    4'b1001: {o1_next,o2_next} = 2'b00;
    4'b1010: {o1_next,o2_next} = 2'b00;
    4'b1011: {o1_next,o2_next} = 2'b00;
    4'b1100: {o1_next,o2_next} = 2'b10;
    4'b1101: {o1_next,o2_next} = 2'b10;
    4'b1110: {o1_next,o2_next} = 2'b00;
    4'b1111: {o1_next,o2_next} = 2'b10;
  endcase
```

Erik's colleague was pleasantly surprised when just a couple of hours after presenting the problem, he received an email stating that validation was complete. Using an FEV tool, Erik had determined that one particular combination of inputs got an incorrect result, and in all other cases, the redrawn circuit was precisely equivalent to the specification table. Luckily, further analysis determined that the one mismatch case was actually a don't-care condition for this particular design, where they could tolerate either a 0 or 1, and thus he had solidly proven that the rewrite was safe.

After this, Erik was sold on the concept of FV. Why was he spending so much time setting up fancy mechanisms to drive particular examples through his models in simulation, when there was technology available to definitively prove correctness of RTL designs? Erik began watching Intel's internal job boards for positions that emphasized this new technology and soon shifted his career in a direction specializing in FV.

FV: THE NEXT LEVEL OF DEPTH

There are several ways to view formal verification in terms of the kinds of basic capabilities it provides, as well as numerous specific techniques to insert FV methods into design flows. We first look at the general motivations and use cases for FV, and then talk more specifically about where it fits into practical design and validation flows.

OVERALL ADVANTAGES OF FV

Even before we discuss specific applications or usage models, you can probably see that analyzing the mathematical space of possible RTL behaviors has many advantages over traditional simulation, emulation, or other validation flows. Among the general advantages of FV methods are:

- *Solving the Right Problem*: While this may be too philosophical for practically oriented engineers, how many times have you asked yourself: how *should* we be verifying correctness of our designs? Many would argue that the ideal way is to mathematically prove they meet their specification. Our tolerance of weaker tools like simulation and emulation has been an unfortunate consequence of technological limitations, and with these limitations now lessening, we should be transitioning out of these older methods wherever possible.

- *Complete coverage*: If we define "coverage" as the proportion of possible design behaviors analyzed, FV inherently provides complete coverage. We saw a great example of this in our motivating anecdote above. Perfect FV is not quite possible on all designs—later we will discuss some limitations due to capacity and constraints—but FV methods still offer complete coverage of some subset of the behavior space, equivalent to running an exponential number of simulation tests.

- *Minimal Examples*: Most FV engines inherently are able to generate minimal examples of desired behaviors. A rare behavior may be possible with 10 cycles after reset, but in a typical random simulation environment, it would show up embedded in a multi-thousand-cycle random run. An FV tool will usually generate the minimal 10-cycle example, making it much easier to understand and debug the rare behavior.

- *Corner Cases*: With FV, any behavior not specifically ruled out is allowed, which means FV tools are very likely to uncover interesting corner cases that would not have been thought of by the user, such as the rare FDIV error that cost Intel so much money. Contrast this with simulation, where the user needs to specify what kinds of input patterns are allowed, often resulting in implicit limitations of which they may not be fully aware.

- *State-Driven and Output-Driven Analysis*: Because FV allows you to constrain the behaviors of your logic at any point in the design, including an internal state or output, it enables us to reason about the behaviors of a design that can or cannot lead to particular states or outputs of interest. This is another major contrast with simulation and emulation, which require actively driven inputs to reach any design state.

- *Understanding Infinite Behaviors*: With FV, the power of mathematical reasoning allows us to ask and answer questions about model behavior over unbounded time periods. For example, we can ask questions about whether a model can be stuck forever without reaching a desired state, or whether it is guaranteed to eventually perform some behavior that cannot be guaranteed in a finite time limit. These questions cannot be effectively addressed by technologies like simulation.

These benefits will become more concrete as we discuss them in terms of specific FV methods in later chapters.

GENERAL USAGE MODELS FOR FV

Based on the overall advantages described above, there are several general ways in which FV is used in real design and validation flows. It can be used to achieve

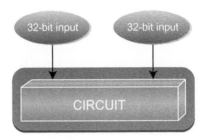

FIGURE 1.4

Small design that is a challenge to fully verify.

complete coverage, ensuring that all possible cases are examined, to confidently prevent issues like the Pentium FDIV error. It can be used for bug hunting, to provide solid coverage for some particular risky area of a design, in cases where full FV is not feasible. It can also be used for design exploration, using the power of mathematical analysis as an aid to better understand RTL behavior.

FV FOR COMPLETE COVERAGE

To further understand the inherent power in FV methods, let's take a moment to consider a simple design verification problem: an adder that has two 32-bit inputs, as illustrated in Figure 1.4.

To fully verify all possible inputs to this design, we would need to simulate a total of 2^{64} possible combinations. If you have a super-fast simulator that can simulate 2^{20} cycles per second (a much faster estimate than is realistic for most current simulators), this means it will take you 2^{44} seconds, or over half a million years to check all possible values. Most likely, your manager has not allocated this much time for your current project. And this does not account for testing sequential behaviors over multiple cycles, which you will probably need for any realistic design. Thus, we can see that something more powerful than simulation is needed in cases where we want truly comprehensive design coverage.

TIP 1.1

When you want to get complete coverage of design behaviors, consider using FV as your primary validation method.

FV for Bug Hunting

As we will see when we describe the methods in more detail, full FV of a design will not always be possible. There may be parts composed of analog logic or other design methods not compatible with formal analysis. There also are complexity limitations that may make complete FV infeasible due to the style or size of the logic. In these cases, simulation cannot be completely replaced.

However, for the subset of a design where FV is effective, this method will provide exponentially more coverage than could be gained from simulation alone. Thus, as a supplement to simulation, FV can still be valuable as a method to find potential bugs that might otherwise have been missed.

TIP 1.2

When you have a design with nontrivial logic and are worried that you will not be able to get sufficient coverage with simulation tests, think about FV as a supplement to simulation.

FV for Exploring Designs

Another major usage of FV is as a tool for exploring RTL design behaviors. FV tools are able to analyze the potential simulation space and figure out a way to produce particular behaviors, based on specifications of the state or output you would like to see. This can be seen as a form of reverse engineering: you do not need to know what design activity (if any) can produce a given state that you request, but the FV tool will figure this out for you. For example, you can provide a query like "Is there any set of inputs that will give a value of 32'ffffffff from my adder?", and FV can find out if there is some theoretically possible sequence of inputs that will get you there.

Contrast this with simulation, where to answer a question based on a desired state or output, you would need to somehow specify what inputs are needed to produce the desired situation, or run lots and lots of random simulation and hope to get lucky. In this simple example, directly figuring out the needed inputs is probably within the domain of your math skills, but there are many common types of designs where inputs are passed in as smaller or encoded segments during multiple cycles, and it might not be feasible to figure out an exact sequence of simulation inputs that will get you the result you want. Using a FV tool frees you from this burden, because it will examine the space of possible simulations and identify one that will get you the desired result or prove it impossible. In other words, when designing tests with FV, you can specify the destination rather than the journey.

TIP 1.3

When you have a design where you can easily specify interesting states or outputs, but it is difficult or time-consuming to specify the sequence of inputs needed to get there, think about using FV.

FV in Real Design Flows

Based on the approaches above, there are a number of specific techniques that have been developed, using modern EDA tools, to leverage FV throughout the

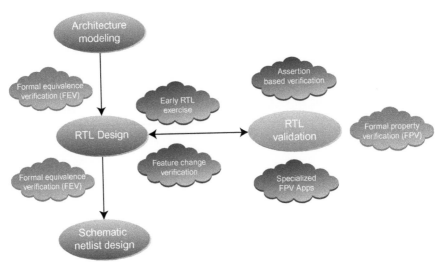

FIGURE 1.5

FV methods emphasized in this book and how they relate to a typical VLSI design flow.

SOC design flow. In this section, we briefly review the major methods that we will discuss in the remainder of this book. Figure 1.5 illustrates the major stages of a VLSI design flow that we are emphasizing in this book, and where the FV methods we describe fit in.

- *Assertion-Based Verification (ABV).* This is the use of assertions, usually expressed in a language like SystemVerilog Assertions (SVA), to describe properties that must be true of RTL. In some cases, properties can fully describe the specification of a design. Using ABV does not in itself guarantee you will be doing true FV, since assertions can also be checked in simulation, and in fact such use accounts for the majority of ABV in the industry today. However, ABV is a key building block that enables FV.
- *Formal Property Verification (FPV).* This refers to the use of formal tools to prove assertions. FPV is a very general technique and can be further subdivided into numerous additional techniques:
  - *Early Design Exercise FPV.* This refers to using FPV's ability to analyze RTL at early stages, in order to help gain insights into initial functionality and find early bugs.
  - *Full Proof FPV.* This is the classic use of FPV to replace simulation and verify that an RTL model correctly implements its specification, described typically as a set of assertions.
  - *Bug Hunting FPV.* This refers to the use of FPV to supplement simulation, in cases where it is not possible to exhaustively verify a design. It can still be a very powerful technique, finding rare corner-case bugs and gaining theoretical coverage exponentially greater than simulation.

- *Unreachable Coverage Elimination.* If your primary validation method is simulation, there will often be some point in the project when a few targeted cover states or lines of code have not been reached, and the validation team is struggling to figure out if they are testable or not. FPV can be used to identify reachable and unreachable states and regions of a design.
- *Specialized FPV Apps.* This refers to FPV as applied to particular problems, such as verifying adherence to a known protocol, ensuring correct SOC connectivity, ensuring correct control register implementation, and finding post-silicon bugs. In each of these cases, attention to the characteristics of the particular problem can improve the productivity of the FPV flow involved.

- *Formal Equivalence Verification* (FEV). This refers to using formal techniques to compare two models and determine if they are equivalent. The models might each be high-level models, RTL, or schematics, or this might involve the comparison between two of these levels of abstraction.
  - *Schematic FV.* This refers to the use of FEV to check that a schematic netlist, resulting from synthesis or hand-drawn at transistor level, properly implements its RTL. This was the first type of FEV to become commercially viable, back in the 1990s, and was a critical enabler for the rise of powerful synthesis tools. Now nearly every company uses this technique, even if they do not do much FV in general.
  - *Feature Change Verification.* With the rising reuse of existing RTL models in SOC design, there are many cases where a piece of RTL is expected to continue to work for currently defined functionality, but has the code modified or changed for new use cases. There are also cases of nonfunctional changes, where we expect functionality to remain exactly the same while the model is changed to fix timing or other issues. FEV can be used to compare the two pieces of RTL, with any new functionality shut off, and make sure the previously existing usage modes will continue to work.
  - *High-Level Model Equivalence Verification.* This refers to the comparison of a high-level model, such as a System C model of the general functionality of a design, to an RTL model. This kind of comparison involves many challenges, since high-level models can be much more abstract than RTL. This is a new and emerging technology at the time of this writing, but it is advancing fast enough that we will include some discussion of this topic in our FEV chapter.

FV METHODS NOT DISCUSSED IN THIS BOOK

There are many other interesting and powerful FV methods available that are seen as new and experimental, or are primarily implemented by academic techniques and have not reached the point where they are well-supported by commercial tools. We are not trying to discourage use of tools in any of these categories—in fact, some have been extensively used at Intel with great success (see [Kai10]). But, due to their newness, requirements for specialized software, or lack of commercial EDA support, they will not be emphasized in this book.

- *Assertion Synthesis.* This refers to the concept of automatically creating assertions rather than requiring users to write them. The assertions may be derived from the RTL itself, from simulation runs, or a combination. This area has just emerged in the past few years, and there is still a lot of debate about its overall value and best usage models, which is why we have chosen to exclude it from this book.
  - *Smart Linting.* This is the simplest type of assertion synthesis, trying to create RTL-derived properties at compile time, and then using lightweight FPV to immediately verify them. For example, a smart linting tool might try to prove that all array accesses are within the declared bounds. Technically, we could discuss this in our FPV section, since it is offered in a push-button fashion by several commercial tools, but we are omitting this method since we have not seen it demonstrate noticeable ROI on our projects.
  - *Structural Assertion Synthesis.* This is a slightly more complex form of smart linting, where assertions are generated for conditions that cannot be formally proven at compile time. They may require additional user constraints or more advanced FPV techniques to correctly prove, or be aimed at, simulation-time checking.
  - *Behavioral Assertion Synthesis.* This method uses simulation traces from real-life simulation tests, presumably written by validators who knew what realistic behaviors of the model to exercise, to derive assertions. Often these can be useful for future verification planning, both FV and simulation, or to point out coverage holes in a project's test suite.
- *Symbolic Simulation.* Symbolic simulation augments the basic concepts of simulation with the ability to simulate variables as well as 0/1 values and to derive Boolean expressions of the results of circuit execution. In some ways, it can be considered another technique for implementing FPV. An advanced form of this method called *symbolic trajectory evaluation* (STE) is used heavily at Intel to verify complex datapath operations, such as floating point mathematics. Unfortunately, STE capability is not provided by any major commercial EDA tool at this time; Intel's usage is all based on internally developed nonpublic tools. There are academic STE tools that can be downloaded, but these are difficult to use in an industrial setting. Thus, describing it in this book would probably be of little use to a practicing engineer not at Intel.
- *High-Level Modeling and Verification.* This is the idea of modeling in some language more abstract than RTL, such as System C, TLA, Murphi, or PROMELA, and then using model-checking or theorem-proving tools to

verify these models. Once again, these are powerful techniques that have been used successfully at Intel, based on experts applying academic or custom-designed tools, but these also lack good commercial EDA support.

- *Software FV.* Being able to formally verify software has been a goal of researchers for a long time, but due to the popularity of high-level and abstract techniques in software engineering, good commercial tools in this area have proven to be an elusive goal. This remains a promising area for growth in FV technology, but due to our focus on hardware design, this is largely beyond the scope of the authors' expertise.

The list above is not exhaustive; formal verification is still an active research area in academia, and interesting new uses of FV continue to be hypothesized and pioneered. Again, however, this book will emphasize practical applications that you can use today, so we will not spend much time on new or speculative applications.

THE EMERGENCE OF PRACTICAL FV

For many years, the formal aspects of modern mathematics, in which new theorems are deduced in a well-defined manner from existing theorems and axioms, have naturally led mathematicians and scientists to speculate on automating portions of their discipline. Since mathematics is ideally completely formal, why shouldn't some kind of machine be able to carry out automated reasoning, deriving new and interesting theorems without human intervention? In a sense, theoreticians have been dreaming of this kind of automation for over 300 years, starting with Gottfried Leibniz's seventeenth-century speculation about a *universal characteristic*. The development of modern computer systems in the twentieth century brought these dreams into the practical realm.

EARLY AUTOMATED REASONING

The first significant automated reasoning computer program was the 1956 Logic Theorist by Alan Newell, Herbert Simon, and J. C. Shaw. It attempted to automatically derive foundational mathematical theorems from basic axioms, and in some cases generated proofs that were judged more elegant than existing manually written proofs by leading mathematicians. Newell, Simon, and Shaw's work inspired a generation of researchers in artificial intelligence and automated reasoning, with ideas and approaches too numerous to discuss here. Initially there were optimistic predictions that Logic Theorist was the beginning of the inevitable rise of fully general, all-purpose artificial intelligence, and soon each of us would have a robot friend at their desk to help solve any difficult logic problems. But gradually researchers began to realize that, at least in the short term, it would be much better to focus on domain-specific systems than to aim for fully general automated reasoning.

APPLICATIONS TO COMPUTER SCIENCE

Academic researchers began discussing automating the solutions to particular computer science problems in the 1960s, beginning with seminal work by R. W. Floyd and C. A. R. Hoare on verifying "partial correctness" and "total correctness," basic types of properties on computer programs. This sparked significant academic interest and follow-up research throughout the 1970s, but unfortunately these techniques were largely seen as not yet scaling enough to support any kind of practical usage in industry. In the 1980s, this work led to the development of *model checking,* the basic technology upon which the techniques in this book are built. The basic idea was that, given a finite state machine and a temporal logic specification, we can use efficient algorithms or heuristics to establish that the machine conforms to the specification. Unlike earlier *theorem proving* approaches, which required users to guide automated reasoning step by step through a proof, model checking was a much more automated technique, where the system would come up with either proofs or counterexamples on its own once the model and constraints were supplied.

Initially this method was promising, but not practical in industry due to the state explosion problem: as we saw in the example in Figure 1.4, even a small number of inputs in a system quickly blow up into an exponential number of combinations. For a while, counts of the number of states in a verified system became an important measure of research quality in this area, as model-checking software teetered just on the verge of practical usefulness. When one of the authors (Erik) was in graduate school at Carnegie Mellon University in the early 1990s, Ed Clarke, one of the foundational researchers in model checking, became infamous among the local graduate students for mystifying pronouncements like "We verified 10^{50} states today!" Students not specialized in this area began referring to him as "the guy with the states." But researchers continued to improve the available algorithms and heuristics throughout the 1980s.

MODEL CHECKING BECOMES PRACTICAL

In the early 1990s, these tools finally began to reach the point where they could be utilized by real companies developing microprocessors, due to advances such as the use of efficient data representation called *binary decision diagrams* (BDDs). Real successes in model checking began to be reported, such as a case when Clarke's student Ken McMillan used model checking with BDDs to find a subtle bug in the "well validated" IEEE Futurebus + standard.

When the Intel FDIV bug became a major public issue in 1994, processor design companies began looking closely at opportunities to use the newly respectable method of FV to improve their validation processes. At first, they needed to hire researchers to develop in-house tools, as there were no real FV options available in the EDA market. Over the next couple of decades, various startups began to emerge, selling different types of formal technology that became more and more usable and efficient in practice.

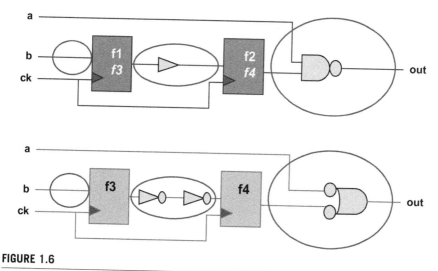

FIGURE 1.6

Breaking up a model into key points at latch/flop boundaries for easy FEV.

The first type of FV to reach commercial viability was the use of FEV for schematic FV, verifying that schematic netlists matched their RTL models. This was a more tractable problem than general FV, due to the convention of making schematics *state matching* with respect to RTL models: for every latch or flip-flop in the RTL, there was a corresponding one in the schematics. Thus, verification could break up the models into small, manageable chunks, the logic between each single pair of state elements, or "key points" (see Figure 1.6).

Gradually, practical FPV tools emerged. These tools attack more general problems, checking that RTL models match a specification, which may not necessarily be state matching, and thus require complex temporal reasoning. The continued development of new automated heuristics has brought this method into the realm of practicality as well.

Today you really can buy an off-the-shelf EDA tool and effectively use it to interact with, understand, and verify your RTL throughout the SOC design flow.

THE STANDARDIZING OF ASSERTIONS

One other development that has helped make FV especially practical in the last decade or so has been the standardization of property description languages. FV tools in the early 2000s or earlier commonly provided their own unique language for specifying properties. Each tool would have some "good reason" why its language was superior to others and some formal arguments showing useful mathematical characteristics of their custom language. However, the ultimate result of all this divergence was that it was very difficult to try out a new or unfamiliar tool. Further, it restricted usage to experts who had the patience to learn a new set of directives and idioms. In addition, many early property languages were designed by researchers and mathematicians, and showed little awareness of styles of expression that are useful for real engineers working on RTL design models.

The first glimmer of hope for getting out of this situation came starting in 2001 with Accelera's Open Verification Library (OVL), a set of standard assertions that could be defined as modules/entities in any design language. These were relatively coarse-grained objects such as *assert_always* (to declare some Boolean condition that would always be true), *assert_implication* (to declare statements in the form "*a* implies *b*"), or *assert_no_overflow* (to declare that a queue should not overflow.) While they did not provide much flexibility, their ability to take arbitrary Boolean inputs largely compensated for this limitation. Since it was standard and had versions that were implemented on top of all major design languages (VHDL, Verilog 2001, SystemVerilog), it became fairly popular in the design world despite its limitations. There were also parallel efforts to standardize other property languages, most prominently the Property Specification Language (PSL).

Starting in 2005, OVL and PSL began to be subsumed by a new assertion language that attempted to balance concerns about mathematical soundness and engineering usefulness: SVA provides a much more flexible way than OVL to specify a variety of assertions, as we will see in Chapter 3. OVL did not completely go away: an SVA implementation of OVL is available, so users who are more comfortable with those coarse-grained assertions can still use them. However, SVA has grown to be the accepted standard for describing properties for FV, and in the present day any serious tool is expected to support this language.

CHALLENGES IN IMPLEMENTING FV

If FV is really as powerful as we have been claiming throughout this chapter, and will continue to claim throughout this book, why isn't everyone already using it? As part of any practical discussion of FV, it is also important for us to point out a few limitations, which have made it a little more challenging to widely deploy.

FUNDAMENTAL LIMITATIONS OF MATHEMATICS

You probably have a vague recollection of some college professor telling you about certain major discoveries in the first half of the twentieth century, showing that there are fundamental limits to what can be mathematically proven. Gödel's Incompleteness Theorem, for example, showed that any formal system at least as complex as basic arithmetic would be either inconsistent or incomplete. He did this by showing that in such a system, one could always construct the mind-bending, but not quite paradoxical, statement "This statement cannot be proven." Think about it for a minute: if it is false, then it can be proven, and the system is inconsistent, allowing proofs of false statements. If it is true, then we have a true and unprovable statement, showing the system's incompleteness. A few years later, Alan Turing produced a similar result in the domain of theoretical computer science, showing that it would be impossible to generate a universal computer program that could definitively tell you whether any other program would eventually halt, or would run forever.

While these results are of theoretical interest, what they really show us in the area of FV is just that a universal tool that would be guaranteed to formally prove the correctness of any specification cannot be developed. They do not preclude the development of practical tools that can handle the vast majority of finite real-life specifications in a well-defined language.

COMPLEXITY THEORY

In addition to asking what fundamentally can or cannot be computed, computer scientists also ask another question: for answers that can be computed, how much time or memory does it take? The subdomain of complexity theory attempts to answer this question by dividing problems into different complexity classes based on how hard they are to solve.

One of the core problems of FV is the *satisfiability (SAT) problem*: given a Boolean expression, is there some set of values of the variables that will cause it to evaluate to 1? For example, consider the following Boolean expression:

```
(a&b&c) | (a&!b&d) | (c&d&e) | (!e&a&b)
```

If asked whether there is a set of values of the variables *a, b, c, d, e* that would cause this expression to evaluate to 1, there is no easy way to answer other than trying out combinations of values, and there are an exponential number (2 to the power of the number of variables) to try. But if someone were to give you a set of values that they claim would work, it is very easy to substitute them and check the claim.

In 1971, Cook's theorem showed that this problem, SAT, is in a class of provably hard problems known as *NP-complete*. This means that mathematicians generally believe that the time to solve it is *exponential* in relation to the size of its input set. Exponential time means that the bound expression contains n in its exponents, as in (2^n) or ($7^{3n} + 5n + 1$). For particular small values of n this may not seem so bad, but if you try substituting a few values you will see that as n grows larger, exponential time tends to quickly grow out of control. In practice, if a problem is NP-complete, this means a program that solves it in full generality and reasonable time for all conceivable cases cannot be implemented.

THE GOOD NEWS

In fact, all the issues above just show us that FV is an engineering challenge. We will never be able to implement an FV system that is 100 percent guaranteed to work well on 100 percent of RTL designs—but how many areas of engineering offer us such guarantees anyway? What they do show is that we will have to base FV tools on the use of *heuristics*: problem-solving strategies that work for some subset of cases but are not guaranteed to work well for every case.

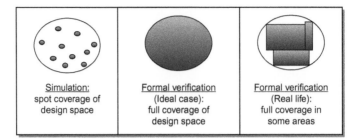

FIGURE 1.7

Coverage level of FV as compared to simulation.

Even in cases where FV is only applicable to a subset of a design, what we usually find is that for the portion where it is applicable, it is equivalent to running an exponential number of simulation tests, fully covering a huge subset of the verification space even if not able to reach the ideal point of complete coverage. Figure 1.7 illustrates this situation.

Thus, the complexity challenges we have mentioned do not outweigh the inherent power and many benefits of FV technology. As you will see throughout this book, current FV tools are effectively combining a powerful set of heuristics to solve the real verification problems that we encounter daily in RTL design, and are growing more powerful every day.

AMPLIFYING THE POWER OF FORMAL

Research during the past two decades has resulted in an amazing variety of heuristics to attack SAT and similar problems, and this is the primary reason why we are able today to take an off-the-shelf EDA tool and use it to analyze a typical VLSI design. It is now commonplace to take an off-the-shelf FPV tool, load a real unit or cluster level RTL design, and be able to do formal analysis immediately.

Because we are working with heuristics, however, you probably will come across cases where you want to run FV on a design even larger than the initial push-button capacity of your tools. Once you are familiar with the basics of the technology, you will find that it is relatively easy to use a variety of tricks that can make seemingly difficult problems easily tractable. Here are some of the general techniques that we use when preparing challenging designs for the use of FV:

- *State Matching*: Most current synthesis tools generate schematics that are (mostly) guaranteed to have a flop-by-flop correspondence with the RTL that generated them. Thus, when doing formal equivalence checking between the RTL and netlists, we can simplify the problem using our knowledge of the corresponding flops in the two designs.

- *Bounded Proofs*: Instead of proving that your design is guaranteed to have correct behaviors for all time, you can prove that all behaviors are guaranteed correct for behavior traces up to some defined length. While this is not as powerful as a full proof of guaranteed functionality, it is still the equivalent of running an exponential number of simulation tests. Thus, it is often quite useful in practice.
- *Proof Decomposition*: We can often improve our FV capacity significantly by making every property as simple as possible. For example, a property in the form "(A OR B) implies C" can be divided into two independent properties "A implies C" and "B implies C."
- *Targeted Verification*: Are you primarily worried about some small set of risky cases, such as what happens when a queue is nearly full or some protocol is nearly complete? You can guide the tool to concentrate on particular parts of the problem space.
- *Size Reductions*: Often we can just represent a small portion of a large memory or cache, reduce datapath width to just a few bits, or reduce the size of parameterized elements, and still analyze our designs in a way that will catch the vast majority of bugs.
- *Case Splitting*: For a design that has many modes or opcodes, do we need to verify them all at once? We can often split the job into a number of simple verification tasks, each checking a subset of the possible behaviors.
- *Design Abstractions*: We can often ignore details of a computation in the context of verifying properties of the overall design. For example, does a counter really need to be incrementing by precisely one every cycle, or does the rest of the logic just care that it generates realistic values each cycle?
- *Data Abstractions*: Perhaps instead of analyzing fully general data patterns, we can specify a simplified subset of possible data to look at, such as most data bits being 0, or all data packets being one of a small set of types.

The descriptions above just give the basic flavor of the various simplification techniques. In upcoming chapters, each of these will be discussed in more detail, and in the context of more specific usage of particular types of FV tools.

GETTING THE MOST OUT OF THIS BOOK

Our goal is to provide real, practical techniques that you can use immediately to improve your design flows. To emphasize this focus on practical usability, we are providing tips in each chapter: quick pieces of practical advice for you to easily review as you skim the text.

TIP 1.4

Pay attention to the tips in each chapter to gain practical advice that you will find useful when attempting FV on your designs.

This chapter, being a general introduction, is somewhat of an outlier, with only a handful of tips. Chapter 2 provides some general background on the internals of FV tools, intended mainly to convince you that these techniques are not black magic, but just solid application of well-founded engineering techniques. You should be able to skip it, but we thought it important to include for those of you who are curious about this topic.

Each of the remaining chapters focuses on real, ready-to-use techniques that can be added to your design flows. We begin by describing the basic building blocks of SVA in Chapter 3 and basic concepts of FPV in Chapter 4. If you are not already familiar with assertions and/or FV to some degree, we do strongly recommend that you read Chapters 3 and 4 carefully, as they provide basic foundations that will be useful in the rest of the book.

We then focus in more detail on FPV techniques in Chapters 5–7, and FEV in Chapter 8. You will probably get the most out of the book if you read all those chapters, though it is probably okay to focus on the ones containing the particular techniques that look most useful to your project.

After that, we conclude with discussion of some advanced topics that will help you in your FV efforts: Chapter 9, "Formal Verification's Greatest Bloopers," discusses the things that can go wrong with FV flows in a typical project, and Chapter 10 contains a toolkit of advanced tricks for dealing with complexity. Both of these chapters can be considered optional, though if you are attempting a serious FV effort, you are likely to find them very useful.

We also have provided a companion website for this book at http://formalverificationbook.com. From there you can download actual code examples that we discuss in many chapters of this book.

Again, don't forget our key point: do not think of FV as a point technique to use at one spot in your validation flow—instead, think of it as a general-purpose toolkit for understanding, interacting with, and verifying your RTL models. In fact, let's close the chapter with this tip:

> **TIP 1.5**
>
> At any point in your design flows where you are dealing with RTL in some fashion, ask the question: can we use FV to improve our methods here?

PRACTICAL TIPS FROM THIS CHAPTER

1.1 When you want to get complete coverage of design behaviors, consider using FV as your primary validation method.

1.2 When you have a design with nontrivial logic, and are worried that you will not be able to get sufficient coverage with simulation tests, think about FV as a supplement to simulation.

1.3 When you have a design where you can easily specify interesting states or outputs, but it is difficult or time-consuming to specify the sequence of inputs needed to get there, think about using FV.

1.4 Pay attention to the tips in each chapter, to gain practical advice that you will find useful when attempting FV on your designs.

1.5 At any point in your design flows where you are dealing with RTL in some fashion, ask the question: can we use FV to improve our methods here?

FURTHER READING

[Acc08] Accelera OVL standard, <http://www.accellera.org/downloads/standards/ovl>.

[Cla09] Edmund M. Clarke, E. Allen Emerson, and Joseph Sifaki, "Model Checking: Algorithmic Verification and Debugging" *Communications of the ACM*, Vol. 52, No. 11, November 2009.

[Coo71] Cook, Stephen "The Complexity of Theorem Proving Procedures," *Proceedings of the Third Annual ACM Symposium on Theory of Computing*, pp. 151–158, 1971.

[Dav65] Martin Davis, ed., *The Undecidable*, Lippincott Williams & Wilkins, 1965.

[Dsi08] Vijay D'Silva, Daniel Kroening, and Georg Weissenbacher, "A Survey of Automated Techniques for Formal Software Verification" *IEEE Transactions on Computer Aided Design of Integrated Circuits and Systems*, Vol. 27, No. 7, July 2008.

[Gup14] Aarti Gupta, M.V. Achutha KiranKumar, and Rajnish Ghughal, "Formally Verifying Graphics FPU", *Lecture Notes in Computer Science*, Vol. 8442, Springer, 2014<http://link.springer.com/chapter/10.1007%2F978-3-319-06410-9_45> pp. 673–687.

[Jon01] Robert Jones, Carl Seger, John O'Leary, Mark Aagard, and Thomas Melham, "Practical Formal Verification in Microprocessor Design" *IEEE Design and Test Journal*, July-August 2001.

[Jon02] Robert B Jones, *Symbolic Simulation Methods for Industrial Formal Verification*, Springer, 2002.

[Kai10] Roope Kaivola, Rajnish Ghughal, Jesse Whittemore, Amber Tefler, Naren Narasimhan, Anna Slobodova, and Sudhindhra Pandav, "Replacing Testing with Formal Verification in Intel® Core™ i7 Processor Execution Engine Validation," HCSS Conference Proceedings, 2010.

[Kro99] Thomas Kropf, *Introduction to Formal Hardware Verification*, Springer Verlag, 1999.

[Kur97] R. P. Kurshan, "Formal Verification in a Commercial Setting," *Proceedings of the Design Automation Conference*, Anaheim, California, June 9–13, pp. 258–262, 1997.

[Mcf93] M.C. McFerland, "Formal Verification of Sequential Hardware: A Tutorial" *IEEE Transactions on CAD*, Vol. 12, No. 5, May 1993.

[Mcm93] Kenneth L. McMillan, *Symbolic Model Checking*, Springer, 1993.

[Mon03] Jean François Monin and Michael G. Hinchey, *Understanding Formal Methods*, Springer, 2003, ISBN 1-85233-247-6.

[Nel02] Stacy Nelson and Charles Pecheur, "Formal Verification for a Next-Generation Space Shuttle," in Second Goddard Workshop on Formal Aspects of Agent-Based Systems (FAABS II), Greenbelt, MD, October 2002. Lecture Notes in Computer Science, Vol. 2699, Springer, http://www.info.ucl.ac.be/~pecheur/publi/VVofIVHM.pdf.

[New56] Allen Newell and Herbert A Simon, "The logic theory machine: A Complex Information Processing System". Offprint (reproduced typescript) from *IRE Transactions on Information Theory IT-2*, September 1956.

[Rob65] John Alan Robinson, "A Machine-Oriented Logic Based on the Resolution Principle" *Journal of the ACM*, Vol. 12, 23−41, 1965.

[Seg92] Carl-Johan Seger, "An Introduction to Formal Verification," Technical Report 92-13, UBC, Department of Computer Science, Vancouver, B.C., Canada, June 1992.

[Sin06] Vigyan Singhal, "Oski Technologies-Formal Verification: Theory and Practice": http://drona.csa.iisc.ernet.in/~deepakd/talks/formal-iisc-0306.pdf.

[Smu91] Raymond Smullyan, *Godel's Incompleteness Theorems*, Oxford University Press, 1991.

[Van99] Jean Van Heijenoort, *From Frege to Gödel: A Source Book in Mathematical Logic, 1879−1931*, iUniverse, 1999.

Basic formal verification algorithms

2

This chapter will provide you with a general idea of the kinds of algorithms that are used in formal verification tools. We intend to convince you that formal verification is not "black magic," but instead a set of smart techniques that really do provide full behavioral coverage without exhaustive simulation. This chapter is intentionally a very basic coverage of the concepts, as whole books have been written on FV algorithms. A more formalized, mathematical presentation can be found in books such as [Cla99] and [Kro99]. We won't be presenting complex definitions and rigorously derived equations, but instead will provide an intuition of how FV tools accomplish their task. If you just want to trust us, you can feel free to skip this chapter and move on to the more practical focus of the remainder of this book. However, understanding the basic ideas of this chapter can give you key insights into what an FV tool is doing when it analyzes your designs.

FORMAL VERIFICATION (FV) IN THE VALIDATION PROCESS

The three central tasks of validation are to *stimulate* a design, to *check* that the design produces results according to its specification, and to measure how much of a design's possible execution space has been simulated and checked (*coverage*). Prior to the manufacturing of a device, validation is most commonly accomplished through running simulations of a register transfer level (RTL) model.

However, even for fairly simple designs, the number of possible distinct input stimulus sequences is seemingly infinite. It's actually an exponential function of the size of the possible inputs, starting state, and runtime, but this tends to feel like infinity for practical purposes. With hardware support such as emulation, simulations can greatly be accelerated, but still the time required to exercise commercial designs for all possible cases would vastly exceed the lifetime of the product. As such, achieving complete coverage of all possible execution sequences is not possible through these methods, and coverage goals are carefully set to include a good representation of characteristic conditions as well as critical and taxing scenarios, to uncover most, but not all, bugs. Meeting coverage goals is not an end in its own right, but the information gathered is a means to help guide validators to target aspects of the design that have not been exercised.

Rather than checking each unique sequence, FV techniques build a data structure that captures the results for all possible stimuli sequences. Checking properties against this structure then verifies required properties against all possible stimuli. This checking can discover deep, complex bugs that would be very difficult to hit using conventional stimulus generation techniques.

This chapter will discuss how we can check an implementation satisfies its requirements using formal models, including a discussion of the basic underlying mathematics of two different techniques: binary decision diagrams (BDDs) and SAT.

A SIMPLE VENDING MACHINE EXAMPLE

Before we get into too much detail on the general techniques, we begin with a small example showing how a clever data structure can be used to transform an apparently exponential-complexity problem into something much more tractable.

Boolean logic is usually represented through truth tables, which describe expected output values of a system in terms of each of their inputs. We can use truth tables to define functions or systems with multiple stimulus arguments and multiple results. For example, the truth table below describes a 1-bit ADD operation (Table 2.1).

The size of truth tables grows quickly as stimuli are added: with each additional input column, we double the number of rows for the number of new

Table 2.1 Truth Table for Simple ADD

Stimulus		Result	
x	y	Sum	Carry
0	0	0	0
0	1	1	0
1	0	1	0
1	1	0	1

Table 2.2 Truth Table for Simple MUX

Stimulus			Result
x	**y**	**z**	**MUX**
0	0	0	0
0	0	1	1
0	1	0	0
0	1	1	1
1	0	0	0
1	0	1	0
1	1	0	1
1	1	1	1

possible stimulus values. Defining a MUX operation, for example, requires twice as many rows as the 2-bit ADD (Table 2.2):

This means that a truth table for n inputs will have 2^n rows; as we discussed in the last chapter, this exponential growth quickly makes it very difficult to analyze with simple tools and techniques.

However, many FV algorithms take advantage of a key insight that mitigates this problem: in real life, such a truth table can often be quite *sparse* in terms of information content, since many rows produce 0 values, and many sets of rows produce the same value. As an example, consider developing a specification for a simple vending machine truth table that determines whether 35 cents has been deposited. (Yes, one of the authors may be revealing their age by hypothesizing such a vending machine, but bear with us for now.) We'll limit our specification to require that the machine only accepts exact change consisting of nickels (5 cents), dimes (10 cents), or quarters (25 cents). Legitimate inputs to the vending machine that should be accepted are:

- One quarter, one dime
- One quarter, two nickels
- Three dimes, one nickel
- Two dimes, three nickels
- One dime, five nickels
- Seven nickels

For these six cases, our truth table result should be 1, and otherwise it should be 0. To keep track of the possible inputs at any time we will need six bits:

- 1 bit to track how many quarters have been entered (0 or 1),
- 2 bits to track how many dimes have been entered (0–3), and
- 3 bits to track how many nickels have been entered (0–7).

To write out a complete truth table, we will need 64 rows (2^6), yet only six rows will produce a 1 result. If we were to allow pennies in our vending machine

Table 2.3 Efficient Truth Table for 35-Cent Vending Machine

Stimulus		Result	
Nickels [2:0]	**Dimes [1:0]**	**Quarters**	**Vend**
3'b000	2'b01	1	1
3'b010	2'b00	1	1
3'b001	2'b11	0	1
3'b011	2'b10	0	1
3'b101	2'b01	0	1
3'b111	2'b00	0	1
Any other pattern			0

specification, we would need to add six more bits to count up to 35 pennies and our table would increase to 4096 rows (2^{12}), but there are only 18 more valid input combinations—a very sparse table! As requirement specifications grow, we need a more compact representation, particularly for presenting to the reader, but also to simplify mechanical reasoning by a computer program.

Rather than enumerate all the rows, we can choose to display a table with only those input rows where the result is 1. In Table 2.3, we provide such a reduced table for the vending machine example; as you can see, the number of rows actually needed is significantly less than the predicted 64.

There are many other minimization techniques and other heuristics to efficiently handle Boolean formulas, which we will describe later in this chapter. By now you should be able to see our key point: by clever choices of algorithms and data structures, a Boolean function, which would seemingly require handling an exponential number of different cases, can often be represented and analyzed in a compact and efficient way.

COMPARING SPECIFICATIONS

To validate a design, we need to compare two specifications; one capturing the design requirements (the "specification") and one the implementation details (the "implementation"). The specification is typically more abstract than the implementation, describing the expected results rather than how the implementing logic is connected together. As we will see in more detail in later chapters, the specification will usually be in the form of a set of properties such as SystemVerilog Assertions (SVA) assertions, an RTL model, or a model in a high-level language like SystemC. The implementation will typically be a more detailed RTL model or a schematic netlist. In some cases, the abstraction gap may be quite small and formal techniques are often used to compare two different implementations for equality, such as after a minor bug fix later in a project.

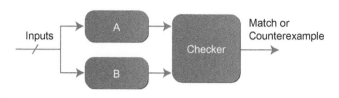

FIGURE 2.1

Simple formal checker definition.

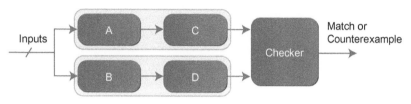

FIGURE 2.2

Checker operating on larger system.

Before discussing in detail the algorithms used by formal verification, we will first provide insight into how a FV tool accomplishes its task. In Figure 2.1, boxes A and B represent specifications that receive the same inputs and whose outputs are compared by a checker. The checker then confirms A and B produce equivalent results. If the checker records the sequence of inputs that resulted in a failure, the checker could provide a counterexample trace demonstrating a case where A and B are not equivalent. This is a *black box* checker because the checker does not observe state or signal values that are internal to A and B (as a *white box* checker could). Though a *black box* checker has less visibility, its definition is impervious to internal changes, making maintenance costs lower than *white box* checkers.

If A and B are simple enough, we may be able to test all possible sequences or use FV to show the two boxes produce equivalent results. We could then use this equivalence proof to simplify other problems. For example, consider the diagram where A and B are components of a larger system (Figure 2.2).

In this example, if we had already proven that A and B were equivalent, we could remove A and B and tackle a simpler problem of showing that C and D were equivalent. The inputs to C and D in this revised scenario would be different and are labeled as *Inputs'* in the figure below. If identifying what *Inputs'* should be is challenging, it may be more convenient to retain a copy of A (or B) that accepts *Inputs* and produces *Inputs'*. By using divide and conquer strategies we can often enable verification of much larger designs than can be verified natively with a FV tool (Figure 2.3).

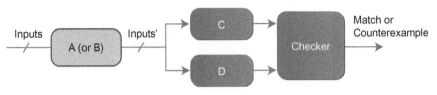

FIGURE 2.3

Focusing on correct subproblem after A and B proven equivalent.

We might imagine that the top box in the diagrams is the requirements specification and the bottom box is the implementation specification. Utilizing a simple checker that compares output streams will enable validation of the two specifications when they possess an equivalent level of detail. For example, we could compare output streams to show a retimed RTL model is equivalent to its original representation. This is an example of formal equivalence verification (FEV), which is discussed later in this book. Generally however, the two specifications are not strictly the same. The requirements specification is an abstracted view of the implementation with many details left out.

CONES OF INFLUENCE

Validation complexity can be reduced if orthogonal requirements are considered separately. For example, if a design includes add and multiply hardware, different simulation runs might be used to focus on the distinct operations. In the case where the design had separate units that performed these two operations, it would be more efficient to include in a simulation only the part of the design needed to verify the targeted operation. Generally, this is not done for simulation testing because it is more efficient to create one validation environment rather than one for each operation. FV tools are designed to support this kind of decomposition and take this idea one step further. FV tools analyze the properties to be verified and then remove from the implementation any logic that does not have an influence on the results described by the properties. This is known as a *cone of influence* reduction. As seen in the example Figure 2.4, there are several boxes that could be removed from the design, as they play no part in the computation of *result*. In large designs, this will greatly reduce the amount of logic considered.

FV tools also support user guided logic simplifications that are not automatically applied. For example, a user might wish to only check cases where an input is a single value (enabling a simplification of the logic). There are a number of other logic *pruning* simplifications that can be applied that don't affect the completeness of a FV check and will be discussed in subsequent chapters. We will now shift attention to the mathematics underlying FV.

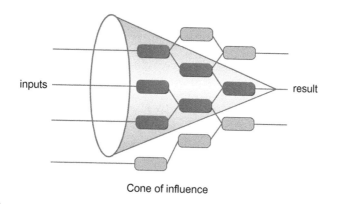

Cone of influence

FIGURE 2.4

Focusing on the cone of influence.

FORMALIZING OPERATION DEFINITIONS

Within a requirements or implementation specification, we use Boolean variables for the inputs, outputs, and state elements that may retain different values over time. We will initially assume that these variables can take on binary values (0 or 1), though it can be useful to add a third unknown value, "X," to indicate we don't know whether the value is 0 or 1. Conventionally, 0 is also interpreted as representing low/off/false and 1 as representing high/on/true. Operations on values or combinations of values can be described in terms of truth tables where the results (outputs and next states) are a function of stimulus arguments (inputs and current states). Since the reader is presumed to be a design or validation engineer proficient in SystemVerilog, we will assume you have a basic understanding of the common Boolean operations: AND (&&), OR (||), NOT (!), and their various negations and variants.

BUILDING TRUTH TABLES INTELLIGENTLY

As we mentioned in the beginning of this chapter, the truth table in Table 2.1 described a 1-bit add operation, and contained four rows. Suppose we want to expand this ADD operation to allow more input variables. With each additional input column, we double the number of rows for the number of new possible stimulus values, leading to exponential growth in the size of a basic truth table: we will require 2^n rows to handle n variables. However, as we saw in the vending machine example, we can take advantage of the sparseness of the actual data to generate much more compact representations of truth tables. By recognizing the fact that we do not need to repeat rows that represent identical or zero results, we can use significantly fewer rows in practice than the naïve exponential calculation would suggest.

Table 2.4 Truth Table with Sequential Logic

Stimulus		Result	
Input	**Sum**	**Sum'**	**Carry**
0	0	0	0
0	1	1	0
1	0	1	0
1	1	0	1

ADDING SEQUENTIAL LOGIC

Truth tables can also capture systems with sequential logic, where the model can store state information that changes over time, by adding input stimulus and output result columns to represent the current and next states of a variable. Though two variables are used, it is convenient to give them the same name with an added suffix tick mark (') to the successor state variable. The table above shows the definition for a 1-bit adder that adds a new input value to its current sum each cycle (Table 2.4).

BOOLEAN ALGEBRA NOTATION

While we can use truth tables to specify behaviors that combine multiple operations, it is much more convenient to write these as formulas using Boolean algebra. We will represent variables with single letter names and occasionally with subscripts. As we discussed above, when a variable is a state variable, tick mark (') suffixes can be used to indicate the successor state. For consistency with the rest of this book, we will use SystemVerilog-style formulas to represent common operations:

```
AND: && (for example, x && y)
OR: || (for example, x || y)
NOT: ! (for example, !x)
```

We will also use other conventions to minimize the need for notation and parenthesis. The NOT operation has the highest precedence, followed by the AND operator. As a concrete example, consider the MUX implementation below (Figure 2.5):

Here, we introduce intermediate variables a, b, and c as outputs of different gates and can describe the implementation as a set of formulas:

```
a == !y
b == x && y
c == a && z
result == b || c
```

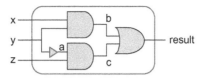

FIGURE 2.5

Simple circuit example.

Table 2.5 Truth Table for Circuit Example

Stimulus			Intermediates			Result
x	y	z	a = NOT y	b = AND(x,y)	c = AND(a,z)	OR(a,c)
0	0	0	1	0	0	0
0	0	1	1	0	1	1
0	1	0	0	0	0	0
0	1	1	0	0	0	0
1	0	0	1	0	0	0
1	0	1	1	0	1	1
1	1	0	0	1	0	1
1	1	1	0	1	0	1

The conjunction of these formulas, the global statement that all of the above four formulas are true, represents the implementation of the design. We can simplify the conjunction by substituting the definition of the intermediate variables into the final equation: a into the definition of c (c == $!y$ && z) and then the definitions of b and c into result. This simplifies the full formula to (Table 2.5):

```
result == (x && y) || (!y && z)
```

For simple functions, like XOR, it can be straightforward to immediately write down a Boolean algebra formula describing the operation. For more complicated functions, like the 35-cent vending machine, we can create a formula by recognizing that if the inputs match any of the six identified combinations, the accepting formula should be true. We can express the requirements specification for the 35-cent vending machine as follows, where quarters are counted with variable q_0, dimes with variables d_0 and d_1, and nickels with variables n_0, n_1, and n_2:

```
(q0 && d0 && !d1 && !n0 && !n1 && !n2) ||
(q0 && !d0 && !d1 && !n0 && n1 && !n2) ||
(!q0 && d0 && d1 && n0 && !n1 && !n2) ||
(!q0 && !d0 && d1 && n0 && n1 && !n2) ||
(!q0 && d0 && !d1 && n0 && !n1 && n2) ||
(!q0 && !d0 && !d1 && n0 && n1 && n2)
```

A formula with this structure is said to be in *disjunctive normal form (DNF)*. Formulas in this form consist of a set of subterms that are ORed (disjunction) together and each of the subterms consists only of variables or their negation that are ANDed (conjunction) together. Since AND is similar to multiplication and OR is similar to addition, this form is also called *sum-of-products form.*

Constructing formulas from truth tables in this manner can be easily automated, and is often useful for building FV tools. We must use caution when doing such rewrites, though, since the resulting formula may be more complicated than needed to compute the desired result. For example, the definition for *result* on the small circuit example in Figure 2.2 was:

```
(x && y) || (!y && z)
```

but when constructing the DNF directly by capturing the rows of the truth table (Table 2.5) that evaluate to 1, we get

```
(!x && !y && z) || (x && !y && z) || (x && y && !z) || (x && y && z)
```

In the next section, we will present Boolean algebra laws that we can use to rewrite a formula into an equivalent formula. Through a sequence of rewrites, we can then show that two formulas are equivalent. Since a judicious rewrite can result in an exponential reduction in overall size of a formula, the ability for a tool to perform such transformations is a core capability that enables successful FV.

BASIC BOOLEAN ALGEBRA LAWS

The table below provides a list of the basic laws that can be confirmed through observations from the truth tables presented previously or by writing out new truth tables. You will see that some, like the commutative law, are the familiar laws you learned for (non-Boolean) algebra in high school math, while others, such as the distribution of addition over multiplication, do not have analogues in non-Boolean contexts. FV engines can make use of these laws to quickly rewrite Boolean formulas into more convenient forms for analysis (Table 2.6).

COMPARING SPECIFICATIONS

To show that an implementation satisfies its requirements requires a proof that the implementation implies the specification:

```
implementation→requirements
```

If the requirement is that the two are precisely equal (produce the same result for all possible input sequences), then we would also need to also show the reverse also true:

```
requirements→implementation
```

Table 2.6 Basic Laws of Boolean Algebra

Commutative Laws	x && y == y && x	$x \mid\mid y$ == $y \mid\mid x$
Associative Laws	x&&$(y$&&$z)$ == $(x$&&$y)$&&z	$x\mid\mid(y\mid\mid z)$ == $(x\mid\mid y)\mid\mid z$
Distributive Laws	x&&$(y\mid\mid z)$ == x&&$y \mid\mid x$&&z	$x\mid\mid(y$&&$z)$ == $(x\mid\mid y)$ && $(x\mid\mid z)$
Inverse Laws	x&&$!x$ == 0	$x\mid\mid !x$ == 1
Identity Laws	x&&1 == x	$x\mid\mid 0$ == x
Idempotence Laws	x&&x == x	$x\mid\mid x$ == x
Annihilator Laws	x&&0 == 0	$x\mid\mid 1$ == 1
DeMorgan's Law	x&&y == $!(!x\mid\mid !y)$	$x\mid\mid y$ = $!(!x$&&$!y)$
Double Negation	$!!x$ == x	

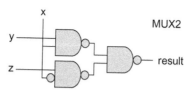

MUX2

result

FIGURE 2.6

Another MUX implementation, which we will call MUX2.

Using the basic Boolean algebra rules, we can rewrite formulas to show that two implementations produce equivalent results. For example, consider the alternative implementation of a MUX in (Figure 2.6).

We can define the implementation with the formula: $!(!(x$&&$y)$&&$!(!x$&&$z))$. To show that this implementation produces the same result as the original implementation, we can apply Boolean algebra rules to rewrite a formula into an equivalent formula. In this case,

- Apply DeMorgan's Law producing: $!!(x$&&$y) \mid\mid !!(!x$&&$z)$
- Remove the double NOT operations producing: $(x$&&$y)\mid\mid(!x$&&$z)$

So, $!(!(x$&&$y)$&&$!(!x$&&$z))$ == $(x$&&$y)\mid\mid(!x$&&$z)$. We now have a new *theorem* that we can add to our list of rewriting rules for future simplifications. At first glance, our design specification for MUX2:

$(x$&&$y) \mid\mid (!x$&&$z)$

is a different than our first MUX design definition:

$(x$&&$y) \mid\mid (!y$&&$z)$

This discrepancy provides a means to make a couple key observations. The variables x, y, and z in our formulas are really placeholders (or *formals*) for the

Table 2.7 Comparing MUX Implementations with x/y Bits Swizzled

Stimulus			Result	
X	Y	z	MUX	MUX2
0	0	0	0	0
0	0	1	1	1
0	1	0	0	0
0	1	1	1	0
1	0	0	0	0
1	0	1	0	1
1	1	0	1	1
1	1	1	1	1

actual input values that will be used in the computation. Using better formal notation to make this clearer, we can restate *MUX* and *MUX2* as:

```
MUX(x,y,z) = (x&&y)||(!y&&z)
MUX2(y,x,z) = (x&&y)||(!x&&z)
```

As placeholders, the input variables can be renamed without affecting the value computed by a function. If we then rename the first variable *a* and the second variable *b* in each formula, and apply commutative laws, we will see that the two definitions do match. Alternatively we could rename x for y and *simultaneously* y for x in the MUX2 specification.

While both implementations can perform the same function, we can't simply replace one for the other without properly connecting the inputs. The error of swizzling input bits can be difficult to detect. In this simple MUX example, for many inputs, a correct result is produced in most cases even after failing to relabel the inputs as discussed above. Only in two input stimulus patterns would an incorrect hookup be detected (see the truth (Table 2.7).

Automated rewriting procedures are available for small digital circuit problems that can find a sequence of transformations to reduce the complexity of a formula and can be used to show two formulas are equivalent. For large problems, both truth tables and Boolean algebra formulas become unwieldy for the automated procedures, even with human guidance.

To address this problem, alternative representations have been found that enable much larger problems to be solved automatically. In the following sections, we will present two structures to represent the behavior of Boolean logic to enable efficient comparisons between different designs and specifications. We will first present BDDs, followed by SAT formulas.

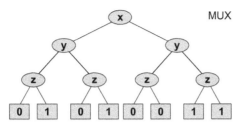

FIGURE 2.7

Simple BDD with no optimizations.

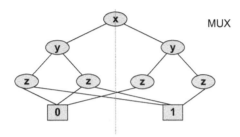

FIGURE 2.8

BDD with terminal nodes merged.

BDDS

BDDs provide a compact way of representing the behavior of many circuits in the form of a binary decision tree. As observed in our example truth tables, there is often a lot of redundancy: many of the rows of the 35-cent vending machine truth table are 0. BDDs provide a structure that enables removal of this redundancy while preserving the behavior of the original design. They also are very powerful for FV applications because they are *canonical*: if we apply a set of standardized rules, we will construct a unique BDD, such that any other equivalent design will have the same BDD representation without any rewriting required. This means that an FV tool can test equivalence between two formulas just by converting both to BDD form and checking to see that the BDDs are identical. This is why the development of BDDs was a key enabler for the first generation of efficient industrial FEV tools.

Figure 2.7 is an example of a BDD for our MUX specification. To find a result for a particular input pattern, follow the left branch of a variable node if the variable is 0 in the pattern and the right branch if the variable is 1.

In this current form, we haven't really bought ourselves a storage advantage over a truth table, since we are still directly representing all of the exponential number of potential execution paths. To minimize the size, we can eliminate many redundancies. First, let us drop all the redundant 0 and 1 terminal nodes (the boxes in the bottom row) (Figure 2.8).

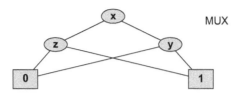

FIGURE 2.9

More compact BDD with identical nodes merged.

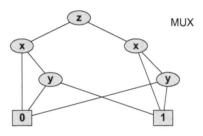

FIGURE 2.10

Less compact BDD due to poor choice of ordering.

Next, observe that decisions made by the two z nodes on the left side of the tree are the same, so the parent y node does not influence the result. Similarly, on the right side of the tree, the z nodes are unnecessary. As a result, we can safely merge these sets of nodes. This results in a much more compact representation, as follows (Figure 2.9):

Critical to the size of a BDD is the order in which variables are added to the tree. Our original MUX was conveniently defined so as to provide a reasonable natural ordering. However, if we were to swap the order we add variables to z, then x, then y, the function remains the same, but we would produce the following BDD (Figure 2.10).

While objectively the new BDD is not terribly complicated (it is only a MUX after all), we have added two additional nodes (a 66% size increase). For more complicated circuits, the size of a BDD can grow exponentially depending on the order of the variables. Heuristic-based algorithms are often good at finding a better order (reordering) that reduces the size of a BDD. For example, there are many cases when matching the order of variables to the topology of a circuit being analyzed can be a very good strategy, leveraging the circuit's clues about nodes whose logic is closely related. Another often powerful heuristic is to try to substitute 0 and 1 values for each primary input, and see which cases (if any) significantly reduce the total logic needed to evaluate the model: such cases indicate variables that should be near the top of the BDD tree. A wide variety of such heuristics is described in [Ric08]. However, just like SAT, the problem of BDD ordering is NP-complete, so for large, complex operations, finding a good BDD ordering can still take exponential time in the worst case. In practice, though, there are many cases when FV tools can efficiently construct BDDs for surprisingly large Boolean functions.

COMPUTING A BDD FOR A CIRCUIT DESIGN

If we had a truth table for a design and a specification, we could immediately go about creating a BDD, performing reduction steps, and confirming that the design and the specification match. However, rarely is a specification or a design expressed as a truth table: especially in the chip design world, it is much more likely presented in the form of an RTL model. Fortunately, we have a set of well-defined rules for creating primitive BDDs corresponding to basic logic operations, and for combining such BDDs to compose operations. If we start with a circuit, we can build up a BDD by adding one logical operation at a time, mimicking the structure of the input model. When the circuit is expressed as a set of Boolean algebra formulas, we can also first apply laws and theorems to minimize its representation.

To see how this works in practice, let's start by looking at the basic BDDs representing AND, OR, and NOT gates (Figure 2.11).

To create a BDD from a circuit, we can use these generic forms to incrementally construct more complex BDDs, one gate at a time. For example, consider the formula $(x\&\&y)||z$, shown in Figure 2.12.

We can construct a BDD for the circuit by replacing x for a and y for b in the generic AND BDD and grafting its 0 and 1 arc to replace the a node arcs of an OR BDD while replacing z for b. The left side of the figure below shows the graft and the right side presents the composition. This process can iterate until we have added all gates in a circuit into a BDD (Figure 2.13).

If we are comparing two different implementations of combinational logic, we can now evaluate whether they compute the same result when the designs have

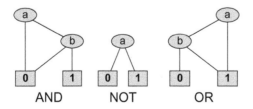

FIGURE 2.11

BDDs for basic gate types.

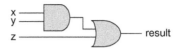

FIGURE 2.12

Circuit computing (x&&y)||x.

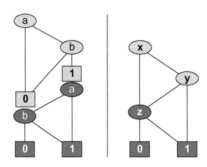

FIGURE 2.13

Combining gate BDDs to build the circuit.

an equal number of inputs and outputs (including state). However, specifications are often more abstract such that there won't be strict equivalence. Furthermore, specifications generally describe systems in terms of their behavior over time rather than their stepwise actions.

MODEL CHECKING

Model checking is the primary technique used by FV tools to analyze the behavior of a sequential system over a period of time. Given a set of requirements defined as temporal logic properties and a finite-state system, a model-checking algorithm can search over the possible future states and determine whether a property is violated.

The search begins by creating a state space BDD for the initial state, where all variables potentially hold any value unless an explicit constraint has been provided. Using system transitions (encoded as BDDs), the state space BDD can be expanded to include all possible next states. This process (called *reachability*) can repeat until all possible future states are added to the BDD. While it can't be predicted how many times the process needs to repeat, a *fixed point* is reached when no new states are added to the state BDD. At this point, the complete set of possible behaviors has been analyzed: applying the transitions further to any of the existing states produces no new states to add.

In the case that a violation is detected, the model checker works backwards from the violating stage back to the initial conditions to create a specific example of how the bad state can be reached. There may be many different ways that the violating state may be reached. Model checkers generally return the shortest possible path, though some can provide multiple paths or other hints to assist in root causing the problem.

A model checker can return the result that the specification is satisfied, return a violation, or not provide either due to a computational explosion, where the tool times out or generates BDDs that use up all available memory.

While BDDs provide a means to fully check that a design meets its specification, there are practical limits on how big a design can be checked. As pointed out previously, BDD models can grow exponentially with each additional input or state element. With a careful ordering of variables, BDDs can be tamed in many cases. For larger designs, time and space blowups often require manual effort or the use of more advanced heuristics to apply case splitting, assume-guarantee reasoning, or use simplifying assumptions to obtain a result. Such strategies can often convert exponential growth into a set of smaller problems that can fit in the space available.

BOOLEAN SATISFIABILITY

The next technique we will present trades off guarantees of complete coverage for all problems, but with the benefit of providing counterexamples much more quickly and being applicable to much larger designs in a much more automated way. It is based on directly attempting to solve the Boolean SAT problem that we mentioned in Chapter 1. While this problem is provably hard in the worst case, researchers have discovered a number of heuristic methods that can often solve SAT in reasonable time on unit-level designs.

To better understand SAT, consider the following specification, where we wish to show the implementation satisfies the requirement:

```
implementation = !(!a&&c || a&&!b)
requirement = !a&&!c || b&c
```

This can be stated as determining whether or not the statement

```
!(!a&&c || a&&!b) ➔ !a&&!c || b&c
```

is a *tautology*: in a tautology, for any inputs, the formula evaluates to true. Rewriting using the definition of implication (p➔q is defined as $!p$ || q) and removing a double negative, this formula can be written as:

```
(!a&&c || a&&!b) || (!a&&!c || b&&c)
```

To prove the formula is a tautology, a truth table could be constructed. The result for each of the eight possible input patterns could be computed, and any row with 0 would be flagged as an error. However, as we are looking to find bugs quickly, it would be more optimal to refocus the solution on the problem of searching for any assignment of variables where the implementation does not satisfy its requirements. This is the essence of the classic SAT problem. For our particular goal of finding counterexamples, we can formulate the objective as finding an assignment of variables such that:

```
!(implementation ➔ specification)
```

If no assignment can be found, then we can conclude the implementation does satisfy the specification.

BOUNDED MODEL CHECKING

BDD-based techniques incrementally build a representation of all possible design next states until a fixed point is reached when the structure contains all possible future outcomes. The algorithm then can compute whether requirements are violated in any of the reachable states. SAT checking instead proceeds by iteratively building an expression to describe all possible execution paths from the design state and concurrently checking that requirements are satisfied at each step. Eventually, either a counterexample is found or the expansion gets too big and the FV engine can no longer determine whether the requirements are satisfied for the current step. Checking on the fly can reveal counterexamples sooner and before exponential expansion becomes a problem.

For simplicity, imagine a design of the *requirement* definition above with the modification that the c variable is a state element. Using priming notation for future values, the new design can be expressed with the expression:

```
c' = !a&&!c || b&&c
```

and visually in the simplified (we'll ignore clocking the register) Figure 2.14.

To expand the expression to capture what values may be assigned to variables in two steps, we need to add a new version of the formula with new (or *fresh*) variables for a, b, and c for the next state. The new added expression would be:

```
c'' = !a'&&!c' || b'&&c'
```

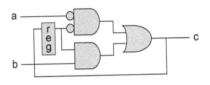

FIGURE 2.14

A simple sequential circuit.

The primed variables a' and b' represent the inputs that arrive at the second step and c'' represents the state that will be stored after the second computation.

This process repeats, adding fresh variables, until the SAT solver runs out of time or space and asserts that the requirements have been satisfied to a particular *bound*, the last successful expansion, or determines at some point that the target formula can be violated. This bound can be interpreted as the number of design execution steps that can be taken from a given start state such that the requirements are satisfied. If a SAT engine reaches a bound of n, this basically means that all possible executions of the design up to n cycles after reset have been analyzed—a powerful result equivalent to running an exponential number of simulations.

Each step can take an increasing amount of time to compute, so it is common for solvers to be run with a maximum bound parameter. After the proof reaches the designated bound, the engine considers it "good enough" and ends the analysis. Whether or not the bound achieved is sufficient for validation requirements is an important question, which we will discuss in future chapters.

SAT solvers require less memory than pure BDD engines and can check much larger models. Additionally, they do not require good BDD variable orderings. The downside to this technique is that no fixed point is computed to tell whether or not all possible execution sequences have been covered. In some circumstances, SAT induction techniques can cover all possible behaviors, but this is not the norm. Since our operational goal at early verification stages is usually to find bugs or analyze possible behaviors quickly, using SAT based techniques is often a win over using BDD techniques.

SOLVING THE SAT PROBLEM

A key observation is that we are trying to find, with as little computation as possible, just one example where an assignment of variables will produce a counterexample. To minimize the computation, it would be advantageous to structure the problem in a way that enables dividing it into simpler subproblems. Ideally, if we can structure it as an AND of many terms, we can determine that an assignment of variables makes the whole formula 0 by showing that just one term evaluates 0. Many SAT algorithms use this method, enabling them to quickly determine a large formula is 0 without having to examine every term.

More formally, given a Boolean logic formula in *conjunctive normal form*, the SAT problem requires we find an assignment of values for each variable such that the result will be 1. The formula is *satisfiable* if such an assignment exists and *unsatisfiable* if no assignment exists.

A formula is in conjunctive normal form (CNF) if it is a conjunction of clauses where each clause is an OR of variables or negated variables. This form is also called product-of-sums form, again viewing AND as multiplication-like and OR as addition-like. For example:

`(a||b||!d)&&(!b||c)&&(a||c)`

is in CNF. Note any Boolean logic formula can be converted into CNF, though the CNF formula may be larger than the original formula. While this form may appear a bit ugly, it has the advantage that it is a gigantic AND of many terms, meaning we just need to show a single term is 0 to falsify it, as discussed above.

Constructing CNF formulas from an RTL representation is straightforward. For each gate, we need to define the relationship between the inputs and the outputs. For example, consider an OR gate with inputs a and b and output c. The requirement on c is that if either a or b is 1, then c is 1. Also, c is 0 when both a and b are low. This can be captured by the requirements:

a ➔ c
b ➔ c
$!(a||b)$ ➔ $!c$

Rewriting using our definitions of implication, we get the CNF formula:

$(!a||c)\&\&(!b||c)\&\&(a||b||!c)$

The reader is invited to create a similar definition for an AND gate. Circuit definitions can be constructed by adding additional conjunctions for new gates and relating the output of one gate to the input of the next by using a common variable name.

To find an assignment of variables, we might construct a truth table and check each possibility. Returning to the example above, we might try assigning variables values starting with $a = 0$, $b = 0$, $c = 0$, $d = 0$. Unfortunately, those assignments produce a 0, so on to another assignment. The solution $a = 0$, $b = 0$, $c = 0$, $d = 1$ doesn't work either. So on we go, until a solution is found or, in the worst case, we've exhausted all 16 (2^n) possibilities.

As the number of variables grows, the time required to solve the problem becomes intractable. As we discussed in the last chapter, the bad news is that there is no algorithm that efficiently provides a solution for all possible formulas. The good news is that the problem has received a lot of attention and there are many known strategies that can do quite well for fairly big problems.

Rather than simply enumerating and testing the exponential number of cases, good SAT strategies utilize the following insights:

- Divide and conquer: Try to solve multiple smaller problems.
- Learn from mistakes (or avoid mistakes): Leverage information from earlier failures in later stages.
- Optimize what's important: Identify critical problems to solve.
- Domain-specific knowledge: Use known characteristics of realistic RTL designs.

These ideas plus some additional creativity have led to significant algorithm improvements enabling SAT to tackle industrial-sized problems. Further, strategies are continuing to evolve that will speed up the time required to solve existing problems and also enable even larger problems to be solved.

THE DAVIS–PUTNAM SAT ALGORITHM

Rather than repeating computations for each possible assignment of all variables in a truth table, a better strategy would be to evaluate the assignment of each variable just once and spawn off two subproblems: one with the formula simplified by replacing the variable with the value 1 and the other replacing the variable with the value 0. This process is repeated for each variable and if at the end, a subproblem evaluates the formula to 1, we have a set of assignments showing the formula is satisfiable. Alternatively, if all subproblems (or their descendants) produce formula evaluations of 0, the formula is unsatisfiable. Here is an outline of the algorithm:

```
SATDivide&Conquer(formula)
  If the formula evaluates to 1
    {Return Success!}
  If the formula evaluates to 0,
    {Return Failure, hope another assignment works.}
  Else
    {split the problem on some variable, v.
      SATDivide&Conquer (formula replacing v with 0)
      SATDivide&Conquer (formula replacing v with 1)
    }
```

In the worst case, the algorithm will recurse until all variables have been assigned, resulting in exponential time cost. However, with each split, one of the assignments will eliminate one of the clauses. For example, if the formula includes the clause (a||!b||c), when a is assigned the value 1, the clause will evaluate to 1, without needing to assign values to any other variables in the clause. The same reduction is possible if variable a is negated in the term, and a is assigned the value 0. Furthermore, once any one of the conjunctive clauses (ANDed terms) evaluate to 0, the entire formula evaluates to 0, so the algorithm can abandon any further variable assignments.

These two different reductions of the search space can be seen in the search graph below that finds solutions for the formula $(a||b||!d)\&\&(!b||c)\&\&(a||c)$. In this search, variable a is chosen for the first split, followed by b, c, and finally, d. Like with BDDs, the left subtrees identify where variables are assigned to 0 and right subtrees where variables are assigned to 1 (Figure 2.15).

Solutions can be collected as the algorithm returns from recursive calls. In the figure, solutions can be found by ascending up the tree from terminal nodes with value 1 and collecting variable assignments (e.g., from the left most terminal node 1: $d=0$, $c=1$, $b=0$, $a=0$). Note that some solutions may not provide an assignment for all variables (the far right solution above does not assign a value to d). In these cases, any unassigned variables can be arbitrarily assigned 0 or 1.

The choice of what variable to split on does impact the size of the search. In the above example, we chose variables in an arbitrary alphabetical order. Had we instead chosen to first split on variable b, there would be one less split required (try it!). Even better here would be to let each subproblem select its own optimal variable. The reader will find that choosing a for one subproblem and c for the other will prune out another split. For this simple problem, an algorithm that made the right choices would cut perhaps 28% of the run time—not a bad improvement, especially if it scaled to larger problems (again, this won't work for all problems). In this case, it might be speculated that variables that appear both with and without negation (e.g., b) might be better choices for splitting because both subproblems will be able to eliminate a clause when a variable is assigned to a value. This is the crux of what the Davis–Putnam algorithm does.

The Davis–Putnam algorithm improves this basic technique by using *resolution*. It simplifies the problem by first finding pairs of clauses where a variable appears as positive and negative. In our example:

    (a||b||!d) && (!b||c) && (a||c)

this is the case for b in the first and second clause. Resolution combines these two clauses into one without variable b and leaves other clauses unaffected.

    (a||b||!d) && (!b||c) becomes (a||!d||c)

This produces the simpler formula:

    (a||!d||c)&&(a||c)

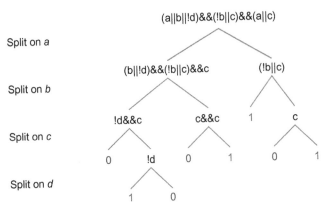

FIGURE 2.15

Solving SAT with a simple search algorithm.

If there were other clauses with variable b, they could be resolved into one clause at the same time as well. This process repeats seeking other candidate variables until there are no further clauses that can be resolved. Once there are no further clauses to resolve, we need to find a variable assignment for the reduced formula and then plug the values back into the original problem to solve for the resolved variables. In our example, we might find the assignment $a = 1$, $d = 0$, $c = 0$. Plugging this partial solution into the original formula, we see that b must be 0.

THE DAVIS LOGEMANN LOVELAND (DLL) SAT ALGORITHM

The Davis–Putnam algorithm can be improved by observing that assignments for variables that appear alone in a subclause (possibly because all other variables were assigned the value 0) can be made without needing to split the problem. Each subclause must evaluate to 1, so the variable value must be 1, unless it is appears in a NOT formula, in which case the value must be 0. Rather than eventually paying the performance cost of splitting on these variables, we can replace the variable in all subclauses sooner with its required value. For example, for the subproblem:

```
(b||!d)&&(!b||c)&&c
```

the variable c stands alone and thus must be 1 if a solution exists. The subproblem then simplifies to:

```
(b||!d)&&(!b)
```

We can then repeat the process assigning b the value 0 (required by the second clause), simplifying the subproblem to $(\overline{d})$, which then requires assigning d the value 0. Thus, using this method, we have completely resolved our SAT instance with no splitting or searching required! This improvement is called *Boolean Constraint Propagation* (BCP). DLL is often referred to as DPLL, perhaps because it is an improvement to the Davis–Putnam algorithm.

Additional SAT Algorithm Improvements

There have been many advances in the basic algorithms, and new improvements continue to be developed in academia and by EDA tool vendors. Since the size of SAT formulas can be quite large, even small efficiency improvements can have a significant impact on finding solutions. The improvements can be characterized as techniques that learn from discoveries made as the search proceeds, localized search techniques, and improved engineering of how the data structures are constructed and processed.

One effective learning technique has been to keep track of conflicts or *conflict clauses*. The idea is to save the discovery of assignments of sets of variables that will lead to failures. Utilizing this information, subsequent backtracking can avoid retrying bad assignments. A further interesting algorithm (known as "Grasp") showed that it can be beneficial to restart the entire search after adding a set of conflict clauses discovered on the first search attempt

Good engineering of the algorithm can also greatly improve performance. Another successful solver ("Chaff") takes the approach of making the frequently used operations very efficient. By optimizing the BCP algorithm and optimizing the decision strategy for speed and recently added clauses, the solver improved speed by 1–2 orders of magnitude.

With the improvements to the underlying algorithm, SAT has become a practical technique to solve interesting industry sized problems. This in turn has motivated research into even better techniques and commercial systems developed by the EDA industry.

CHAPTER SUMMARY

FV explores the complete space of possible design behaviors, unlike testing, simulation, and emulation techniques, which can be used to find and eliminate errors, but cannot demonstrate the absence of design flaws. Where FV can be applied, full coverage is achieved, increasing confidence in a design. However, FV is solving problems that have been proven to be *NP-complete* or worse, meaning there is no hope of a general efficient algorithm that will always guarantee a timely solution. Yet decades of research have led to today's generation of FV tools that really are able to analyze real industrial designs in reasonable time.

The magic of FV is created by efficient data structures to capture all possible behaviors a design may take, combined with efficient algorithms that search over the space to find counterexamples for when design requirements aren't satisfied. As we saw in the vending machine example, we can often exploit symmetry and patterns to store a Boolean function much more efficiently than a naïve counting of the bits would indicate. We also can leverage a solid understanding of the laws of Boolean algebra to provide many opportunities to rewrite formulas in equivalent ways that are useful for our formal search algorithms. By combining efficient but flexible representations of Boolean logic with a clever set of data structures and search strategies, modern FV tools can operate efficiently on many real-life functions with hundreds or thousands of variables.

For some problems that require complete coverage (such as floating point arithmetics), the appropriate strategy is to use BDD techniques, which provide a complete analysis at the expense of likely complexity issues on larger models. SAT-based FV strategies instead search for counterexamples as design behavior is incrementally expanded. Compared with using BDDs, SAT techniques are more automated, faster, and can work on larger designs. The downside to SAT techniques is that they are tailored towards bounded analysis, which is equivalent to simulating all behaviors possible in a certain number of execution cycles after reset, rather than fully analyzing all behaviors out to infinity. In practice, adequately large bounds on real designs can be achieved fairly regularly with a modest amount of effort.

Because designs may exhibit very different behaviors, a verification system that can utilize a variety of different techniques is highly desirable. On any given model, some approaches may hit complexity issues (run out of memory or time) while others do not. Together, the many heuristics and algorithms developed over the years have brought us to the modern stage where FV really is practical. By using today's generation of modern FV tools, a practicing engineer can leverage these powerful algorithms to understand and verify a wide variety of industrial designs.

FURTHER READING

[And99] H. R. Andersen, "An Introduction to Binary Decision Diagrams," Lecture Notes, IT University of Copenhagen, 1999.

[Cla99] Edmund M. Clarke Jr., Orna Grumberg, and Doron A. Peled, *Model Checking*, MIT Press, 1999.

[Cla08] Koen Claessen, Niklas Een, Mary Sheeran, and Nkklas Sorensson. "SAT-solving in practice." Workshop on Discrete Event Systems, Goteborg, Sweden, 2008.

[Hut00] Michael R.A. Huth, and Mark D. Ryan, *Logic in Computer Science, Modeling and Reasoning about Systems*, Cambridge University Press, 2000.

[Kro99] Thomas Kropf, *Introduction to Formal Hardware Verification*, Springer Verlag, 1999.

[Mos01] Matthew W. Moskewicz, Conor F. Madigan, Ying Zhao, Lintao Zhang, and Sharad Malik, "Chaff: Engineering an Efficient SAT Solver", Design Automation Conference (DAC), 2001.

[Ric08] Michael Rice and Sanjay Kulhari, "A Survey of Static Variable Ordering Heuristics for Efficient BDD/MDD Construction", Technical Report, University of California at Riverside, <http://alumni.cs.ucr.edu/~skulhari/StaticHeuristics.pdf>.

[She98] M. Sheeran and G. Stålmarck, "A Tutorial on Stålmarck's Proof Procedure", Formal Methods in Computer Aided Design (FMCAD), 1998.

Introduction to systemverilog assertions

3

Assertion-based design verification is an absolute necessity in today's large, complex designs ... Every design engineer should be adding assertion checks to his design!
—**Ben Cohen et al,** *SystemVerilog Assertions Handbook*

In order to leverage the power of formal verification (FV) to prove correctness of your design, you must first have a way to express what it means for your design to be correct. The most popular way to do this is through *properties*, specified in *assertions*, using the SystemVerilog Assertions (SVA) language. Although there are numerous specification methods in the industry and academia, such as the Property Specification Language (PSL) language and the Open Verification Library (OVL) assertion library that we mentioned briefly in Chapter 1, SVA has effectively become the industry standard over the last decade for specifying register transfer level (RTL) assertions.

Thus, before we explore FV techniques in detail, we need to start by learning the SVA language. The discussion in this chapter assumes you are already familiar with the SystemVerilog modeling language in general. In keeping with the theme of this book, our emphasis will be on assertion constructs that are most relevant to FV, though SVA assertions are also very useful in a simulation context. This will also be a very brief introduction, emphasizing the most useful features of the language and giving you just enough information and examples to effectively use them. If you want to know the full syntax definitions, every available language feature, or other details, there have been some excellent full-length books written entirely on SVA, including [Coh13] and [Cer14]. We do believe, however, that the information in this chapter will be sufficient to enable your productive use of SVA assertions.

In this chapter, we will be describing the SVA language as described in SystemVerilog Language Reference Manual (LRM) IEEE Standard 1800−2012. For brevity and clarity, in the remainder of this chapter we will refer to this document simply as the LRM.

BASIC ASSERTION CONCEPTS

To clarify our discussion for this chapter, we will use a concrete target model to describe the concept and usage of SVA assertions. Once we describe such a concrete model, it is much easier to introduce concepts such as the basic types of verification statements.

A SIMPLE ARBITER EXAMPLE

The model we use is a simple arbiter design, as shown in Figure 3.1.

This is an arbiter that has four requesting agents, each able to request a shared resource using one bit of the req signal. The gnt signal indicates which agent is currently authorized to use the resource. There is also an opcode input, allowing certain commands that override the normal behavior of the arbiter, such as forcing a particular agent to get priority, or cutting off all access to the resource for a period of time. There is an error output as well, to signify that a bad opcode or illegal sequence of opcodes has been sent. The interface code for a top-level System Verilog (SV) module implementing this design is shown below.

```
typedef enum logic[2:0] {NOP,FORCE0,FORCE1,FORCE2,
        FORCE3,ACCESS_OFF,ACCESS_ON} t_opcode;
module arbiter(
    input logic [3:0] req,
    input t_opcode opcode,
    input logic clk, rst,
    output logic [3:0] gnt,
    output logic op_error
);
```

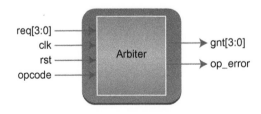

FIGURE 3.1

Arbiter example.

WHAT ARE ASSERTIONS?

At the most basic level, an *assertion* is a statement about your design that you expect to always be true. In the case of our arbiter, a simple example might be the fact that you never expect a grant to agent 0 when it was not requested:

```
check_grant: assert property (!(gnt[0] && !req[0])) else $error("Grant
without request for agent 0!");
```

As we will see in the discussions below, assertions can get much more complex than the simple Boolean expression above, involving logical implications and potential statements about values changing over time.

When running a simulation on a model, your simulator will usually flag an error when it detects that any SVA assertion in your code is not true. In the above example, if we ever see `gnt[0] == 1` and `req[0] == 0` in simulation, the message `Grant without request for agent 0!` will be displayed.

When running a formal property verification (FPV) tool, assertions are treated as proof targets: the goal of the tool is to mathematically prove that your RTL model can never violate this assertion.

There are two other types of properties we should understand before diving into the technical details: assumptions and cover points.

WHAT ARE ASSUMPTIONS?

Assumptions are similar to assertions, but rather than specifying the behavior of a device under test, they usually specify conditions that are intended to represent constraints on the verification environment. Often these represent conditions that are externally guaranteed to be true, due to inputs or other environmental factors. For example, perhaps we expect that our arbiter will only see legal non-NOP opcodes arrive at its `opcode` input:

```
good_opcode: assume property (opcode inside {FORCE0,FORCE1,FORCE2,
FORCE3,ACCESS_OFF,ACCESS_ON}) else $error("Illegal opcode.");
```

For simulation, an assumption is treated in exactly the same manner as an assertion: the simulator checks to see whether the current simulation values violate the specified condition, flagging a violation and printing the message if not. But keep in mind that the conceptual meaning is still somewhat different from an assertion failure: a failed assumption usually means something is wrong in the testing environment, testbench code, or a neighboring design module, while a failed assertion usually indicates a problem in the design under test. (This is not strictly required though, as it is legal to have an assumption involving internal design nodes, a situation we will discuss in more detail in future chapters.) In the example *good_opcode* above, it would indicate that the testbench is incorrectly driving an illegal opcode into the design.

In FV, there is a major difference between assumptions and assertions. Just like its name implies, an assumption is something that the tools assume to be true. An assumption is taken as an axiom and used to prove the truth of the assertions. Without assumptions, FV tools start by allowing any possible values to arrive at the inputs of the model they are analyzing; the assumptions are the primary method by which the user guides these values toward allowable behaviors. In most cases, a good set of assumptions is a requirement in order to eliminate consideration of unrealistic behaviors and correctly prove the assertions on a design.

WHAT ARE COVER POINTS?

An SVA cover point is specified in a similar way to assertions and assumptions, but it has a somewhat different meaning. While assertions or assumptions are expected to always be true, a *cover point* is something that is only occasionally true: it is specifying some kind of interesting condition that we want to make sure we are testing. For example, in our arbiter, we probably want to make sure that we are testing the possibly challenging case where all our agents are requesting the resource at once:

```
cover_all_at_once: cover property
        (req[0]&&req[1]&&req[2]&&req[3]);
```

In simulation, most users check cover points collectively: the tool or scripts save information to a database whenever a cover point is hit, and in the end the user can examine the total coverage after running all the simulation tests in their test suite. You usually want to make sure that each of your cover points is hit at least once; if not, this reveals a potential hole in your testing.

For FV, cover points also play an important role. Although FV theoretically covers all possible behaviors of your system, remember that you can specify assumptions or other input requirements that limit the possible traffic considered. This leads to a danger of *overconstraint*: you may accidentally specify assumptions that rule out interesting classes of traffic to your system. As a result, making sure that your FPV environment is able to reach all your cover points is a critical step in FV. We will discuss this more in the upcoming chapters on FPV.

CLARIFICATION ON ASSERTION STATEMENTS

As you may have noticed in the examples above, assertions, assumptions, and cover points are all specified with basically the same mechanisms in SVA. Thus, most of the mechanics of defining them are the same for all three types of constructs. For clarity, we concentrate on assertions in the remaining text of this chapter; keep in mind, however, that most of our discussion applies to assumptions and cover points as well. You should be able to use the techniques described in the remainder of this chapter equally for describing all three types of constructs. The term *assertion statement*, used here the same way it is defined in the LRM [IEE12], can equally refer to assertions, assumptions, or cover points.

SVA ASSERTION LANGUAGE BASICS

The SVA assertion language can be viewed as several layers of increasing complexity, as shown in Figure 3.2.

- *Booleans* are standard SystemVerilog Boolean expressions. A Boolean expression may be a single logic variable or a formula such as (req[0]&&req [1]&&req[2]&&req[3]) in the cover point example above.
- *Sequences* are statements about Boolean values (or other sequences) happening over time. They are dependent on a clearly defined clocking event to define time passing. For example, the following sequence represents a request followed by a grant in two clock cycles:

  ```
  req[0] ##2 gnt[0]
  ```

- *Properties* combine sequences with additional operators to show implication and similar concepts, to express some behavior expected to hold in a design. For example, a property might state that if we receive a request followed two cycles later by a grant, it implies that the grant will de-assert at the next cycle:

  ```
  req[0] ##2 gnt[0] |-> ##1 !gnt[0]
  ```

- *Assertion Statements* are statements using one of the keywords *assert*, *assume*, or *cover*, causing an SVA property to be checked as an assertion, assumption, or cover point. A property has no effect unless it is used in some kind of an

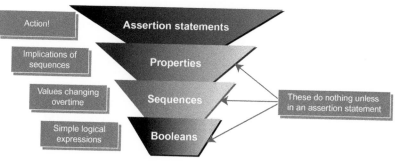

FIGURE 3.2

Layers of the SVA assertion language.

assertion statement. For example, an assertion statement that causes the property above to be checked might read:

```
gnt_falls: assert property(req[0] ##2 gnt[0] |->
           ##1 !gnt[0]);
```

We will discuss sequences, properties, and assertion statements in more detail in the remainder of this chapter. But before we move on, there is one more key concept we need to introduce: *immediate* and *concurrent* assertions.

- *Immediate* assertion statements are simple assertion statements that are checked whenever they are visited in procedural code. They allow only Boolean arguments, have no mechanisms for clocking or reset, and do not support many advanced property operators. As a result, they cannot check conditions that require awareness of the passage of time. In SVA, an immediate assertion is indicated by an assertion without the keyword *property*, as in:

```
imm1: assert (!(gnt[0] && !req[0]))
```

- *Concurrent* assertion statements are always evaluated relative to one or more clocks and can describe behavior that spans time, and allow numerous additional operators that support advanced statements about logical implication over time intervals. As a result, they are much more generally useful than immediate assertion statements. In SVA, a concurrent assertion is indicated by including the keyword *property* in the assertion, as in:

```
conc1: assert property (!(gnt[0] && !req[0]))
```

Although concurrent assertion *conc1* looks similar to immediate assertion *imm1*, their evaluations have some important differences. While the immediate assertion is evaluated whenever it is visited in procedural code, the concurrent assertion is only evaluated at edges of a well-defined clock. This will become clearer as we describe the two assertion types in more detail.

IMMEDIATE ASSERTIONS

Immediate assertions are the simplest kinds of assertion statements. They are generally considered part of SystemVerilog procedural code and are evaluated whenever they are visited during code evaluation. They have no concept of clocks or reset (aside from any clock/reset that may control their enclosing procedural block) and thus are incapable of verifying behavior that spans over time. They are also vulnerable to the usual hazards of SystemVerilog procedural code, including "delta-time" glitches, where they can be affected by temporary values in the middle of a time step, due to multiple evaluations of procedural (*always* or *always_**) blocks.

In general, we recommend using concurrent assertions instead of immediate assertions whenever possible. There are several reasons for this recommendation:

- Using assertions that are relative to known clocks, a feature directly supported by concurrent assertions, helps to keep the expected behavior clear and well understood.
- The delta-time hazard, where immediate assertions may report on temporary values that will change by the end of a time step, can result in invalid reports of failures and make debugging more difficult.
- Since immediate assertions are not stated relative to a clock unless located in a clocked procedural block, changes in your model or testbench's timing behavior can create unpredictable results.

However, there are certain cases where immediate assertions are required:

- In functions or other truly unclocked structures: you may want to add an immediate assertion inside a function; for example, to check the safety of its arguments or check a calculation.
- For state-matching formal equivalence verification (FEV) tools: As we will see in Chapter 8, state-matching FEV tools break the logic into combinational logic cones, and thus many of them can handle only unclocked assumptions for proving equivalence.

For these reasons, we are describing immediate assertions here rather than skipping them altogether. But keep in mind that they must be used with caution and are recommended only in the above cases.

TIP 3.1

Use concurrent rather than immediate assertions, unless you are in a truly unclocked context such as a function, or you are specifically writing assumptions to aid state-matching FEV tools.

WRITING IMMEDIATE ASSERTIONS

While immediate assertions should usually only be used in cases we have described above, it is important that you use them correctly when you do need them. We recommend that you always use the variant of immediate assertions known as *final deferred immediate assertions*. A final deferred immediate assertion statement is relatively simple to describe: just use `assert final` followed by any Boolean expression, with an optional label before and failure message after. (If you are working with Electronic Design Automation (EDA) tools that have not yet adopted the latest LRM, you may need to use the *observed deferred immediate assertion* `assert #0` instead, which behaves the same in most common cases. See LRM clause 16.4 for more details on these constructs.) So if we want to write an immediate assertion to check that we are not granting access to agent 0 when they did not request it, we could write this statement:

```
grant0_ok: assert final (!(gnt[0] && !req[0])) else
    $error("Grant without request for agent 0.");
```

The label `grant0_ok` is an optional name for the assertion; most EDA tools will auto-generate a name if no label is present, but we recommend always including one.

The action block `else $error ...` is also optional, with most simulation tools generating default messages for assertion failures if it is not present. But we recommend always including something meaningful here, for aid in simulation debug.

This assertion could be placed within an `always` block in any module where the `gnt` and `req` signals are visible, or inside a function with access to these signals. We could also place it outside an `always` block within a module; in this case, it is treated as if in an implicit `always_comb` block. Whenever its procedural code is executed, the assertion will be checked.

COMPLICATIONS OF PROCEDURAL CODE AND MOTIVATION FOR ASSERT FINAL

The way that procedural code, mainly `always` blocks, is executed in SystemVerilog can be a surprise to many users—even some who have been designing in the language for years. What you need to keep in mind are three key concepts:

- Within a single `always` block, statements are executed in the order in which they appear, like software code.
- There is no guaranteed ordering for multiple `always` blocks; they can be executed in any order.
- If a signal in the sensitivity list of an `always` block changes (due to the execution of another `always` block or other type of assignment), it is executed again during the same time step.

These can result in some behaviors for immediate assertions that will surprise users without a detailed familiarity with the LRM. This is why the more recent versions of the language introduced the concept of *deferred assertions*. These are a form of immediate assertion that follows a special rule: if the procedure in which they exist is executed multiple times during a single simulation time step, only the result of the final execution will be reported. (The actual rule is a little more complicated, involving the concept of SystemVerilog "simulation regions," but rather than getting sidetracked with a full description of SV, we'll refer you to the LRM for the details.)

To make this clearer, here is an example of a very poorly written fragment of RTL code, which uses non-deferred immediate assertions:

```
always_comb begin : add_1_to_evens
    if (f_even(i) && i < 9) begin
      i = i + 1;
       a1: assert (i > = 10) else $error("i is %0d",i);
    end
end
always_comb begin : add_1_to_odds
    if (f_odd(i) && i < 10) begin
      i = i + 1;
       a2: assert (i > = 10) else $error("i is %0d",i);
    end
end
```

Let's assume that `f_even` correctly returns true for even numbers, and `f_odd` correctly returns true for odd numbers, as their name implies. If `i` somehow was assigned a value less than 10 somewhere, the above pair of *always* blocks would together be executed over and over, alternately increasing `i` by 1 each time, and we would see an assertion failure each time `i` is incremented but not yet at its maximum:

```
Assertion failure in myfile.v:40: i is 4
Assertion failure in myfile.v:34: i is 5
Assertion failure in myfile.v:40: i is 6
Assertion failure in myfile.v:34: i is 7
Assertion failure in myfile.v:40: i is 8
Assertion failure in myfile.v:34: i is 9
```

The user would find the above messages very confusing, since at the end of any time step in their simulator, they would see that `i` is always at least 10. The intermediate values that were changing during the time step triggered these assertions. This is why deferred assertions were introduced: for a deferred assertion, in any simulation time step, only the result of the final execution of each assertion in a given procedure is reported. In the case of the example above, if each `assert` were replaced with an `assert final`, then we would see no violations: at the final execution of each procedure for any given time step, either *i* would have a legal value, or no assertion would be checked.

For this reason, we recommend that whenever you do use immediate assertions, you use the deferred variety.

TIP 3.2

If you must use an immediate assertion, make it a deferred immediate assertion, by using `assert final`, or by using `assert #0` if your tools do not yet support the p1800−2012 standard.

LOCATION IN PROCEDURAL BLOCKS

There is one more complication of immediate assertions that we should discuss. An immediate assertion operates on whatever values its variables hold at the time its line is executed. This may differ from the values the signals settle upon at the end of the procedure. Here is an example of a procedure with a poorly placed immediate assertion:

```
always_comb begin
    gnt = 4'b0;
    no_conflict: assert final ($onehot0(gnt));
    if (|req)
      gnt = f_compute_grant (req);
end
```

In this example, the assertion `no_conflict` has been written to check that there is always at most one grant. But because it was placed before the `f_compute_grant` call, it will actually never detect a failure, even if there is an error in the `f_compute_grant` function: at the time the assertion line is reached, the value of `gnt` will always be the 0 assigned on the line before. The following version makes much more sense:

```
always_comb begin
    gnt = 4'b0;
    if (|req)
      gnt = f_compute_grant (req);
    no_conflict: assert final ($onehot0(gnt));
end
```

You need to keep in mind that the `final` qualifier for an immediate assertion only signifies the use of the final execution of its enclosing `always` block during each time step; it does not indicate that it detects the final value for its variables. If you find this confusing, there is no need to worry: you can sidestep the issue in most cases by simply following a rule of thumb to put any immediate assertions at the end of the procedure or function.

TIP 3.3

In cases where you need to use an immediate assertion, put it at the end of the procedure or function that calculates its key values.

BOOLEAN BUILDING BLOCKS

Before we close our discussion of immediate assertions, we should examine the various Boolean building blocks provided by the SystemVerilog language. These are not strictly for assertions, but are useful shorthand that can enable us to write clearer and more succinct assertions for common situations. They are especially useful in that they can be applied to both immediate and concurrent assertions. In most cases, their meanings are relatively self-explanatory, so rather than explain them in detail here, we will just supply Table 3.1 to summarize the constructs that we have found most useful in assertion contexts.

CONCURRENT ASSERTION BASICS AND CLOCKING

As we discussed in the last section, most of the assertions that you write for FPV purposes will be *concurrent assertions*. These assertions support clear specification of clocks and resets, and are capable of examining the behavior of values over time. Before we discuss the more complex sequence and property concepts, which allow us to specify complex behaviors over a period of time, we will begin by introducing concurrent assertions on simple Boolean expressions, so we can discuss the basics of how their timing works. Here is an example of a concurrent assertion for checking that, at any rising edge of the clock `clk` outside reset, we have an acceptable non-NOP opcode:

```
safe_opcode: assert property (
    @(posedge clk)
    disable iff (rst)
    (opcode inside {FORCE0,FORCE1,FORCE2,FORCE3,ACCESS_OFF,ACCESS_ON}))
    else $error("Illegal opcode.");
```

From this example, we can see that the syntax for concurrent assertions differs from immediate assertions in several obvious ways:

- The assertion statement is declared with the keywords `assert property`.
- We include an optional clock specification, with a relevant edge.
- We include an optional reset specification, using the keywords `disable iff`.

Table 3.1 Useful Boolean Building Blocks in the SystemVerilog Language

Construct	Meaning	Usage example
`$countbits` (*expression, val1, val2, ...*)	Count occurrences of specified bit	`num_gnts = $countbits (gnt, 1'b1)`
`$countones` (*expression*)	Count bits that are equal to 1	`num_gnts = $countones (gnt)`
`$onehot(`*expression*`)`	Return true iff precisely one bit is 1	`safe_gnts = $onehot (gnt)`
`$onehot0(`*expression*`)`	Return true iff no bits are 1, or precisely one bit is 1	`safe_or_no_gnts = $onehot0(gnt)`
expression `inside` *list*	Return true iff expression is in list	`safe_opcode = opcode inside {ADD,SUB,MUL}`

In this example, we are checking a simple Boolean formula. Functionally, the key difference between this assertion and a similar immediate assertion is that this one is checked only at the given clock edge, and that this one is ignored during its reset (`disable iff`) condition.

We should also note that because a concurrent assertion can define its own clocking and reset, concurrent assertions usually make the most sense to use outside procedural code, separate from an `always` block. You can include them in procedural code as well, but we recommend avoiding this usage, as it can introduce complex relationships between assertion and procedure timing. (See LRM section 16.14.6 if you want to learn the full details of this usage.)

TIP 3.4

Concurrent assertions are best placed outside your procedural code (that is, outside of your `always` blocks) to avoid confusion about which values are checked.

Before we go into greater depth on the many ways to implement more powerful concurrent assertions, we should carefully examine the clock and reset conditions: it is important you understand these in order to fully comprehend what a concurrent assertion is checking.

SAMPLING AND ASSERTION CLOCKING

Concurrent assertions operate on what is known as the *sampled value* of their arguments. Essentially, at any simulation time step, the sampled value of each variable is the value that variable attained at the end of the previous simulation time step.

In Figure 3.3, we see a signal *sig1* with values that change at various times, and a concurrent assertion:

```
sig1_off: assert property (@(posedge clk1) !sig1);
```

At first glance, the reported values for the assertion might seem strange, because a naïve reader would think that the assertion should simply be true whenever `sig1` is

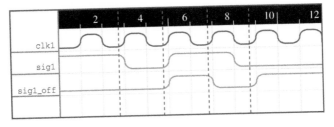

FIGURE 3.3

How values are sampled for concurrent assertions.

false. But actually, the assertion results are only calculated at each positive edge of the clock, and as we stated above, they always examine the value sampled at the end of the previous time step, just before that edge. So we see results indicating:

- At phase 4, `sig1` has just gone to 0, but it was 1 before the rising edge of `clk1`, so the assertion uses the value of 1 and fails.
- At phase 6, `sig1` has just gone to 1, but it was 0 before the rising edge of `clk1`, so the assertion uses the value of 0 and passes.
- At phase 8, `sig1` was 1 before the clock edge as well as after, so the assertion uses the value of 1 and fails.
- At phase 10, `sig1` went to 0 in plenty of time before the rising clock edge, so the assertion uses the value of 0 and passes.

Although this might be disconcerting at first, a few minutes of reflection will reveal that this will, at worst, lead to off-by-one reporting of assertion failures; as long as this sampling rule is consistent for all values used in the concurrent assertion, any failures defined by its logic should behave as expected, as long as the failing values are visible just before an edge of the relevant clock. We should also note that many EDA tools compensate for this inherent off-by-one behavior in their output, so the particular tool you are using may or may not actually report failures after the signal transitions in this way. But if they are compliant with the rules of the language, they will consistently use these sampled values to calculate assertion results.

TIP 3.5

Don't worry if reports of concurrent assertion failure times in some EDA tools seem to be one cycle later than the failure-causing values. This is a consequence of SVA's definition of sampling.

The place where this sampling behavior can lead to trouble is if you put concurrent assertions in procedural code or include terms that use unclocked elements, such as software calls, and create situations where sampled and non-sampled values might be combined in one assertion. This is another reason for our earlier tip to put your concurrent assertions outside procedural code.

SAMPLED VALUE FUNCTIONS

As helpful building blocks to construct concurrent assertions, SVA also provides a set of *sampled value functions*, built-in functions that operate on sampled values in the same way as concurrent assertions. For example, suppose we want to make sure that whenever there is no grant, there was no request on the previous cycle. We could write the assertion like this:

```
no_grant_ok: assert property (@(posedge clk)
        (|gnt) || !$past(|req));
```

This assertion checks the desired condition. Both the req and gnt values are sampled just before the positive edge of clk, and the $past function examines the value of its argument one cycle earlier. These functions all inherit the clock of the assertion statement, sequence, or property where they are used, though they may also be passed explicit clock arguments.

The most useful sampled value functions, with summaries and usage examples, are shown in Table 3.2. Here we show the simple forms that are most commonly used: refer to LRM section 16.9.3 for the details and full set of options.

One slight wrinkle to watch for when using these functions is the issue of X or Z values. Many modern simulators support 4-valued runs that include these values, and this feature has been added to some FV tools. According to the LRM, a transition from X to 1 counts as a rise for *$rose*, and from X to 0 counts as a fall for *$fell*. If you are targeting a validation environment that allows these values and you do not want transitions from X/Z to count as a rise or fall, you should probably be using sequence notation, as described in the next section, rather than these shorthand functions.

CONCURRENT ASSERTION CLOCK EDGES

As you have probably inferred from the discussion in the previous sections, the clock to be used by a concurrent assertion is an important consideration when creating the concurrent assertion. This clock is expressed with a clock specifier such as @(posedge clk1). The clock expression is what determines which values are sampled, and can create unexpected behavior if the wrong clock is used. A common mistake is to omit an edge and use an expression like @(clk1): this makes an assertion act on positive and negative clock edges, effectively examining each phase rather than each cycle. For a latch-based design, this may

Table 3.2 The Most Useful Sampled Value Functions

Function	Description
$past(*expr*)	Sampled value of expression one clock earlier
$past(*expr, n*)	Like $past(*expr*), but look *n* clocks earlier instead of one
$rose(*expr*)	Returns 1 iff LSB* of sampled value of expression is 1, and one clock earlier it was non-1
$fell(*expr*)	Returns 1 iff LSB of sampled value of expression is 0, and one clock earlier it was non-0
$stable (*expr*)	Returns 1 iff sampled value of expression equals value at previous edge
$changed (*expr*)	Returns 1 iff sampled value of expression does not equal value at previous edge

LSB stands for Least Significant Bit.

sometimes be the true user intent, but more commonly, a posedge is really needed. If a slow clock is passed in to an assertion, it may be ignoring short-term values that last only a single phase of a faster clock. If sampled value functions such as $past are used, or sequence delays (which we will describe in the next section) are used, choosing a different clock can actually change the number of cycles that are counted.

In Figure 3.4 we can see the different behaviors of an assertion with the same logical expression, !sig1, but with different clocks passed in.

```
check_posedge: assert property (@(posedge clk1) !sig1);
check_anyedge: assert property (@(clk1) !sig1);
check_posedge4: assert property (@(posedge clk4) !sig1);
```

In particular, we see that:

- At phase 4, the check_posedge and check_anyedge assertions have detected the zero value of sig1, but the check_posedge4 assertion has not, since we do not yet have a positive edge of clk4.
- At phase 7, the check_anyedge assertion has detected the one-phase glitch of sig1, but neither of the other two detects it, since this pulse does not persist until any positive clock edge.
- At phase 14, we see that all three assertions are passing, since sig1 had a value of 0 before positive edges of both clocks.

Ultimately, the key lesson here is that you should be sure to understand what clocks you are using for your assertions, and why. Do you want to detect one-phase "glitch" values, or ignore them? Do you want to look for every change relative to your fastest clock or really only care about some slower clock used to sense outputs?

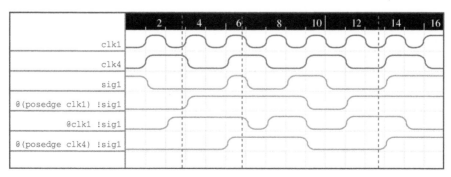

FIGURE 3.4

Sampling behavior for different assertion clocks.

> **TIP 3.6**
>
> Think carefully about the proper clock for your assertions and be sure to include the posedge or negedge qualifier if applicable.

CONCURRENT ASSERTION RESET (DISABLE) CONDITIONS

In addition to clocks, concurrent assertions also allow you to specify reset conditions using disable iff. The main goal here is to shut off assertion checking during reset: on most modern designs, you can expect some level of arbitrary "garbage" values in your design at reset, and you probably do not want to deal with the noise of invalid assertion failures due to these arbitrary values. So an assertion is considered to be trivially passing whenever its disable condition is true.

A complication with assertion resets is that they are an exception to the sampling behavior described in the past few sections: assertion reset is *asynchronous*, with an assertion being shut off immediately any time its disable condition is met. The consequence of this is that you should not try to be clever and insert miscellaneous logic within your disable clause: because this is timed differently from the rest of the assertion, you are likely to get confusing and unintended results. For example, consider the following two assertions, both trying to state that outside of reset, if you have at least one grant, you should have a request:

```
bad_assert: assert property (@(posedge clk)
    disable iff
      (real_rst || ($countones(gnt)==0))
    ($countones(req)>0));

good_assert: assert property (@(posedge clk)
    disable iff (real_rst)
    (($countones(req)>0) ||
        ($countones(gnt)==0)));
```

At first glance, these might look logically equivalent: both are assertions that say you must either not have any grants, or you must have at least one request currently high. But because bad_assert puts the gnt signal in the disable condition, which is not sampled, it will actually be looking at gnt values one cycle earlier than the req values, causing a failure to be missed on the waveform shown in Figure 3.5.

In Figure 3.5, there is clearly a problem in phase 6, where there is a grant with no request. The assertion good_assert will report this failure on phase 8, using the sampled values from just before the relevant rising edge of clk1.

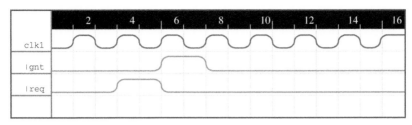

FIGURE 3.5

Missed failure due to miscellaneous logic in the disable clause.

The assertion bad_assert is disabled for every phase except 6. The sampled values just before the phase 8 rising edge show |req false, but the current value of gnt (used instead of the sampled value, due to the disable clause) disables the checking of this assertion.

> **TIP 3.7**
>
> In the reset (disable iff) of an SVA assertion, only use actual resets: signals that globally shut off major parts of the model for long periods of time. Using miscellaneous logic in the reset term can give confusing results due to the asynchronous behavior.

SETTING DEFAULT CLOCK AND RESET

As we conclude our examination of SVA clocking and reset for concurrent assertions, there is one more important language feature to discuss. You have probably noticed from our examples so far that specifying the clock and reset of an assertion can seem a bit wordy:

```
good_assert: assert property @(posedge clk)
        disable iff (rst)
        (|req || !(|gnt)) else $error("Bad gnt.");
safe_opcode: assert property (
    @(posedge clk)
    disable iff (rst)
    (opcode inside {FORCE0,FORCE1,FORCE2,FORCE3,ACCESS_OFF,ACCESS_ON}))
    else $error("Illegal opcode.");
```

Fortunately, SVA offers a way to set a global clock and reset for the concurrent assertions in a module, so they can be written once and cover multiple assertions. You declare a default clock with a default clocking statement and a default reset with a default disable iff statement. If these defaults are declared, they apply to all assertion statements in the current module, except those that explicitly include a different clock or reset. Thus, the following code is equivalent to the two assertions above:

```
default clocking @(posedge clk); endclocking
default disable iff (rst);
good_assert: assert property
        (|req || !(|gnt)) else $error("Bad gnt.");
safe_opcode: assert property (
    (opcode inside {FORCE0,FORCE1,FORCE2,FORCE3,ACCESS_OFF,ACCESS_ON}))
    else $error("Illegal opcode.");
```

The asymmetric syntax between the `default clocking` and `default disable iff` statements above is not a typo: `default clocking` requires an `endclocking`, while `default disable iff` does not. (Don't ask us why, it's a quirk from the initial language design that we're now stuck with.) In the common case where you have many assertions that use the same clocks and resets, declaring these defaults in each assertion-containing module can significantly improve readability of your assertion code and also prevent the mistakes we have seen in the past few sections from misuse of clock and reset.

TIP 3.8

When you are writing many assertion statements that use the same clocks and resets, be sure to use `default clocking` and `default disable iff` statements to declare the clocks and resets once, instead of including them in every individual assertion.

By the way—now that we have described the usage of these default constructs, coding examples in this chapter and the following chapters will usually not bother to specify the explicit clock and reset for each assertion. When reading any code fragment in the remainder of this text, you should assume an appropriate `default clocking` and `default disable iff` are in effect. This way, we can write our examples much more cleanly, without redundant details of clocking and reset visible in every assertion line.

SEQUENCES, PROPERTIES, AND CONCURRENT ASSERTIONS

Now that we have introduced the basics of concurrent assertions and showed how their clocking works, we can finally get to the most powerful aspect: the ability to state behaviors happening over time and to use the multiple layers of the language to build up complex sequences and properties.

SEQUENCE SYNTAX AND EXAMPLES

A sequence is a specification of a set of values occurring over a period of time. The basic operation used to build a sequence is a delay specifier, in the form ##n (for a specific number of clocks) or ##[a:b] (indicating a variable delay between a and b clocks.) The special symbol $ can be used for the upper bound of a sequence, specifying a potentially unlimited number of cycles. A sequence is said to be *matched* when its specified values have all occurred. A sequence with a variable delay may have multiple overlapping matches during any execution trace. Figure 3.6 shows a few examples of simple sequences.

Another common sequence operation is the repetition operator [*m:n]. This indicates that a subsequence is to be repeated a certain number of times. Again, the upper bound may be $, indicating a potentially unlimited number of repetitions. Figure 3.7 shows some illustrations of using this operator.

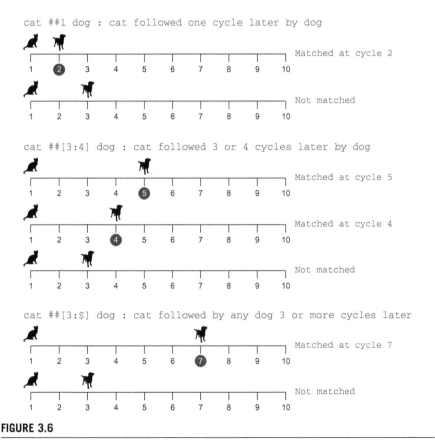

FIGURE 3.6

Basic sequence examples.

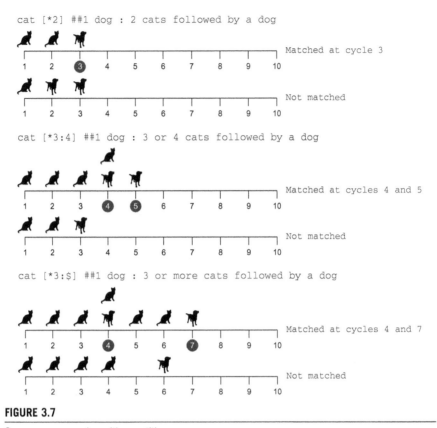

FIGURE 3.7

Sequence examples with repetition.

Sequences may be logically combined using the and or or operators. (Note that these are distinct from SystemVerilog's || and && operators, which provide logical ANDing or ORing for Boolean expressions.) When using the and operator, we are indicating that both sequences are starting at the same time, though their endpoints may mismatch. For the or operator, one of the two sequences must be matched. Also useful are the throughout operator, which checks that some Boolean expression remains true for the whole execution of a sequence, and the within operator, which checks that one sequence occurs within the execution of another. Figure 3.8 shows some examples using these operators.

A final set of sequence operators that is commonly useful are the *goto repetition* operators, [->n] and [=n]. These indicate that some value occurs exactly *n* times in the sequence, though these occurrences may be nonconsecutive and have arbitrary other activity in between. The simple goto [->n] matches at the final occurrence of the value, while the nonconsecutive goto [=n] allows an arbitrary

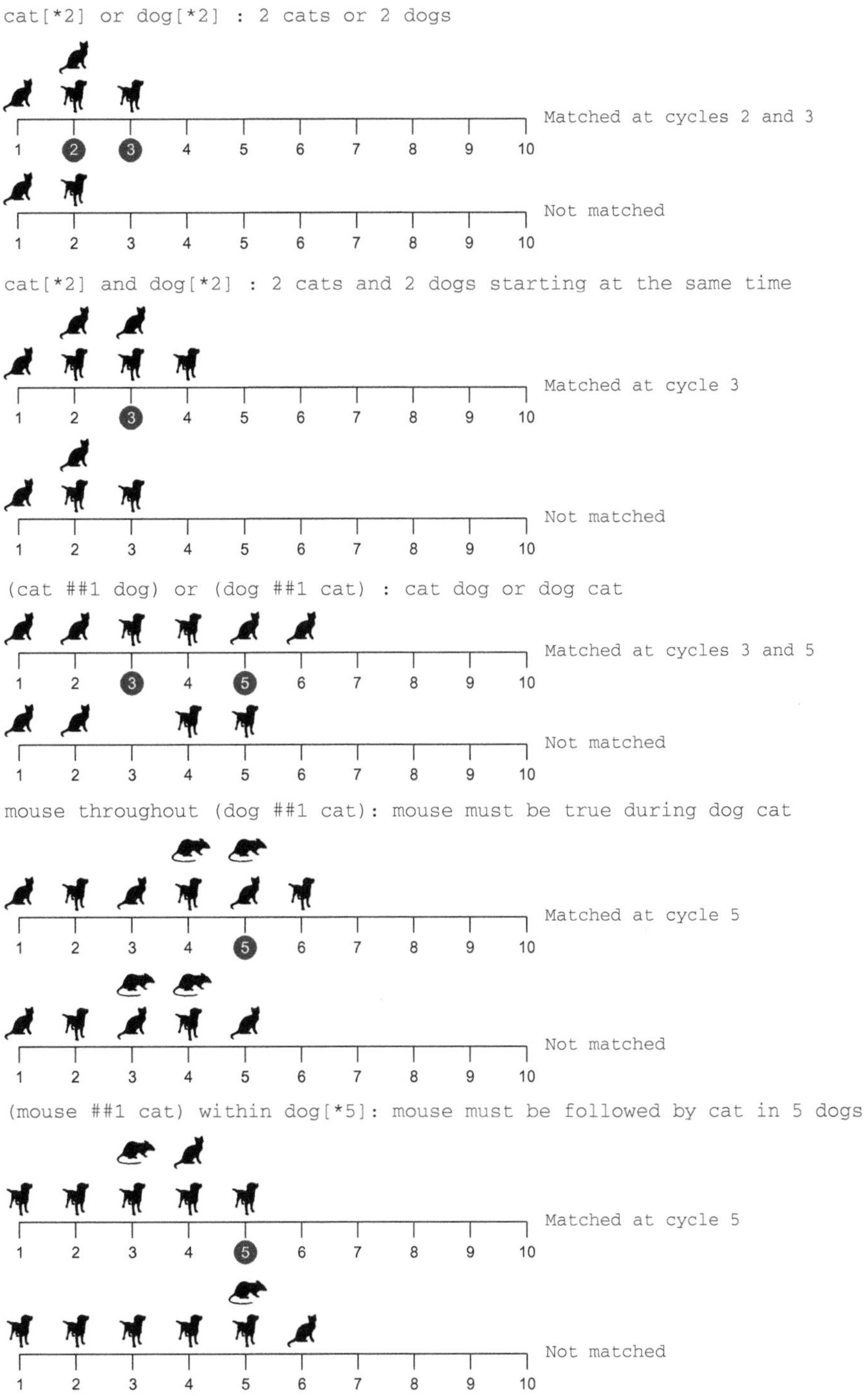

cat[*2] or dog[*2] : 2 cats or 2 dogs

Matched at cycles 2 and 3
Not matched

cat[*2] and dog[*2] : 2 cats and 2 dogs starting at the same time

Matched at cycle 3
Not matched

(cat ##1 dog) or (dog ##1 cat) : cat dog or dog cat

Matched at cycles 3 and 5
Not matched

mouse throughout (dog ##1 cat): mouse must be true during dog cat

Matched at cycle 5
Not matched

(mouse ##1 cat) within dog[*5]: mouse must be followed by cat in 5 dogs

Matched at cycle 5
Not matched

FIGURE 3.8

Sequence examples with more operators.

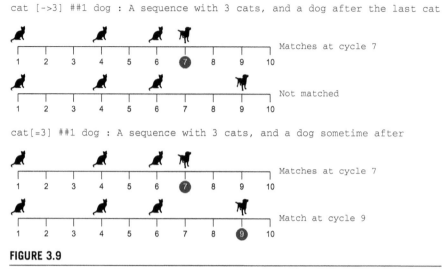

cat [->3] ##1 dog : A sequence with 3 cats, and a dog after the last cat

cat[=3] ##1 dog : A sequence with 3 cats, and a dog sometime after

FIGURE 3.9

Sequence examples with goto operators.

amount of additional time after the last occurrence. Figure 3.9 shows some examples of these.

Remember that sequences are not useful unless part of an assertion statement; the simple examples above are technically code fragments, not useful statements. Asserting a sequence as an assertion or assumption is not usually meaningful (we will discuss this more in the next subsection on properties), but sequences are very useful for building a cover property. Here are some examples of cover assertion statements that might be useful in our arbiter example:

```
// cover case where agent 0 req gets granted in 1 cycle
c1: cover property (req[0] ##1 gnt[0]);
// cover case where agent 0 req waits >5 cycles
c2: cover property ((req[0] && !gnt[0])[*5:$]
        ##1 gnt[0]);
// cover case where we see a FORCE1 arrive sometime
//        while req0 is waiting
c3: cover property (opcode == FORCE1) within
((req[0] && !gnt[0])[*1:$]);
```

Using sequences instead of $rose/$fell

When describing sampled value functions in the last section, we mentioned that if you want to check for rising or falling values without counting transitions from X, you could use sequence notation instead of $rose or $fell. The sequence expression (!mysig ##1 mysig) is similar to $rose(mysig), except that it will not trigger on a transition from X to 1: it strictly checks that `mysig` is 0 for a clock, then 1 for the next clock. Similarly, you can use `(mysig ##1 !mysig)` instead of `$fell(mysig)`, to avoid triggering on transitions from X to 0.

PROPERTY SYNTAX AND EXAMPLES

The most common types of properties are created using *triggered implication* constructs, *sequence | - > property* and *sequence | = > property*. The left hand side, or *antecedent,* of an implication must be a sequence. The right hand side, or *consequent*, can be a sequence or a property. The difference between the two operators is that | - > checks the property on the same clock tick when the sequence is matched, while the | = > operator checks one tick later. Triggered properties are vacuously true (that is, true for trivial reasons) on cycles where their triggering sequence is not matched. Figure 3.10 shows some examples of simple properties and traces where they are true and false at various times.

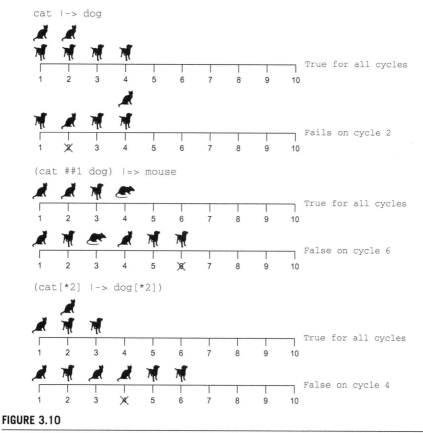

FIGURE 3.10

Property examples.

We should also make an important point here about these triggered implication properties: they provide a very important advantage for validation, as opposed to other ways to write logically equivalent properties. This is because many EDA tools take advantage of the information about the triggering condition. For example, an overlapping $|$-$>$ operation is often logically equivalent to a simple Boolean operation, as in the example below:

```
a1_boolean: assert property (!cat || dog);
a1_trigger: assert property (cat |-> dog);
```

However, with the triggered version, EDA tools can provide an advantage in numerous ways, to provide improved debug features.

- Simulation debug tools can indicate cycles when the assertion was triggered, as well as when it passed or failed.
- FV tools can generate an implicit cover point to check whether the triggering condition is possible. This also allows them to automatically report when an assertion is proven *vacuously:* it cannot be violated because the triggering condition cannot be met.

Thus, we recommend that whenever you have multiple potential ways to write a property, you try to state it as a triggered implication if possible.

TIP 3.9

Use triggered properties ($|$-$>$, $|$=$>$) in preference to other forms of properties when possible. This enables many EDA tools to provide specialized visualization and debug features.

Another set of useful tools for constructing properties are the *linear temporal logic* (LTL) operators. A full discussion of LTL operators is probably more detail than you need at this point, so we will refer you to LRM section 16.12 if you wish to learn the full story. But LTL operators are critical if you want to create "liveness properties": properties that specify aspects of potentially infinite execution traces. Probably the most useful LTL operators in practice are s_until and s_eventually. For the most part, these operators are exactly what they sound like: s_until specifies that one property must be true until another property (which must occur) is true, and s_eventually specifies that some expression must eventually be true. The s_ prefix on these operators stands for "strong," indicating that in an infinite trace the specified conditions must happen at some point. (You can omit the s_ prefix to get "weak" versions of these operators, which means that an infinite trace that never hits the condition is not considered a violation.) Infinite traces may sound odd if you are used to simulation, but they can be analyzed by FV tools; we will discuss this issue more in upcoming chapters. Figure 3.11 shows some examples of these LTL operators.

One more very useful class of properties is negated sequences. SVA sequences have a not operator, to enables us to check cases when the sequence is not matched.

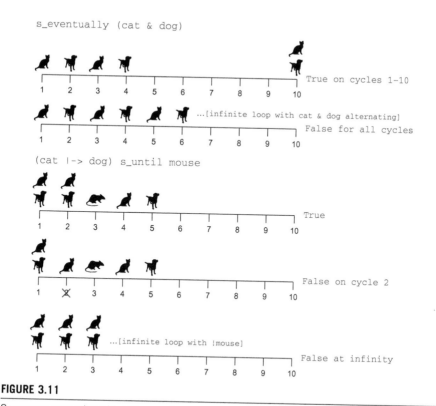

FIGURE 3.11

Sequence examples with LTL operators.

We did not include this in the sequence section above because technically a negated sequence is a property object, not a sequence object. This means that it cannot be used as the left-hand side of an implication operator. However, a negated sequence is often very useful as a property to check that some unsafe condition never occurs. Here are some examples of negated sequences used as properties. Figure 3.12 shows some examples of these.

Like sequences, properties are not actually meaningful unless included in an assertion statement; once again, the examples above are just fragments at this point. Here are some examples of assertion statements that might be useful in our arbiter model.

```
// assume after gnt 0, req 0 falls within 5 cycles
req0_fall_within_5: assume property
    ($rose(gnt[0]) |=> ##[1:5] $fell(req[0]));
// assert that any request0 is granted within 20 cycles
gnt0_within_20: assert property
    ($rose(req[0]) |-> ##[1:20] gnt[0])
```

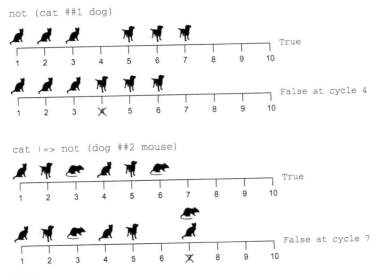

FIGURE 3.12

Negated sequence examples.

```
// assert that any grant on 0 is eventually withdrawn
gnt0_fall: assert property
    ($rose(gnt[0]) |-> s_eventually (!gnt[0]));
```

NAMED SEQUENCES AND PROPERTIES

Until now, we have been using sequences and properties directly in assertion statements, which is the most common mode of use. But sometimes you might want to encapsulate an advanced set of behaviors as a named object for more convenient reuse. SVA provides the ability to create named sequence and property objects for this purpose. These are similar to module declarations, but they take an optional set of untyped arguments. To define a named sequence, you just need the keyword sequence followed by its list of formal arguments, then the expression of the sequence, followed by an endsequence. Similarly for properties, you just need the keyword property followed by its list of formal arguments, then the expression of the property, followed by an endproperty. The property or sequence can then be instantiated in an assertion statement, or in another property/sequence, by using its name and passing in appropriate arguments. Here are some simple examples of a named sequence and property and how they might be used:

```
sequence within_5_cycles(sig);
    ##[1:5] sig;
endsequence
property b_within_5_after_a(a,b);
```

```
    a |-> within_5_cycles(b);
endproperty
// assertions a1 and a2 below are equivalent
a1: assert property (gnt[0] |-> ##[1:5] !req[0]);
a2: assert property (b_within_5_after_a(gnt[0],!req[0]));
```

TIP 3.10

If you are including a nontrivial amount of logic in any assertion statement, consider defining named sequences and properties to enable cleaner and more modular code.

ASSERTIONS AND IMPLICIT MULTITHREADING

Now that you know how to describe complex behaviors that happen over time, a question has probably occurred to you: what happens if multiple behaviors overlap? For example, suppose we implement a version of the arbiter that accepts each request as a one-cycle pulse and expects a grant precisely 10 cycles after any request. Here is an example assertion describing this behavior for agent 0:

```
delayed_gnt: assert property (req[0] |-> ##10 gnt[0]);
```

Due to the 10-cycle gap between the request and the grant, though, it is possible that another request will arrive within that window. That second request should also get a grant precisely 10 cycles after it arrived. So in effect, we need two overlapping evaluations of this assertion. Fortunately, SVA assertions provide built-in multithreading: multiple instances of an assertion or sequence may be in progress at any given time, with a new one triggered each time its starting conditions are met. The waveform shown in Figure 3.13 illustrates how this happens.

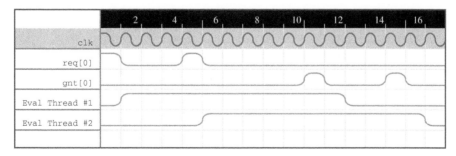

FIGURE 3.13

Parallel evaluation threads for assertion `delayed_gnt`.

In Figure 3.13, we can see that the first evaluation thread is launched after the request pulse on `req[0]` in cycle 1, and completes when the corresponding grant is seen in cycle 11. Similarly, the second thread is launched after the request in cycle 5, and ends after seeing the corresponding grant in cycle 15. Even though these two evaluations of the assertion are happening at the same time, they do not interfere with each other: if the grant had failed to arrive at cycle 11 or at cycle 15, a failure would have been reported.

Of course, like many powerful language features, this implicit multithreading is a double-edged sword: be careful not to create assertions with a triggering condition that happens often, or you risk creating a situation where the system must potentially analyze new threads created every single cycle, significantly impacting both FV and simulation performance. For example, the following assertion would have ended up creating new threads on nearly every cycle (all except cycles 1 and 5) in Figure 3.13:

```
notreq: assert property (!req[0] |-> ##10 !gnt[0]);
```

WRITING THE PROPERTIES

At this point, you know enough about the basics of assertions to write a wide variety of useful assertion statements. But in practice, how do you decide when and how to write assertions? In this final section of this chapter, we give you some general guidelines on adding assertions to your RTL models. This initial discussion is fairly general; in future chapters, we will return more specifically to examples of assertions that are especially useful in FV. There are three main project phases when you would typically define assertion statements needed in your code: during design specification, during RTL development, and during validation.

Planning properties at the specification phase

You should begin thinking about assertion statements when you are generating the high-level specifications for your design. Whenever you are describing a concrete requirement that will describe the behavior of signals in your design, think about whether it is something that you could potentially write as an assertion. Actually coding an RTL assertion at this early phase might not make sense, but you should find some way to indicate in your specification that you are at a point where an assertion is appropriate, so the correct assertion can later be inserted by an RTL developer or validator when the code is available. This can be as simple as a comment "ASSERTION" at the start of relevant paragraphs.

Also remember to think about potential cover points at this stage: both typical conditions that will be useful as a general sanity check on your validation, as well as interesting corner cases that you are worried your validation might miss.

> ### TIP 3.11
>
> Begin thinking about potential assertions and cover points in your specification/requirements phase, and mark potential assertions in the documents you create before RTL development.

Embedded properties during RTL development

During RTL development, you have a critical opportunity to capture your own thought processes in a permanently reusable way. Most commonly, RTL authors add comments to their code to describe why they are implementing it in a certain way. Assertions, however, can be thought of as "executable comments"—while they help to clarify the code, they also provide checks, during both simulation and FV, that the original intentions remain accurate. For example, compare the following two fragments of code:

```
// Fragment 1
// We expect opcode to be in the valid range; bad
// opcode would result in bypassing these lines.
// Also, don't forget to test each possible value.
assign forced_nodes = f_get_force_nodes(opcode);

// Fragment 2
op_ok: assert property
    ((opcode > = NOP)&&(opcode < = ACCESS_OFF));
generate for (i = NOP;i < = ACCESS_OFF;i ++) begin: b1
  test_opcode: cover property (opcode == i);
end
endgenerate
assign forced_nodes = f_get_force_nodes(opcode);
```

You can see that while both convey the idea that we expect opcodes in a valid range, and both demand us to test each possible opcode value, only Fragment 2 does these in an enforceable way. When the RTL is passed on to a future project for reuse, virtually a certainty in today's world of System-On-Chip (SOC) design, the new users will see assertion failures in simulation or FV if they use it in a way that violates the original author's assumption. And if the new user accidentally disables some opcodes that were available in the original design, the new validation team will discover some cover points that are not hit.

One other aspect of embedded assertion writing that is important to point out here is the use of assertions rather than assumptions. In general, you need to be careful about writing assumptions: because they constrain the space of possible values used for FV, a poorly chosen assumption can be counterproductive or dangerous. Whether a particular statement needs to be an assertion or an assumption depends on the hierarchy level where you are running FV, and most modern FV tools allow you to dynamically change a particular set of assertions to assumptions at the tool level. Also, assertions and assumptions are equivalent during simulation. Thus, we recommend that when writing embedded assertion statements during RTL development, you just write assertions and cover points, rather than assumptions.

TIP 3.12

As you are developing RTL, whenever you are about to write a comment about expected values or behavior of signals, think about whether it can be stated as an SVA assertion. If so, write the assertion, thinking of it as an "executable comment" for better long-term enforcement of your expectations.

TIP 3.13

As you are developing RTL, whenever you are about to write a comment about kinds of testing that need to be done, think about whether it can be stated as an SVA cover statement. If so, write the cover statement, thinking of it as an "executable comment" for better long-term enforcement of your expectations.

TIP 3.14

When writing embedded SVA statements, use assertions rather than assumptions. If a statement truly needs to be an assumption, this can be changed later dynamically in your FV tool.

Validation-focused properties

The other major project phase when you will typically be writing assertions is for validation purposes. This is typically the style of property writing that you will do for focused FV efforts, as we will see in upcoming chapters. When your focus is on validation, use the specification for your block as a starting point, and write assertions that restate the specification in an SVA format. For example, here is a possible specification of our arbiter block:

- When `opcode == FORCEn`, agent n gets the grant.
- When `opcode == ACCESS_OFF`, nobody gets a grant.
- The `op_error` signal is 1 if opcode is invalid, otherwise it is 0.
- When `opcode == NOP`, arbitration works as follows:
    - If nobody has a grant, the lowest-numbered requesting agent (0, 1, 2, 3) gets the grant.
    - When the grant holder lifts the request, the next agent that requested gets the grant.

When we have such a specification, we should usually try to write "end-to-end" assertions that will specify how our design's outputs look in terms of its inputs. These will be the most effective in helping to find if some unexpected or overlooked part of our design causes incorrect behavior. While white-box assertions based on internal nodes can also be useful validation and debug aids, using these exclusively can be dangerous because they focus on the designer's low-level thought processes instead of the overall design intent.

> **TIP 3.15**
>
> For validation, write high-level "end-to-end" assertions, based on your specification, that say how the outputs will behave depending on the inputs. Also write accompanying cover points that will check that your major usage cases are validated.

Also, depending on the complexity of our design, we need to keep in mind that it is often the case that a simple set of assertions may be difficult to write; we may also need some SystemVerilog modeling code to track the state or compute intermediate values. This is fine: don't be afraid to add queues, state machines, or similar modeling along with your assertions, to enable you to properly track design behavior. At the same time, be careful about cases where the modeling gets complex enough to add noticeable simulation cost: you may need to use `ifdefs` to mark some code as formal-only if this becomes an issue.

> **TIP 3.16**
>
> When writing high-level assertions and cover points based on your specification, be sure to add modeling code when appropriate. However, also pay attention to simulation profiling reports to detect cases where complex modeling is starting to have a noticeable simulation cost, and consider restricting such modeling and related assertions to only be used in FV.

Now let's look at the actual assertions we would write for our arbiter, based on each of the specification conditions.

- When `opcode == FORCEn`, agent `n` gets the grant.

This one seems very straightforward—but even with this simple requirement, we can see an initial ambiguity. Does our arbiter provide grants instantaneously, or is there a delay? We should probably improve our specification to state this directly. For now, we will expect a one-cycle delay between a request/opcode and a grant. We also need to be careful to include the implicit requirement here that other agents do not get the grant. We should also add appropriate cover points to make sure we validate cases where we use this functionality: many EDA tools will generate automatic covers for the direct triggering condition, but we may also want to add an explicit check that we can see cases where the force request is active and we get the grant. Thus, this requirement leads to the following assertion statements:

```
parameter t_opcode fv_forces[3:0] =
        {FORCE3,FORCE2,FORCE1,FORCE0};
generate for (i = 0; i < = 3;i++) begin: g1
    forcei: assert property (
        (opcode == fv_forces[i]) | = >
        (gnt[i] == 1) && ($onehot(gnt))) else
        $error("Force op broken.");
    cover_forcei: cover property (
        (opcode == fv_forces[i])
            && (gnt[i] == 1));
end
endgenerate
```

Now for the next two requirements:

- When opcode == ACCESS_OFF, nobody gets a grant.
- The op_error signal is 1 if opcode is invalid, otherwise it is 0.

These two are fairly straightforward. But be careful on the error condition: we need to not only assert that invalid opcodes give us an error, but also that valid opcodes do not give us an error. To make this easier we create an instrumentation signal *fv_validop* as shown below. We also add some related cover points.

```
accessoff: assert property (
        (opcode == ACCESS_OFF) | = >
        (|gnt == 0)) else
        $error("Incorrect grant: ACCESS_OFF.");
logic fv_validop;
assign fv_validop = (opcode inside {FORCE0,FORCE1,FORCE2,
            FORCE3,ACCESS_OFF,ACCESS_ON});
error0: assert property (fv_validop | = > !op_error);
error1: assert property (!fv_validop | = > op_error);
cover_nognt: cover property (|gnt == 0);
cover_err: cover property (!fv_validop ##1 !op_error);
```

The final set of requirements form the core of the arbiter operation.

- When opcode == NOP, arbitration works as follows:
  - If nobody has a grant, the lowest-numbered requesting agent (0, 1, 2, 3) gets the grant.
  - When the grant holder lifts the request, the next agent that requested gets the grant.

Here we will illustrate the use of some instrumentation functions, simple SystemVerilog function statements, to determine the next agent in the round robin ordering for the assertion. Note that this is probably redundant with some logic in the design; this is fine, since we are trying to double-check our critical implementation logic.

TIP 3.17

When writing assertions for validation, it is okay to write instrumentation code that mimics some calculation in your design. If doing this, we recommend keeping the validation code in a separate file and using some naming convention like an *fv_* prefix on all instrumentation objects to avoid confusion between the real design and instrumentation logic.

```systemverilog
// Return which bit of a one-hot grant is on
function int fv_which_bit(logic [3:0] gnt);
  assert_some_owner: assert final ($onehot(gnt));
  for (int i = 0; i < 4; i++) begin
    if (gnt[i] == 1) begin
      fv_which_bit = i;
    end
  end
endfunction
// Compute next grant for round-robin scheme
function logic [3:0] fv_rr_next(logic [3:0] req,
          logic [3:0] gnt);
  fv_rr_next = 0;
  for (int i = 1; (i < 4); i++) begin
    if (req[(fv_which_bit(gnt) + i)%4]) begin
      fv_rr_next[(fv_which_bit(gnt) + i)%4] = 1;
      break;
    end
  end
endfunction
// If nobody has the current grant, treat as if agent 3 had it (so agent
0,1,2 are next in priority).
rr_nobody: assert property (((opcode == NOP) &&
  (|gnt == 0) && (|req == 1)) |=>
  (gnt = fv_rr_next(req,4'b1000))) else
    $error("Wrong priority for first grant.");
// If ANDing req and gnt vector gives 0, req is ended.
rr_next: assert property (((opcode == NOP) &&
  (|gnt == 1) && (|req == 1) && (|(req&gnt) == 4'b0)) |=>
  (gnt == fv_rr_next(req,gnt))) else
    $error("Violation of round robin grant policy.");
```

We would also generate some related cover points for the above example, checking that grants to each of the agents are possible, but for the sake of brevity we do not describe them in detail here.

Before we finish with the assertions to implement on this block, it is also a good idea to take a step back, look at the specification, and see if there are any unstated safety conditions that were so obvious that nobody bothered to state them. This is a common problem in specifications: there are often implicit notions about a particular type of design that are so well understood by the engineering community that we "do not need" to state them. In this case, you may have already spotted that in this detailed arbiter specification, we have never mentioned one core safety property that should be true of any arbiter:

- We never grant the resource to more than one agent at a time.

This one is easy to state as an assertion, so we should go ahead and do it. Our other assertions might imply it at some level, but there is really no downside to formally stating such a clear and direct requirement.

```
safety1: assert property ($onehot0(gnt)) else
        $error("Grant to multiple agents!");
```

Remember to review your plans for such missing requirements whenever writing a set of assertions for a new model.

TIP 3.18

When you write specification-based validation assertions, also think about high-level unstated safety conditions that may be implicitly part of the design intent.

Connecting the properties to your design

Once you have written your assertions and cover points, you must insert them into your RTL model. The most direct way to do this is simply to paste them inside the code of your top-level module. If you are writing embedded assertions as you design the code, inserting them in the actual RTL as you write it does make the most sense. However, if you are writing assertions later for validation purposes, you may not want to touch the original RTL code directly.

SystemVerilog provides a nice feature to enable you to connect externally written code inside a module: the `bind` statement. Binding allows you to separate design code from verification code. A bind essentially forces a remote module to instantiate another module inside it, and be treated just like any other submodule instance. This enables you to put a set of validation assertions in a standalone module and then connect it to your model.

To illustrate the use of `bind` statements, the following two code fragments are equivalent:

```
// Fragment 1: Directly instantiate FV module
module arbiter(...);
...
   fv_arbiter fv_arbiter_inst(clk,rst,
          req,gnt,opcode,op_error);
endmodule

// Fragment 2: Bind FV module
module arbiter(...);
   ...
endmodule
// This line may be below or in another file
bind arbiter fv_arbiter fv_arbiter_inst(clk,rst,
          req,gnt,opcode,op_error);
```

Thus, the original RTL code may be cleanly maintained, while validation code is written independently and connected later.

TIP 3.19

If you want to add validation assertions without touching the original RTL code, take advantage of SystemVerilog's `bind` statement.

SUMMARY

In this chapter, we introduced the basics of SVA. We learned about the three types of assertion statements: assertions, which state a requirement of your design; assumptions, which state an expectation from a design's external environment; and cover points, which describe expected testing conditions for a design. We then discussed the major features of the SVA language that are most likely useful for FV, including:

- Immediate assertions, which are useful in unclocked situations and for FEV tools.
- Boolean building blocks including `$countones`, `$countbits`, `$onehot`, `$onehot0`, and the inside operator.
- Concurrent assertions, clocked assertions that are the most useful for FPV. These are timed using well-defined "sampling" behavior that can be tricky for beginners.
- Clocking and reset for concurrent assertions, including the ability to set default clock and reset values using `default clocking` and `default disable iff`.

- Sequence operations, including ##[m:n] delay operators, [*n], [->n], and [=>n] repetition operators, and the and, or, and throughout operators.
- Property operations, including triggered implications |-> and |=>, LTL operators s_until and s_eventually, and negated sequences as properties.
- Sampled value functions, including $past, $rose, $fell, $stable, and $changed.
- Named sequence and property objects.
- Implicit multithreading aspects of SVA properties.

We then introduced the two main phases of a project where you are most likely to be writing assertions: during RTL development, when you want to use assertions as a type of executable comment, and during validation, when you should emphasize end-to-end specification-based assertions. We created a set of specification-based assertions for our arbiter example and showed how it might be connected to a model using SystemVerilog's bind feature.

Now that you know the basics of assertions, in the next few chapters we will introduce their most powerful application: *FPV*.

PRACTICAL TIPS FROM THIS CHAPTER

3.1 Use concurrent rather than immediate assertions, unless you are in a truly unclocked context such as a function, or you are specifically writing assumptions to aid state-matching FEV tools.

3.2 If you must use an immediate assertion, make it a deferred immediate assertion, by using assert final, or by using assert #0 if your tools do not yet support the p1800−2012 standard.

3.3 In cases where you need to use an immediate assertion, put it at the end of the procedure or function that calculates its key values.

3.4 Concurrent assertions are best placed outside your procedural code (that is, outside of your always blocks) to avoid confusion about which values are checked.

3.5 Don't worry if reports of concurrent assertion failure times in some EDA tools seem to be one cycle later than the failure-causing values. This is a consequence of SVA's definition of sampling.

3.6 Think carefully about the proper clock for your assertions and be sure to include the posedge or negedge qualifier if applicable.

3.7 In the reset (disable iff) of an SVA assertion, only use actual resets: signals that globally shut off major parts of the model for long periods of time. Using miscellaneous logic in the reset term can give confusing results due to the asynchronous behavior.

3.8 When you are writing many assertion statements that use the same clocks and resets, be sure to use default clocking and default disable iff statements to declare the clocks and resets once, instead of including them in every individual assertion.

3.9 Use triggered properties ($|$ - >, $|$ = >) in preference to other forms of properties when possible. This enables many EDA tools to provide specialized visualization and debug features.

3.10 If you are including a nontrivial amount of logic in any assertion statement, consider defining named sequences and properties to enable cleaner and more modular code.

3.11 Begin thinking about potential assertions in your specification/requirements phase, and mark potential assertions in the documents you create before RTL development.

3.12 As you are developing RTL, whenever you are about to write a comment about expected values or behavior of signals, think about whether it can be stated as an SVA assertion. If so, write the assertion, thinking of it as an "executable comment" for better long-term enforcement of your expectations.

3.13 As you are developing RTL, whenever you are about to write a comment about kinds of testing that need to be done, think about whether it can be stated as an SVA cover statement. If so, write the cover statement, thinking of it as an "executable comment" for better long-term enforcement of your expectations.

3.14 When writing embedded SVA statements, use assertions rather than assumptions. If a statement truly needs to be an assumption, this can be changed later dynamically in your FV tool.

3.15 For validation, write high-level "end-to-end" assertions, based on your specification, that say how the outputs will behave depending on the inputs.

3.16 When writing high-level assertions based on your specification, be sure to add modeling code when appropriate. However, also pay attention to simulation profiling reports to detect cases where complex modeling is starting to have a noticeable simulation cost, and consider restricting such modeling and related assertions to only be used in FPV.

3.17 When writing end-to-end assertions for validation, it is okay to write instrumentation code that mimics some calculation in your design. If doing this, we recommend keeping the validation code in a separate file and using some naming convention like a *fv_* prefix before all FV objects to avoid confusion between the real design and instrumentation logic.

3.18 When you write specification-based validation assertions, also think about high-level unstated safety conditions that may be implicitly part of the design intent.

3.19 If you want to add validation assertions without touching the original RTL code, take advantage of SystemVerilog's `bind` statement.

FURTHER READING

[Cer09] E. Cerny, S. Dudani, D. Korchemny, E. Seligman, and L. Piper, "Verification Case Studies: Evolution from SVA 2005 to SVA 2009," Design and Verification Conference (DVCon) 2009, February 2009.

[Cer14] Eduard Cerny, Surrendra Dudani, John Havlicek, and Dmitry Korchemny, *SVA: The Power of Assertions in SystemVerilog*, 2nd Edition, Springer, 2014.

[Coh13] Ben Cohen, Srinivasan Venkataramanan, Ajeetha Kumari, and Lisa Piper, *SystemVerilog Assertions Handbook, 3rd Edition with IEEE 1800–2012*, VhdlCohen Publications, 2013.

[Fos04] Harry Foster, Adam Krolnik, and David Lacey, *Assertion Based Design*, 2nd Edition, Springer, 2004.

[IEE12] "IEEE Standard for SystemVerilog—Unified Hardware Design, Specification and Verification Language," IEEE Computer Society, IEEE, New York, IEEE Std 1800–2012.

[Meh13] Ashok B. Mehta, *SystemVerilog Assertions and Functional Coverage: Guide to Language, Methodology and Applications*, Springer, 2013.

[Sut06] Stuart Sutherland, "Getting Started with SystemVerilog Assertions," DesignCon Tutorial, 2006.

[Vij05] Srikanth Vijayaraghavan and Meyyappan Ramanathan, *A Practical Guide for SystemVerilog Assertions*, Springer, 2005.

Formal property verification

4

Formal will dominate verification.
—Kathryn Kranen

Now that we have introduced the fundamental concepts of formal verification (FV), we are ready to discuss the FV technique you are likely to see earliest in your register transfer level (RTL) design flow: formal property verification (FPV). At its most basic level, FPV is the process of verifying properties, usually expressed as assertions or cover points, on an RTL model. But FPV can be much more than this: it is the foundation for a new way of interacting with your RTL models, fundamentally different from the traditional simulation-based methods you are probably familiar with. Once you learn how FPV is different and have been able to fully internalize this new paradigm, many new possibilities arise for improving your design and verification processes.

In this chapter, we explore the various ways in which FPV differs from simulation, and show how FPV requires a fundamentally different style of interaction with the tools and with your design. We then discuss the various usage models of FPV and the design types that are most suitable for these techniques. From this, we move on to exploring how to bring up an FPV environment on a real model and how to address the various difficulties you are likely to encounter when first using this technique on a particular design.

When you finish this chapter, you should be ready to bring up an initial FPV environment on an RTL model of your own.

WHAT IS FPV?

At its highest level, FPV is a method for proving whether a set of properties, defined in SystemVerilog Assertions (SVA) (see Chapter 3) or a similar language, is satisfied by a given piece of RTL. The inputs to FPV are:

- An RTL model.
- A set of properties to prove: assertions and cover points.
- A set of constraints: assumptions, plus clock and reset definitions.

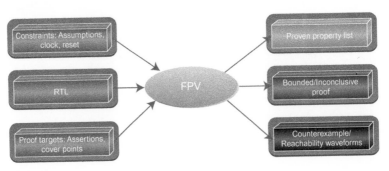

FIGURE 4.1

FPV tool execution.

An FPV tool mathematically analyzes the space of all possible logical execution paths on the target model, based on the constraints passed in. Unlike simulation, it is not checking particular signal values: all possible values that are legal under the current constraints are checked at once.

The outputs of FPV typically include:

- A list of proven properties: proven assertions and unreachable cover points.
- For each disproved assertion or reachable cover point, a waveform showing a case of failure/reachability.
- A list of bounded or inconclusive proofs: assertions and covers that were not definitely proven or disproven.

Note that an inconclusive proof can still be a very useful result, as we will discuss in later sections, though not as desirable as a full proof. As we discussed in Chapters 1 and 2, because FPV is solving problems that are mathematically hard, no tool can guarantee full proofs on every design.

Figure 4.1 illustrates a high-level view of an FPV tool execution. To further clarify what FPV is doing, let's examine a conceptual view of the "execution space" of a typical design. Figure 4.2 illustrates an example execution space. You can think of each point in the figure as representing a set of values for all the state elements (latches and flops) in the RTL design.

In Figure 4.2, we see:

- *The full space of all possible RTL state values.* The outer rectangle represents all possible values that could be assigned to nodes in the RTL design.
- *The reset states.* The possible starting states of the system based on setup information from the user.
- *The reachable states.* This oval represents all possible states of the system that are actually possible to reach when starting in the reset state.
- *Assumptions.* Each assumption constrains the possible behaviors of a design, ruling out some portion of the state space. The assumption ovals indicate parts of the state space ruled out by assumptions. We can see that sometimes

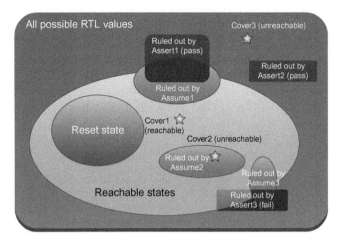

FIGURE 4.2

State space analyzed by FPV.

assumptions (redundantly) rule out part of the unreachable space, which is why these can extend outside the reachable states.

- *Assertions.* Each assertion makes a statement about the model's behavior, effectively defining some subset of the design space as not legal for this model. The assertion boxes represent sets of states that are defined as illegal by the model's assertions.
  - Assert1 passes because, although its set of illegal states intersects with the set of reachable states, all states in the intersection are ruled out by assumptions.
  - Assert2 passes because the illegal states it defines are all outside the model's reachable state space.
  - Assert3 fails because some of the illegal states it defines are within the reachable state space and not ruled out by assumptions.
- *Cover Points.* Each cover point defines a class of good states that we want to make sure are reachable in the current verification environment. The stars mark sets of states defined by the model's cover points.
  - Cover1 is reachable since it contains states within the reachable state space.
  - Cover2 is unreachable since all its states are ruled out by assumptions.
  - Cover3 is unreachable since it lies entirely outside the reachable state space.

An FPV tool essentially takes a model, a set of properties, and a set of constraints, and attempts to determine where each lie within this state space. As we will see in the coming chapters, this basic technology can be used as the foundation for many different types of tasks in a typical System-On-Chip (SOC) design and verification flow:

- *Design exercise FPV.* Use the power of formal technology to explore the basic behaviors of a design without creating a simulation testbench.
- *Bug hunting FPV.* Target a complex block that is also being validated by other means, such as simulation, but create properties to check for corner cases that simulation may have missed.
- *"Traditional" full proof FPV.* Target a complex or risky design block, and create and prove properties to verify that it meets its specification.
- *Application-specific FPV.* Target some particular aspect of design functionality, such as control registers, top-level debug bus connectivity, or new feature insertion, and prove that this aspect has been designed correctly.

But before we study each of these usage models in full detail, let's review the basic concepts of FPV. Then we will explore the fundamental ways in which it interacts with RTL differently from traditional simulation-based methods.

EXAMPLE FOR THIS CHAPTER: COMBINATION LOCK

To illustrate how FPV works in practice, we use a concrete example: a piece of RTL representing a combination lock.

As shown in Figure 4.3, this is a simple combination-style lock to secure a door that takes a four-digit decimal input and requires a set of three specific numbers on consecutive clock cycles to open. The combination that opens the lock is hardcoded in the RTL. (You can find many conceptual flaws in this design, such as the silliness of hardcoding a combination value in RTL, or the oddity of requiring a user to enter a new number during each of three processor cycles in a row.

FIGURE 4.3

Simple combination lock.

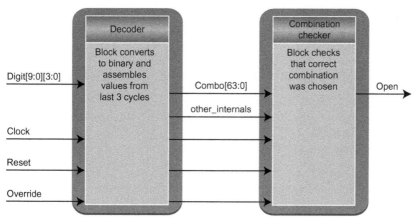

FIGURE 4.4

Block diagram of combination lock RTL.

```
module combination_lock (
    input bit [9:0] digits [3:0],
    input bit override,
    input bit clk, rst,
    output bit open
    );

    bit [63:0] combo;
    decoder d1(clk, rst, digits, combo);
    combination_checker c1(clk, rst, combo, override,
    open);
endmodule
```

FIGURE 4.5

Top-level RTL for combination lock example.

Keep in mind that we just want to demonstrate the basics of FPV, not become home-security millionaires.) We also add an "override" input to cover cases where some kind of physical key can be inserted as an alternative to entering the combination. A basic block diagram and top-level RTL description are shown in Figure 4.4 and Figure 4.5, respectively.

BRINGING UP A BASIC FPV ENVIRONMENT

Using this simple example, let's take a look at what it takes to bring up an initial FPV environment. In a real design/verification context, you would first want to do some careful planning and pre-verification work based on your overall motivation for running FPV, but we will defer a discussion of the planning aspects and details of the various usage models until future chapters. For the moment, we just want to bring up the FPV environment, and see how the tool would interact with a real model.

For now, we will consider ourselves to have some modest validation goals:

- Verify that the lock can open with the correct combination, as specified in some constants {COMBO_FIRST_PART, COMBO_SECOND_PART, COMBO_THIRD_PART}.
- Verify that no incorrect combination can open the lock.

Given these goals, what do we need to do in order to start using an FPV tool? Assuming we already understand the interface and know we have synthesizable RTL that can legally be compiled, we need to create a basic set of cover points, assumptions, and assertions, and then create a reasonable proof environment. As with most examples in this book, the SystemVerilog code is downloadable from our website at http://formalverificationbook.com; to save space and focus on the more interesting aspects, we are not providing a full listing in this text.

Compiling your RTL

The main target of an FPV run is a compiled RTL model. Compiling RTL for most FPV tools is not too different from compiling for simulation or synthesis tools. However, for all modern FPV tools (as of this writing), the RTL models used in FPV must be synthesizable. If you're a typical designer creating RTL targeted for synthesis, this requirement is probably something you have dealt with in other contexts. You do need to be aware of this constraint, as it usually rules out SystemVerilog elements including:

- Explicit time delays (#n) in the code. However, SVA ## delay constructs in sequences and properties are fine.
- Object-oriented testbench constructs such as classes and methods.
- Transistors, weak assignments, and similar nonlogical circuit elements.

If you find that constructs like those above are so integral to some part of your code that you cannot eliminate them, chances are that you are looking at an analog or behavioral module, and may need to reconsider your choice of FPV targets or create a synthesizable representation of the logic. Current FPV tools are designed and optimized for synthesizable RTL. This is not as much of a limitation as it may appear, since the *bind* construct that we discussed in Chapter 3 allows nonsynthesizable validation code, often resulting from popular simulation-based validation methodologies like Open Verification Methodology (OVM) and Universal Verification Methodology (UVM), to be cleanly separated from your synthesizable models. Thus, with proper planning, you should be able to keep your synthesizable code separate from any nonsynthesizable code in order to fully enable FPV.

> **TIP 4.1**
>
> If you are using a simulation-based validation methodology like OVM or UVM that may generate nonsynthesizable code, use the SystemVerilog *bind* construct to keep your validation modules separate from your synthesizable RTL. This will enable you to use FPV as well as simulation.

Creating cover points

In some projects without much FPV experience, cover points have been treated as an afterthought for FPV, but we consider this to be a critical mistake. In an FPV tool, hitting a cover point helps to confirm that, in the proof environment you have currently set up, typical behaviors that you would expect from the system are possible. We have seen some extreme cases where FPV users have created pages of useful assertions while neglecting cover points, shown the assertions are all proven, and told their managers that they were done with a major verification project—only to find later that due to some minor issue, such as using the wrong polarity of reset, the percentage of design logic that was actually verified was in the single digits. Thus, we recommend that you follow this key principle:

> **TIP 4.2**
>
> Begin any FPV effort by creating a set of reasonable cover points for your model, representing typical and interesting activity, as well as the minimum expected specification and behavior coverage for your team's verification goals.

There is no simple formula for the appropriate set of cover points, because it is very dependent on your exact design and its most interesting aspects. Common conditions you often want to cover include:

- Each of the documented flows is possible: translate each waveform diagram in your specification document into an SVA sequence.
- Each input and output can assume a set of interesting values.
- Each type of transaction/operation can successfully complete.
- Each state of your state machines is possible.
- Each queue can reach empty and almost-full states.
- Examples of each expected error type that must be handled or reported gracefully by your design.

In the case of our combination lock example, the problem is on the simple side. Hence, there are not likely to be that many cover points we would need. However, we should be sure to include ones such as these:

- It's possible for our lock to be locked or unlocked.

```
c1: cover property (open == 0);
c2: cover property (open == 1);
```

- Each input on the dial can legally take on each digit, without causing some kind of contradiction in the model.

```
generate for (i = 0; i < 3; i++) begin
  for (j = 0; j < 9; j++) begin
    // We use a one-hot encoding
    c3: cover property (digit[i][j] == 1);
      end
    end
```

One other issue to keep in mind is that while cover points are useful, we need to remain cautious about creating excessive numbers that overburden our proof process. For example, instead of our c3 loop above independently checking that we can cover each digit once, we might want to add 10,000 assertions to check that all specific combinations of digits are possible. Most likely, such an exhaustive check is unnecessary in this case, unless we have specific reason to suspect an issue in this area. On the other hand, if there were special-case requirements for certain values, we would want to make sure to cover each of those critical values.

Creating assumptions

Next, we need to create assumptions: statements about the basic behaviors of our model's inputs. This will enable the FPV tools to focus on valid portions of our problem space. A key point about assumptions that is important to keep in mind in any FPV process is:

TIP 4.3

You will never think of exactly the right assumptions you need in advance. Start out with a small set of clearly needed assumptions, rather than trying to be exhaustive from the beginning. It's okay to start out with too few assumptions: identifying the truly necessary assumptions is part of the FPV debug process.

In fact, the majority of human engineering time spent in FPV is taken up by viewing waveforms and refining assumptions based on new cases to rule out. So initially, it is best to only choose a small set of clearly needed assumptions based on the interface of our model. In the case of our combination lock example, you may recall that we had an input based on a one-hot encoded model of each of four decimal digits:

```
input bit [9:0] digits [3:0];
```

Based on this modeling, we want to ensure that in each of the four-digit slots, only one digit is active.

```
generate for (i = 0; i < 4; i++) begin
  a1: assume property ($onehot(digits[i]));
  end
```

We will likely come across more assumptions that we need for this model, but we can figure that out during the debug process. If you read the description of the model carefully, you may have spotted one already. For now, we leave it out intentionally, so we can "discover" it later during debug.

Creating assertions

Assertions are the traditional focus of FPV. They are the statements about a design that we wish to prove. Ideally, we will be able to use FPV tools to ensure that our assertions are true for all possible simulations on our model. However, when initially bringing up an FPV environment on a design, we need to keep one important principle in mind:

TIP 4.4

When first bringing up a model, viewing cover point traces is much more important than trying to prove assertions.

To understand why this is true, think for a minute about how you would react in the following scenario: you spend a few hours setting up an FPV run, finally press the button to have it prove the assertions, and it comes back with a message "All assertions proven." Would you have a clear idea what was done? Would you be able to convince a skeptical boss, or a skeptical self, that some verification had actually happened? Would you have clear evidence that risky corner cases were covered?

In fact, there is a definite chance that you accidentally overconstrained the model, ruling out interesting traces with overly aggressive assumptions. This is why we mentioned above that focus on cover points is critical when setting up an FPV process. Because cover points force the tool to generate waveforms, representing potential simulations that are supported by the current proof environment, these cover points create confidence that the tool really is exploring the proof space.

Since we have already discussed the cover points, let's now come up with some assertions for our combination lock model. The most critical ones are probably that the correct combination does indeed open the lock, and that wrong ones do not. Ideally, we would like to write assertions based on our inputs, and checking our outputs. We can write an end-to-end assertion for our correct-combination property using an SVA sequence:

```
sequence correct_combo_entered;
  (digits == COMBO_FIRST_PART) ##1
  (digits == COMBO_SECOND_PART) ##1
  (digits == COMBO_THIRD_PART);
endsequence
  open_good: assert property (correct_combo_entered |=> open);
```

We need to be careful here about properly reflecting our conditions: we really want an "if and only if" check here, which has two parts. We do not only want to prove that a good combination opens the lock; we want to prove that *only* good combinations open the lock. This means we also need an assertion that if any combination is bad, it does not open the lock.

There are several ways to write this property. What we really want to prove is that if any individual part of the three-cycle combination is wrong, the lock will not open. So rather than one monolithic property, it might make more sense to create three simpler properties.

```
open_ok2: assert property (
  open |-> $past(digits,3) == COMBO_FIRST_PART));
open_ok1: assert property (
  open|-> $past(digits,2) == COMBO_SECOND_PART));
open_ok0: assert property (
  open |-> $past(digits,1) == COMBO_THIRD_PART));
```

In general it is much easier to debug simple assertions than complex ones: we will be able to see directly which logical condition is failing, instead of having to contend with multiple ones being mixed together.

> **TIP 4.5**
>
> Make every assertion as simple as possible and prefer multiple small assertions to one (logically equivalent) large one.

If we chose to ignore this tip and just wanted a single assertion, we could have written something like `open_ok_complex` below, to state that it is illegal to have an open lock after any incorrect combination.

```
open_ok_complex: assert property (open |->
  ($past(digits,3) == COMBO_FIRST_PART) &&
  ($past(digits,2) == COMBO_SECOND_PART) &&
  ($past(digits,1) == COMBO_THIRD_PART));
```

The above property is just as correct as our earlier three properties, though if it fails, we will have to do more work to debug: we will need to examine the waveform to determine which of the three parts actually failed before moving on to identify the root cause.

Clocks and resets

There are two more key pieces of setup information needed to create an FPV environment: clocks and resets. Clocks are critical because, as you saw in the last chapter, SVA sequences and concurrent assertions always exist relative to some clock. With most FPV tools, you can supply the name of some input as the primary clock, and the tool will assume it is driven with a standard clock pattern: 010101.... If you have multiple clocks, you can use tool commands to specify their relative frequencies.

If you are dealing with a clock generated inside your RTL model, it can be a little trickier. Remember that FPV requires synthesizable code, as mentioned above, so we cannot use an actual representation of a *phase-locked loop* (or PLL, a nonsynthesizable analog piece of hardware that generates clocking) as the source of its clock. In such a case, you would need to blackbox the PLL and then treat its clock output as a primary input to the model. We will see examples like this when we discuss blackboxing in the next chapter.

In the case of our combination lock example, there is a simple clock input. We can just specify that directly to our FPV tool with a tool-specific command that will probably look like:

```
clock clk
```

Resets are important because we need to always consider the initial state of a model. Could our combination lock just happen to be open at the start of our verification, in which case anything we dial would leave it in the "open" state? Maybe, but it would be silly to spend time debugging cases where we just happened to start with such a broken initial state. Most likely there is some defined sequence, maybe as simple as holding the reset signal high for a specified number of cycles, which gets our design into a known starting state, so we can do intelligent verification that would match real-life behavior.

In our particular example, we see that the combination lock just has a single reset input. Let's create a simple reset sequence that holds it to 1 for 100 cycles to be safe. The command (again tool-specific) will probably look something like this:

```
reset rst = 1 0-100
```

Running the verification

Now that we have put together all the elements of our proof environment, we are ready to actually run the FPV tool and look at some results. The FPV tool will figure out the starting state of our design based on our reset specification, and then analyze the space of all possible logic executions that start in that state. It will attempt to find a trace, or potential simulation, for each cover point we have specified, and attempt to prove that each assertion can never be violated. The results we expect are:

- For each passing cover point, an example trace showing one way it can be covered.
- For each failing assertion, an example trace showing one way it can be violated.
- For each passing assertion or failing cover, a statement that the tool has proven it passes or is uncoverable.

- A list of assertions or covers that have bounded proofs, where they were not fully proven, but are proven for all traces up to length n for some value of *n*. (We will discuss these in more detail in later chapters.)

Let's examine what might happen in a run of a typical FPV tool on one implementation of our `combination_lock` model. (We actually did this using a commercial tool, but here and in the remainder of this book, we are translating the results and discussion to generic formats, to avoid having to debate merits of particular vendors.) Our first run receives the result shown in Table 4.1.

A naïve user's first inclination might be to look at this and say, "Our assertions are failing; there must be something wrong with the RTL." But you shouldn't rush into debugging failing assertions as your first step: this is a common mistake. We had the foresight to create some good cover points, so shouldn't we first do some sanity-checking and make sure the cover traces look reasonable? Remember, cover points are there to help you demonstrate some example waveforms that show expected behaviors: let's use them to figure out if the behavior appears sensible, or if we missed something critical when setting up our environment.

TIP 4.6

Before you start debugging assertion failures, observe the waveforms of your major cover points and make sure they match the expected behavior of your RTL.

Cover point `c1` was written to demonstrate a case where the lock is not open. Its waveform is pretty simple; we just come out of reset and see that the lock is not open, as shown below in Figure 4.6.

Since this looks reasonable and did not add much insight, now we can move on to the more interesting cover point `c2`, indicating a case where the lock is open. We can immediately suspect an issue here, because as you may recall, our design is supposed to take three cycles to enter a full combination, but the tool claims it can open the lock in two cycles. A look at the waveform, as shown in Figure 4.7, can show us what is happening.

Table 4.1 Result of Initial FPV Run

Property	Status
`combination_lock.c1`	covered: 1 cycle
`combination_lock.c2`	covered: 2 cycles
`combination_lock[*][*].c3`	covered: 1 cycle
`combination_lock.open_good`	fail: 4 cycles
`combination_lock.open_ok2`	fail: 4 cycles
`combination_lock.open_ok1`	fail: 3 cycles
`combination_lock.open_ok0`	fail: 2 cycles

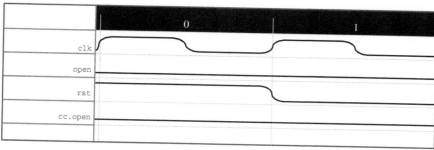

FIGURE 4.6

Cover waveform for cover point c1.

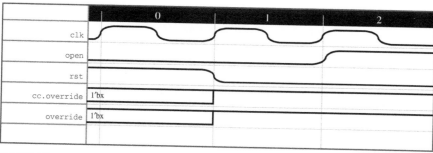

FIGURE 4.7

Coverage waveform for cover point c2.

Looking at this waveform, we can now see how the lock was opened on cycle 2: we forgot about the override input. By setting this override to 1, we can open the lock at any time. There are two main ways to fix this:

1. Account for override in our assertions and covers. For example, we could replace

   ```
   c2: cover property (open == 1);
   ```

   with

   ```
   c2: cover property ((open==1) && !$past(override));
   ```

2. Ignore override for the purpose of this verification environment. In this case, rather than modifying each assertion and cover to account for the override, we would just add one new assumption:

   ```
   fix1: assume property (override == 0);
   ```

Depending on our verification goals, either of the above solutions might be appropriate. If the override logic is considered interesting, new, or a potential source of bugs for some other reason, we should probably use solution 1 and work to account for it in our other properties. However, if we do not consider the override logic interesting or risky, or do not want to focus on it for the purpose of our current verification, solution 2 is easier to implement. For the moment, let's use solution 2. Once we add this assumption and rerun, we get a much more reasonable waveform for c2, shown in Figure 4.8.

The c3 waveforms (not shown here) are relatively simple ones, and quick inspection reveals that their cover traces are reasonable.

Now that we are at a point where we are getting decent cover traces, we should rerun the verification in case some of our recent changes affected overall results, aside from the particular properties we just looked at. In our particular example, the new result we get can be seen in Table 4.2.

Since we are hitting our cover points with reasonable traces, it is now time to take a look at our assertion failures. We can ask our tool to bring up a failure trace, or counterexample, for one of the failing assertions. The one for assertion open_good is shown in Figure 4.9.

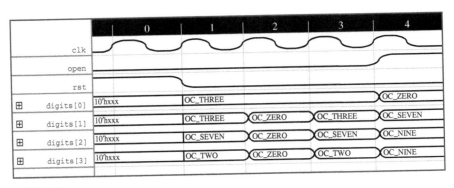

FIGURE 4.8

New waveform for cover point c2 after override fix.

Table 4.2 Result of FPV Run after Adding Assumption

Property	Status
combination_lock.c1	covered: 1 cycle
combination_lock.c2	covered: 4 cycles
combination_lock[*][*].c3	covered: 1 cycle
combination_lock.open_good	fail: 4 cycles
combination_lock.open_ok2	fail: 4 cycles
combination_lock.open_ok1	fail: 4 cycles
combination_lock.open_ok0	fail: 4 cycles

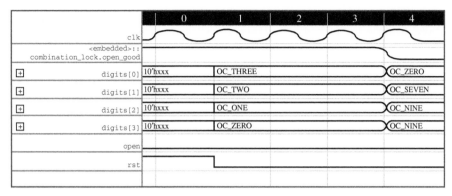

FIGURE 4.9

Counterexample trace for assertion open_good.

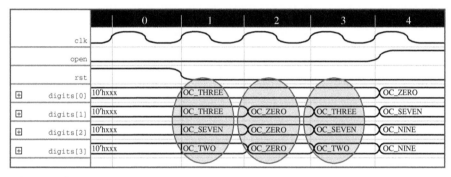

FIGURE 4.10

The c2 cover waveform revisited, showing digits' input values that open the lock.

In this example, we can check the code against the values in the waveform to verify that the "digit" inputs are matching the constants in the code—but they don't seem to be the values that actually open the lock. In fact, the suspiciously regular constants {3210, 3210, 3210} (when converted from one-hot binary to the decimals they represent) we initially have in the RTL were actually just placeholders, and do not correctly define the values needed. This is actually not such a rare situation when dealing with real-life RTL. But how can we figure out the correct combination?

It has likely occurred to you by now that we already have the answer to this question: our cover point c2 covers the condition we want, displaying a specific waveform where we can see the correct values for each cycle that will result in the lock opening in our design, as highlighted in Figure 4.10.

From this cover waveform, we can read the three cycles of combination values needed to open the lock, {2733, 0003, 2733}, and correct the constants in our RTL. This is a great demonstration of the power of FV: we didn't need to directly figure out the detailed inputs that would get the result we wanted; we just specified a cover point, and the FPV tool found a way to get us there. Once we change the constants to the correct values and rerun the verification, we see the result shown in Table 4.3.

We can see that our open_good property now passes, showing that the combination mentioned in the constants does open the lock. But our bad* assertions are failing, showing that it is also possible for other combinations to open it as well. This is another situation that would be challenging in simulation: how many random runs would it take until we stumbled upon one of the alternate combinations that incorrectly opens our lock? Since we're using FPV, we can just click a button and bring up a counterexample, as shown in Figure 4.11.

Looking closely at the values of our digits inputs on the relevant cycle for this assertion, we see they represent the combination {2735}. Suspiciously, it differs from the expected {2733} only in the last digit. After we examine

Table 4.3 FPV Results after Combination Value Corrected

Property	Status
combination_lock.c1	covered: 1 cycle
combination_lock.c2	covered: 4 cycles
combination_lock[*][*].c3	covered: 1 cycle
combination_lock.open_good	Pass
combination_lock.open_ok2	fail: 4 cycles
combination_lock.open_ok1	fail: 4 cycles
combination_lock.open_ok0	fail: 4 cycles

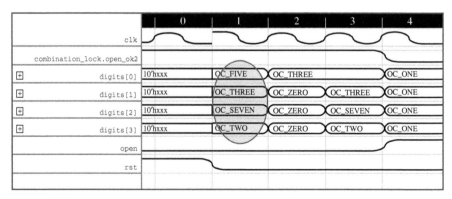

FIGURE 4.11

Counterexample for assertion open_ok2, showing unexpected values that open the lock.

Table 4.4 FPV Results after RTL Bugs Are Fixed

Property	Status
combination_lock.c1	covered: 1 cycle
combination_lock.c2	covered: 4 cycles
combination_lock[*][*].c3	covered: 1 cycle
combination_lock.open_good	pass
combination_lock.open_ok2	pass
combination_lock.open_ok1	pass
combination_lock.open_ok0	pass

counterexamples for bad1 and bad0, we can see a similar issue, leading us to find a remaining RTL bug that effectively allows multiple alternative values for the last digit of the combination. After we fix this and make a related change to the constants, we finally get a fully clean run, as shown in Table 4.4.

HOW IS FPV DIFFERENT FROM SIMULATION?

Now that you have a basic idea of what an FPV tool does, we can take a closer look at how FPV differs from simulation. You may recognize at this point that while both FPV and simulation are methods for interacting with and testing your RTL designs, they differ in a number of fundamental ways. Before we dive more deeply into how you would effectively use an FPV tool, which we will discuss in the next few chapters, we should take a step back and clarify the various differences between FPV and simulation. It is important to have a solid understanding of these differences in order to maximize your FPV productivity and to understand the situations when each type of tool is best applied.

To start with, we should look at how the different types of SVA verification statements are handled in simulation and FPV. As you may recall from Chapter 3, there are three main types of verification statements that typically appear in RTL code: assertions, assumptions, and cover points. Table 4.5 shows how each of the types of verification statements are treated differently in simulation and FPV.

These differences are inherent to the ways the two types of tool operate. A simulation tool always runs on specific test vectors, checking that the current values behave as expected for each assertion and assumption in the code, and checking whether they hit a cover point. An FPV tool analyzes the space of possible simulations as limited by the assumptions. This means that it is performing a much more complex task and can find if there is any possible way to violate an assertion or hit a cover point.

These basic differences in design and philosophy result in a number of consequential differences in practice, which engineers new to FPV often find somewhat surprising. Table 4.6 shows some of the differences that we have found to be the most jarring during early FPV adoption. The items in this table are not meant to

Table 4.5 Verification Statements: FPV and Simulation Differences

Statement type	Simulation	FPV
Assertion	Report if any test values used in current tests have violated the assertion.	Report if it is possible for any set of test values to violate the assertion.
Assumption	Report if any test values used in current tests have violated the assumption.	Use the assumptions to limit the space of possible test values.
Cover point	Report how many test values used in current tests have exercised the cover point.	Report if it is possible for any set of test values to exercise the cover point.

Table 4.6 Key Practical Differences between FPV and Simulation

Key area of difference	Simulation	FPV
What types and sizes of models can be run?	Up to full-chip level, and both synthesizable and behavioral code.	Unit or cluster level, or full-chip with lots of removed logic, and synthesizable code only.
How to reach targeted behaviors?	*Describe the journey:* generate input values to create desired behaviors.	*Describe the destination:* specify target property or state, tool finds if it's reachable.
What values are checked?	*Specific values:* simulator checks design based on user-specified inputs.	*Universe of all possible values:* tool analyzes space of legal values under current constraints.
How do we constrain the model?	*Active constraints:* we implicitly constrain the model by limiting the values passed in during simulation.	*Passive constraints:* use assumptions to rule out all illegal cases.
How are constraints on internal nodes handled?	*Forced values:* a live constraint on an internal signal affects only downstream logic.	*Back-propagation + Forward-propagation:* a constraint affects the universe of possible values, in its fanin and fanout logic.
What do we use for debug?	*Single trace:* when a simulation fails, you need to debug what was simulated.	*Example from FPV space:* the tool presents one example from a family of possible failures.
How long are typical traces?	*Thousands of cycles:* typically need to represent full machine startup and do many random things before hitting complex bug.	*Tens of cycles:* FPV usually generates a minimal path to any target, resulting in much smaller traces with little extra activity.

be an exhaustive list. This is merely an initial summary of the most common areas that users sometimes find it challenging to internalize. Let's look at each of these differences in greater detail.

WHAT TYPES AND SIZES OF MODELS CAN BE RUN?

The first difference we are highlighting is one of the most challenging: while simulation can handle models of virtually any size up to full-chip, due to its near-linear complexity, FPV requires a smaller model. Thus, FPV usually must be targeted at a cluster or unit level. As of this writing, the recommendation is to aim for a model size of less than 40,000 state elements.

This capacity limitation should not be too surprising: remember that FPV is doing something much more powerful, analyzing the space of all possible simulations on the model rather than just particular values. This effectively gives you the same result as running an exponential number of simulations on the design.

You should not take this to mean that FPV is impossible on large models though. It merely indicates that if using a larger model, we need to use intelligent techniques to focus on just the relevant parts of a model, rather than just feeding the entire model into the tool. A number of techniques can be used to reduce model complexity for FV; we will explore these methods in more detail in future chapters.

The key point to remember here is that by using techniques like the one above, we have been able to reliably run FPV on much larger models than you would initially expect, including targeted FPV verification tasks on full-chip models in some cases.

HOW DO WE REACH TARGETED BEHAVIORS?

The next difference we have highlighted between simulation and FPV is the way we specify our validation process: what information do we have to give the tool in order to complete our validation goal? To make this more concrete, think about the case where we hit the problem that our lock could have multiple valid combinations that open it.

Simulation

In a typical simulation environment, you need to design a testbench that drives active values to the model. So we need to supply a procedure for deciding what random values to drive and then check if any of the values exercise our desired conditions.

In our combination lock example, if you are worried about trying to find alternate combinations that will incorrectly open your lock, you will need to design your testbench to drive lots and lots of random values, hoping to luckily guess the random one that results in incorrectly seeing `open == 1` on the output. In this example, where each attempt at opening the lock requires three cycles during which 10^4 possible values are being driven on each cycle, we will need to go through $10^{4 \times 3}/2$, or about 500 billion, simulation cycles on average before we stumble upon the needed result.

Furthermore, even after spending all those simulation cycles to find the alternate combination, and then fixing the bug, we will still have no idea whether other alternate combinations exist. We will have to run a trillion cycles for complete coverage.

FPV

As discussed above, for FPV we just define the properties, and then ask the tool to figure out if it they are always true:

```
open_ok2: assert property (
  open |-> $past(digits,3) == COMBO_FIRST_PART));
open_ok1: assert property (
  open|-> $past(digits,2) == COMBO_SECOND_PART));
open_ok0: assert property (
  open |-> $past(digits,1) == COMBO_THIRD_PART));
```

Once these properties are defined, the FPV tool can attempt to find some legal execution trace that violates the given assertions. There is no issue of needing multiple iterations: a single FPV run, in principle, covers the entire verification space. Assuming it does not hit a complexity problem, the tool will return with either a proof that no such alternate combinations exist, or a concrete counterexample showing some alternate combination that successfully opened the lock.

Best of all, once we have fixed our initial bug and believe no more alternate combinations exist, all we have to do to be sure is run FPV once more on the same properties after the RTL fix. If the tool reports that the properties now pass, no simulations or further FPV runs are needed.

WHAT VALUES ARE CHECKED?

The third major difference we are highlighting is in the set of values that are checked by each methodology.

Simulation

Each simulation run is checking a particular set of values that are driven through the model. Even if you have a fast random simulation environment, it is still only checking a specific, finite set of values. So if you review the results of a simulation run that didn't succeed in opening the lock, you can never be sure that no other value would succeed. When you look at a generated waveform, you always need to ask the question, "What other values did we check, or should we check, on these signals?"

FPV

Again, FPV is checking the universe of all possible values, not just specific ones. If an FPV run completes on our model and claims that no invalid combination opens the lock, then we know that no set of invalid values, under our current model constraints, can possibly reach the open condition. This is a very powerful result, but also has a downside: it means that if a model is not properly constrained by assumptions, many impossible execution paths may effectively be checked as well, causing false negatives where an assertion fails on an unrealistic example. As a result, a significant proportion of any FPV effort will consist of identifying constraints needed to make sure only realistic values are being checked and eliminating false failures.

How do we constrain the model?

Our discussion above about simulating "all" cases oversimplified a bit: in real-life verification, we usually need to add constraints, limitations on the actual values we drive into the model. There are many typical reasons to constrain a model:

- Some values may be impossible to generate.
- Some values may inherently never be chosen by the environment.
- Some values may be disallowed due to documented limitations that users are expected to follow.
- Some values may represent aspects of the design that are not the focus of our current verification.

In the case of our combination lock example, remember our issue with the `override` input, a signal that bypasses the locking mechanism and forces the lock to open. For a validation environment in which we are trying to check issues with the correctness of the combination(s), we need to force this to 0, as mentioned above:

```
fix1: assume property (override == 0);
```

Simulation

In simulation, we usually set up the environment to only drive legal values to our signals. In this case, we need to set up our simulation drivers so they will always give the value 0 to our `override` signal. If using a random simulation, we might be able to use a semi-passive method like the SystemVerilog `constraint` operator, which may superficially seem similar to using formal assumptions. However, even in this case, the simulator is still driving a set of specific values.

If our simulation tests pass, we know that for some subset of possible values under our constraints, our design is correct. There is no intention or attempt to cover all possible values that are legal under the constraint.

FPV

In FPV, we do not set up the environment to specifically drive active values: once again, FPV inherently covers the entire verification space. Instead, we need to add assumptions to rule out illegal values. In other words, we provide constraints to eliminate parts of the verification universe that are not valid for our current set of checks. Once we do this, the FPV environment covers the full verification space minus the subset ruled out by our assumptions.

If our FPV proofs succeed, we are guaranteed that the tool has tested for all possible values under our constraints. It didn't just check a sampling of values where `override` was 0, but covered all possible cases where this was true.

How are constraints on internal nodes handled?

Another, more complex, problem is what happens if we constrain internal nodes. For example, suppose we have some knowledge of the larger system in which this combination lock appears. We may know that all combinations, once the three cycles of decimal digits are combined and decoded into a 64-bit binary value on the internal signal, will be less than some known value `MAX_COMBO`. Is there an easy way we can represent this constraint on the internal `combo` signal, rather than having to create a more complex set of constraints on the digits passed into the `digit` input?

Simulation

We may force legal values on the internal `combo` node by having our simulation tool directly drive values to that node. However, this will affect only downstream logic: the subsequent logic in the combination checker will be affected by our new values, but the values on the `digit` input and within the decoder will be completely unrelated. When we look at waveforms, we will have to be careful to recognize that any values upstream from the internal `combo` signal, or parallel signals that are generated from its source logic at the same time, are effectively garbage values that we need to ignore.

FPV

In the case of FPV, any constraint effectively restricts the universe of possible simulations. So if we constrain an internal node, it doesn't just affect downstream logic: it effectively back-propagates, causing us to only see values on its drivers that are consistent with the constraint. Thus, we can put the following simple assumption on the `combo` signal:

```
assume property (combo <= MAX_COMBO);
```

With this assumption, we are guaranteed that any values we see on the `digit` input in an FPV environment will be consistent: they will be valid values that, when sent into the decoder block, will result in legal values of `combo` obeying the

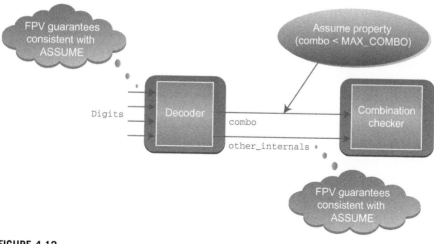

FIGURE 4.12

Effects of constraining an internal signal in FPV.

assumption. The same is true of other internal signals generated from the same source logic. Figure 4.12 below illustrates this situation:

Note that this method of constraining an internal node can in some sense be considered cheating: what if the decoder has bugs where it receives a legal set of inputs, but then wrongly decodes it into a combo value that exceeds MAX_COMBO? We will not detect such bugs if we run FPV with this internal assumption. It would force us to ignore all cases where the decoder outputs a value greater than MAX_COMBO. On the other hand, if we have inherited a mature, well-tested decoder block and are really more interested in formally checking the downstream logic, this might be considered an acceptable risk.

TIP 4.7

If you are finding it very difficult to write good input assumptions for an FPV task, remember that assumptions can be written in terms of decoded/intermediate internal signals. This does carry the risk, though, that the logic driving these signals is not fully covered by your verification.

What do we use for debug?

A key issue with all validation tools is how to debug the failures. Runs that just report that all checks/proofs completed successfully are nice, but it takes a lot of iteration to get there—the typical user of either formal or simulation tools spends a lot of time debugging waveform diagrams. There are fundamental differences between the kind of debug waveforms we get for simulation and FPV models.

Simulation

A failure waveform received from a random simulation is inherently a single instance of model failure. It shows the result from one particular run, and getting a substantially different run may take many random cycles. For example, suppose we look at a cover point wave from our combination lock example and decide it is illegal because the input was not constrained properly to give a valid combination. To solve this, we would have to modify our test environment and then launch a new set of random simulations, hoping that we hit upon another failure case. But we will never be sure that we have or have not correctly ruled out the illegal combinations, unless we happen to hit another bad value randomly during our testing, or run the impractical number of simulation cycles required for complete coverage.

FPV

The waveform generated by a FPV run seems similar to a simulation waveform, in that it shows a set of concrete values in the model happening over time. But there is a key difference: an FPV waveform is a representative of a family of possible failures found by the proof engines. This means that if the user finds something they want to change, such as the need for an assumption affecting the input values, they can add a constraint to this effect and ask the engine to re-solve. The tool will either return with a waveform that still meets the requested cover case with the new constraints or attempt to prove that the additional assumption rules out all such cases.

How long are typical traces?

Another difference between simulation and FPV that is very noticeable to new users is the length of typical debug waveforms.

Simulation

A typical simulation waveform will contain thousands of cycles. There is probably some complex model reset, followed by many cycles of random or irrelevant activity until a particular test condition or failure is reached. The actual cause of the failure may be buried somewhere in the middle of this long simulation, with the actual cycle of the root cause difficult to derive. It is often very challenging during debug to examine thousands of cycles of data and determine exactly which ones are specifically relevant to the current failure.

This also can present a significant challenge when aiming to verify that a bug has been fixed: how much of the detail of these thousands of cycles must be preserved in order to properly reproduce the bug? And again, how can we be sure that the bug fix is complete, rather than a partial fix that would reproduce the same problem with a slight tweak to the waveform?

FPV

In FPV, a typical failure trace will be very short, in many cases just 10−20 cycles after reset. This can frighten an unprepared user who is more familiar with simulation—but is actually very useful. The shorter length is mainly because most FPV engines search for a minimal example that can reach an assertion failure: thus, the FPV waveform gets right to the point, without wasting extra cycles on random activity that is unnecessary for the current example. Typical FPV tools also show much shorter reset sequences. They usually detect the minimum amount of reset needed until the model state stops changing, as opposed to simulations, which tend to use much looser bounds to determine the needed reset length.

DECIDING WHERE AND HOW TO RUN FPV

Now that you know the basics of how FPV works, you are probably eager to dive in and apply it to some of your own designs. You should make sure that you are clear on your verification goals, and try to start with designs that are most amenable to FPV. Of course we do not want to discourage you from trying FPV tools on challenging designs (a topic we discuss more in upcoming chapters), but you will probably find your FPV skills will develop most effectively if you start from simple, clear cases where FPV is optimal, and work your way upward from there.

Motivations for running FPV

Remember from the beginning of this chapter that we mentioned several major use models for FPV tools. Now we have built enough background to examine them each in a bit more detail. Here we will take a first look at when and why we would use each method, while in the next three chapters we visit each of these methods in more detail.

- *Design exercise FPV.* Use the power of formal technology to explore the basic behaviors of a design without needing to create a simulation testbench.
- *Bug hunting FPV.* Target a complex block that is also being validated by other means, such as simulation, but create properties to check for corner cases that simulation may have missed.
- *"Traditional" full proof FPV.* Target a complex or risky design block, and create and prove properties to verify that it meets its specification.
- *Application-specific FPV.* Target some particular aspect of design functionality, such as control registers, top-level debug bus connectivity, or new feature insertion, and prove that this aspect has been designed correctly.

Using design exercise FPV

As mentioned above, design exercise FPV refers to our usage of FPV techniques to explore the basic behaviors of a design without creating a simulation testbench.

At first, this concept might seem a little odd. Originally, FV methods were introduced as a form of "last-mile" verification, an effort to cover unusual or hard-to-reach corner cases that might otherwise be missed—and most likely that is what first motivated you to look at FV. So why are we talking about using formal to explore "basic behaviors" of a design?

To understand this, we should think about what happens when first creating an RTL model of a new design. If you are a typical design engineer, you are used to the fact that when you complete your first version of the model, it is very difficult to exercise it. You need to write some simulation testbench code to drive interesting values and often need to wait for adjoining modules from other owners to be ready for integration into some higher-level testing environment. If you do write some local testbench code, most likely it is just doing barebones exercise of some common cases. But what if your design has interesting states that can only be reached by many cycles of specific inputs? To get to any interesting destination state in your system, you have to write a testbench that drives the right values in cycle-by-cycle.

FPV provides a new ability here: specifying the destination rather than the journey. Because it mathematically explores the entire space of possible simulations, it will find a way to reach any state in your system that is reachable. You just need to specify the desired state through an SVA assertion. We saw the power of this method in our combination lock example above: with a simple cover point cover property (open == 1), we are able to find the combination that opens the lock. A single FPV run can generate a long, complex sequence of inputs that would have required many hours of testbench development otherwise—you can think of FPV used in this context as an instant testbench generator.

In addition, since FPV can be run at the level of any compilable module, individual designers can use it to find bugs early before other designers have completed their adjacent modules, or before the validation team has generated the expected testbench collateral. Because the cost of bugs grows exponentially throughout the design process, this can make a huge difference in overall development time.

You should consider doing design exercise FPV if:

- You are writing new RTL and want to see how it behaves in simple cases, or verify its basic functionality.
- You are trying to do early verification before needed collateral, such as adjacent units or testbenches, is ready.
- You have a partial design and want to see how it behaves in conjunction with some known assumptions about the unimplemented portion.
- You have inherited some legacy RTL code that is not fully documented, and you want to understand its typical behaviors.
- You are exploring the suitability of FPV on a new RTL design, as a preliminary step toward bug hunting or full proof FPV.

> **TIP 4.8**
>
> If you are working on new RTL, need to do early verification before a testbench is ready, want to better understand a partially finished design, need help understanding a legacy RTL model, or are just beginning to explore the possibility of validation-focused FPV for your design, consider using design exercise FPV.

Using bug hunting FPV

Bug hunting FPV is closer to the traditional notions you probably have of FV: a technique for finding potential corner-case issues in a design that you might miss through other methods. The idea here is that you are writing assertions representing the required behaviors for your design and using FPV to find potential cases where your RTL could violate them. This method is typically used if there is a part of your design that is seen as especially risky due to large numbers of corner cases, and you want extra confidence in your verification even after running your full set of random simulations.

You should consider doing bug hunting FPV if:

- You are working on a design containing many corner cases and want an extra level of validation confidence.
- You have been running regular simulations on your design, and some part of it repeatedly has new errors showing up during random tests.
- You have already done design exercise FPV on your model, so increasing your FPV coverage by adding additional targeted assertions is relatively low cost.
- You have a mature/reused model that mostly does not need further verification, but you have added a new feature that you want to verify with confidence.

> **TIP 4.9**
>
> If you are validating a design with many corner cases, have been seeing many bugs in random tests, have completed design exercise FPV with success and want to do further validation, or have just added a feature to a mature model, consider bug hunting FPV.

Using full proof FPV

Full proof FPV is the usage model that corresponds most closely with the original motivation for FV: generating mathematical proofs that your design is 100% correct. In this usage model, you will attempt to write properties that define your complete specification and then prove that all those properties will be true of your design.

Full proof FPV is the most effort intensive, as it involves trying to completely prove the functionality of a design. But it carries a huge benefit: if you correctly run your full proofs and include measures to check that your assumptions are reasonable, you can be confident that you have fully verified your RTL and do not need to spend any effort on running simulations or other validation methods. (There are certain cases where your full proofs may not be valid, as we will discuss in upcoming chapters. However, this is true to some level of approximation.)

Because full proof FPV can be a substantial effort, we always recommend that you start with design exercise FPV, then expand it to bug hunting and finally full proof FPV. Your design exploration and bug hunting will function as initial sanity-checks that you have chosen a design with size and style that are appropriate for FPV, and with logic that is of a complexity level that is reasonable for FPV tools.

You should consider running full proof FPV on your RTL if:

- You are provided with a detailed reference specification that is expected to be implemented.
- You have a design that conforms to standard interfaces where packages of pre-verified FPV collateral are available.
- Your design is defined by a set of tables that fully encapsulate the expected behavior.
- You have a part of your RTL that needs bulletproof verification to reduce design risk.

TIP 4.10

If you have a detailed reference specification or tables that fully define your desired behaviors, have standard interfaces that provide a significant amount of prepackaged FPV collateral, or strongly require bulletproof specification on a part of your design due to known risks, consider full proof FPV.

Using application-specific FPV

When we talk about application-specific FPV, we cover a collection of different techniques where FPV can be used effectively to solve a particular problem. In these cases, we can take advantage of a detailed understanding of the problem to generate well-known property types, address inherent complexity issues, or otherwise leverage problem-specific collateral to make FPV easier. We discuss this in more detail in Chapter 7. To give you the general flavor, here are some common types of application-specific FPV:

- *Reusable protocol verification.* You can use FPV to verify that the interface behaviors of your design comply with some known protocol, such as a common bus specification.

- *Unreachable coverage elimination.* You can use FPV to identify cover points in your design, which are provably unreachable, so they can be excluded from the measures of coverage in your simulation environment.
- *Post-silicon bug reproduction.* Using FPV to reproduce bug sightings seen in silicon can be very powerful. This kind of usage can take advantage of the fact that the user is trying to produce a small, well-defined set of behaviors, rather than attempting general-purpose FPV. FPV is a powerful method to find a legal way that RTL can reach an observed unexpected behavior.
- *Top-level connectivity verification.* This refers to the use of FPV to verify that the top-level connections from your SOC's pin ring to internal units are correct for a given set of control register or other parameter values. Though this circuitry tends to be logically simple, there tend to be too many possible combinations to efficiently check with simulation.
- *Control register verification.* You may want to use FPV to check that the control registers implemented in your design correctly follow their access specifications. For example, some may be read-only, some may be write-only, or some may only be accessible under certain conditions.

TIP 4.11
If you are working in an area such as reusable protocol verification, unreachable coverage elimination, post-silicon debug, connectivity verification, or control register verification, leverage application-specific FPV methods, tools, and environments.

The most important piece of advice regarding when to use application-specific FPV is to be careful that you are not using general-purpose FPV solutions when an application-specific solution is available for your current problem. In fact, this is worthy of calling out as another general tip:

TIP 4.12
Before spending time on setting up a general-purpose FPV environment for your block, check to see if a domain-specific solution exists for the problem(s) you are currently addressing.

If you fail to follow this advice, you will likely end up doing significant amounts of unnecessary work when setting up your FPV run, and are likely to miss important assertions or checks that are encapsulated in the domain-specific solution.

SUMMARY

In this chapter, we have introduced you to the concept of FPV, a powerful general technique for determining whether a set of properties, expressed as SVA assertions, is valid on a given RTL model. We then walked through an example FPV run on a small combination lock model and examined how the tool would report some simple types of bugs on this model and how we would fix them.

We then continued with a discussion of the practical differences between simulation and FPV from a user point of view, and how these would impact your use of FPV tools in practice. The main areas of difference include:

- What types and sizes of models can be run? Simulation is typically run up to the full-chip level, while FPV generally requires smaller models or extensive blackboxing.
- How to reach targeted behaviors? Simulation requires testbenches to specify the journey, generating the correct sequence of input values for a desired behavior, while FPV allows us to specify the destination.
- What values are checked? Simulation is checking specific test values, while FPV covers all values not ruled out by constraints.
- How do we constrain the model? Simulation requires active constraints because it generates specific inputs, while FPV uses assumptions to passively rule out all illegal inputs.
- How are constraints on internal nodes handled? Simulation hacks the logic and allows inconsistent input and output values, while FPV ensures that all values anywhere in the model are consistent with its assumptions.
- What do we use for debug? Simulation generates a specific trace, while FPV shows an example from a large space of possible traces.
- How long are typical traces? Simulation typically generates thousands of cycles of random traffic to produce a failure, while FPV gets right to the point and often generates waveforms of tens of cycles.

Finally, we discussed the major usage models for FPV and gave you a preview of the main usage models we will be discussing in the next few chapters: design exercise FPV, bug hunting FPV, full proof FPV, and application-specific FPV.

PRACTICAL TIPS FROM THIS CHAPTER

4.1 If you are using a simulation-based validation methodology like OVM or UVM that may generate nonsynthesizable code, use the SystemVerilog *bind* construct to keep your validation modules separate from your synthesizable RTL. This will enable you to use FPV as well as simulation.

4.2 Begin any FPV effort by creating a set of reasonable cover points for your model, representing typical and interesting activity, as well as the minimum expected specification and behavior coverage for your team's verification goals.

4.3 You will never think of exactly the right assumptions you need in advance. Start out with a small set of clearly needed assumptions, rather than trying to be exhaustive from the beginning. It's okay to start out with too few assumptions: identifying the truly necessary assumptions is part of the FPV debug process.

4.4 When first bringing up a model, viewing cover point traces is much more important than trying to prove assertions.

4.5 Make every assertion as simple as possible and prefer multiple small assertions to one (logically equivalent) large one.

4.6 Before you start debugging assertion failures, observe the waveforms of your major cover points and make sure they match the expected behavior of your RTL.

4.7 If you are finding it very difficult to write good input assumptions for an FPV task, remember that assumptions can be written in terms of decoded/intermediate internal signals. This does carry the risk, though, that the logic driving these signals is not fully covered by your verification.

4.8 If you are working on new RTL, need to do early verification before a testbench is ready, want to better understand a partially finished design, need help understanding a legacy RTL model, or are just beginning to explore the possibility of validation-focused FPV for your design, consider using design exercise FPV.

4.9 If you are validating a design with many corner cases, have been seeing many bugs in random tests, have completed design exercise FPV with success and want to do further validation, or have just added a feature to a mature model, consider bug hunting FPV.

4.10 If you have a detailed reference specification or tables that fully define your desired behaviors, have standard interfaces that provide a significant amount of prepackaged FPV collateral, or strongly require bulletproof specification on a part of your design due to known risks, consider full proof FPV.

4.11 If you are working in an area such as reusable protocol verification, unreachable coverage elimination, post-silicon debug, connectivity verification, or control register verification, leverage application-specific FPV methods, tools, and environments.

4.12 Before spending time on setting up a general-purpose FPV environment for your block, check to see if a domain-specific solution exists for the problem(s) you are currently addressing.

FURTHER READING

[Cla99] Edmund Clarke, Orna Grumberg, and Doron Peled, *Model Checking*, MIT Press, 1999.

[Mon14] Normando Montecillo, "How I Unwittingly Started Broadcom's Formal Verification User Group," Deepchip blog, November 2014, http://www.deepchip.com/items/0544-02.html.

[Sin06] Vigyan Singhal, Oski technologies-formal verification: theory and practice, http://drona.csa.iisc.ernet.in/∼deepakd/talks/formal-iisc-0306.pdf.

Effective FPV for design exercise

5

*Fortunately, design errors detected earlier in the design cycle can be
corrected far more easily and at a smaller cost than those detected later.*
Lionel Bening and Harry Foster, *Principles of Verifiable RTL Design*

In the previous chapter, we discussed the basics of formal property verification (FPV), and how it differs from simulation. Now we are going to dive in more detail into one of the key areas where FPV is used in practice: early design exercise. This means we are using FPV to do verification on a new or recently changed register transfer level (RTL) model, with the goal of quickly and efficiently discovering potential bugs and unexpected behaviors of our design.

As we mentioned in the previous chapter, FPV has some key advantages for this task over more traditional methods like simulation. In early stages, a designer is often working with a low-level module that does not yet have a simulation testbench built, or whose testbench depends on adjacent modules that are not yet developed. If developing a custom simulation testbench, most designers are most likely to write very basic code that only tests a few example flows and values, rather than putting in the effort to comprehensively cover corner cases. This barebones approach can result in significantly increased costs later on, because it is well known that finding and fixing a bug late in a project can be exponentially more expensive than if that bug had been discovered earlier.

FPV's ability to specify the destination rather than the journey, to describe some condition or property and ask the tool to figure out how to get there, provides a key advantage in enabling early bug hunting. To a designer used to having to write specific tests to cover for issues, this ability to generate an "instant testbench" covering tricky corner cases can seem almost miraculous. Numerous design engineers have told us that using this design exploration mode enabled them to almost instantly find design mistakes that otherwise would have taken several months for the (simulation-based) validation team to notice and correct. Some common situations when you are likely to consider using design exercise FPV are:

- You are writing new RTL and want to see how it behaves in simple cases or verify its basic functionality

119

- You are trying to do early verification before needed collateral such as adjacent units or testbenches are ready
- You are exploring the suitability of FPV on a new RTL design, as a preliminary step toward bug hunting or full proof FPV
- You have a partial design and want to see how it behaves in conjunction with some known assumptions about the unimplemented portion.

This chapter describes the practical issues in setting up a design exercise FPV environment and effectively using it on your model. We illustrate this process on an example design to provide a direct demonstration of our major points.

EXAMPLE FOR THIS CHAPTER: TRAFFIC LIGHT CONTROLLER

For our illustration of design exercise FPV, we pay homage to the unwritten law that every discussion of properties or validation must invoke an example of a traffic light controller at some point. As in our other examples, we use a simple design with some intentional flaws to illustrate the usage of FPV—if you use our RTL to control a real traffic light, please do not hold us responsible for any resulting vehicular damage.

Figure 5.1 illustrates the concept of what we are designing here: a set of state machines to control the lights at a four-way intersection, with a few simple requirements in the specification:

- Precisely one direction must have a non-red light at any given time. (The cars coming from that direction have right-of-way for both straight driving and left turns.)

FIGURE 5.1

Four-way intersection with traffic lights.

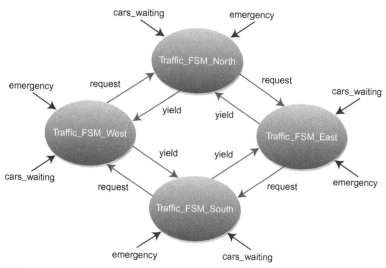

FIGURE 5.2

Traffic controller design.

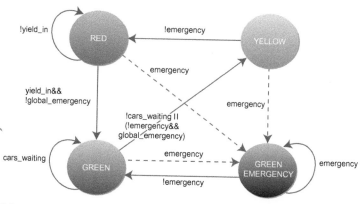

FIGURE 5.3

Traffic light state machine.

- If a car is waiting, it eventually gets a green light.
- An "emergency" signal radioed from an approaching ambulance can force a particular direction to turn green within two cycles.

We will implement this system using a set of state machines, one for each of the traffic lights, with a top-level module that instantiates each of the four traffic state machines, handles top-level environmental inputs and outputs, and connects them properly so control can be safely passed between the lights. Figure 5.2 illustrates the top-level design of our controller, Figure 5.3 shows the

```
module light_fsm(input int index,
                 input logic clk,rst,
                             cars_waiting, emergency,
                             request_in,global_emergency,
                             yield_in,
                 output logic request_out,yield_out,
                 output t_light light);

t_state cur_state, next_state;
always @(posedge clk) begin
     cur_state <= next_state;
end
// Compute next state
always_comb begin
    // nonemergency case
    case (cur_state)
        RED   :  next_state = (yield_in) ? GREEN : RED;
        GREEN :  next_state = (!cars_waiting && request_in) ?
YELLOW : GREEN;
        YELLOW:  next_state = RED;
        default: next_state = BOGUS;
    endcase

    // emergency overrides
    if (emergency) begin
        next_state = GREEN_EMERGENCY;
    end else if (cur_state == GREEN_EMERGENCY) begin
        next_state = GREEN;
    end else if (global_emergency) begin
        if (cur_state == GREEN)
            next_state = YELLOW;
    end
end
// Assign outputs
always_comb begin
    request_out = (cur_state == RED) && cars_waiting;
    yield_out = (cur_state == YELLOW);
    light = (cur_state == RED) ? L_RED :
            (cur_state == YELLOW) ? L_YELLOW :
            L_GREEN;
end
endmodule
```

FIGURE 5.4

SystemVerilog code for traffic state machine.

state machine that is replicated at each light, and Figure 5.4 shows the basic code that implements it. (The full SystemVerilog model can be downloaded from our book website at http://formalverificationbook.com if you would like to try it yourself.)

As you can see from the figures above, this system contains four state machines implementing a kind of round-robin protocol, where one light can be green or yellow at a time, and each light grants the permission for the next light to turn green based on two conditions:

- There is a request from the next light's finite-state machine (FSM), due to cars waiting at that direction. This is shown with the `request_out`/`request_in` signals.
- There are no cars coming from the current direction. This is shown with the `cars_waiting` signal.

Even though this is a relatively small design, there are multiple communicating state machines, which is a situation that commonly results in unexpected interactions. As a result, you are likely to desire some form of simple testing and sanity-checking at early design stages. This is also one of the situations where design exploration using FPV is ideal: you can specify particular situations or combinations of states you want to see, and unlike simulation, you do not have to figure out the cycle-by-cycle inputs needed to arrive at those desired states.

TIP 5.1

FPV-based design exercise is a powerful tool for exploring possible behaviors of interacting state machines.

CREATING A DESIGN EXERCISE PLAN

Remember, the idea of design exercise is that we are in an early stage of development, and want to quickly get confidence in the basic functionality of our design. Thus, planning for design exercise should be relatively lightweight; we do not want to put the same level of effort into this as we would in a full verification plan. However, we should try to start with a clear understanding of our goals, an outline of the kinds of properties we will be looking at, a staging plan for how to gradually increase the level of complexity, and success criteria for determining when we have done sufficient design exercise.

TIP 5.2

Create a design exercise plan when beginning design exercise FPV. This should be very lightweight when compared to a full verification plan. But you should be sure to specify your goals, outline your major properties, include a complexity staging plan, and include exit criteria.

With the above description in mind, now we will create the design exercise plan for our traffic light controller.

DESIGN EXERCISE GOALS

There are several goals that are typical for an early design exercise plan. Since we are dealing with a model that includes FSMs, we should start by thinking specifically about useful goals when exercising this design style. Whenever dealing with a state machine design, the most obvious exercise goal is to make sure we can visit every legal state. So this is our first goal for the traffic light controller: make sure that each of its FSMs can reach every legal state.

Taking this idea a step further, we might think about trying to exercise each possible cross-product of multiple states on the four state machines in our model. We need to be careful though; in this particular design, there actually are not very many cross-products that make sense due to the requirement that only one light be in a non-red state at any given time. So for now we will omit state cross-products from our plan.

TIP 5.3

When doing design exercise on a state machine-based design, an important goal is to try to exercise each legal state. Also consider checking cross-products of states if multiple FSMs are involved.

Another goal we should think about is inherent in the concept of design exercise, but sometimes overlooked due to excessive focus on assertions: we want to observe typical flows through our design. If we have a specification document, chances are that it contains some waveform diagrams showing typical behaviors: we want to make sure our design is actually capable of these behaviors. Thus, our first goal is to be able to see waveforms showing the normal behavior of our traffic light system. Figure 5.5 shows an example of a waveform that might appear in our spec document, demonstrating the "flow" of traffic control around the four lights, which we hope to replicate in an FPV environment.

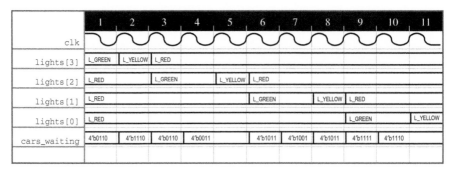

FIGURE 5.5

Spec waveform showing typical traffic light transitions.

> **TIP 5.4**
>
> Try to observe typical behaviors and flows in your design, such as waveform diagrams you might find in a specification document.

Finally, we would like to make sure we initially obey each of the actual requirements in the spec: only one non-red light, eventual green lights for cars that are waiting, and automatic green lights for emergency conditions. In the case of a more complex spec, we might select only a subset of requirements to be targeted at design exercise stage. Remember that our goal here is not full validation of our design, but just the ability to have a basic level of confidence.

> **TIP 5.5**
>
> You should also include goals related to specific requirements of your design. But be careful not to turn your lightweight design exercise into an attempt at full verification: defer more complex properties to later stages of the validation process.

MAJOR PROPERTIES FOR DESIGN EXERCISE

Once you have an idea of your goals, you should decide on the major properties you want to include in your design exercise environment. At this point, we are just trying to describe the properties in plain English for planning purposes—the SVA syntax details can come later.

The first, and most critical, properties for design exercise are the cover points. Remember that our overall objective is to see the design in action and sanity-check real waveforms, so cover points are arguably more important than assertions for this application of FPV. The goals above should directly lead us to defining some cover points to create for our model. As we stated in our plan, we want to begin by making sure we can cover each of the states in our FSMs.

Next, we want to define a cover property to reach each interesting behavior that was described in the spec waveforms. For this exercise, let's assume the only spec waveform is the light transition waveform illustrated in Figure 5.5, where each of the lights in turn becomes green, then yellow, then red. Note that there is a good chance we will get lucky and get a waveform illustrating this condition from our simple state-based cover points above. But to be sure, we should plan a sequence-based cover that represents the major points of this waveform directly.

Next we need to define the safety properties that will actually represent adherence to our spec. In this case, we just have properties corresponding to the three main specification points we described when presenting the problem:

- Precisely one direction must have a non-red light at any given time.
- If a car is waiting, it eventually gets a green light.
- An "emergency" signal radioed from an approaching ambulance can force a particular direction to turn green within two cycles.

Keep in mind that our goal here is to verify the basic safety of typical behaviors, not necessarily to do a full formal proof of model correctness. Thus, the design exercise plan does not need to include 100 percent of the properties implied by the spec, just a reasonable subset of the simpler ones.

TIP 5.6

Try to include basic specification-derived properties in your design exercise plans, but avoid the pitfall of turning this into a full proof plan: your goal is to choose properties that will not be too difficult to write and verify.

Finally, we should think about assumptions we might need on our inputs, in order to ensure reasonable behavior about the external environment. Remember that you should not obsess about assumptions at early stages: you will never think of all the right ones in advance, and you should expect to spend the early stages of your debug process "wiggling," or examining failure waveforms and using them to improve the assumptions.

We should keep in mind, though, that if we have a common interface that has been used in other designs that have undergone formal verification (FV), it is likely that pre-written property sets are available. For example, several companies sell FV property packages for commonly used bus protocols; whenever you are working on a design that incorporates a common protocol, be sure to take advantage of available property sets. Chances are that the assertions in such property sets are more detailed than you want at the design exercise stage, but the assumptions can help you quickly create a functional FPV environment.

TIP 5.7

If reusing or complying to a common interface, check whether pre-written interface property sets are available from others in your company, or from an external vendor.

In the case of our traffic light controller, we have a relatively simple interface where this consideration does not apply. Since we do not initially see any obvious input assumptions that are needed, we will not define any for now.

COMPLEXITY STAGING PLAN

As we have discussed in previous chapters, FPV can be challenging for large or complex designs. When preparing to run FPV on a model, we need to put some advance thought into potential complexity issues. It may be the case that your design includes elements, such as embedded caches, which inherently add a lot of state without being logically interesting, and we want to make sure those are not an impediment to the FPV runs. There are many advanced techniques for dealing with complexity on large models, which we will discuss in future chapters since they are usually more applicable to full proof FPV than initial design exercise. But when preparing for design exercise, you should look for simple opportunities to make the problem more tractable. Here are the main types of complexity techniques you are likely to use at this stage:

- *Blackboxes*: A *blackbox* is a portion of a model that you choose to ignore for FV; usually this is a standalone submodule such as a memory or counter. Blackboxing a portion of a model effectively eliminates its logic from consideration; the FPV tool acts as if any arbitrary value may appear on its outputs.
- *Cut points:* A *cut point* is an individual signal in a model whose driving logic is being ignored. For example, suppose you are outputting the result of a complex mathematical calculation, but are just interested in checking whether the data is transported correctly rather than rechecking your math. In that case, you could make the result signal a cut point. The FPV tool would then act as if the result could attain any arbitrary value.

Both of the above techniques are *underconstraints*: they make your proofs more general. In effect, you are over-approximating the model, by not considering the details in some part of the logic. You are guaranteed that if you can prove an assertion in a model with blackboxes or cut points, it is going to be true of the full model as well.

> ### TIP 5.8
>
> When setting up a model for design exercise, check for opportunities to safely reduce complexity using blackbox or cut point techniques.

The major downsides of these methods are:

- Validation gaps: no properties of the logic within the blackbox are being checked. You will need to be careful to have a clear understanding of where in your process these designs are being validated.
- False negatives/covers: FPV may generate waveforms that could not occur in real life, by assigning values to your cut point or blackbox outputs that are not realistic. You should be careful to only use these techniques when you truly do not care about the particular signal values.

But at this stage, if you can find opportunities to use these techniques to eliminate uninteresting logic in a design you are exercising, your FPV runs are likely to be much more efficient and your productivity may be significantly higher. In the case of our current example, the traffic light controller, some examples of these techniques that we might consider are:

- Blackbox some of the traffic state machines? We have four identical state machines in our design, as you saw in Figure 5.2. Would it make sense to hide the logic of three of them and just verify one in isolation? In this particular case, we conclude that this is not a suitable method, since the round-robin interaction between the multiple state machines is a key component of what we want to check.

- Cut some of the signals between the state machines, such as the `request` or `yield` lines? This is probably not a good idea for the same reason: the interaction between the state machines is at the core of the protocol.

So, in our traffic light controller design, we will not be using any blackboxes or cut points.

However, there is another class of complexity optimizations we should consider: *overconstraint*. This is the concept of assigning a constant value or limited range of values to some signal(s) in the design. Like the underconstraining techniques above, it can reduce the FPV complexity, increasing the chance that our tool can handle our model. However, unlike the underconstraints, this method makes the model more specific rather than more general, so it may result in missing some interesting potential behaviors or bugs. This is a consequence of its beneficial effect: it restricts the set of behaviors being tested, making it easier for the tool to initially concentrate on a smaller set of problems.

For design exercise, we are not claiming to provide bulletproof correctness for the design, so using initial overconstraints to simplify the problem for the user is highly encouraged. You will find it much more straightforward to understand and debug the behaviors you observe in FPV if you begin with a simple model with a limited set of behaviors. After you have exercised the simple model and observed and debugged a variety of behaviors, you can then gradually reduce your overconstraints and add support for more complex behaviors.

TIP 5.9

At the start of design exploration, use overconstraint judiciously to enable design exploration on a simplified model and have a staging plan to gradually add increased functionality.

Some examples of common overconstraining simplifications that are often done to enable more convenient design exercise are:

- Turn off special modes such as low power, scan, or clock gating.
- Restrict the set of available opcodes or transaction types.
- Assume errors or exception conditions will not happen.
- Force almost all bits of a data bus to be 0, so only handfuls carry active data.

In the case of our traffic model, there is one obvious simplification we can do to rule out a "special" mode: assume the *emergency* inputs will always be zero. This will enable us to first understand and verify the behavior of our traffic light controller in the typical nonemergency cases. Then, once we are confident in the basic functionality, we can remove this overconstraint and verify the emergency conditions as well.

Keep in mind that adding overconstraints to your model can be dangerous in the long term, if you add them to embedded code and forget about them. Because they are intentionally excluding legal behaviors, you need to be very careful that later validation-focused FPV efforts do not accidentally pick them up. This could result in them missing the fact that they are not fully covering their expected behavior space, though this danger is minimized if they are also following our recommendations about creating good cover points. We suggest a naming convention, such as preceding the assumption names with *fv_overconstrain*, to mark these intentional overconstraints that should later be removed.

TIP 5.10

Use a naming convention, such as a prefix *fv_overconstrain*, to mark intentional overconstraints that enable early design exercise but should later be removed for more rigorous verification.

One other aspect of this overconstraint technique we should point out is that you do have the ability to add assumptions on internal nodes instead of primary inputs. This can often be very useful, as we described in Chapter 4, enabling us to create simpler assumptions at the expense of some level of formal rigor. In this case, the traffic controller we described has an internal *global_emergency* signal that is high if any of the multiple emergency inputs comes in; so we can just write a single assumption on that signal. The risk here is minimal, since we are planning to remove this assumption at the later stages of design exercise in any case.

TIP 5.11

When doing design exercise FPV, be sure to take advantage of FPV's ability to back-propagate assumptions on internal nodes, where this would enable you to simplify your assumption creation.

EXIT CRITERIA

Now that we have specified our goals, properties, and staging plan, we also need to define the exit criteria: when are we done with design exercise? This might seem like a redundant question at first. We have defined our goals, so we are done when we have completed our goals, right? However, we again need to keep in mind that design exercise is often intended as an early check to improve the quality of models passed to the validation team. Thus, we may want to allow ourselves to complete design exercise based on weaker conditions than full completion of our original goals. Some examples of reasonable exit criteria might be:

- *Time limit:* Spend a week on design exercise, trying to find and solve as many bugs or incorrect behaviors as we can during that time.

- *Coverage:* Make sure we have covered all the basic behaviors expressed in our cover point goals, without necessarily guaranteeing we have verified all our assertions.
- *Full Exercise:* We want to formally verify all the properties in our exercise plan before passing the design on to the validation team.

A time limit or coverage-based goal is most likely reasonable for designers scheduled to deliver RTL on a tight deadline, with the understanding that a validation team will then more fully verify the model. Choosing a full exercise goal may be the most appropriate if we are using design exercise as a piloting stage for potentially full FPV verification that is planned later.

We should also specify whether we need to be at a particular level in our staging plan: will we be satisfied if we have only exercised nonemergency conditions, or do we really want to have a good understanding of the emergency behaviors as well? We can decide either way, but should be clear about what we are willing to accept. Doing more thorough design exercise might take longer, but is likely to save validators more time later on.

PUTTING IT ALL TOGETHER

The design exercise plan for our traffic light controller, based on the various considerations we described in the last few subsections, is illustrated in Table 5.1 below. As you can see, it is relatively simple compared to a real validation plan: this is intentional, as design exercise should be a relatively lightweight process compared to full validation.

Table 5.1 Design Exercise Plan for Traffic Light Controller

Goals	Show that we can reach each state of our traffic FSMs. Replicate the behaviors shown in the spec waveform. Verify that we obey the three key specifications.
Properties	Cover each state of each FSM. Cover the traffic-handoff waveform from the specification. Assert that only one direction may have a non-red light at any given time. Assert that if a car is waiting, it eventually gets a green light. Assert that the *emergency* signal can force a particular direction to turn green within two cycles.
Complexity Staging	No good blackbox or cut point opportunities. Overconstraint: add initial assumption that *global_emergency* is 0. We can relax this assumption after basic covers and nonemergency-related assertions are proven.
Exit Criteria	We want to exercise all covers and prove our three targeted assertions under both emergency and nonemergency conditions.

SETTING UP THE DESIGN EXERCISE FPV ENVIRONMENT

Once again, we need to set up a proper environment for exploring this model. As you may recall from the previous chapter, there are several components to setting up a useful FPV environment:

- A synthesizable SystemVerilog model
- Cover points to explore interesting behaviors
- Assumptions to constrain the inputs
- Assertions to check for desired properties
- Reasonable clocks and resets for the design

The first requirement, a synthesizable SystemVerilog model, needs no further discussion; the code for our traffic light controller is synthesizable, so we are ready to go.

COVER POINTS

Since we planned the cover points within our design exercise plan, we just need to translate our abstract concepts into actual SVA code. We start with the requirement to cover all our FSM states, by defining this cover point to be inserted in each of our state machines:

```
generate for (i = RED; i < = GREEN_EMERGENCY; i++) begin :g1
  state1: cover property (cur_state == i);
end
endgenerate
```

Next, we want to cover the traffic-handoff waveform from our specification. To review, the waveform is the one shown earlier in Figure 5.5.

We have a few options here. We could meticulously specify the values of each signal on every cycle. However, if we have a good understanding of our spec, we should be able to pick out the signals that are critical to the current transaction. In this case, the most important aspect is that we see each light become green in turn. We also need to decide how exact to match the timings in the waveform: is it really intended that we precisely specify a 2-cycle gap between green lights, or is the real timing slightly variable? Usually you will have to judge this based on the text in your specification document. In this case, we will allow the timing to vary slightly and decide that the following top-level cover point is a good representation of our intention:

```
cover_wave: cover property ((lights[3] == L_GREEN)##[1:4]
                            (lights[2] == L_GREEN)##[1:4]
                            (lights[1] == L_GREEN)##[1:4]
                            (lights[0] == L_GREEN));
```

ASSUMPTIONS

As we discussed earlier, we expect to create the majority of assumptions while debugging initial traces, so we actually do not have many assumptions to create at this point. But as part of our initial staging plan, we are going to initially force the traffic light controller into nonemergency status. So we need an assumption for this:

```
fv_overconstrain_emergency: assume property
(global_emergency == 0);
```

ASSERTIONS

Next, we create the assertions we specified in our goals. Note that it is acceptable to have a few lines of modeling code to go along with each assertion when this makes sense, though if we find ourselves writing extensive amounts of additional code, we should question whether the assertion is appropriate for design exercise.

- Assert that precisely one direction must have a non-red light at any given time. This is an assertion we should place at the top level of our model, since it involves signals from multiple directions.
  ```
  // Calculate num_greens and num_yellows for assertions
  always_comb begin
    num_greens = 0;
    num_yellows = 0;
    for (int i = 0;i < 4;i++) begin
        if (lights[i] == L_GREEN) num_greens++;
        if (lights[i] == L_YELLOW) num_yellows++;
    end
  end
  safety1: assert property ((num_greens + num_yellows) == 1);
  ```
- Assert that if a car is waiting, it eventually gets a green light. This assertion should be in each of the individual traffic FSMs.
  ```
  liveness1: assert property (
              ((cur_state == RED) && cars_waiting) |->
                                  s_eventually(cur_state == GREEN));
  ```
- Assert that the *emergency* signal can force a particular direction to turn green within two cycles. This is another assertion that belongs in each of the traffic FSMs.
  ```
  emergency1: assert property (emergency |->
                          ##2 (light == L_GREEN));
  ```

There is one more assertion we need to create, based on a safety condition implied by the specifics of our RTL. You may have noticed that in our state machine code in Figure 5.4, we defined a BOGUS state to indicate invalid state machine values; we should make sure we never hit this.

```
nobogus: assert property (cur_state != BOGUS);
```

While this was not in our plan, that is often the case with safety properties that were either written by the RTL authors or added as we reviewed the RTL. We should try to verify these as well as the higher-level specification-based properties, when they are available.

> **TIP 5.12**
>
> Try to insert safety properties inline in your RTL when applicable during RTL design or review. These can be useful to include in your FPV runs and often help to uncover errors closer to the root cause than high-level specification properties.

CLOCKS AND RESETS

We need to define the clocking and reset conditions for our model. In the case of our traffic light controller, we just have simple top-level inputs `clk` and `rst`. We just need to use the appropriate tool-specific commands to inform our FPV tool that these are the clock and reset signals for our model.

SANITY-CHECKS

Once we have put together our design exercise environment, we should start up our tool and load the model. One important task before we move on is to double-check that we have a reasonable level of complexity. Most FPV tools have a command to display the structural complexity after compiling a model. Our current guideline is to aim for models of less than 40,000 state elements, though we have seen cases where models of much larger sizes were handled successfully. This number is very rough, and likely to grow as the technology further advances.

In the case of our traffic light controller, the tool reports 310 flops, so we are not too worried about complexity. If we had gotten a number above our 40,000 threshold, we probably would want to take a step back at this point and review opportunities for blackboxes, cut points, or further overconstraint to simplify the model.

WIGGLING THE DESIGN

Now that we have planned our design exercise and created our FPV environment, we are ready to finally run FPV and use it to exercise our design. Before we dive in and look at the initial runs on our traffic light controller, though, we should begin by discussing these first stages of design exercise FPV: the *wiggling* process.

THE WIGGLING PROCESS

The term *wiggling* refers to the first stages of debug in any FPV process: the attempt to advance from the stage of getting small, silly-looking waveforms to the point of viewing interesting traffic on a design. Many users new to FPV are scared off when they bring up the waveforms resulting from their first run, and see 1-cycle counterexamples or cover waveforms. Don't fall into this trap: short counterexamples in early stages of FPV are fine and expected!

TIP 5.13

Don't be afraid of seeing short, even 1-cycle, waveforms in early FPV stages. This is a normal part of the wiggling process.

Remember, as we discussed in the last chapter, short waveforms are the natural result of using a technique that searches for the quickest possible way to reach any cover point or violate any assertion. Because most FPV engines inherently look for the shortest possible waveform meeting the user conditions, they will naturally find very short waveforms when any of the following conditions are met:

- The defined reset sequence fails to reset some state elements, so they can potentially wake up in an arbitrary configuration.
- Incorrect clocking or clock gating has been defined, so elements of the design are not reset at all and thus can wake up in an arbitrary configuration.
- Some assumptions that should be placed on the inputs have not been defined, causing some inputs to arrive in an arbitrary configuration that is not realistic for the current design.

Remember that for any case in which the values of a state element or signal are not defined, constrained, or clearly determined by the RTL, a formal engine will cleverly choose values that very quickly reach cover points or violate assertions. This is a major contrast with simulation-based validation, where you expect most rare bugs or behaviors to be embedded in many thousands of cycles of random activity. While this can be surprising to new users, it is actually a key advantage of FPV: the tool gets right to the point and finds a way to reach the desired values as early as possible.

When you see these short waveforms, you should check them to understand why they really do reach the cover points or violate the assertions. You should then think about the potential root causes mentioned above: reset, clocking, or missing assumptions. As we have mentioned before, you are virtually guaranteed to have missed some needed assumptions or configuration parameters, so should expect several iterations of wiggling on any design before generating interesting FPV waveforms. Don't get discouraged if you need to repeat the process several times: some of our FPV experts estimate 10−20 wiggles (iterations of debugging short waveforms) need to happen on a typical interesting RTL unit before seeing useful behaviors. Of course, due to the simplicity of our traffic light controller, we will be seeing fewer iterations in this chapter's discussion.

WIGGLING STAGE 1: OUR FIRST SHORT WAVEFORM

Now that we understand the basic concept of wiggling, we can begin the wiggling process on our traffic light controller example. In the previous chapter, we emphasized the fact that in early stages of FPV, cover points are much more important than assertions: you want to ensure that you can observe expected flows and behaviors, and see waveforms that are in line with your specification. We consider this point so important that we'll repeat the tip here:

TIP 5.14

Begin any FPV effort by creating a set of reasonable cover points on your model, representing typical and interesting activity.

A common mistake people make at this stage is to start by trying to prove the assertions, with cover points as a secondary consideration. But if the assertions are proven at this stage, what does it really tell us? Since a proven assertion doesn't generate any waveform, it would be hard to decide whether our FPV environment is effectively exercising the design. On the other hand, observing cover waveforms will directly tell us whether basic flows through our model are happening as expected.

Thus, in our first FPV run, let's concentrate on the instances of cover point *state1*, the cover point that shows each of our states are reachable, for each state machine and state. For the moment, we will also concentrate on FSM instance 0, since all four of our FSMs are symmetric. Our first run results in output something like this (Table 5.2).

Table 5.2 Initial Output of FPV Run on Cover Points

Property	Status
light[0].prop_loop[RED].state1	cover: 1 cycle
light[0].prop_loop[YELLOW].state1	cover: 1 cycle
light[0].prop_loop[GREEN].state1	cover: 1 cycle
light[0].prop_loop[GREEN_EMERGENCY].state1	cover: 1 cycle

Looking at this output, we can quickly spot the fact that something is not quite right. First, all the covers are covered in one cycle; as mentioned above, this is likely to indicate incorrect reset constraints or missing assumptions in early wiggling stages. Secondly, you may recall that for complexity staging, we created an assumption that prevents the emergency signal from arriving—so we would expect the GREEN_EMERGENCY state to not yet be coverable at all. To debug this, we can start by looking at the waveform for the most problematic cover point, the one for GREEN_EMERGENCY, shown in Figure 5.6 below:

We have used the tool option to display the reset cycles in the waveform—this is usually the best way to debug a 1-cycle FPV result. Many FPV tools hide the reset cycles by default, to avoid the distraction of constantly reviewing a well-understood reset sequence.

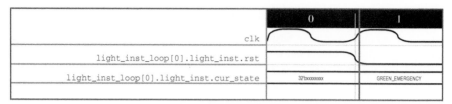

FIGURE 5.6

Initial cover waveform for GREEN_EMERGENCY state.

TIP 5.15

When dealing with very short waveforms from an FPV tool, be sure to turn on the tool option to display reset cycles.

In the Figure 5.6 waveform, we can see the core issue: during reset, the state is undetermined (X), leaving it free to attain any legal value in the first cycle afterward. Taking a closer look at the RTL in Figure 5.4, we can see that we have indeed neglected to reset the main state flops:

```
always @(posedge clk) begin
    cur_state <= next_state;
end
```

This is an easy issue to rectify though; we just need to add logic that resets the FSM state in response to the reset signal. So we can modify the model as follows:

```
always @(posedge clk or posedge rst) begin
  if (rst) begin
    cur_state <= RED;
  end else begin
    cur_state <= next_state;
  end
end
```

Now the state of each of our traffic state machines will be set properly, and we can have the FPV tool run our initial checks again. (You may have already spotted a subtle problem with the above lines. That's okay; we are purposely introducing another error here to illustrate the wiggling process.)

DEBUGGING ANOTHER SHORT WAVEFORM

Following the fix mentioned above, we can reload the model into our FPV tool and again attempt to verify our initial cover points. This time, we get a slightly different result (Table 5.3).

Table 5.3 Cover Point Results After First Fix

Property	Status
light[0].prop_loop[RED].state1	cover: 1 cycle
light[0].prop_loop[YELLOW].state1	NOT covered
light[0].prop_loop[GREEN].state1	NOT covered
light[0].prop_loop[GREEN_EMERGENCY].state1	NOT covered

Now three of our four states cannot be covered at all! While we expected the GREEN_EMERGENCY state to be uncovered, the uncovered YELLOW and GREEN states are a surprise. This is somewhat problematic, as we hope that approaching cars might eventually get a green light.

Debugging uncovered cover points can be a little tricky: since the tool has proven that we cannot reach them, how do we get a waveform to look at? Usually, the best method is to look at one of the related cover points that you are able to cover (or create a simple one if none are available), and look at how the signals related to your cover point are behaving. In this case, since we can cover the RED state, we begin by looking at the waveform generated for that case, as shown in Figure 5.7.

Initially, this waveform does not seem very enlightening, merely showing us that the state was reset to RED. We know that a RED state on cycle 1 is expected, since that was the reset value; thus querying the signal drivers in this waveform will not be interesting. But since the other states were not covered, that shows that we probably are stuck at this state forever. So let's create a slightly more

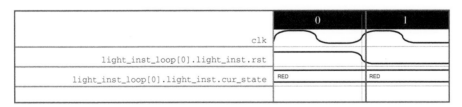

FIGURE 5.7

Cover waveform for RED state.

interesting cover point that shows us staying RED for several further cycles and try to figure out why this is happening by using our FPV tool's debug features to trace the drivers of the continuous RED value at later cycles.

TIP 5.16

When debugging unreachable cover points, start by using or creating a simple cover point that is reachable and gradually add complexity to it, in order to get more insight into your design's behavior.

For our example, seeing the RED state for five cycles should be more than sufficient:

```
test_cover: cover property ((cur_state == RED)[*5]);
```

After generating a trace for this new cover point, we use the FPV tool's debug features to add the drivers of our `cur_state` signal, and now we can get a much better insight into what is happening, as shown in Figure 5.8.

When we look at the signals in the waveform, we see that the *yield_in* signal coming to the state machine is critical in enabling a transition out of the RED state. As we review the design, we can see that this actually makes sense: you may recall, from our top-level design in Figure 5.2 and the state machine definition in Figures 5.3 and 5.4, that there are *yield* signals between the four traffic state machines. One of them can transition to a GREEN state only if the next one was previously GREEN and then yielded its ownership of the traffic by setting its *yield* signal as it transitioned back to RED.

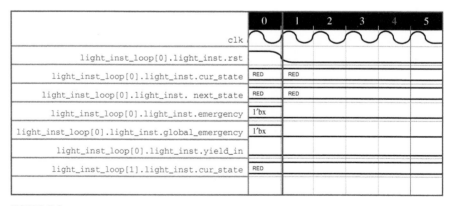

FIGURE 5.8

Waveform with drivers traced for RED State after cycle 1.

So now we see the root of the problem: for any of the four state machines to transition to GREEN, another one would have had to be GREEN first, and then set its *yield* signal. But our current design resets all lights to RED at the beginning, so nobody ever becomes GREEN. We need to modify our reset conditions so one of the lights does reset to GREEN:

```
parameter t_state RESET_STATE[3:0] = {GREEN,RED,RED,RED};

always @(posedge clk or posedge rst) begin
    if (rst) begin
      cur_state <= RESET_STATE[index];
    end else begin
      cur_state <= next_state;
    end
end
```

After this change, we can rerun our FPV tool and get more sensible results for the cover points (Table 5.4).

Table 5.4 Cover Point Results After Reset Fix

Property	Status
light[0].prop_loop[RED].state1	cover: 1 cycle
light[0].prop_loop[YELLOW].state1	cover: 8 cycles
light[0].prop_loop[GREEN].state1	cover: 7 cycles
light[0].prop_loop[GREEN_EMERGENCY].state1	NOT covered

Remember that the GREEN_EMERGENCY state being uncovered is acceptable at this point, since we have used an assumption to turn off the *emergency* condition. Now that we have some longer traces for our basic cover points, it is a good time to look at the waveforms and make sure we can see the kind of traffic we expect. Choosing the YELLOW one, we can see the kind of flow we expect for this system in Figure 5.9.

Now we can see the expected flow of each direction reaching the GREEN state in turn, a nice typical view of how this system really should be acting. In fact, we have essentially covered our cover_wave property, matching the waveform given in the specification document, without really trying. We should continue with a full run that checks all our cover points, including cover_wave and the state covers for each of the traffic state machines 1, 2 and 3. (Until now, we have been focusing on state machine 0.) This run doesn't result in any major surprises, and all the nonemergency cover points are now covered. Since we now have interesting waveforms and everything is no longer being covered in one cycle, we can consider ourselves to be past the early wiggling stage and can begin some more interesting design exploration.

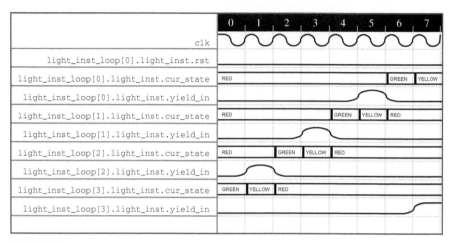

FIGURE 5.9

New waveform covering a YELLOW state for light 0.

EXPLORING MORE INTERESTING BEHAVIORS

Now that we are past the first stages of FPV, it is time to get to the real point of this design exploration process, to examine and experiment with various behaviors of our design and get a feel for how it acts under various conditions. We still have some assertions in our original design exercise plan that we have not verified yet, so we should be sure to check those. But before that, we also should not be afraid to create additional cover points on the fly, inspired by the first set of behaviors we observe. Part of the power of formal design exploration is that you can easily tweak the various possibilities of design and environment behavior, checking out ideas that occur to you based on your initial observations.

> **TIP 5.17**
>
> Try to create new assertions and cover points, not necessarily matching something from your design exercise plan, as new ideas and questions occur to you during formal design exploration.

ANSWERING SOME NEW QUESTIONS

In our case, after observing the cover waveform in Figure 5.9 showing the hand-off of the green light to each FSM in turn, it might occur to us:

- Are we sure the cycle will repeat? Maybe we made some subtle mistake that will get us stuck after each color has occurred once.
- Conversely, are these transitions always going to occur so soon, or is it possible for a light to be stuck at one state for a long time?

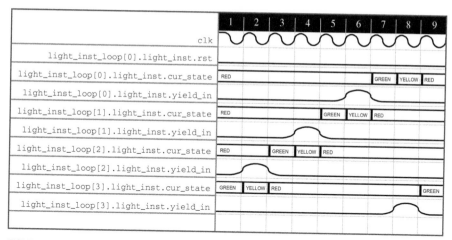

FIGURE 5.10

Waveform showing a full cycle of green lights and the start of another.

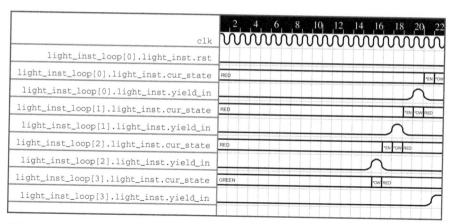

FIGURE 5.11

Waveform showing long periods of red lights.

To answer these questions, we can create some more cover points in our state machines that were not in the original plan:

```
cover_interesting1:  cover   property   ((cur_state == GREEN)   ##1
(cur_state! = GREEN) ##[1:$] (cur_state == GREEN));
cover_interesting2: cover property ((cur_state == RED)[*20]);
```

When we run the tool, we are able to see that we can get reasonable cover waveforms for both these conditions, as shown in Figures 5.10 and 5.11.

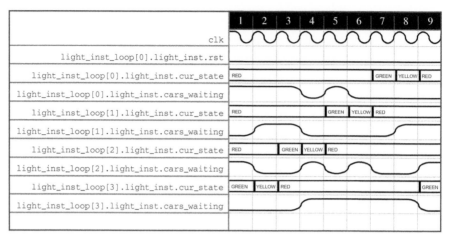

FIGURE 5.12

Discovering disappearing cars in our model.

Since these behaviors seem reasonable, we should also spot-check some of the other activity in the design: we have ideas of the expected values of various other signals, such as `cars_waiting`, `yield_out`, and so on, and it would be nice to make sure they are also acting in accordance with our expectations about these flows. After adding the `cars_waiting` signal to our `cover_interesting1` waveform, we actually do spot something unexpected, as shown in Figure 5.12.

Somehow the `cars_waiting` signal is falling on its own, showing there is no longer a car waiting, even when its light is still RED. Is this sensible behavior for traffic? Perhaps we live in a state where U-turns are legal, and due to the poorly designed traffic light controllers, cars turning around without waiting for the green light are a common occurrence. But it is much more likely that we should expect cars to remain waiting until their light is green. This odd behavior doesn't seem to cause any bugs that we have discovered yet, but still, we want to be viewing and testing realistic examples. So we add one more assumption to our state machine design:

```
no_vanishing_cars: assume property ((cars_waiting && (cur_state ==
RED)) | = > cars_waiting);
```

With this new assumption, we now see more sensible waveforms, where cars only disappear from a direction's waiting queue after they have seen a green light, as shown in Figure 5.13.

Now we are building up a nice library of interesting behaviors to share with fellow designers, architects, and validators. At early stages of design, this kind of exploration can be very important to motivate discussion of further design decisions and provide feedback help direct further refinements to the specification. We should continue adding signals and reviewing waveforms until we have good confidence in the basic functionality and flows we intended.

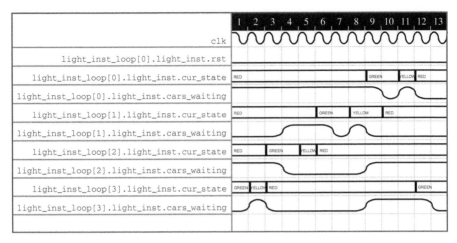

FIGURE 5.13

With new assumption, cars wait for a yellow or green light.

On this simple design, let's assume we have answered all our basic questions for now and move on to examining proofs of our assertions.

PROVING THE ASSERTIONS

Until now, we have been using the FPV tool as a kind of instant testbench generator, having it find particular waveforms that we can examine by hand. But as we have discussed in previous chapters, the greatest power of FPV is the ability to prove assertions: this can provide us formal confidence that bad behaviors will never occur in any possible simulation. In our example, we have only defined a small number of assertions so far. Our initial attempt to prove them returns a result like the following (again, due to the multiple symmetric state machines, we are initially just showing the results for state machine 0) (Table 5.5).

The first two are passing, which is a good result: we know we cannot violate the basic safety condition of multiple active directions of traffic, and we know

Table 5.5 Results of First Proof Attempt on Assertions

Property	Status
safety1	pass
lights[0].nobogus	pass
lights[0].emergency1	vacuous pass
lights[0].liveness1	fail: 2

that we cannot enter a BOGUS state. The vacuous pass for `emergency1` indicates that we cannot violate it, but for a trivial reason: its preconditions can never be met. Remember, this is how we defined this property:

```
emergency1: assert property (emergency |->
    ##2 (light == L_GREEN));
```

It is a triggered implication, stating that if the emergency signal is high, then we must get a green light within two cycles. But we know that in our current configuration, we will never get the emergency signal high—we assumed that was impossible, in order to simplify our early stages of design exploration:

```
fv_overconstrain_emergency: assume property (global_emergency == 0);
```

Thus we are satisfied for now with the `emergency1` property's vacuous status, though this is something we should revisit when we later remove this assumption.

The most interesting result from these initial prove attempts is the failing property `liveness1`. This was the property stating that a waiting car will eventually get a green light:

```
liveness1: assert property (
    ((cur_state == RED) && cars_waiting) |->
        s_eventually(cur_state == GREEN));
```

Since the property failed, that means there is some set of conditions under which a light may be red forever while cars are waiting for it, certainly not a desirable feature of a traffic light controller. To understand why this is happening, we can examine a counterexample waveform generated by the FPV tool, as shown in Figure 5.14.

At first, it might seem odd that a 2-cycle waveform can appear as a counterexample here: since this was a *liveness* property, specifying an infinite condition using the `s_eventually` operator, shouldn't the counterexample have to be infinite? Actually, this is an infinite example: when disproving a liveness property, FPV tools generate a waveform consisting of two parts: a *prefix* and a *loop*.

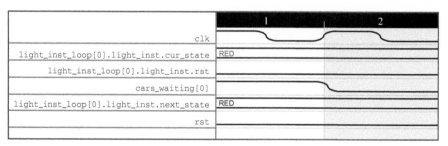

FIGURE 5.14

Failure waveform for liveness1 assertion.

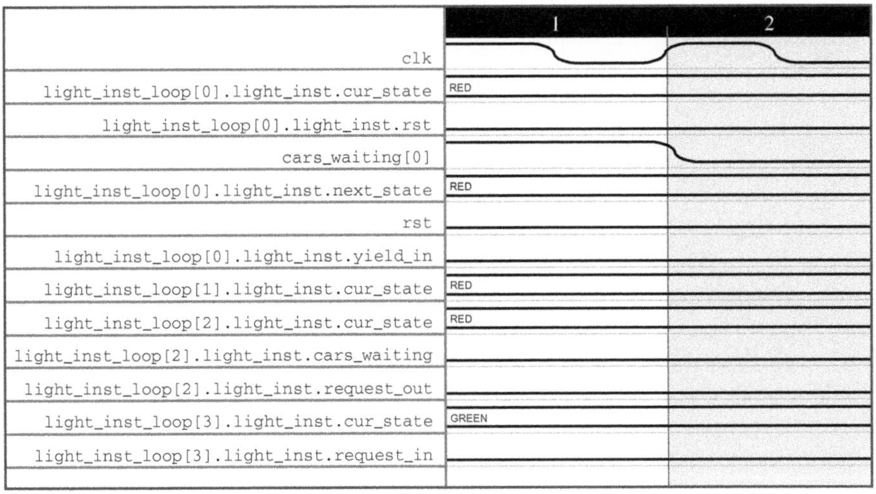

	1	2
clk		
light_inst_loop[0].light_inst.cur_state	RED	
light_inst_loop[0].light_inst.rst		
cars_waiting[0]		
light_inst_loop[0].light_inst.next_state	RED	
rst		
light_inst_loop[0].light_inst.yield_in		
light_inst_loop[1].light_inst.cur_state	RED	
light_inst_loop[2].light_inst.cur_state	RED	
light_inst_loop[2].light_inst.cars_waiting		
light_inst_loop[2].light_inst.request_out		
light_inst_loop[3].light_inst.cur_state	GREEN	
light_inst_loop[3].light_inst.request_in		

FIGURE 5.15

Determining the root cause of the endless red light in Figure 5.14.

The prefix is a finite waveform, only one cycle in our case, which occurs once in the counterexample. The loop, shown by the different shading on cycle 2, is a sequence of events that is understood to repeat for an infinite amount of time. So this waveform is telling us that after the events in cycle 1 occur, those in cycle 2 can occur repeatedly for an infinite amount of time, causing our s_eventually condition to never be satisfied. In this case, after the car arrives at the red light in cycle 1, that light can remain red in cycle 2 and every cycle afterward.

We are not done, though, because we really want to understand why it is possible that the loop in cycle 2 occurs. We should look at the fanin of that RED state to figure out why it is possible for it to last forever. After adding a few levels of fanin in the FPV tool, we can trace the root cause as shown in the new waveform in Figure 5.15.

This leads to an interesting insight. Remember that we had a round-robin protocol for the lights, where each direction yields the green light to the next one if two conditions are met:

- There are no cars coming from the current direction.
- There is a request from the next light's FSM, due to cars waiting at that direction.

In this waveform, we can see that the poor drivers at light 0 are stuck because light 1 never got the green light, which is because light 2 never got the green light... because light 2 never *requested* the green light! The cars_waiting signal at light 2 is permanently 0, showing that no car ever arrives there, so that direction never requests the green light. Thus, light 3 permanently holds onto the green, seeing no reason to ever release it.

Thinking about this a little more, we can see that the round-robin protocol will effectively be infinitely halted if either of the two conditions above remains 0 for infinite time. This is a useful insight: in effect, we have found a fundamental flaw in our central protocol, a way for one malicious light to prevent others from turning green. We need to decide based on project requirements whether this requires a major redesign, or whether we have just omitted some assumptions that will be true of our design's environment.

In this case, let's decide that in real life, there will always be cars coming from every direction, and there will always be a guarantee of a gap in traffic as well. Thus, rather than redesigning our controller, we just need to add some FPV assumptions. This is fine—as we have mentioned before, the vast majority of time spent in FPV is in efforts to understand corner-case waveforms produced by the tool and decide whether we need to tighten our assumptions or have a real design bug.

TIP 5.18

Continuing to "wiggle," adding more assumptions after examining counterexample waveforms, is an expected part of the FPV process. Only a small minority of counterexample waveforms lead to actual bugs, but many more lead to new insights about your design requirements.

To solve the problem in our case, we need each direction to eventually get `cars_waiting = 1`, so it will request the light, and also need to guarantee that each direction will eventually get `cars_waiting = 0`, so it will release the light. So we can add these assumptions to each of the directions our model:

```
traffic_gap1: assume property (cars_waiting |=> s_eventually
(!cars_waiting));
traffic_gap2: assume  property  (!cars_waiting  |=>  s_eventually
(cars_waiting));
```

Once we add these assumptions and rerun the proofs, our properties all pass. On more complex designs, we would expect numerous iterations before reaching this stage. But now we have good confidence that our basic protocol works, and there are no tricky combinations of inputs that can result in violating our basic safety rules or causing a deadlocked traffic system. Before we declare victory and go home, though, we need to remember the initial compromise we made to simplify the problem: ignoring the emergency conditions.

REMOVING SIMPLIFICATIONS AND EXPLORING MORE BEHAVIORS

When we were planning the verification of our traffic light controller, we added one overconstraint, the assumption that the emergency signals would be tied to 0.

```
fv_overconstrain_emergency: assume property (global_emergency == 0);
```

It was very useful to be working under this constraint so far: we were able to explore and verify the basic traffic light protocol and design, without having to worry about the complication of the emergency condition. But now that we have completed the basic verification, it is time to examine our model's behavior under more complex conditions.

After removing this constraint, we rerun our FPV tool on all our assertions and cover points, to get an initial idea of any problem spots. We expect that all our cover points will be reached, since if they were reached under an overconstraint condition they should certainly still be reachable when it is removed. We see that this is true of our model, with the addition that the GREEN_EMERGENCY states can now be covered (Table 5.6).

Table 5.6 Cover Point Results After Removing Constraint

Property	Status
light[0].prop_loop[RED].state1	cover: 1 cycle
light[0].prop_loop[YELLOW].state1	cover: 4 cycles
light[0].prop_loop[GREEN].state1	cover: 3 cycles
light[0].prop_loop[GREEN_EMERGENCY].state1	cover: 2 cycles
light[0].cover_interesting1	cover: 5 cycles
light[0].cover_interesting2	cover: 20 cycles

The lengths of some of the cover traces have gone down, which is interesting, but not completely unexpected since we have widened our range of possible behaviors. We should examine the waveforms for each of these cover points and make sure we are seeing somewhat realistic flows and values occurring. Let's assume we have done that and move on to the question of the assertions.

The assertions are more interesting now: we are now allowing a vast range of additional behaviors, based on arbitrary occurrence of emergency conditions, so it is likely that some new corner case will be found that can violate one of them. Examining the assertion results at the top level and for traffic FSM 0, we find that this is indeed the case (Table 5.7).

Table 5.7 Assertion Results After Removing Constraint

Property	Status
safety1	fail: 2
lights[0].nobogus	pass
lights[0].emergency1	pass
lights[0].liveness1	fail: 4

The failure of our basic safety property safety1 is the biggest concern. This was the property that ensures traffic from multiple directions is not getting yellow

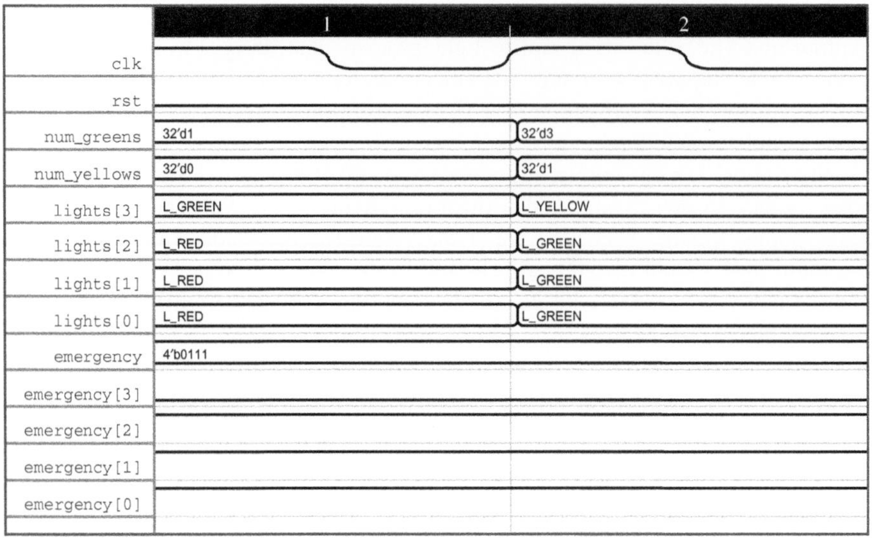

		1	2
clk			
rst			
num_greens	32'd1		32'd3
num_yellows	32'd0		32'd1
lights[3]	L_GREEN		L_YELLOW
lights[2]	L_RED		L_GREEN
lights[1]	L_RED		L_GREEN
lights[0]	L_RED		L_GREEN
emergency	4'b0111		
emergency[3]			
emergency[2]			
emergency[1]			
emergency[0]			

FIGURE 5.16

Multiple green lights caused by emergency condition.

or green lights at once. If this is violated, then there is a major issue with our design. Looking at the failure waveform for this property can give us some insight (Figure 5.16).

Oops, it looks like our emergency protocol has two fundamental flaws. First, we can see from the *lights[3]* and *lights[2]* values that if a light is green and an emergency signal arrives in another direction, the other direction will get a green light while the first is still yellow, causing a potential collision. This is a fundamental bug in our code: we need to make sure the emergency transition to green is delayed by a cycle, to allow for the yellow light. In addition, we can see that multiple emergency signals can arrive at once, causing each of their directions to turn green at the same time! There is no way to justify a prohibition of this as an environmental assumption, since the whole point of emergency vehicles is that they can come at any time; we need to modify our design to do some kind of arbitration when this condition occurs.

In real life, at this stage we would be making a fairly major change to our RTL, to add this arbitration protocol. We might be tempted to immediately rerun our FPV with the emergency mode on, so we can check this latest change. However, it is probably safer to first re-add our simplification assumption *fv_overconstrain_emergency*, so we can first verify in a simpler environment that these major changes did not disrupt the nonemergency condition. After we have confidence that nothing there is broken, it makes more sense to return to this unconstrained environment.

> **TIP 5.19**
>
> If you have a simplified environment with overconstraining assumptions, be sure to reuse it to test any major design changes before removing the overconstraint. This can significantly simplify your debug process.

FACING COMPLEXITY ISSUES

One other potential challenge to keep in mind is that some of our assertions may turn out to be very difficult to generate acceptable results on, due to hitting complexity issues. For example, we may see this result when trying to prove one of our assertions (Table 5.8):

Table 5.8 Assertion Result for Complexity Case

Property	Status
safety1	timeout/bound 5

For one of our assertions, *safety1*, the proof engine was not able to fully determine its success or failure, and timed out while only having proven it to a bound of five. This means that it is proven true only for potential executions of 5 cycles or less, not a very good result.

As we have mentioned above in our discussion of complexity staging, there are several simple techniques available to reduce design complexity. You can add blackboxes or cut points, hiding some of the logic for verification purposes. You can also attempt to use overconstraint to limit the design to certain modes or data types. We will see in later chapters that a number of more aggressive techniques are available.

However, when you are running in design exercise mode, you usually do not want to spend a lot of time dealing with complexity. Of course, if the majority of your properties are hitting these issues with timeouts and low bounds, you do need to take a step back and look for potential complexity reduction opportunities, or perhaps add more intermediate steps to your complexity staging plan. On the other hand, if you are able to prove or explore the majority of your assertions and cover points, you should probably put aside the ones with complexity issues, flagging them for more attention when you reach the validation-focused FPV stages we will discuss in the next chapter.

> **TIP 5.20**
>
> If you are facing complexity issues with a small number of assertions in design exercise FPV, flag them for more attention in later validation-focused FPV stages.

SUMMARY

In this chapter, we have reviewed the typical process of using FPV for early design exercise, using our example of a traffic light controller. We saw that this lightweight process involves several steps:

- Design exercise planning: start out with a clear understanding of your design exercise goals, major properties you want, your complexity staging plan, and your exit criteria. Try to find opportunities to overconstrain your design to simplify your initial exploration.
- Setting up your design: once you have the general plan, create cover points, assumptions, and assertions. Then build your model in an FPV tool, and sanity-check the complexity.
- Once you have your design running in the FPV tool, expect very short waveforms in your initial runs. You need to go through several rounds of "wiggling," examining waveforms and adding related assumptions, before getting interesting waveforms.
- After you have interesting waveforms, examine your cover traces and debug your failing assertions. Be sure to add new properties inspired by questions that occur to you when examining initial waveforms.
- Once you have confidence in your initial properties, gradually relax the overconstraints and try them again, debugging any new issues that come up due to the expanded range of behaviors you are exploring.

What value has this form of exercise brought to our design and validation process? We can see a number of critical benefits from going through this process:

- We have explored many typical behaviors and flows for our design, generating waveforms that can be used for reference and illustration in future discussions.
- We have uncovered environmental assumptions and requirements that are critical for our design to work properly, but were not explicitly stated ahead of time.
- We have validated that in nonemergency conditions, our protocol meets our requirements for all possible inputs, by proving assertions exhaustively with our FPV tool.
- We have discovered some real bugs in our design and realized that we need some major changes to the emergency protocols in our system.

Most critically, we have done all the above in an early design or validation stage on our local model, rather than having to use higher-level simulation environments at greater cost later in our project. Due to this use in very early project stages, we have potentially provided an exponential increase in the efficiency of finding bugs and generating clean RTL models.

PRACTICAL TIPS FROM THIS CHAPTER

5.1 FPV-based design exercise is a powerful tool for exploring possible behaviors of interacting state machines.

5.2 Create a design exercise plan when beginning design exercise FPV. This should be very lightweight when compared to a full verification plan. But you should be sure to specify your goals, outline your major properties, include a complexity staging plan, and include exit criteria.

5.3 When doing design exercise on a state machine-based design, an important goal is to try to exercise each legal state. Also consider checking cross-products of states if multiple FSMs are involved.

5.4 Try to observe typical behaviors and flows in your design, such as waveform diagrams you might find in a specification document.

5.5 You should also include goals related to specific requirements of your design. But be careful not to turn your lightweight design exercise into an attempt at full verification: defer more complex properties to later stages of the validation process.

5.6 Try to include basic specification-derived properties in your design exercise plans, but avoid the pitfall of turning this into a full proof plan: your goal is to choose properties that will not be too difficult to write and verify.

5.7 If reusing or complying to a common interface, check whether pre-written interface property sets are available from others in your company, or from an external vendor.

5.8 When setting up a model for design exercise, check for opportunities to safely reduce complexity using blackbox or cut point techniques.

5.9 At the start of design exploration, use overconstraint judiciously to enable design exploration on a simplified model and have a staging plan to gradually add increased functionality.

5.10 Use a naming convention, such as a prefix *fv_overconstrain*, to mark intentional overconstraints that enable early design exercise but should later be removed for more rigorous verification.

5.11 When doing design exercise FPV, be sure to take advantage of FPV's ability to back-propagate assumptions on internal nodes, where this would enable you to simplify your assumption creation.

5.12 Try to insert safety properties inline in your RTL when applicable during RTL design or review. These can be useful to include in your FPV runs and often help to uncover errors closer to the root cause than high-level specification properties.

5.13 Don't be afraid of seeing short, even 1-cycle, waveforms in early FPV stages. This is a normal part of the wiggling process.

5.14 Begin any FPV effort by creating a set of reasonable cover points on your model, representing typical and interesting activity.

5.15 When dealing with very short waveforms from an FPV tool, be sure to turn on the tool option to display reset cycles.

5.16 When debugging unreachable cover points, start by using or creating a simple cover point that is reachable and gradually add complexity to it, in order to get more insight into your design's behavior.

5.17 Try to create new assertions and cover points, not necessarily matching something from your design exercise plan, as new ideas and questions occur to you during formal design exploration.

5.18 Continuing to "wiggle," adding more assumptions after examining counterexample waveforms, is an expected part of the FPV process. Only a small minority of counterexample waveforms lead to actual bugs, but many more lead to new insights about your design requirements.

5.19 If you have a simplified environment with overconstraining assumptions, be sure to reuse it to test any major design changes before removing the overconstraint. This can significantly simplify your debug process.

5.20 If you are facing complexity issues with a small number of assertions in design exercise FPV, flag them for more attention in later validation-focused FPV stages.

FURTHER READING

[Ben01] Lionel Benning and Harry Foster, *Principles of Verifiable RTL Design*, Springer, 2001.

[Ran11] Rajeev Ranjan, Claudionor Coelho, and Sebastian Skalberg, "Beyond Verification: Leveraging Formal for Debugging," Design Automation Conference 2011.

[Ran09] Rajeev Ranjan, et al., "Towards Harnessing the True Potential of IP Reuse," DesignCon 2009.

[Ste12] Daryl Stewart, "Formal for Everyone," Formal Methods in Computer Aided Design 2012.

Effective FPV for verification

## 6

> *[With formal verification,] people are able to take designs, plan about what they can verify in a design, while they are building a test bench run regressions, measure progress, measure coverage, and in the end check off and sign off and say we are completely done.*
>
> **Vigyan Singhal, *Oski Technologies***

Now that we have explored the basic methods of formal verification (FV) through design exercise, we are well poised to discuss and explore more validation-oriented modes of formal property verification (FPV). In the previous chapter, we explored the power of formal technology and observed how design exercise can help users to better understand their register transfer level (RTL) designs. In this chapter, we are going to dive into a couple of more advanced design verification techniques: *bug hunting FPV* and *full proof FPV*. The bug hunting mode of FPV is typically applied on a reasonably complex block where complimentary validation methods such as simulation or emulation are expected to be used as well. The goal of FPV on such a block would be to target complex scenarios and discover subtle corner cases that are unlikely to be hit through simulation. Full proof FPV, the traditional goal of the original FPV research pioneers, generally targets complex or risky designs with an intention to completely prove that the design meets its specification. If done properly, full proof FPV can be used to completely replace unit-level simulation testing.

When planning validation-focused FPV, you need to decide on your goals: whether to use it to supplement other forms of validation and hunt for bugs, or to use as the primary method of validation and completely verify the design formally. If you are inexperienced with FPV, we usually recommend that you start with RTL exercise, then advance to a bug hunting effort and choose whether to expand to full proof based on your initial level of success. After some experience, you should be better able to judge which mode of FPV suits your design best.

The remainder of this chapter describes the practical issues in setting up a robust FPV environment and effectively using it on your model for bug hunting and full proof scenarios. This includes a good understanding of the extended wiggling process, to refine your assumptions iteratively, and build a strong FPV environment. You will also need to think about coverage issues and to include the use of good cover points to justify that you are truly verifying your interesting design space. We illustrate this process on an example design to provide a direct demonstration of our major points.

DECIDING ON YOUR FPV GOALS

First, if you are thinking about validation-focused FPV, you need to make sure you choose an appropriate design style to work with. FPV is most effective on control logic blocks, or data transport blocks. By "data transport," we mean a block that essentially routes data from one point to another. This contrasts with "data transformation" blocks, which perform complex operations on the data, such as floating point arithmetic or MPEG decoder logic: most FPV tools cannot handle these well. Light arithmetic operations, such as integer addition and subtraction, are often acceptable for the current generation of tools, but you will probably need other forms of validation for major blocks involving multiplication, division, or floating point methods.

TIP 6.1

For validation-focused FPV, choose blocks that primarily involve control logic or data transport, with data transformation limited to simple operations like integer addition.

Before we embark on deciding the FPV goal for the design under test (DUT), we need to understand more clearly what we mean by bug hunting FPV and full proof FPV.

BUG HUNTING FPV

Bug hunting FPV is a technique to hunt for potential corner-case issues in a design that we might miss through other techniques. The most important design requirements are written as assertions, and you prove that illegal assertion-violating conditions are not possible, or use the FPV tool to discover the existence of such scenarios in the design. This method is typically used if part of your design is seen as especially risky due to large number of corner cases and you want extra confidence in your verification even after running your full set of random simulations. It is common to resort to bug hunting FPV when hitting simulation coverage problems at a late design stage to ensure that there are not any tricky corner cases waiting to be exposed.

Some of the common situations that would lead you to choose bug hunting FPV are as follows:

- You are working on a design containing many corner cases, such as a large piece of control logic with several interacting state machines, and want an extra level of validation confidence.

- You have been running regular simulations on your design, and some part of it repeatedly exposes new errors during random tests.
- You are verifying a critical component of your design, and similar blocks have a history of logic bugs escaping to late stages or to silicon.
- You have already done design exercise FPV on your model, so increasing your FPV coverage by adding additional targeted assertions has a relatively low cost.
- You have a mature/reused model that mostly does not need further verification, but you have added a new feature that you want to verify with confidence.
- You have a bug that was found with a random test in a higher-level simulation testbench and you are finding it tough to reproduce the same bug at unit level because you would need a complex and rare set of input conditions.

Here, FPV is used as supplement to simulation. You are free to allow some level of overconstraining or some other compromises, as discussed in the design exercise context in the previous chapter. Don't shy away from adding constraints that limit you to exercise only a part of the complete set of possible behaviors, the part you wish to focus on, or where you suspect a lurking bug. This is absolutely acceptable when you are doing bug hunting FPV.

TIP 6.2

When planning for bug hunting FPV, use overconstraint as needed to simplify the model you work on in order to focus on your current problem areas.

This is a medium effort activity, more effort intensive than design exercise FPV but simpler than full proof FPV, and can function as a decent compromise between the other two forms.

FULL PROOF FPV

Full proof FPV is the usage model that corresponds most closely with the original motivation for FV research: generating solid proofs that your design is 100% correct. Full proof FPV is a high-effort activity, as it involves trying to prove the complete functionality of the design. As a result, the return on such investment is high as well: you can use it as a substitute for unit-level simulation. Thus, you can save the effort you would have spent on running simulations or other validation methods. A design completely proven through FPV, with a solid set of assertions to fully define the specification, along with solid and well-reviewed sets of cover points and assumptions, provides as much or more confidence than many months of random regressions on a full simulation environment. This method also reduces the risk of hard-to-find misses and nightmares due to corner-case behaviors not anticipated during test planning, which are often experienced in late stages of traditional validation.

You should consider running full proof FPV on your RTL if:

- You are provided with a detailed reference specification that is expected to be implemented.
- You have a design that conforms to standard interfaces where packages of pre-verified FPV collateral are available or the set of needed constraints is clearly documented.
- Your design is defined by a set of tables that fully encapsulate the expected behavior.
- You have a part of your RTL that needs bulletproof verification to reduce design risk.
- You have completed an initial effort at bug hunting FPV, and it was successful enough that you believe you can expand your assertion set and reduce your overconstraints to cover the full specification.
- You have successfully run full proof FPV on similar blocks in the past and are confident you can develop a similar verification plan.

STAGING YOUR FPV EFFORTS

Because full proof FPV can be a substantial effort, we always recommend that you start with design exercise FPV, expand it into bug hunting, and gradually march toward the full proof mode. Your design exercise will function as an initial sanity-check that you have chosen a design whose size is appropriate for FPV, and whose logic is of a complexity level that is reasonable for FPV tools to handle. As we discussed in the previous chapter, design exercise enables you to do a relatively lightweight planning effort, and quickly get some hands-on results that will give you confidence in the tool's ability to handle your design. Once you observe decent results by extensive wiggling, are confident about the environment you created, and are satisfied that you have fulfilled the goals in your design exercise plan, it is time to transition to bug hunting.

When ready to begin bug hunting, you should begin by creating a bug hunting verification plan. Once you have created this plan, start adding more complex assertions to the design and verify them, doing further wiggling, improving your modeling, and refining constraints as needed. It is perfectly fine to have your design overconstrained in the bug hunting mode, though you will often be gradually removing those constraints to find larger classes of bugs. After you have achieved the goals in your bug hunting plan, it is time to consider full proof FPV.

When planning full proof FPV, you need to be very careful about the full coverage of the design. Make sure you are starting with a solid specification document (or demand one from your architects), and be sure that your planning includes not only a full set of assertions, but also a broad set of cover points that can instill confidence in the verification effort spent. There is always an issue of logical holes lurking—some of which you would have never thought of if not examining cover points. In some cases, commercial tool features can help with coverage information as well. But even when you have tool features to help check coverage, you need to carefully think through the needed set of cover points: no tool can completely substitute for human design intuition.

Now we will look more into the steps involved in achieving your FPV goals, as we walk through the core ideas of bug hunting FPV on the basis of a simple arithmetic logic unit (ALU) design example.

EXAMPLE FOR THIS CHAPTER: SIMPLE ALU

For our illustration of design exercise FPV, we resort to yet another common example in the formal world, a simple ALU. As in our other examples, we use a simple design with some intentional flaws to illustrate the usage of FPV—no guarantees that it would not create another FDIV bug.

Figure 6.1 illustrates the basic block diagram of the ALU under consideration, with a few simple requirements in the specification:

- The logical unit computes simple logical operations: OR, AND, and NOT.
- The arithmetic unit computes simple arithmetic computations: addition, subtraction, and compare.
- The results are accompanied by the respective valid signals *logresultv/ arithresultv* and the final selection to the output is based on the operation.
- The computation takes three clocks to produce results at the output ports.
- There are four threads running in parallel computing on a large vector; in other words, the below logic is replicated four times.

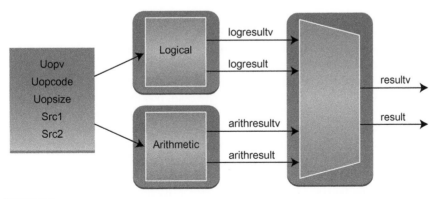

FIGURE 6.1

Simple ALU.

(The full SystemVerilog model can be downloaded from the book website at http://formalverificationbook.com if you would like to try it yourself.)

You can see from Figure 6.1 that the operations are computed in parallel and hence there is an opportunity for simple power savings that is embedded as a part of the design. Only the selected computation logic is active, while the other portion of the unit can be effectively *clock-gated*, cut off from the clock lines to prevent logic transitions and reduce overall power usage. The top-level code for this design is shown in Figure 6.2.

For brevity, only the instantiations and final connections are depicted here. The ALU considered here also has debug-related signals that are not shown in the above code. The μops (micro-operations) can operate on three different data sizes (DSIZE), whose encodings are also defined.

UNDERSTANDING THE DESIGN

Remember that before you enter a validation-focused FPV effort, whether bug hunting or full proof, you should begin with design exercise FPV, as we discussed in the previous chapter. This will play a critical role in helping to judge the general feasibility of FPV on the chosen design, based on a lightweight initial effort. For the remainder of this discussion, we will assume that design exercise FPV has already been completed on the ALU, and we are looking to expand our efforts into bug hunting and eventually to full proof FPV.

> ### TIP 6.3
>
> When first trying FPV on any new design, start with lightweight design exercise FPV (as described in Chapter 5) to verify basic behaviors and FPV feasibility before moving to more elaborate validation-focused FPV efforts.

When transitioning from design exercise to bug hunting FPV, the first step is identifying the right DUT block for verification. As we have discussed in previous chapters, FPV tools have a fundamental limitation on the amount of logic they can meaningfully consume to provide verification feedback. This is because, by very definition, the formal tools explore all possible behaviors exhibited by design block being tested, which is a computationally expensive problem. In addition, the performance of FPV engines can vary widely based on the internal structure of the logic, independent of model size, so it is best to avoid pushing against the maximum capacity of the engines when it can be avoided. Thus we should not feed the formal tools arbitrarily large design blocks to test.

To make the best use of the tool's limited capacity, we carve out the most interesting parts of a design when choosing our DUT. There needs to be a good balance between having the flexibility in choosing an arbitrary piece of logic and

```
// uopcode definitions
   parameter OPAND = 5'b00000;
   parameter OPOR  = 5'b00001;
   parameter OPXOR = 5'b00010;
   parameter OPADD = 5'b01000;
   parameter OPSUB = 5'b01001;
   parameter OPCMP = 5'b01011;
   //
   parameter DSIZE08 = 2'b00;
   parameter DSIZE16 = 2'b01;
   parameter DSIZE32 = 2'b10;
   parameter MAXDSIZE = DSIZE08;
   // Top-level wrapper module
   module alu0(
           Clk,
           uopv,
           uopcode,
           uopsize,
           src1,
           src2,
           resultv,
           result,
                dfts1ovrd,
   dftdata,
   defeature_addck
                );
logical logical (
                .Clk ( Clk ),
                .uopv ( uopv ),
                .uopcode ( uopcode ),
                .uopsize ( uopsize ),
                .src1 ( src1 ),
                .src2 ( src2 ),
                .logresultv ( logresultv ),
                .logresult ( logresult ),
                .dftdata (dftdata),
                .dfts1ovrd(dfts1ovrd)
                 );

arithmetic arithmetic (
                .Clk ( Clk ),
                .uopv ( uopv ),
                .uopcode ( uopcode ),
                .uopsize ( uopsize ),
                .src1 ( src1 ),
                .src2 ( src2 ),
                .arithresultv ( arithresultv )
                .arithresult ( arithresult )
                .defeature_addck(defeature_addck)
            );
resultv = logresultv | arithresultv;

`MUX2_1( result,
        logresultv, logresult,
        arithresultv, arithresult )
end
endmodule // alu0
```

FIGURE 6.2

SystemVerilog code for simple ALU.

choosing a DUT that is large enough and well-documented enough that creating a verification plan is clear.

In the case of our ALU example, the design contains four parallel copies of the ALU, one for each thread. But if our primary focus is on the ALU functionality, rather than the thread dispatching logic at the top level, it probably makes the most sense for us to focus on the ALU logic itself, verifying one single generic ALU instance rather than the top-level model that has four of them. This provides us significant potential complexity savings, with one quarter the logic to analyze of the full model.

TIP 6.4

Carefully carve out the logic you want to verify with FPV and limit the design to a size that can be handled by the tools. A good rule of thumb with current-generation tools is to aim for less than 40,000 active state elements (latches and flip-flops).

The number of state elements we describe may sound somewhat limiting, but keep in mind that in most cases you will be blackboxing large embedded memories, as we will discuss in the complexity section below.

Once you have identified the DUT that you are choosing for the bug hunting effort, the next step is to make sure you have a good understanding of your model. You should start by looking at a block diagram of your proposed initial DUT, and by doing the following:

- Determine the approximate sizes, in number of state elements, for each major submodule. Many EDA tools can display this information for compiled models.
- Identify the blocks you would like to target with FPV. Remember to consider both the design sizes and the style of logic: control logic or data transport blocks tend to work best with FPV tools.
- Identify blackbox candidates: submodules that you might be able to eliminate from consideration if needed. Try to blackbox blocks whose logic is least likely to meaningfully affect your primary targets. You also need to think about the potential effort required to create interface assumptions that model that block's output behavior, if it affects your targets.
- Identify major external interfaces that need to be properly constrained.

The above items are not always very easy to determine, of course. If you have simulation waveforms available from the current design or a similar design from a previous project, you should also examine them for guidance. These waveforms can help you determine which parts of your interfaces are active during typical transactions, and whether critical activity takes place on the interfaces of your proposed blackboxes.

For our ALU, we would probably generate a diagram something like Figure 6.3. Here we are assuming that the arithmetic logic has been identified as a primary risk area, so we want to be sure that our FPV environment ultimately tests this logic.

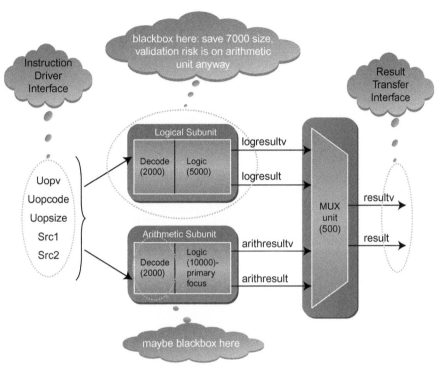

FIGURE 6.3

ALU block diagram with block sizes, interfaces, and blackbox candidates clarified.

Once we have generated this diagram and understand the basic design flow, blocks, and interfaces of our model, it is time to work on the bug hunting FPV plan.

TIP 6.5

When beginning the bug hunting or full proof FPV planning process, start with a block diagram of your unit, including the sizes of all major blocks, and label the interfaces, blackbox candidates, and areas of verification focus. This diagram will provide a critical foundation for your verification plan.

CREATING THE FPV VERIFICATION PLAN

Let's assume that we have chosen to undertake FPV because we want to exhaustively check the corner cases of the arithmetic logic and achieve more confidence in the functionality of the design. We should try to start with:

- A clear understanding of our goals.
- The kinds of properties we will be looking at, including cover points that should be hit.

- A staging plan for how to initially overconstrain the verification and gradually remove the overconstraints.
- A decomposition strategy to be deployed, if needed, to deal with the level of complexity.
- Success criteria for determining when we have done sufficient FPV.

TIP 6.6

Create a verification plan when beginning a validation-focused FPV effort. This should describe the logic to be verified, properties and cover points, staging plan, decomposition strategy, and success criteria.

The verification plan is subject to change; you should be able to take the feedback from the initial FPV runs and tune your plan to drive the rest of the verification effort. The plan should be easily translatable to the FPV environment, which would involve creating properties that could be constraints (assumptions), functional checks (assertions), and sanity-checkers (covers). Don't be surprised to see this refinement loop being executed many times, as new issues and learnings are uncovered, which motivate fine-tuning the verification plan and the FPV environment. At all stages, the cover points help you to continuously sanity-check that you are still observing interesting activity in your design.

FPV GOALS

One of the main goals of bug hunting FPV is to expose the corner-case issues that would be hard to hit through simulations. To better enable the examination of corner cases, we should try to create properties involving each of the major functions of our design, or of the part of our design we consider to have the greatest risk. For the ALU example in this chapter, we might consider verifying all opcodes for a specific class of operations and specific cases of DSIZE, while in full proof mode we would consider all the cases: the cross-product of all DSIZEs and all opcodes.

Most of the design behaviors would be defined in the specification document. If doing bug hunting FPV, we can use this as a guide to the most important features. If doing full proof FPV, we should carefully review this document, and make sure its requirements have been included in our FPV plan.

Based on the considerations above, we can come up with the initial set of goals for our bug hunting FPV on the ALU:

- Verify the behavior of the arithmetic unit, in the absence of any unusual activity such as power-gating or scan/debug hooks, for the default DSIZE 08.
- If time permits, expand to check the logical operators as well and additional DSIZE values.
- Once all the above checks are complete, consider adding checks for the power-gating and scan/debug features.

MAJOR PROPERTIES FOR FPV

As per the verification plan, you should decide on the major properties you want to include in your FPV environment. At this point we should describe the properties in plain English for planning purposes; the real coding in SystemVerilog Assertions (SVA) will follow later.

Cover points

As explained earlier, for any FPV activity, the cover points are the most critical properties at early stages. We begin with writing covers of typical activity and interesting combinations of basic behaviors. We would start with defining a cover property for each opcode and flow that was described in waveforms in the specification document.

Figure 6.4 shows an example of a waveform that might appear in our specification, demonstrating the flow of arithmetic and logic operations, which we aim to replicate in the formal environment.

In addition to replicating applicable waveforms from the specification, we should plan on cover points to execute arithmetic operations, and see how the design responds for a predefined set of inputs. So our initial cover point plan might look like this:

- Create cover points that replicate each waveform in the specification that illustrates arithmetic unit behavior.
- Cover each arithmetic operation (ADD, SUB, CMP) with nonzero inputs, alone and back-to-back with another arbitrary operation.
- Cover cases of each operation above with specific data that exercises all bits.

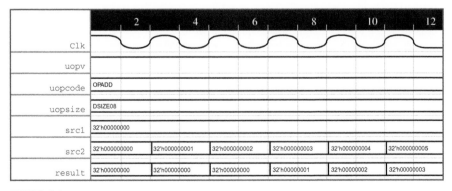

FIGURE 6.4

Specification waveform we would like to cover.

Assumptions

Next we need to consider assumptions. In bug hunting mode, we want to target specific behaviors of the design, which would mean that we might be applying constraints so that behaviors are restricted to checking operations of the choice. We should not shy away from overconstraining while trying to verify specific behaviors. Remember that we might not be able to come up with the right assumptions in the first attempt, and hence we might be spending some time wiggling to converge on all needed assumptions. This is a common practice for any model bring-up. In our case, the initial assumptions for our planned overconstraints on the environment would include:

- Assume the *uopsize* input is always DSIZE 08.
- Assume dfx (scan) inputs are shut off.
- Assume all operations are arithmetic, not logical.

We should also examine the interfaces we have identified in our block diagram: we will need to make sure our assumption set properly models the behaviors of each of these interfaces. In the case of our simple ALU, we have identified the Instruction Driver Interface and Data Transfer Interface as the points of interaction between our model and the outside world. For this simple example, these interfaces do not have any complex protocol requirements to model with assumptions.

In more complex cases, the interfaces from the design under consideration might align to a standard protocol specification, such as USB, AXI, or AHB, or match a block from a previous design or version. Thus, you may have a set of reusable assumptions (and assertions) that define a protocol, or be able to leverage a similar interface assumption set from a previous project. Be sure to take advantage of any reuse opportunities. In our simple ALU example, we do not have such a case.

TIP 6.7

Explore the opportunity of reusing standard properties whenever applicable to your units: this can save you significant time when bringing up an FPV environment.

If the interfaces are complex to describe in terms of standalone assertions, and we do not have reusable collateral, we might also consider developing reference models, as discussed in the next subsection.

Assertions

Apart from cover points and assumptions, we obviously need to define one more type of property: our assertions, or proof targets. As discussed above, these should largely be inspired by the specification document, which is the official definition of what we are supposed to be validating.

Here are the types of assertions we generate for this example:

- Assert that when a valid operation arrives, a valid output appears in three cycles.
- Assert that each operation generates the expected results: if we select ADD, the output should match the sum of the inputs, and so forth.

Note that both the properties above are end-to-end properties based on the specification: they talk about desired outputs in terms of expected inputs. In more complex designs, you may want to supplement these with *whitebox assertions* that check intermediate activity on internal nodes. While it is often the case that you can fully describe your specification with end-to-end properties, these will also be likely in many cases to be the most logically complex, encompassing large amounts of logic to prove and challenging the formal engines. We should keep this in mind and think about also creating more local assertions on internal modules and verifying intermediate steps of our computation if we run into complexity issues. We still want to specify the end-to-end properties, but having these smaller properties available during wiggling may significantly improve the efficiency of the debug process.

In addition, as we look at the above assertions, it might appear that they are a bit challenging to write as a bunch of standalone properties. Therefore, this might be a good point to start thinking about reference models.

Reference modeling and properties

So far we have described the property planning in terms of simple standalone cover points, assumptions, and assertions. But depending on the logic that is being validated, the DUT may have a varying degree of complex interaction with the neighboring logic. We often handle this by creating SystemVerilog modules that mimic the behavior of the surrounding logic, and generate the expected results at any given time step. These kinds of modules are known as reference models.

TIP 6.8

If you start generating a lot of assumptions or assertions with complex interactions, consider creating a reference model and basing the properties on its behavior.

So when should we create a reference model and when would a simpler collection of SVA assumptions or assertions be sufficient?

For assumptions, the creation of an abstraction of the surrounding logic should be guided by the failure scenarios exposed during the verification process. This is because it is almost impossible to know in advance the set of constraints sufficient for a given DUT. The constraints that are necessary depend not only on the interaction between the DUT and surrounding logic, but also on the specifications that are being validated. If adding constraints to the model requires lots of bookkeeping, it is best to develop a reference model that captures this abstraction in a very simple way. In situations that do not require lot of bookkeeping and information tracking from past events, a collection of simple SVA assumptions is usually sufficient. Often it is hard to be sure from the beginning whether you need to represent the full complexity of the neighboring unit in constraints for correct behavior, or if a small set of basic assumptions will suffice. Thus, we usually recommend starting with simple assumptions, which can evolve into an abstracted reference model of the surrounding logic at later stages if required.

TIP 6.9

Start with simple constraints on the inputs and slowly evolve into an abstracted reference model of the surrounding logic, if required.

However, we should think about potential reference models we might need, and plan for them as necessary. If you have some interface that follows a complex protocol, you are likely to need a reference model. Looking at our specification, we see that in this case there are not many requirements on the inputs. But if our interfaces were more complex, we might look at the Instruction Driver Interface and the Result Transfer Interface and consider what it would take to create reference models.

In addition to environmental reference models for assumptions, we should also think about the possible need for functional reference models for assertions. This is often a solid way to verify complete operation. In general, the RTL implementation of the design would need to take into consideration the timing requirements, debug-related hooks, clock gating, and other requirements. The reference model to be written for FPV can be abstracted to some degree: we need not consider any such requirements and can concentrate just on the functional aspect of the design. We refer to such partial or abstract models of the logic as *shadow modeling*. These partial shadow models are in general very helpful for the bug hunting FPV and can later be expanded to a complete abstraction model if full proof FPV is needed. A simple assertion that the RTL output will always be equal to the abstract model output would then give you a sense of formal completeness, for the portion of the logic that we model.

TIP 6.10

Don't be afraid to model the code from the specification. A simple assertion that the model output is equal to the implementation output is often a solid way of proving a design formally.

Again, in this case we have a relatively simple model, but you can easily envision cases where we are carrying out a multistep arithmetic operation that would be messy to specify in assertions. In this case, we might want to think about modeling the behavior of our ALU operations independently, and just compare the expected results to those from our real model. So we might add to our verification plan:

• If specifying the assertions proves complex, consider a shadow model to generate the expected result from each arithmetic operation based on the inputs.

ADDRESSING COMPLEXITY

As part of our FPV plan, we should consider possible actions to reduce the size or complexity of the design, and make it more amenable to FV. This may or may not be necessary, but based on initial size or difficulties in convergence of some properties in our FPV design exercise environment, we should make an early judgment on whether some complexity issues might need to be addressed in the initial FPV plan. We also need to keep in mind the possibility that our initial assertions might prove quickly, but as we add more complex assertions or relax some overconstraints to expand the verification scope, we might need to address the complexity. In Chapter 10 we discuss advanced complexity techniques you can use on challenging blocks when issues are observed during verification, but here we discuss a few basic techniques you should be thinking about at the FPV planning stages.

Staging plan

You should always be careful about trying to verify the fully general logic of your unit from the beginning: while it might seem elegant to try to verify all the logic in one shot, in many cases it will make your FPV process much more complex for the tools, in addition to making debug more difficult. We encourage you to start with an overconstrained environment, focusing on the most risky areas or operations identified in the design.

To maximize the value of our verification environment, we should have a solid staging plan in place to relax the constraints step by step, gradually building our bug hunting FPV into a full proof run. So first we might restrict our verification to one particular data size, DSIZE08, by adding an assumption that the data size has a constant value. Once this restricted environment is stable and debugged, we can relax this condition and try to achieve the same level of confidence as before with more possibilities enabled.

As previously discussed, we also want to ignore the Design For Testability (DFT) functionality and the logic submodule in our initial verification. If we succeed in verifying the arithmetic subunit, our main area of focus, with all data sizes, we optionally might want to consider adding these additional functions back in to the model.

• For the first stage of FPV, we want to focus on the arithmetic submodule, with DFT deactivated and data size DSIZE08.
• At the next stage, we hope to verify the module for all data sizes.
• Depending on the success of the above stages, we may later verify the DFT and logical blocks.

Blackboxes

In addition to considering overconstraints, we should also think about submodules that are good candidates for *blackboxing*, which means they would be ignored for FPV purposes. We should refer again to our block diagram here, where we have identified the sizes of each major submodule and marked likely candidates for blackboxing. In general, if your block contains large embedded queues or memories, these are prime candidates for blackboxing, though we do not have such elements in the case of our ALU.

When choosing blackboxes, we need to be careful to think about the data flow through our block and what the effects of a blackbox might be. Since we are initially focusing on arithmetic operations, our first identified blackbox, the logic unit, is mostly harmless: the operations we focus on will not utilize this unit. So we will plan on blackboxing this initially, to help minimize the complexity.

- Initially blackbox the logic subunit.

However, remember that the outputs of a blackbox become *free variables*—they can take on any value at any time, just like an input, so they might require new assumptions. For our ALU, we need to add a new assumption when blackboxing the logic unit, so it does not appear to be producing valid logic results for the final MUX:

- Since we are blackboxing the logic unit, add an assumption that *logresultv* is always 0.

We also identified a secondary potential blackbox target: the decoding block at the front end of the arithmetic subunit. If we have a formal design exercise environment up already (which we recommend as the starting point of an FPV effort, as discussed earlier), it might be useful to bring up a few cover points with the additional blackbox active, and sanity-check the waveforms generated in our FPV tool to get an idea of the additional assumptions that might be required. Such an example is shown in Figure 6.5 below.

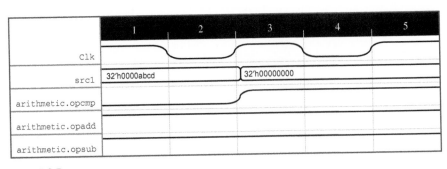

FIGURE 6.5

Effect of blackboxing on the outputs of a decoder.

What do we observe now? A few cycles after the start of our waveform, we see a case where all the arithmetic operations are enabled at the same time. This is an unwanted situation and there is no guarantee of any correct result at the output of the block. If you analyze the situation now, we have cut out the block that sanitizes the opcode and generates one and only one operation for a clock cycle. Now all the outputs of the decoder block are free to choose any values and hence we observe something that looks like an insane behavior. We would need to rectify this situation by adding some new assumptions related to the blackbox, or back off and conclude that the decoder is not a good blackbox candidate. Hence, we need to be extra cautious in choosing the blocks in the design we want to blackbox. Since we already determined that this blackbox is not truly necessary, we are probably better off keeping this logic in the model for now.

Essentially, this problem stemmed from the fact that our blackbox candidate was directly in the path of the operations we are checking; we can see that this is much more likely to require some more complex additional assumptions if we blackbox it. In addition, right now our total state count in the un-blackboxed portion of the ALU is comfortably below our target range (40,000 state elements), so we can avoid this additional blackbox unless it is needed. Thus we should initially plan on not blackboxing this subunit, though we can still keep that in mind as a possibility in case we hit complexity issues.

TIP 6.11

When thinking about blackboxing a submodule, look at waveforms involved in common operations, extracted from simulation or design exercise FPV cover points, to help decide whether you would need complex assumptions to model relevant outputs.

Structural abstraction

Another useful complexity reduction technique is data/structural abstraction, where the size of logical structures is reduced: for example, by reducing the number of buffer entries or restricting the width of a data bus. Structural abstraction not only reduces the size of the logic, and hence the state space, that the tool has to search; it also allows the tool to reach interesting microarchitecture points in the flow at much lower bounds. For example, if there are several corner cases in the microarchitectural flows when a buffer/queue is full, then reducing the size of the buffers from 40 to 4 will allow the tool to explore behaviors around "queue full" at a much lower bound.

TIP 6.12

Structural abstractions not only reduce the size of the logic and the state space, but also allow the tool to reach interesting microarchitectural points at much lower bound.

These data/structural abstractions are usually very simple and can be fully automated. It is a good idea to work with the RTL designers to parameterize the sizes of various buffers and arrays. The reduced sizes of the buffers should be nested in an *ifdef* block in the RTL that could be enabled only for FPV. This will allow the FPV user to take advantage of the parameterized values to work with an abstracted RTL model.

TIP 6.13

Work with your designer early in the design cycle to parameterize the RTL code such that it becomes easy for you to reduce structure sizes during FPV.

For our ALU example, we are in good shape because we have MAXDSIZE as a parameter. Perhaps the mode with an 8-bit maximum size is not really something required in our final product, but having it there lets us do our initial verification in a simpler, smaller environment that is likely to reveal the vast majority of potential bugs.

• Set parameter MAXDSIZE to DSIZE08 for our initial FPV runs, allowing some logic minimization at compile time.

QUALITY CHECKS AND EXIT CRITERIA

A passing proof does not necessarily mean that the DUT satisfies the property under all possible input scenarios. Proof development is prone to human errors: it involves the process of debugging failures, adding constraints and modeling to the proof environment, and guiding the process toward the final validation goal. It is crucial that we have quality checks in place to catch these errors or proof limitations as quickly as possible. The major factors that must be considered to judge FPV quality include:

• Quality of the property set being proven: Does the set of assertions provide a good representation of the targeted specification, and exercise all relevant parts of the model?
• Quality of the constraints: Assumptions, blackboxes, and other tool directives are limiting the proof space. Are we sure that we are not ignoring critical behaviors and hiding bugs?
• Quality of the verification: Did the FPV tool achieve a full proof, or a bounded proof at a depth that ensures high quality?

The first fundamental component of FPV quality depends on actually targeting the important aspects of your design. You should make sure that you review your assertions, assumptions, and cover points with architects and design experts. This review should check that you have assertions and cover points for each major piece of functionality you are trying to verify, and that your assumptions are reasonable or correspond to intentional limitations of your FPV environment. If using FPV as a complement to simulation, you should focus on the risk areas not covered by your simulation plan and make sure these are covered in your FPV plan.

TIP 6.14

Make sure that you review your assertions, assumptions, and cover points with architects and design experts, as part of the validation planning process. Include FPV in the validation plan, and check that the properties you create are covering the aspects of functionality not being covered by simulation.

Another major goal of quality checks is to make sure that you do not have any proofs passing *vacuously,* or due to having assumptions and other tool constraints that are so strong they rule out normal design behaviors or deactivate important parts of your RTL model.

As we have discussed in previous chapters, the best way to gain confidence in coverage and prevent vacuity is a good set of cover points. There is a common statement among the FPV experts: "Tell me the cover points and not the assertions to check if your FPV activity is complete." Most tools auto-generate a trigger condition cover point for any assertion or assumption in the form $A \mid \negmedspace> B$, to check that the triggering condition A is possible. These auto-generated precondition covers are useful, but make sure you do not fully depend on them: good manually written cover points that capture a designer's or validator's intuition or explicit examples from the specification are much more valuable.

Another simple test that we recommend for projects with little previous FPV experience is to insert some known bugs (based on escapes from similar designs) and try to reproduce them as part of the process of confirming nonvacuity of your proof environment. This can be especially effective in convincing your management that your environment really is contributing to the validation effort, which can often be an area of doubt if they are primarily seeing reports of successful proofs.

TIP 6.15

Carefully check that your cover points, including both automatically generated assertion/ assumption triggers and manually created covers that represent major design operations, are passing. If not, it means you have a likely vacuity issue.

The third major aspect of verification quality is the strength of the verification itself. In the ideal case, your FPV tool will give you full proofs of your assertions, which give you confidence that no possible execution of any length could violate them. However, in practice, you will be likely to have many assertions that are only able to get bounded proofs. In general, this is perfectly acceptable and, in fact, many Intel projects complete their FPV goals using primarily bounded rather than full proofs. Remember that a bounded proof is still a very powerful result, showing that your assertion cannot fail in any possible system execution up to that number of cycles after reset, in effect equivalent to running an exponential number of simulation tests. The main challenge here is that you need to be careful that you have good proof bounds that do not hide important model behaviors.

Checking that your cover points are passing, with trace lengths less than the proof bound of your assertions, is your most important quality check. Conceptually, this shows that the potential executions considered in the proofs include the operation represented by that cover point. Usually it is best to have your assertions proven to a depth of at least twice the length of your longest cover point trace to gain confidence that your proofs encompass issues caused by multiple consecutive operations in your design.

> **TIP 6.16**
>
> If you are using bounded proofs, make sure that your assertions are proven to a depth greater than your longest cover point trace, preferably at least two times that trace length.

Reconciling your assertions and assumptions with simulation results is another important quality check if you have a simulation environment available that contains the unit under test. Some tools allow you to store a collection of simulation traces in a repository and check any new assumption added against the collection of the simulation traces. This will give early feedback on whether the assumption being added is correct. This should be followed by a more exhaustive check of all the assumptions against a much larger collection of simulation tests as part of your regular regressions. Remember that SVA assumptions are treated the same way as assertions in dynamic simulation: an error is flagged if any set of test values violates its condition. Make sure that these properties are triggered in the simulation runs, which can be reported for SVA by most modern simulation tools. Think carefully about your overconstraints though: some subset of your assertions and assumptions may not make sense in simulation. For example, since we assumed that the DFT functionality is turned off, we need to make sure to choose a subset of simulation tests that do not exercise these features.

> **TIP 6.17**
>
> Make sure that you attach the FPV assumptions as checkers in the dynamic simulation environment, if available, so that you can gather feedback about the quality of your formal environment.

We also should mention here that many commercial FPV tools offer automatic coverage functionality, where they can help you figure out how well your set of formal assertions is covering your RTL code. The more advanced tools offer features such as expression coverage or toggle coverage, to do more fine-grained measurement of possible gaps in your FPV testing. Naturally, we encourage you to make use of such tools when available, since they can provide good hints about major gaps in your FPV environment. However, do not rely solely on such tools: no amount of automated checking can substitute for the human intuition of creating cover points that represent your actual design and validation intent.

> ### TIP 6.18
>
> Use automated coverage features of your EDA tools to gain additional feedback about coverage, but do not treat these as a substitute for a good set of human-created cover points based on your design and validation intent.

Exit criteria

We started with defining our goals of the FPV, followed by wiggling the design and exploring it, created a verification plan aligning to the end goal, defined the properties to hit our goal, formulated the staging plan, and understood the abstractions to be done. Now we need to define the exit criteria to confidently exit out of the activity on the design. In order to enable these exit criteria, we suggest you try to continuously measure the forms of quality we describe above, tracking the progress on each of the quality metrics, as well as tracking your proportion of properties passing, and your progress in your staging plan. Assuming you are continually measuring your quality, some natural examples of reasonable exit criteria could be:

- *Time Limit*: Define a time suitable to exit out of the exercise. While it is common to spend a week on design exercise, we would suggest you spend at least two to three weeks on bug hunting FPV, depending on the complexity of the block considered. When you start seeing more value from the bug hunting mode, exposing new bugs or getting more confidence on some corner cases, you should definitely consider full proof FPV for the block. If moving to full proof mode, you should probably expect at least a doubling of the long-term effort. This will likely pay for itself, of course, if full proof FPV enables you to reduce or eliminate unit-level simulation efforts.
- *Quality*: We can define our exit criteria based on progress in the quality categories defined above. We may have to modify these quality checks for the current stage in our staging plan: each stage will have some subset of known limitations in our verification quality. If our aim is bug hunting and we have a complementary simulation environment, we may not require that we complete all stages, or we may allow some percentage of property completion rather than full completion of the current verification stage. In general, your quality exit criteria may include:
  - Quality of the property set being proven: Make sure the validation plan has been fully reviewed, we have created all the assertions and cover points planned, and all of the assertions are passing.

- Quality of the constraints: Make sure all our cover points are passing and no assumptions are failing in simulation regressions.
- Quality of the verification: Make sure all bounded proofs are reaching an acceptable bound, as judged in relation to the cover points. You may also include some criteria related to the automatic coverage reported by your FPV tools, if available.

- *Success Trail Off:* As with many validation tasks, sometimes you may reach a point of diminishing returns, where you are starting to see less return on your investment after your FPV environment reaches a certain level of maturity. It is common that after a period of initial wiggling to improve assumptions, you will experience several weeks of rapid bug finding, gradually trailing off as the design matures. You may want to set some criterion related to this pattern, such as ending bug hunting FPV when you have a week go by with all proofs passing to the expected bound and no bugs found by new properties.

So for our exit criteria in our bug hunting FPV plan for the ALU, we might choose these:

- We exercise all our specified covers and prove our arithmetic unit assertions for correct ALU functionality to a bound of 50 cycles, under our chosen overconstraint conditions.
  - Due to the logical depth of this design, we expect that all covers will be covered in fewer than 25 cycles; if this turns out not to be the case, we need to reevaluate the bound of 50 above.
- Our assumptions are passing in available simulation runs.
- Time limit: two weeks.

Putting it all together

The FPV plan for our ALU, based on the various considerations we described in the previous subsections, is illustrated in Table 6.1. This is a bit more involved than the simple design exercise plan in the previous chapter. Don't let this scare you off—planning is a critical part of any FV effort. As an example, a consulting firm that ran a "72-hour FPV" stunt at a recent conference (see [Sla12]), where they took a unit sight-unseen from a customer and tried to run useful FPV within 72 hours, actually spent the first 12 hours of this very limited time period studying their design and planning their verification approach.

Running bug hunting FPV

Now that we have come up with a good verification plan, it is time to begin the verification. We will skip discussion of the basics of loading the model into an FPV tool since that has been covered in the previous chapter and because our starting assumption was that you have already developed a design exercise FPV environment for this model. Part of this would include supplying the necessary

Table 6.1 Bug Hunting FPV Plan for ALU

Goals	Verify the correct behavior of the arithmetic unit, in the absence of any unusual activity such as power-gating or scan/debug hooks, for the default DSIZE 08.
Properties	Create cover points that replicate each waveform in the spec that illustrates arithmetic unit behavior.
	Cover each arithmetic operation (ADD, SUB, CMP) with nonzero inputs, alone and back-to-back with another arbitrary operation.
	Cover cases of each operation above with specific data that exercise all bits. Assume dft (scan) inputs are shut off.
	Assume all operations are arithmetic, not logical.
	• If initial assumptions prove complex to write, consider a reference model to drive the input logic that ensures only two valid instructions are driven per cycle.
	Since we are blackboxing the logic unit, add an assumption that the logic subunit result valid signal *logresultv* is always 0.
	Assert that when a valid operation arrives, a valid output appears in three cycles.
	Assert that each operation generates the expected results: if we selected ADD, the output should match the sum of the inputs, etc.
	• If specifying the assertions proves complex, consider a reference model to derive the expected result from each operation.
Complexity staging	Initial stages: Blackbox logical subunit. Set parameter MAXDSIZE to DSIZE08. Assume that DFT is inactive.
	If too complex: Blackbox decoder too and add appropriate assumptions.
	Stages for improving verification quality if time permits:
	• Allow all DSIZE values.
	• Allow DFT functionality.
	• Un-blackbox logic subunit.
Exit criteria	We exercise all covers and prove our arithmetic unit assertions for correct ALU functionality, to a bound of 50 cycles, under the overconstraint conditions we have specified above.
	Our assumptions must be passing in simulation regressions.
	Time limit: 2 weeks. If we achieve the above goals before then, opportunistically expand to further FPV stages by backing off the complexity compromises above.

tool directives for our initial set of complexity compromises, as mentioned in the FPV plan. This will vary depending on your particular FPV tool, but should result in commands something like this in your control file:

```
# blackbox logic unit
BLACKBOX inst*.logical
# Turn off dft
SET dftslowrd = 0
```

Now we will walk through some of the more interesting steps of the initial bug hunting verification.

INITIAL COVER POINTS

One of our basic sets of cover points was to check that we are covering each arithmetic operation.

```
generate for (j = OPADD; j < = OPCMP; j++) begin: g1
    arithmetic1: cover property
                    (( uopcode == j) ##3 (resultv != 0) );
    end
endgenerate
```

Covering these properties would make sure that all the opcodes can potentially be used in our environment. Proving these cover points and reviewing the waveforms would confirm the fact. Let's assume that our initial covers on these are successful, and we have examined the waveforms.

Next we want to verify a cover point so that, for one particular set of data, the design returns an expected value. We will choose one nontrivial value for an opcode and data and check if the design is behaving sanely. We don't intend to ultimately specify all the values for each operation, since that would defeat the basic claim of formal that you wouldn't need to provide any vectors. But these basic covers are written to give a basic understanding of the design correctness rather than complete coverage.

```
add08: cover property ( ( uopv &
        uopcode == OPADD &
        uopsize == DSIZE08
    ) ##1
    ( src1 == 32'h8 &
      src2 == 32'h4
    ) ##2
    result == 32'hC);
```

The specification enforces that the operation should be initiated one clock cycle before the actual data is applied and the result computation takes two cycles after the data is read in. Execution of this cover will expose us to the basic correctness of the design, and now we are poised to explore much further.

As discussed earlier, we are starting on a piece of RTL that is in the middle of verification churn and we don't expect very basic bugs. This is just the first set of covers to see if our environment is set up correctly and we can take it ahead. We will probably want to add more cover points, inspired by additional interesting cases we observe while debugging FPV waveforms, as we advance further in our bug hunting.

EXTENDED WIGGLING

The process of wiggling is discussed in detail in Chapter 5. We can expect around 10−20 wiggles on a typical unit before we start seeing useful behaviors. It might take even more for complex units. For the simple unit considered in this chapter, we might reach a sane state much earlier in the wiggling cycle. Chances are that we have gone through some wiggling already if we have previously completed FPV design exercise on this unit, so we should not be starting totally from scratch.

We shall begin with the wiggling process on our simple ALU. Just to reiterate, cover points are of paramount importance rather than assertions during the initial stages of FPV. We want to ensure that the basic flows and behaviors we observe in the waveforms are in line with the expectations. One more repetition of this tip is provided here so that we don't miss the importance of this fact.

> ### TIP 6.19
>
> Begin any FPV effort by creating a set of reasonable cover points on your model, representing typical and interesting activity.

We shall not make the common mistake of first starting to prove the assertions, as we already know that covers are much more important at the start of wiggling, and not a secondary consideration. We start by trying to prove the basic cover points we described above, checking that each operation is possible and that a sample ADD operation works correctly on one specific set of values (Table 6.2).

Now one of the arithmetic operations is not covered. This is a bit surprising, as we expect all operations to yield correct results in three clock cycles. Remember that an uncovered cover point indicates that some design behavior cannot be reproduced under our current proof setup and assumptions. This means that the failed cover point does not generate a waveform, so debugging it can be

Table 6.2 Initial Cover Point Results on ALU

Property	Status
alu0.g1[OPADD].arithmetic1	Cover: 8 cycles
alu0.g1[OPSUB].arithmetic1	Cover: 8 cycles
alu0.g1[OPCMP].arithmetic1	Not covered
alu0.add08	Cover: 8 cycles

a bit tricky. There are several methods we can use to get observable waveforms that might give us a hint about why a cover failed:

- Look at the waveform of a related but slightly different cover point to look for unexpected or incorrect model behaviors.
- Create a partial cover point that checks a weaker condition than the original cover point.
- If the cover point involves several events happening in an SVA sequence, remove some of the events and observe the resulting simpler cover point.

In this case, the failing cover point is relatively simple, so it makes the most sense to use the first method above to bring up the waveform for an already covered cover point and look for unexpected or incorrect model behaviors. Bringing up the waveform for the OPADD operation, we are surprised to see a wrong condition being covered here, as shown in Figure 6.6.

As you have probably observed, this is not correct. We expect the output to become 0x0C for the source inputs of 0x8 and 0x4, after three clock cycles. Here, we see that the result value has been always 0x0C since reset, and hence the cover passes. When we debug further, the reason for the result value being constant is that the state element for the result is not resettable—the flop output can come out with any value. In other words, formal analysis has discovered a rare corner-case scenario, where a nonreset flop gets lucky and randomly achieves desired values.

TIP 6.20

Don't get carried away by initial cover passes. Take an extra step to view and analyze if the intention is truly replicated in the waveforms.

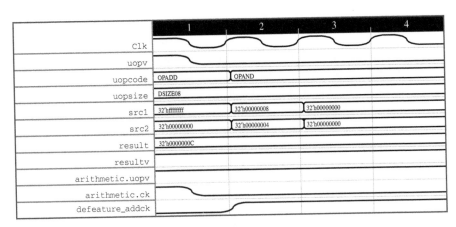

FIGURE 6.6

Cover waveform for alu0.g1[OPADD].arithmetic1.

We also observe that the valid bit for the result is also high throughout and the clock for the flop element is completely gated. We bring in the equation for the clock signal and see that a "defeature bit" signal for the design, which we had not been thinking about as an issue initially, is being driven high after a certain time. Typically, we might speak to the block designer or architect to find out what this defeature bit means: in this case, let's assume they tell us that this bit will be driven to zero in most real-life usages, so the validation team can safely deprioritize cases where this bit is 1.

Now, we need to fix these two issues:

1. Make the flop resettable.
2. Overconstrain the design by adding an assumption that the defeature bit is 1'b0.

Once we complete these modifications to our environment and rerun, we should see a real pass, where the cover waveform truly represents the activity we expect. We may also want to amend our FPV plan to document the fact that we added a new overconstraint. But alas, a new failure for the same cover point forces a second round of wiggling to analyze the failure. Repeating the process of observing the waveform for a different but related cover point, we get the waveform shown in Figure 6.7.

We now see that an add operation is taking more than the two clock cycles we expected: it is precisely taking one more clock cycle. This is a definite bug in the design and needs to be fixed. Once we fix the design and rerun, all the cover points pass. After observing the waveforms for each of the passing cover points, and paying especially close attention to the one that had previously been failing, we can convince ourselves that the design is behaving reasonably for our set of cover points.

Now, we turn our attention to the assertions. While we could write a set of standalone assertions checking each operation, this seems like a case where it

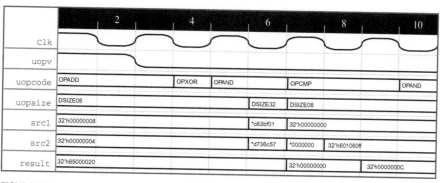

FIGURE 6.7

Cover waveform for `alu0.g1[OPADD].arithmetic1` at a later debug stage.

might make more sense to create a reference model instead, calculating the expected result for each operation. There is a level of abstraction we can apply here, making this more of a shadow model than a full behavioral model: we want to calculate the core results of the logic, without including any of the complexities of a real design such as pipelining, scan, or debug logic. We can also take advantage of overconstraint decisions we made for the initial bug hunting, such as our choice to initially focus on DSIZE 08. In this case, we might initially generate something like this:

```
module my_arithmetic ( Clk, uopv, uopcode, uopsize, src1, src2, resultv,
result );
input Clk;
input node uopv;
input node [3:0] uopcode;
input node [2:0] uopsize;
input node [31:0] src1;
input node [31:0] src2;
output node resultv;
output node [31:0] result;
always_comb isuop = (uopcode == OPADD | uopcode == OPSUB
| uopcode == OPCMP );
always_comb begin
  opadd = ( uopcode == OPADD );
  opsub = ( uopcode == OPSUB );
  opcmp = ( uopcode == OPCMP );
end
always_comb begin
  unique casex ( 1'b1 )
    opadd : result0 = src1 + src2;
    opsub : result0 = src1 - src2;
    opcmp : result0 = (src1 > src2);
  endcase
end;
`MSFF( result1, result0, Clk );
`MSFF( result2, result1, Clk );
`MSFF( result, result2, Clk );
endmodule // my_arithmetic
```

Once the above module is instantiated or bound inside our main ALU, we can add the following assertion to check that the result in the real RTL matches our reference model:

```
assert_equi_check: assert property (uopv |-> ##3 (result ==
my_arithmetic.result ) );
```

We have written here a very simple model for operations. A simple assertion that the two units should generate the same outputs would cover all possible input combinations and, even more important, give complete coverage of the whole data space for these operations (under our known assumptions and overconstraints). This reference model only covers a subset of operations and data sizes, but is correct for the parts that it covers, assuming the corresponding RTL model is properly constrained to not use other parts of the logic.

Now that we have written our reference model and are satisfied with the waveforms on our initial coverage points, it is time to try the proofs. When we run with this setup, we see another failure, shown in Figure 6.8.

When we reanalyze the failure, we see that the data on *src1* is not being used for the computation, but instead *dftdata* is used. This comes in because we haven't disabled the DFT (scan) functionality correctly, despite having planned to do this as one of our initial overconstraints. DFT signals are generally debug-related signals that feed in some sort of pattern through a separate port and help in debug of the existing design, so when running FPV without DFT turned off, it is common to observe cases where the tool figures out clever ways to use it to generate bad results for an assertion. We stated above that we used an overconstraining assumption to set signal *dftslowrd* to 0, but as we figure out after examining the waveform, this is an active-low signal, and we really need to set it to 1. Once we add the correct DFT constraints, and complete several more rounds of wiggling to work out details that need to be fixed in the assumptions, we get to a point where we have the assertion *assert_equi_check* passing. Because this is a comprehensive assertion that covers many operations, we should also be sure to review our cover point traces again after the assertion is passing.

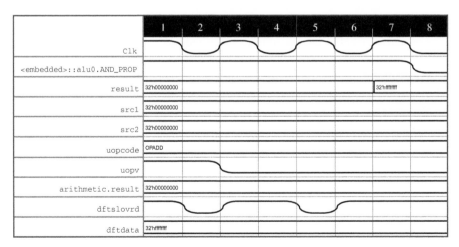

FIGURE 6.8

An initial assertion failure waveform for our model.

Having completed our initial goals in the verification plan, we can consider improving our verification coverage by relaxing some of the initial compromises we made earlier.

A good start would be to relax the constraint that disabled the defeature bit, a last-minute constraint we added based on issues discovered during debug. Since this was a late compromise rather than part of our initial FPV plan, it would be good to find a way to account for it and properly verify its functionality. Instead of driving it to 0, now we should remove this overconstraint and allow it to assume arbitrary values of 0 or 1. This will require figuring out what the expected behavior is for the model under various values of this signal, and refining our reference model to take this new functionality into account.

If that goes well, we then can target the items mentioned in our complexity staging plan to further expand the scope of our verification: allowing all DSIZE values, allowing DFT functionality, and un-blackboxing the logic sub-module. Each of these changes will likely require expanding our reference model (or adding a second, parallel reference model) to include these new aspects of the behavior.

As you have probably figured out by now, this is a relatively simple example overall for FPV. This example is taken to show the power of modeling the code and use it for verification. For most real-life units, the wiggling would take many more iterations to reach a stage of useful verification. Don't be afraid of having to go through 20 "wiggles" to get useful behaviors!

By now, we have good confidence in the environment and the ability to check for various operations.

EXPANDING THE COVER POINTS

After completing each major stage of our FPV effort, we need to take another look to make sure that we are able to reach various interesting microarchitectural conditions and we are not restricting the model unnecessarily. The initial set of cover points helped us in assessing the quality of the environment we started with and understanding more of the design. The final cover points, inspired by a combination of our knowledge of the specification and our experience debugging the interesting corner cases found during the FPV effort, give us the required confidence that we have not left any stone unturned during our exercise. The cover points are our primary indication of the quality of the verification performed.

Covers at this point of the design are mostly "whitebox." We should not hesitate to observe internal transitions and known critical conditions of the internal logic. At a minimum, you should be able to translate most of your simulation coverage specifications into SVA cover points and verify. There might be some areas of the design that remain uncovered because we ruled them out through the assumptions. Hence, these covers are very important in assessing the extent of our journey in achieving our FPV goals.

Remember that when relaxing overconstraints and expanding our verification space, we should review our basic cover points once more, since any relaxation of constraints could result in major changes to overall functionality. Chances are some of our basic operations might be covered in different ways, or the cover points might become less useful. For example, when we turn on DFT logic, which allows arbitrary values to be scanned in for each major state element, we may find that suddenly every cover point is covered by a trivial example where DFT turns on and just happens to scan in the correct value. We will need to carefully modify the cover points so they still are truly covering the intended functionality.

REMOVING SIMPLIFICATIONS AND EXPLORING MORE BEHAVIORS

Let's assume we have reached the point where we are confident in the verification of the arithmetic logic and have now un-blackboxed the logical subunit, at the same time removing our earlier assumption that restricted us to arithmetic operations. We have likely added an assertion that checks that operations always have the proper latency in our top-level model.

```
Resultv_correct_wrt_uopv: assert property ( uopv |-> ##3 resultv );
```

When we try to prove the above assertion, we might get the counterexample shown in Figure 6.9.

As you can see, there is an opcode 5'h10 that is not defined in the list of acceptable opcodes for the design. Thus, the design behaves erroneously when we try to enable the check for all opcodes in one shot. This is another common

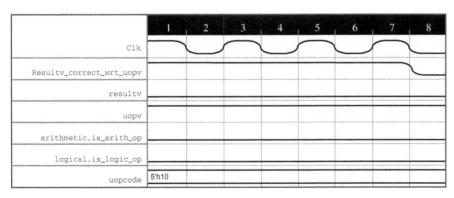

FIGURE 6.9

Counterexample showing the case where no valid result is generated.

situation when relaxing some assumptions and expanding the verification space: allowing a wider variety of legal behaviors has opened the door to a wider variety of illegal behaviors. Thus, we need to add another assumption:

```
Legal_opcode: assume property
    ( valid_arithmetic_op ( uopcode ) ||
      valid_logical_op (uopcode) );
```

THE ROAD TO FULL PROOF FPV

Once you are experienced with running FPV on your models, you can start planning from the beginning for full proof FPV, with bug hunting as the initial stage of your plan. If you are less experienced, you first want to embark on bug hunting FPV, and may think about expanding to full proof based on the success of these efforts. Could you verify all the requirements of the specification, making simulation-based unit-level verification redundant for your current module?

In the case of our ALU example, it looks like full proof FPV might indeed be a reasonable target. Once we have gone through all the steps identified in our complexity staging plan and found that adding more generality to our proofs did not cause a complexity explosion, we can take a step back and ask the question: can we make this a full proof environment and back off from our simulation effort?

Be careful before making this leap: because our initial plan was based on bug hunting, we have some important questions to ask about the completeness of our verification. When focusing on bug hunting, it was sufficient to come up with a small set of interesting properties, which helped us to find and reveal some set of bugs. In general, we must plan for a greater level of rigor in our quality checks to have confidence in full proof FPV. We need to ask the harder question: do we have a complete set of properties, which fully checks all the requirements of our design specification? Remember, just because your FPV run includes the entire RTL model, or mechanical measures of coverage from your tool claim that all lines are exercised, it does not mean that you have fully verified the specification.

TIP 6.21

Remember, just because your FPV run includes the entire RTL model, it does not mean that you have fully verified the specification. You need to check that your assertion set is complete.

In most cases, your main specification is an informal document written in plain English (or another nonmachine language), so there is no easy way to answer this question directly. You must carefully review this document, and make sure that each requirement listed is translated to an assertion, or can be described as nontranslatable. You also need to check that your assertions are as strong as necessary to fully enforce your specification. For example, suppose instead of our assertion requiring a latency of 3, we had written an assertion like the one below that just said we would eventually get an answer:

```
resultv_correct_sometime: assert property
    (uopv |-> s_eventually(resultv));
```

This would seem to be checking the correctness of our ALU, and might help us to find some bugs related to completely dropped operations, but actually would be failing to fully check the latency requirement.

Checking assumptions and cover points is also a critical part of this review. You must make sure all major operations are covered by your cover points, in order to ensure that you are not leaving any gaps in the verification. You should also review your assumption set and make sure it is not unexpectedly ruling out analysis of any part of the specification. Once you have done this, be sure to present your proposed set of specification properties to your design architects and get their buy-in that your verification plan truly is complete.

In the case of our ALU, the overall functionality is very well-defined: we have a set of operations, and for each one, we need to make sure it generates proper output based on its inputs. We also need to check for the corner-case exceptions such as DFT, which we excluded from the initial bug hunting FPV, and make sure our unit operates correctly under these circumstances. We should make sure that we create assertions describing correct operation of each of these exceptions, as well as cover points to double-check that each one can be exercised under our final set of assumptions.

Do not let the need for increased rigor scare you away from attempting full proof FPV. As long as you pay close attention to the requirements of your design specification, this is often very feasible at the unit level, and can be a much smaller overall effort than validating through a comprehensive simulation testbench. In any case, the need for careful reviews is not really a new requirement introduced by FPV: the same concerns and hazards, such as the danger of incomplete or overly weak checking, apply to simulation and other validation methods as well. Full proof FPV has been successfully run on selected units on many projects at Intel and has been found to result in significantly higher design quality for lower effort in the long run.

SUMMARY

In this chapter, we have reviewed the typical process of using FPV for bug hunting and full proof mode, using our example of a simple ALU. Bug hunting is the use of FPV as a supplement to other validation methods, to detect hard-to-find corner-case issues. Full proof FPV is the attempt to fully prove your specification, completely replacing other validation methods.

You should start by trying to identify a good target unit for FPV. Try to find a piece of logic that will have under 40,000 state elements, after appropriate black-boxing of large memories and other state space reductions. Then you should look at a block diagram, identifying your primary verification focus areas, marking the sizes of individual subunits, and labeling major interfaces and potential blackbox candidates. Using this information, you should then create an FPV plan, including major goals, important properties, complexity compromises and staging, and a good set of exit criteria.

We walked through this process on our ALU example, showing how we would come up with an initial bug hunting plan, and demonstrating some of the initial steps as we begin to put this plan into action. Naturally a real-life verification effort would likely have many more wiggling steps than we could describe in the text of this chapter, so our goal was just to demonstrate the general idea. Once we showed how the initial steps of this verification might be completed, we went on to discuss how we could expand this to a full proof FPV effort, which could potentially replace simulation-based verification for this unit.

PRACTICAL TIPS FROM THIS CHAPTER

6.1 For validation-focused FPV, choose blocks that primarily involve control logic or data transport, with data transformation limited to simple operations like integer addition.

6.2 When planning for bug hunting FPV, use overconstraint as needed to simplify the model you work on, in order to focus on your current problem areas.

6.3 When first trying FPV on any new design, start with lightweight design exercise FPV (as described in Chapter 5) to verify basic behaviors and FPV feasibility before moving to more elaborate validation-focused FPV efforts.

6.4 Carefully carve out the logic you want to verify with FPV and limit the design to a size that can be handled by the tools. A good rule of thumb with current-generation tools is to aim for less than 40,000 active state elements (latches and flip-flops).

6.5 When beginning the bug hunting or full proof FPV planning process, start with a block diagram of your unit, including the sizes of all major blocks, and label the interfaces, blackbox candidates, and areas of verification focus. This diagram will provide a critical foundation for your verification plan.

6.6 Create a verification plan when beginning a validation-focused FPV effort. This should describe the logic to be verified, properties and cover points, staging plan, decomposition strategy, and success criteria.

6.7 Explore the opportunity of reusing standard properties whenever applicable to your units: this can save you significant time when bringing up an FPV environment.

6.8 If you start generating a lot of assumptions or assertions with complex interactions, consider creating a reference model and basing the properties on its behavior.

6.9 Start with simple constraints on the inputs and slowly evolve into an abstracted reference model of the surrounding logic, if required.

6.10 Don't be afraid to model the code from the specification. A simple assertion that the model output is equal to the implementation output is often a solid way of proving a design formally.

6.11 When thinking about blackboxing a submodule, look at waveforms involved in common operations, extracted from simulation or design exercise FPV cover points, to help decide whether you would need complex assumptions to model relevant outputs.

6.12 Structural abstractions not only reduce the size of the logic and the state space, but also allow the tool to reach interesting microarchitectural points at much lower bound.

6.13 Work with your designer early in the design cycle to parameterize the RTL code such that it becomes easy for you to reduce structure sizes during FPV.

6.14 Make sure that you review your assertions, assumptions, and cover points with architects and design experts, as part of the validation planning process. Include FPV in the validation plan, and check that the properties you create are covering the aspects of functionality not being covered by simulation.

6.15 Carefully check that your cover points, including both automatically generated assertion/assumption triggers and manually created covers that represent major design operations, are passing. If not, it means you have a likely vacuity issue.

6.16 If you are using bounded proofs, make sure that your assertions are proven to a depth greater than your longest cover point trace, preferably at least two times that trace length.

6.17 Make sure that you attach the FPV assumptions as checkers in the dynamic simulation environment, if available, so that you can gather feedback about the quality of your formal environment.

6.18 Use automated coverage features of your EDA tools to gain additional feedback about coverage, but do not treat these as a substitute for a good set of human-created cover points based on your design and validation intent.

6.19 Begin any FPV effort by creating a set of reasonable cover points on your model, representing typical and interesting activity.

6.20 Don't get carried away by initial cover passes. Take an extra step to view and analyze if the intention is truly replicated in the waveforms.

6.21 Remember, just because your FPV run includes the entire RTL model, it does not mean that you have fully verified the specification. You need to check that your assertion set is complete.

FURTHER READING

[Agg11] P. Aggarwal, D. Chu, V. Kadamby, and V. Singhal, "Planning for End-to-End Formal with Simulation Based Coverage," Formal Methods in Computer Aided Design (FMCAD) 2011, Austin, TX, USA.

[And12] Thomas Anderson and Joseph Hupcey III, "Top 10 Tips for Success with Formal Analysis," EDA Designline, 2012, http://www.embedded.com/print/4372876.

[Bus13] Holger Busch, "Qualification of Formal Properties for Productive Automotive Microcontroller Verification," Design and Verification Conference (DVCon) 2013.

[Kim14] NamDo Kim, Junhyug Park, Vigyan Singhal, and HarGovind Singh, "Sign-off with Bounded Formal Verification Proofs," Design and Verification Conference (DVCon) 2014.

[Sel08] E. Seligman et al., "Zero Escape Plans: Combining Design, Validation, and Formal Methods for Bulletproof Stepping Validation," Design and Verification Conference (DVCon) 2008, February 2008.

[Sla12] Pippa Slayton, "DAC 2012 Oski Challenge: Wrap-Up and Video," http://www.oskitechnology.com/blog/dac-2012-oski-challenge-wrap-up-video.html.

[Tal10] Kesava R. Talupuru, "Formal Methods to Verify the Power Manager for an Embedded Multiprocessor Cluster," Design and Verification Conference (DVCon) 2010.

FPV "Apps" for specific SOC problems

7

In addition to running much faster than simulation, formal apps provide exhaustive checks that expose corner-case bugs simulation might miss.
—Richard Goering, Cadence blogger

The past few chapters have focused on general-purpose formal property verification (FPV), where you create a set of assertions and cover points and use FPV tools to formally analyze their consistency with the register transfer level (RTL). As we have seen, this is a very powerful technique, and useful in several ways throughout your RTL design flow: for early design exercise, for bug hunting, for bulletproof verification of complex logic, or for replacing unit-level simulation for full validation signoff. However, there is a huge class of FPV applications that were missed in this discussion: FPV *apps*, or domain-specific uses of FPV that provide targeted solutions for specific problems.

What is an FPV app? The boundary between traditional FPV and an FPV app tends to be somewhat fuzzy. But as we define it, the distinguishing features of an app are:

- *Specific domain*: We are applying FPV to some specific part of the design process, or to some specific type of design, rather than just writing general-purpose assertions.
- *Less knowledge required*: Someone who does not have much experience with general-purpose FPV should find that learning and leveraging this FPV app is easier than gaining a full knowledge of FPV.
- *Customizable*: An FPV expert should be able to provide simple scripts, on top of existing FPV tools, that enable nonexperts to efficiently use the app. We should also be able to present the results in different ways from standard FPV, to make it more meaningful to experts in the domain of the particular app. Numerous vendors will likely have prepackaged scripts or tools that can save you this effort.

One other point we should mention is that many vendors have provided new apps that work by extending the capabilities of FPV engines. For example, some have enabled 3-valued logic and detection of X propagation, and some have

189

developed property synthesis tools that automatically generate assertions based on simulation traces or static RTL analysis. We are not disputing the usefulness of these tools, but in this chapter, we want to focus on techniques that you can easily enable using standard off-the-shelf model-checking tools. Thus, apps that require new enhancements to core FPV engines are beyond the domain of this discussion. (If you're curious about other types of apps, your favorite vendor will be happy to talk your ear off about these new tools.)

Even staying within the domain of simple apps that can be enabled with standard FPV tools, there are numerous ways you can use FPV to enhance productivity across the design flow. The ones we highlight are specific examples that have seen some degree of success in the industry; do not assume our particular selection means that other apps will not be of use to you as well. FPV should really be thought of as a general toolkit for interpreting and manipulating RTL logic, not just a specific point tool, and it is a key enabler for applications in many areas. In fact, we can be fairly certain that by the time you read this, someone will have presented a conference paper describing another FPV app that we had never thought of. The ones we highlight here include reusable protocol verification, unreachable coverage elimination, connectivity verification, control register verification, and post-silicon debug.

REUSABLE PROTOCOL VERIFICATION

Reusable protocol verification is exactly what it sounds like: the use of FPV properties that describe a particular communication protocol. Since the protocol is reusable, we do not want to reinvent the wheel and recreate the set of protocol-defining properties with every design; we should create a set of SystemVerilog Assertions (SVAs) for our protocol once and then reuse in future designs as needed. You will want to strongly consider reusable protocol FPV in the following situations:

- You are trying to verify that a new RTL model complies with a well-defined protocol.
- You are doing general FPV on a model that has interfaces that should obey a well-defined protocol.
- You have defined a protocol, do not yet have RTL that implements it, and want to explore and sanity-check some typical protocol waveforms.
- You have defined a protocol that is highly parameterized to enable numerous configurations and want to provide a companion set of properties that share these parameters to support validation.

Before we start talking about this application of FPV, we need to mention one important point: for commonly used protocols, there is often FPV-compatible verification IP available for purchase from EDA vendors. Be sure to take a close look at the marketplace offerings before you start creating your own set of properties; otherwise, you may waste a lot of effort duplicating something that was easily available.

TIP 7.1

If using a well-defined protocol, check whether a set of protocol-related properties is available for purchase before investing a lot of effort into manually creating properties.

Assuming the above was not the case, or you did not have the budget to purchase formal protocol IP externally, you will need to define the properties yourself. In this section, we provide some basic guidelines for defining a standard property set for long-term reuse. Initially, if doing tentative FPV experimentation or design exploration, you might want to create quick and dirty properties rather than thinking about the long term. But if you are working with a protocol that is expected to appear in multiple designs, you will probably benefit significantly from following the advice in this section.

To clarify the discussion, we will describe a simple example protocol and show how we could create a set of reusable properties to go with it. This is a simple client-server protocol that obeys the following rules:

1. Each client has an 8-bit *opcode* and *data* signal going out to the server. The opcode field has a nonzero opcode when making a request.
2. The *req_valid* signal goes to 1 to indicate a request. The *req_valid*, *req_opcode*, and *req_data* remain constant until the *rsp_valid* signal, coming from the server, goes high.
3. The server responds to each request in a constant number of cycles, which may be between 2 and 5 depending on the implementation, as specified by SystemVerilog parameter *SERVER_DELAY*.
4. When the *rsp_valid* signal goes high, it remains high for 1 cycle.
5. One cycle after the *rsp_valid* signal is seen, the client needs to set *req_valid* to 0.

Figure 7.1 illustrates the signals involved in this protocol.

BASIC DESIGN OF THE REUSABLE PROPERTY SET

In most cases, we recommend defining any reusable property set as a standalone SystemVerilog module, which can be connected to the rest of the design using the *bind* construct. As we have seen in Chapter 3, the *bind* keyword in SystemVerilog allows a submodule to be instantiated in any module without having to modify that module's code. Below is an example of the header code for our reusable property set, described as a standalone module.

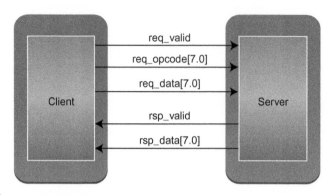

FIGURE 7.1

Simple protocol to demonstrate reusable protocol FPV.

```
module client_server_properties(
    input logic clk, rst,
    input logic req_valid,
    input logic [7:0] req_opcode,
    input logic [7:0] req_data,
    input logic rsp_valid,
    input logic [7:0] rsp_data);
    parameter SERVER_DELAY = 2;
...
```

Note that all the signals involved in the protocol are inputs here. This will usually be the case, since we are trying to observe the behavior of the protocol, not actually modify any behaviors of the design.

Another important detail of this design is the use of a SystemVerilog parameter to represent aspects of the protocol that may hold multiple possible values, but are constant for any given implementation. We could have made *server_delay* an input instead of a parameter, but this would potentially allow it to change at runtime in some implementation, which is specifically disallowed by the rules of the protocol. Another option would be to make it an input and use an assumption to hold it constant, but since each individual protocol-using product is likely being designed based on a single specified value, a parameter seems like a more natural choice here.

TIP 7.2

When representing aspects of a protocol that are constant for any given implementation, use a SystemVerilog parameter rather than a signal or variable.

Once we have fully defined the module, we need to bind it with the design under test (DUT). We could be checking an RTL model of the client, of the server, or of the full system; in the next section we discuss some complications this can cause. But assuming for illustration purposes that we want to connect these properties to the module *client_model*, we could do it using a *bind* statement like this:

```
bind client_model client_server_properties (.*);
```

Note that the use of .* assumes that we have set the names of each interface signal to be the same in both our property module and in the design module *client_model*. If we have changed any signal names, we would need a standard set of port mappings in the form .<port>(<signal>), as in any submodule instantiation.

The above *bind* will create the same effect as if we had instantiated our module inside the design module.

PROPERTY DIRECTION ISSUES

Now that we have described the outline of the module, we need to start writing the properties. But as we begin to write them, we encounter a basic issue: should they be assertions or assumptions? For example, rule 1 tells us "The opcode field has a nonzero opcode when making a request." Which of the following is the correct implementation of this rule?

```
rule_1a: assert property (req_valid |-> req_opcode != 0)
else $display("opcode changed too soon");
rule_1b: assume property (req_valid |-> req_opcode != 0)
else $display("opcode changed too soon");
```

A bit of reflection will reveal that either of these might be correct. There are numerous modes in which we may want to use our properties:

- *Verifying an RTL model of a client.* In this case, the client generates the *req_opcode* signal, so we should be trying to prove this property as an assertion.
- *Verifying an RTL model of the server.* In this case, we should provide assumptions of correct client behavior, so this property should be an assumption.
- *Testing an RTL model of the full system.* In this case, we want to test both sides, so the property should be an assertion.
- *Exploring the protocol itself.* This means we are looking for the kind of waveforms that result when assuming correctness all our properties. In this case, we need to make the property an assumption.

The best answer is that the property might need to be either an assertion or assumption, depending on the particular application of our property set. One method we can use to provide this flexibility is through SystemVerilog parameters and macros. We need to add some parameters to define the mode in which we are building the property set, then use these flags to decide whether each property is an assertion or assumption, as in the following example:

```
parameter CLIENT_IS_DUT = 1;
parameter SERVER_IS_DUT = 0;
parameter SYSTEM_IS_DUT = 0;
parameter THIS_IS_DUT = 0;
`define CLIENT_ASSERT(name, prop, msg) \
    generate if (CLIENT_IS_DUT | SYSTEM_IS_DUT) begin \
      name: assert property (prop) else $error(msg); \
    end else begin \
      name: assume property (prop) else $error (msg); \
    end \
    endgenerate
`define SERVER_ASSERT(name, prop, msg) \
    generate if (SERVER_IS_DUT | SYSTEM_IS_DUT) begin \
      name: assert property (prop) else $error(msg); \
    end else begin \
      name: assume property (prop) else $error (msg); \
    end \
endgenerate
```

Once we have this basic infrastructure defined, our property then becomes:

```
`CLIENT_ASSERT(rule_1, req_valid |-> req_opcode != 0,
       "opcode changed too soon");
```

Now, by choosing the proper set of parameter values to pass into our property module when invoking it, we can set up our *bind* statement to enable testing of the client RTL, server RTL, both, or neither. The properties for the remainder of our rules are then relatively straightforward to define, as long as we are careful to recognize which side is responsible for implementing each requirement:

```
`CLIENT_ASSERT(rule_2a, $rose(req_valid) |=> (
      ($stable(req_valid)) [*SERVER_DELAY]),
      "request changed too soon");
`CLIENT_ASSERT(rule_2b, $rose(req_valid) |=> (
      ($stable(req_opcode))[*SERVER_DELAY]),
      "request changed too soon");
`CLIENT_ASSERT(rule_2c, $rose(req_valid) |=> (
      ($stable(req_data))[*SERVER_DELAY]),
      "request changed too soon");
`SERVER_ASSERT(rule_3, $rose(req_valid) |=>
      ##SERVER_DELAY rsp_valid,
      "rsp_valid failed to rise");
```

```
`SERVER_ASSERT(rule_4, $rose(rsp_valid) |=>
    $fell(rsp_valid),
    "rsp_valid held too long.");
`CLIENT_ASSERT(rule_5, $rose(rsp_valid) |=>
    $fell(req_valid),
    "req_valid held too long.");
```

Note that for the rule 2 properties above, we also followed one of the tips in our earlier chapters and expressed the complex property as multiple simple properties, to separately check the stability of each field. This will likely make debug much simpler in cases where the assertions fail in simulation or FPV.

TIP 7.3

When dealing with a two-way protocol, use parameters and macros to enable your properties to be either assertions or assumptions depending on the configuration.

VERIFYING PROPERTY SET CONSISTENCY

Now that we have created an initial property set, we need to ask the question: is this property set consistent? In other words, does it enable the behaviors we associate with our protocol, in expected ways? We need to have a good answer to this question before we start binding it to RTL models for verification purposes. To do this, we need to prepare a self-checking environment where we will observe cover points and prove assertions implied by our protocol.

TIP 7.4

When defining a reusable property set for a protocol, a critical step is to run a standalone self-checking environment on your property set, before integrating it with any RTL design models.

First, as with any FPV effort, and as discussed in the previous three chapters, we need to create a good set of cover points. In this case, there are a few obvious ones to start with:

```
req_possible: cover property (##1 $rose(req_valid));
rsp_possible: cover property (##1 $rose(rsp_valid));
req_done: cover property (##1 $fell(req_valid));
```

Note that we added an extra ##1 to the beginning of each of these, to avoid false coverage success due to possible bogus transitions at the end of reset, since it is likely that these external inputs would be unconstrained during reset.

We should also create more detailed sequence covers, so that we can see that our vision of the full flow of our protocol is possible. Often these will be inspired by waveforms we have seen in the specification. One example for our case might be:

```
full_req_with_data: cover property (($rose(req_valid) &&
(req_data != 0)) ##SERVER_DELAY $rose(rsp_valid) ##1 $fell(req_valid));
```

TIP 7.5

Create a good set of cover points for your reusable property set, just like you would in any FPV effort.

We also should create some additional assertions: properties we believe to be implicit in our protocol, which should be assured if our other properties are implemented correctly. These will be only for checking our checker, so they should be protected in a section of code that will be ignored except when the checker itself is the verification target. For example, in our protocol, we know that if the opcode changes, it cannot be during a valid request, so we might create the following assertion:

```
generate if (THIS_IS_DUT) begin
    self_check1: assert property ($changed(opcode) |->
                                  !$past(req_valid));
end endgenerate
```

Now we have sufficient infrastructure that we can run our FPV tool on our property set module standalone, under the *THIS_IS_DUT* configuration. All our protocol-defining properties will be assumptions, so we will generate the space of behaviors that are permitted by our protocol. We can then view the cover traces and check the assertion proofs, to be sure that our set of properties is defining our protocol properly. We should spend some time looking at the generated cover waveforms, and make sure they are correctly depicting the protocol envisioned in our specification. If we see that some of the cover points are unreachable, or reachable only in ways we did not anticipate, this will indicate that there is some flaw or inconsistency in our property set that we need to further investigate.

TIP 7.6

In any reusable property set, create redundant self-checking properties representing behaviors that should be true of the protocol, and use this to verify the consistency and correctness of the property set.

Note that this self-consistency environment can also serve another purpose: it is a way to examine the behavior of our protocol independent of any particular RTL implementation. This can be very valuable in early protocol development and also can be a useful way to experiment with potential changes to the protocol before dealing with the complications of RTL. It can also help with judging whether behaviors described in external bug reports are truly permitted by the protocol, leading to better insight as to whether there is a core protocol bug or an issue with a particular RTL implementation. Thus, we strongly recommend that you closely collaborate with your protocol architects when developing this kind of property set and make sure to leverage it for future protocol analysis as well as RTL verification.

TIP 7.7

Remember that your protocol property set's self-consistency environment can also be a useful tool for experimenting with and learning about the behavior of the protocol, independently of any particular RTL design.

CHECKING COMPLETENESS

Another question that needs to be answered about any protocol property set is: is it complete? Does it fully capture the intent of the protocol? In many cases, this question cannot be answered except by a human who understands the protocol: most protocols we have seen are defined by plain English specifications, rather than something formal enough to be directly translatable into a set of assertions. In fact, we cheated a bit when we stated the requirements in terms of a set of well-specified rules a few subsections back. It is more likely that our requirements would initially arrive in a form something like this:

> When the client sends a request, as indicated by the rise of the req_valid signal, the server waits an amount of time determined by an implementation-dependent delay (which shall be between 2 and 5) to respond with a rsp_valid signal....

At first glance, it might appear that we are stuck with having to manually translate specifications into discrete rules for the purpose of creating assertions. However, if you can convince your architects and designers to annotate the specification, it might be possible to do slightly better. The idea is to add some known marker text, along with a stated rule, to parts of the specification that would indicate a potential assertion. If you are using a word processor with an annotation feature, you can avoid messing up the text directly. For example, the first sentence above would be connected to an annotation:

> RULE rsp_valid_delay: rsp_valid rises within 2 to 5 cycles (constant for each implementation) after req_valid.

Each rule annotated in the specification has a tag, *rsp_valid_delay* in this case. Then we just need to ensure, using a script, that each tagged rule in the specification has a corresponding tagged assertion (with assertion tags indicated in a comment line above each assertion) in the property module. One SVA assertion might cover several rules from the specification, or several might cover the same rule; this is acceptable as long as each rule is covered. For example:

```
// RULES: rsp_valid_delay, opcode_valid_data_const
`CLIENT_ASSERT(rule_2a, $rose(req_valid) |=> (
        ($stable(req_valid))[*SERVER_DELAY]),
        "request changed too soon");
`CLIENT_ASSERT(rule_2b, $rose(req_valid) |=> (
        ($stable(req_opcode))[*SERVER_DELAY]),
        "request changed too soon");
`CLIENT_ASSERT(rule_2c, $rose(req_valid) |=> (
        ($stable(req_data))[*SERVER_DELAY]),
        "request changed too soon");
```

> **TIP 7.8**
>
> Define a set of annotations in your protocol specification that enable you to connect rules defined by your specification to assertions in your property module, and use scripts to find any potential holes.

This method will not ensure total completeness—there is still a major human factor involved—but it does help ensure that your property module will attempt to cover each of the rules thought important by the protocol architects.

UNREACHABLE COVERAGE ELIMINATION

The next FV app we discuss is unreachable coverage elimination (UCE). UCE is the method where we examine coverage goals that simulation has failed to reach despite many runs of random testing and try to use FPV to identify theoretically unreachable ones so they can be eliminated from consideration. In other words, we are using FPV to aid our analysis of simulation efforts, rather than as an independent validation tool in itself. You should consider running UCE in cases where:

- Your primary method of validation is simulation, and you have coverage goals that simulation is failing to reach.
- You want to automatically eliminate as many cover points as possible before starting manual review and test writing to cover the missing cases.

In the simplest case, where your coverage is defined by SVA cover points in the RTL code, running UCE is really just the same as doing targeted FPV runs. Just choose the parts of your design containing unreached cover points, and launch a standard FPV tool on those. You do need to be careful about choosing hierarchy levels at which your FPV tool can load the model.

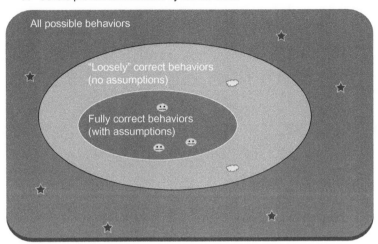

☺ Truly reachable cover points.

☁ Unreachable covers missed by formal UCE (trace found).

★ Covers proven unreachable by formal UCE.

FIGURE 7.2

Behavior of formal UCE without assumptions.

Running FPV for UCE purposes is much easier than doing "real" FPV runs as discussed in Chapters 5 and 6, because you do not need to worry as much about writing assumptions. The reason is that assumptions narrow the space of possible behaviors of your design, so running without them in UCE is a conservative choice. If you run without assumptions, you are being overly generous in the behaviors allowed—which means that if some cover point is unreachable even in this case, you are certain that it is globally unreachable. Figure 7.2 illustrates this situation.

We can see that although some unreachable cover points may not be caught without a full set of FPV assumptions, there is still a good chance that many will be caught without them. The key point is that we minimize the danger of throwing out a good cover point, since we are exploring a space wider than the real behaviors of our design. However, we do need to take care to use a reasonable definition of the design's clocks and reset for our formal runs; you will likely find that a reset trace from simulation is a good FPV starting point. Overall, a good strategy on a project that is having trouble achieving simulation coverage is to do lightweight FPV runs on major blocks, and use these to identify an initial set of unreachable cover points.

TIP 7.9

If you have a project that is stressing simulation-based validation and failing to reach some of its cover points, a lightweight UCE FPV run can help eliminate some of them.

Once a cover point is found unreachable, you need to further examine it to decide if that matches the design intent. In many cases, an unreachable cover point may be part of an old feature or block that was inherited in the RTL, but is not part of the currently intended functionality, and can be safely eliminated from the list of coverage targets. If, however, the designers believe that the point should be reachable, then the unreachable cover may indicate a real design bug. In that case, you probably want to debug it with FPV to better understand why your cover point cannot be reached, as we discussed when talking about cover points in Chapter 6.

THE ROLE OF ASSERTIONS IN UCE

While we can get some decent information from a simple assumption-free UCE FPV run, we can do even better if we are using a design that contains assertions. Since our premise is that if you are doing UCE, you are late in the project cycle and trying to close simulation coverage, we are probably safe in assuming that you have high confidence (resulting from many simulation runs) in the assertions that are present in your code. Since this is the case, we can create a much better UCE FPV run by converting many of those assertions to assumptions. Most modern FPV tools have commands allowing such a conversion.

This might seem a bit strange at first, since we are likely constraining many noninput nodes for testing. But remember that in FPV, an assumption is a constraint on the universe of legal simulations: in effect, we are telling the FPV tool that in any simulation, it should only consider inputs that will result in our assertions being true. This is exactly what we want since we know that none of the valid simulation tests are violating any assertions. In effect, we have further restricted our space of possible simulations, which may now allow us to prove even more cover points unreachable, as shown in Figure 7.3.

We should point out that since simulation-focused assertions are not usually created with formal rigor in mind, they are not likely to provide the full set of assumptions that defines all legal behaviors. This is why the central oval in Figure 7.3 does not coincide with the assertions-as-assumptions region around it. However, simulation-focused assertions can do an excellent job of constraining the behaviors considered by UCE FPV and better enabling a validation team to stop wasting time trying to hit truly unreachable coverage points.

One other issue to be aware of is the fact that too many assumptions can create a complexity issue for FPV. If you find that blindly converting all assumptions to assertions creates performance problems, you may want to instead manually select an interesting subset to use in your UCE FPV run.

TIP 7.10

If doing a UCE FPV run on a model containing simulation-focused assertions, use your FPV tool's commands to convert assertions to assumptions for the FPV run.

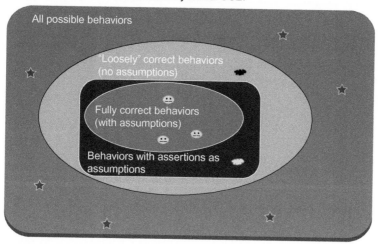

☺ Truly reachable cover points.
☁ Unreachable covers missed by formal UCE (trace found).
🐛 Cover proven unreachable after assertion used as assumptions.
★ Covers proven unreachable by formal UCE.

FIGURE 7.3

UCE FPV with assertions converted to assumptions.

COVERGROUPS AND OTHER COVERAGE TYPES

We have focused our discussion on SVA cover points, the straightforward assertion-like coverage constructs that are automatically evaluated by any FPV tool. But what about other coverage types such as SystemVerilog covergroups, or line/statement/branch coverage? In the best case, your FPV tool will have features to evaluate these kinds of coverage as well, and detect some subset of unreachable coverage constructs, such as dead code, automatically. But in cases where it does not, you will need to consider using scripts (or manual work) to create SVA cover points logically equivalent to your other constructs.

CONNECTIVITY VERIFICATION

Formal connectivity verification refers to the usage of an FPV tool to verify correctness of the top-level connections created during assembly of multiple components, such as in the case of an SOC. The idea of using a FV tool to check connectivity might initially sound strange; in fact, the authors initially dismissed the idea when it was first broached at Intel a few years ago. Don't most designs have simple correct-by-construction scripts that guarantee correct connectivity using methods much simpler than FPV engines?

Actually, a modern design can involve connecting dozens of independently designed IP blocks, through top-level multiplexing blocks that can direct external pins to different functional blocks, with varying delays, depending on the value of various control registers. This means that there are many corner cases where combinations of control values and pin routings interact with each other. Designers want to have strong confidence that their validation provides full coverage. Traditionally this has been addressed by simulation, but it means that many hours of simulation are required after each connectivity change to cover all cases.

FPV is an ideal solution here, since it inherently covers all corner cases, and this MUXing logic is very simple in comparison to other FPV problems. Most connectivity conditions can be converted to straightforward assertions of the form:

```
pin1: assert property (
    (ctrl_block.reg[PIN_SEL] == 1) |-> ##DELAY
    (ip_block.pin1 == $past(top.pin1,DELAY)));
```

Once these assertions are generated, they can often be proven in seconds on typical SOCs. This results in a major productivity difference, allowing almost instant feedback for designers instead of the previous multi-hour delay due to running a comprehensive simulation suite. Thus, connectivity FPV is increasingly being seen as an easy-to-use technique that is fundamental to the SOC assembly flow. It can be implemented using simple scripts on top of a standard FPV tool, in addition to the fact that several tools on the market offer features to support this method directly.

TIP 7.11

If you are assembling a design that has conditional connections between top-level pins and numerous internal IPs, consider using FPV for connectivity verification.

There are a few issues, however, that you do need to be aware of when setting up a connectivity FPV run: setting up the correct model build, specifying the connections, and possible logic complications.

MODEL BUILD FOR CONNECTIVITY

The first issue that you need to think about when setting up connectivity FPV is: building the model. Until now, we have emphasized in most discussions of FPV that you will typically run on a unit or partial cluster model, due to known limitations of tool capacity. However, connectivity FPV usually makes the most sense if run at a full-chip level. Fortunately, this is not usually a major obstacle, since in most cases the full-chip connectivity models can blackbox almost all logic

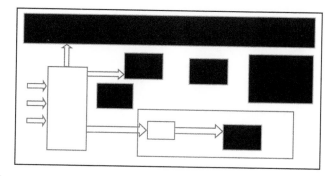

FIGURE 7.4

Full-chip model with blackboxes for connectivity.

blocks: remember that we are just verifying the paths from top-level pins to major block boundaries. Figure 7.4 illustrates a typical full-chip model after blackboxing for connectivity verification:

As you can see in Figure 7.4, most major logic blocks can be blackboxed, with only a small subset actually needed for connectivity verification.

One common mistake when first building such a model is to start by trying to build a full-chip model with no blackboxes, then blackbox what is needed for simplification. This may be a reasonable strategy with typical simulation or floor planning tools, but tends to cause major problems with FV tools. Due to the inherent limitations of FPV capacity, such a tool will often not even be able to compile an un-blackboxed full-chip model. It is much better to start by building a "shell" model, with just the top level of your chip represented and all its submodules blackboxed. Once this is built, gradually un-blackbox elements of your design that you know are participating in top-level connectivity: control registers, MUXing blocks, and so on.

> **TIP 7.12**
>
> When building a model for connectivity FPV, start by building your top-level chip with all submodules blackboxed, then un-blackbox the modules that participate in top-level connectivity selection and MUXing.

It is okay if you accidentally leave something blackboxed unnecessarily at the end of this process, since you will ultimately catch this while debugging your failing connectivity assertions. If some blackboxed element happens to fall inside a connectivity path, your FPV tool will report a bogus connectivity bug (due to treating the output of the blackboxed block as a free output), and you will discover the issue. There is no way such an extra blackbox could create a false positive, where a real error is missed. Figure 7.5 illustrates this situation.

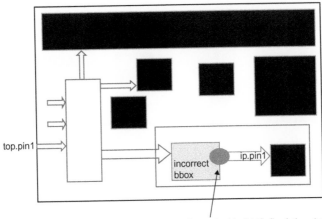

FPV can assign arbitrary value to bbox output to falsify (ip.pin1 == top.pin1)

FIGURE 7.5

FPV will catch accidental extra blackbox in a connectivity FPV build.

Table 7.1 Connectivity Specification

Signal	Control register	Control value	Destination signal	Delay range	Other cond.
top.s1	regblk.r1	0	top.blk1.s1	2	—
top.s1	regblk.r1	1	top.blk2.s1	3	!top.scan

SPECIFYING THE CONNECTIVITY

Aside from building the proper model, the other major component of the connectivity FPV setup is specifying the actual connectivity requirements. Essentially, for each top-level signal that is to be connected to the boundaries of one or more IP blocks, and each value of the relevant control registers, we need:

- Destination signal at some IP block boundary.
- Delay or range of delays (if any) permitted.
- Additional control conditions.

Most teams find it convenient to express this in some kind of spreadsheet format, as in Table 7.1.

Many EDA tools define spreadsheet formats like this that can be natively read by their tools and implicitly converted to assertions, and later back-annotated during debug to simplify the overall process. However, even without such a feature, it is relatively easy to create a script that would translate the table above into assertions like the following:

```
s1_conn_0: assert property ((regblk.r1 == 0) |->
    ##2 top.blk1.s1 == $past(top.s1,2));
s1_conn_1: assert property (
    (regblk.r1 == 1) && (!top.scan) |->
    ##3 (top.blk2.s1 == $past(top.s1,3)));
```

These assertions can then be proven like any standard FPV assertions. The logic to connect SOC signals tends to be a rather simple set of MUXes and delay elements, so assertions like these are typically proven very quickly by most modern FPV tools.

POSSIBLE CONNECTIVITY FPV COMPLICATIONS

As mentioned above, the connectivity properties tend to involve very simple logic compared to typical FPV runs. However, there are still various complications that users of this type of flow have tended to encounter. The most common ones we have seen are low-level pad cells, complex interface protocols, and top-level constraints.

The first issue involves the fact that the top-level interface signals of a typical SOC design need to pass through pad cells to reach the outside world. These cells are often excluded by design teams from most RTL logic flows, because they represent very simple logic but possibly complex electrical and physical issues. Thus their authors, who are usually backend experts, tend to use nonsynthesizable SystemVerilog constructs such as explicit transistors and weak assignments. (If you usually work at a logic level like the authors, there is a good chance you have never seen these constructs. That is okay—at least one of the authors first learned about some of these while debugging connectivity FPV!) Since FPV tools cannot handle such constructs, they will result either in compilation errors or in bogus reports of combinational loops. Thus, to enable sensible connectivity FPV, you may need to replace low-level pad cell SystemVerilog modules with simpler logical representations. For example, you may see a cell like this, probably with less helpful comments:

```
module ugly_pad(vcc,vss,in1,out1)
    // Transistor structure that doesn't change logic
    bufif1(tmp,in1,vcc);
    // Weakpull for cases when pad not in use
    assign (weak0,weak1) out1 = vss;
    // Real action of pad
    assign out1 = tmp;
end
```

To enable connectivity FPV, you will need to modify it so you can get a synthesizable logical view when needed:

```
module ugly_pad(vcc,vss,in1,out1)

    `ifdef FPV
        assign out1 = in1;
    `else
        // Transistor structure that doesn't change
        bufif1(tmp,in1,vcc);
        // Weakpull for cases when pad not in use
        assign (weak0,weak1) out1 = vss;
        // Real action of pad
        assign out1 = tmp;
`endif
end
```

In general, you need to be careful when modifying any logic as part of an FPV effort, but usually the logic of these types of cells is conceptually simple. Be sure to review any changes with the cell's original author or an equivalent expert, of course, to be sure your modifications are logically sound.

> **TIP 7.13**
>
> If you are having trouble compiling pad cells or getting reports of unexpected combinational loops during connectivity FPV, you may need to create a logical view of some of your pad cells.

The second common challenge of connectivity FPV is the issue of programming the control registers. Normally we expect that connectivity logic will be relatively simple and not require very deep reasoning by formal engines. However, if testing conditional connectivity based on control register values, there may be more complexity due to some logical protocol being needed to program the values of these registers. You may find that you already have a good set of assumptions for this protocol, especially if using a common protocol assertion set as discussed earlier in this chapter, reducing the effort needed to create more assumptions. This could still leave you with a high-effort run by the formal engines to analyze the programming of the control registers in every connectivity proof though.

A key insight that can help to address this issue is that, when doing connectivity FPV, your goal is not really to prove the correctness of the control register programming. Presumably other parts of your validation effort, either formal or simulation runs, are already focusing on this area in greater generality anyway. When running connectivity FPV, you are just trying to prove correctness of the connectivity logic. Thus, it is likely acceptable to abstract the control registers: make them *cut points,* telling the FPV tool to ignore their fanins and let them take on an arbitrary value, then add assumptions to hold them constant for each formal run. This way you will prove that for any given constant value of the control registers, the connectivity is correct, even though you are not spending effort in this run to prove the correctness of the register programming logic.

TIP 7.14

If your connectivity FPV runs are slowed down by the logic that programs control registers, consider making those registers cut points and assuming them constant so you can focus on just checking the connectivity logic.

The last common complication with connectivity FPV that we discuss is the problem of top-level constraints. As with any FPV run, you will often find that the first time you attempt it, you will get false failures reported due to lack of assumptions. There is really nothing special about this problem in the connectivity context; the only difference is that you may need to deal with top-level mode pins that did not affect your block-level runs. Often you will have to assume that a top-level scan or debug mode is off, or that high-level "vss" and "vcc" pins actually do represent a logical 0 and 1. You may also face issues due to multiple clocks in the design; if some IP blocks use different clock domains or clocks that have passed through a blackbox, you need to correctly inform the FPV tool of their frequency in relation to the model's main clock. Treat this like any other FPV run and work with experts in the proper area to examine your initial counter-examples and identify relevant top-level assumptions or clocking specifications.

TIP 7.15

You may need to wiggle your first few attempts at connectivity FPV and add top-level assumptions or modify clocking specifications, just like any other FPV effort.

CONTROL REGISTER VERIFICATION

Nearly every modern design has some set of control and status registers, address-able blocks of data that can be read or written at runtime to set major control parameters or get status about the operation of the SOC. These registers each contain several fields, which can have a variety of access policies: some are read-only, some are write-only, some can be freely read or written, and some can only be accessed if certain control bits are set. It is usually very important that these access policies are correctly enforced, both to ensure correct functionality and to avoid issues of data corruption or leakage of secure information. We also need to ensure that registers cannot overwrite or interfere with each other's values.

Control registers can sometimes be subject to tricky errors that are hard to find in simulation. For example, suppose two unrelated read-write registers are

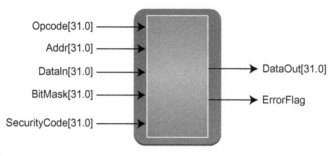

FIGURE 7.6

Basic interface of a control register block.

accidentally assigned the same address, and write attempts to the two can overwrite each other. If they are unrelated, it is possible that none of the random simulation tests will happen to use both the registers at the same time, and thus it is very easy to miss this issue. As a result, it has become increasingly popular in the industry to replace simulation-based testing with FPV-based applications to exhaustively verify control register functionality. Like the connectivity problem, the control register problem is one that tends not to be as complex as other types of control logic, often enabling FPV tools to handle it very efficiently. However, there are a lot of possible combinations of operations that make exhaustive simulation-based testing inconvenient or infeasible.

A typical control register block interface is shown in Figure 7.6. As you can see in the figure, a control register block is usually accessed by providing some kind of opcode indicating a read or write operation, an address and data for the transaction, and some kind of security code (usually generated elsewhere on the chip) to signal the type of access that is authorized. There is also a bit mask to limit the access to specific subfields of a register. Typical outputs include a data out bus, to service requests that read data, and an error flag to signal that an illegal access was attempted.

Most modern FPV tools provide optional apps to directly handle control register verification, often with support for the emerging IP-XACT specification language (see [IEE09]), but in any case it is relatively easy to write scripts to set up the FPV run directly. You just need to design an input format that represents the expectations of your control registers and convert this into SVA assertions.

TIP 7.16

Consider using FPV to verify that your control registers are all correctly read and written according to their specified access policies.

SPECIFYING CONTROL REGISTER REQUIREMENTS

Typically, a simple spreadsheet format can be used to specify the requirements on control registers. For each register, you need to specify

- Symbolic name
- Address
- RTL signal that stores the register value (if available)
- Security access authorization
- List of fields

Then, for each field, you need

- Symbolic name
- Bit range in register
- Access type
- Default (reset) value

There are a number of access types supported for typical registers. Here are some of the most common ones:

- Read-Write (RW): Register can be freely read or written.
- Read-Only (RO): Register can only be read. This is often used to communicate status or hardware configuration to the outside world. (Often there is specific internal logic that can write to it, as in the *fault_status* example above, but through the register access interface it can only be read.)
- Write-Only (WO): Register can only be written. This is a common case when setting runtime parameters.
- Read-Write-Clear. (RWC): Register can be read, but any write attempt will clear it. This is sometimes useful if communicating status information to the outside world, and we want to provide a capability to externally reset the status.

In Figure 7.7, we illustrate a few lines of a typical control register specification spreadsheet.

Register	Address / Field Name	RTL Signal / Field Range	Security/ Access	Dflt
ARCH_VERSION	0010	cregs.rf.arch_reg[31:0]	05	
	arch_major	15:0	RO	1
	os_version	31:16	RW	7
FAULT_LOGGING	0020	cregs.rf.fault_log[16:0]	01	
	fault_status	15:0	RWC	0
	fault_logging_on	16	WO	1

FIGURE 7.7

Portion of a typical control register specification spreadsheet.

In this example, we have two registers, each with two fields. The first, ARCH_VERSION, is at address 0010 and has security authorization code 05. It has two 16-bit fields. The *arch_major* field, with default value 1, is RO, probably used to communicate a hardcoded chip version to the user. The *os_version* field is RW, probably so it can be modified by software, and has default value 7. The second, FAULT_LOGGING, is a 17-bit register at address 0020 with security authorization code 01. It contains a 16-bit *fault_status*, through which the design can communicate some status information to a user, with default value 0. Its type is RWC, so the user can clear it with a write attempt. It also contains a WO *fault_logging_on* bit, through which a user can activate or deactivate fault logging, defaulting to 1.

We should probably comment here on why there is a spot in the table in Figure 7.7 for the internal RTL signal for each register. If we are trying to verify correct accesses through the register interface as shown in Figure 7.6, why should we care about the internal nodes? While verifying externally is the ideal, we need to keep in mind the fact that for many register types, there are major limitations to what we can verify through the external interface. For example, if a register is WO, we can never externally see the result of the write that sets its value, so what kind of assertion could we write on its correctness? Thus, whitebox style assertions, which look at the internal register node as part of the verification, often make the most sense for control registers.

Once you have decided on the specification of your control registers, you can use this information to generate SVA assertions.

SVA ASSERTIONS FOR CONTROL REGISTERS

There are many types of assertions that can be generated to check the correctness of control register accesses. Here we describe the ones that we typically use to check registers with the common access types described above (RW, RO, WO, and RWC). Each of the assertion classes below is generated for every applicable register and field. With each, we illustrate one of the assertions that correspond to the specification in Figure 7.7.

In general, you should be examining your company's specification for its control registers, and generating assertions related to each defined operation for each register type. Don't forget to include assertions both that correct operations succeed, and that incorrect operations do not modify the register value.

We are also assuming here that our design only allows writes at a field granularity (we should enforce this with separate assertions/assumptions), so we don't have to account for messiness due to differing bit masks. Thus, for a given access attempt, each field is either totally enabled or totally disabled.

- *Correct Reset Value.* (All types.) We should check that each register field has the correct default value after reset.
  ```
  assert property ($fell(rst) |-> cregs.rf.arch_reg[31:16] == 7);
  ```

- *Always Read the Reset Value* (RO). Since the field is RO, all reads should get the reset value.
  ```
  assert property ((Opcode == READ) && (Addr == 0010)
      &&SecurityDecode(SecurityCode,Opcode,05)
      && (BitMask[15:0] == 16'hffff) | = >
      (DataOut == 1));
  ```
- *Correctly Ignore Writes.* (RO). After a write attempt, field value is unchanged.
  ```
  assert property ((Opcode == WRITE) && (Addr == 0010)
      && (BitMask[15:0] != 0) | = >
      $stable(cregs.rf.arch_reg[15:0]);
  ```
- *Unauthorized Operation.* (All). Security code does not allow the current operation, so flag error and don't change register.
  ```
  assert property ((Addr == 0010) &&
      !SecurityDecode(SecurityCode,Opcode,05)| = >
      $stable(cregs.rf.arch_reg[31:0] &&
      ErrorFlag);
  ```
- *Correct Value Read.* (RO, RW). Reads from the designated address successfully get the field's value.
  ```
  assert property ((Opcode == READ) && (Addr == 0010)
      && SecurityDecode(SecurityCode,Opcode,05)| = >
      DataOut[15:0]==cregs.rf.arch_reg[15:0]);
  ```
- *Correct Value Written.* (WO, RW). Writes to the designated address successfully set the field's value.
  ```
  assert property ((Opcode == WRITE) && (Addr == 0010)
      && SecurityDecode(SecurityCode,Opcode,05)
      && (BitMask[31:16] == 16'hffff) | = >
      (cregs.rf.arch_reg[31:16] ==
      $past(DataIn[31:16]));
  ```
- *No Read from WO.* (WO) A read attempt on a write-only field should result in all zeroes on the data bus.
  ```
  assert property ((Opcode == READ) && (Addr == 0020) &&
      (BitMask[16] == 1'b1) | = >
      DataOut[16]==0);
  ```
- *RWC Clears Correctly.* (RWC) A write attempt correctly clears an RWC register.
  ```
  assert property ((Opcode == WRITE) && (Addr == 0020)
      && SecurityDecode(SecurityCode,Opcode,01)
      && (BitMask[15:0] == 16'hffff) | = >
      (cregs.rf,fault_log[15:0] == 0));
  ```
- *No Data Corruption.* (All) A nonwrite operation, or a write to another field or address, does not modify a field's value.
  ```
  assert property ((Opcode != WRITE) || (Addr != 0020)
      || (BitMask[15:0] == 0)) | = >
      $stable(cregs.rf.fault_log[15:0]));
  ```
- *Read-Write Match.* (RW) If we write to the field, and we read it later on, we receive the value we wrote. This is technically redundant given the

above assertions, but this lets us focus on observing the full expected flow for a RW register. It also has the advantage of being the only assertion in this set that can check write correctness without relying on whitebox knowledge of the internal register node, which may be needed in some cases where the internal implementation is not fully transparent or documented.

```
assign write_os_version = (opcode == WRITE) &&
       (Addr == 0010) &&
       (BitMask[31:16] != 0);
assign write_os_version_val = (DataIn[31:16]);
always @(posedge clk) begin
  if (write_os_version) begin
    write_os_version_val_last = write_os_version_val;
end end
assign read_os_version = (opcode == WRITE) &&
                  (Addr == 0010) &&
                  (BitMask[31:16] != 0);
assert property (write_os_version ##1
   (!write_os_version throughout read_os_version[->1]) |=>
       DataOut[31:16] == write_os_version_val_last);
```

The list above is not fully exhaustive, because many designs offer other register access types, locking mechanisms to limit access to certain registers, security policies that require additional inputs, and similar features. But the set of assertions we recommend here is a good starting point. Also, since most of these are expressed as triggered assertions, in most FPV tools they will automatically generate a good set of cover points showing that we can cover each typical access type.

TIP 7.17

If using FPV to verify control registers, first check to see if this feature is offered natively by your FPV tool. If not, examine your company's specification for its control registers, and generate assertions related to each defined operation for each register type. Don't forget to include assertions both that correct operations succeed, and that incorrect operations do not modify the register value.

MAJOR CHALLENGES OF CONTROL REGISTER VERIFICATION

There are a number of challenges you are likely to face when setting up control register FPV. You need to properly select the verification level and the initial FPV environment for the control register FPV run. In addition, you need to account for multiple register widths and internal hardware writes.

- *The Verification Level.* In many cases, you might initially find it natural to run control register FPV at the level of your unit/cluster interface or at the same level as your other FPV verification environments. However, it is often the case that some complex external protocol must be decoded in order to form the simple register access requests implied by Figure 7.6. You need to consider whether you really need to be re-verifying your top-level decode logic: in most cases, this is well verified elsewhere, and there is no point in analyzing the same logic while doing control register FPV. Thus, in most cases, control register FPV is best run at the interface of a control register handling block, with interface signals like those in Figure 7.6. Naturally, you should separately ensure that the top-level decode logic is verified somewhere, either through its own FPV run or through other validation methods.

TIP 7.18

Run control register FPV at the level of some block that has a register-oriented interface with address, opcode, and data inputs/outputs, rather than including top-level decode logic.

- *The FPV Environment.* Along the same lines as the above comment, focus on an FPV environment that just contains your register handling block. Also, be sure to remove any assumptions you created to constrain control registers in other FPV environments: these can overconstrain your control register verification, reducing the coverage of real cases, and cause your cover points to fail.

TIP 7.19

Keep the control register FPV environment focused on this local block. Also, remove any assumptions that constrained control registers for your full unit verification.

- *Multiple Access Widths and Register Aliasing.* In some designs we have seen, registers may be up to 64 bits wide, but the register file can be addressed in 32-bit chunks. This means that for a wide register, an access to bits [63:32] at an address A is equivalent to an access to bits [31:0] at address $A + 1$. This requires care when writing the assertions: for example, it is no longer true that a write to a different address will not modify the register (as in our "No Data Corruption" assertion above), because a write to the next higher address can change its upper bits. There may also be cases of more general register aliasing in your design, where two registers with different logical addresses may refer to the same internal node, and you should be careful to account for such cases as well.

- *Hardware Write Paths.* You may have noticed that we mentioned the concept of status registers, which can be written to internally by the hardware to indicate status or events occurring on the chip. This mode of access will likely cause failures of many of the assertions above, which implicitly assume that all registers are accessed through the explicit interface in Figure 7.6. In fact, Figure 7.6 omits the detail that the hardware can internally write to registers through a separate interface; Figure 7.8 provides a revised picture that includes these.

The simplest method is to add an assumption that the internal hardware interface is inactive during control register FPV, in order to verify that the register specifications are correct with respect to the external interface. Alternatively, you can do more comprehensive verification by creating reference models of your registers that account for this alternate access path.

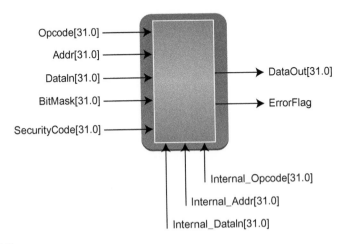

FIGURE 7.8

Register file with internal writes.

POST-SILICON DEBUG

The final application we will look at in this chapter is FPV for post-silicon debug. At first, this usage model might sound surprising, since RTL FPV is generally thought of as a pre-silicon design and validation tool. In fact, however, FPV is ideally suited for "last-mile" debug in cases where we need to diagnose and fix a post-silicon bug sighting.

As you would expect, FPV is not really useful when diagnosing lab sightings at the full-chip level, or when looking at electrical or timing issues, which are beyond the domain of RTL verification. But when you have isolated a bug to the cluster or unit level and suspect that you are dealing with a core RTL logic issue, FPV is ideally suited for reproducing and understanding the suspected bug. This is because of the principle you have seen us mention numerous times in this book: FPV lets you specify the destination rather than the journey. If a logic bug is observed in post-silicon, it is a key indicator that your validation environment was previously incomplete, so you need some tool that can find a new trace based on the observed bug.

TIP 7.22

Consider using FPV in cases where a post-silicon bug sighting is suspected to be a logic bug, especially if pre-silicon validation was simulation based. If your random simulations missed a bug, you probably need FPV's capability to back-solve for a set of inputs leading to a particular behavior.

In practical terms, this means that if you can characterize a suspected bug sighting at the RTL, in terms of a particular pattern of signal values on outputs or scanned state signals, you should be able to describe it as an SVA sequence. You can then use FPV to solve for a legal input pattern that would generate this sequence. If you succeed, then you will be able to see the bug occurring at the RTL, and you can test suspected fixes to see if they will eliminate the problem. If FPV proves that the bug pattern is not reachable, then you are able to rule out the suspected logic bug, and focus on other issues such as timing problems.

To make this discussion more concrete, let's assume you are looking at a CPU model containing the arithmetic logic unit (ALU) from Chapter 6, reviewed again in Figure 7.9.

Furthermore, we will assume that a post-silicon sighting has been reported, where after several addition operations, the *resultv* output goes to 1 and outputs a bogus result during an "off cycle" when no operation is happening. Just for fun, we will also assume that this ALU is complex enough that we could not run FPV on a model containing the whole thing. How would we go about debugging this sighting with FPV?

BUILDING THE FPV ENVIRONMENT

We are assuming here that you have reached a point in your initial post-silicon debug efforts where you have developed a basic understanding of your defect

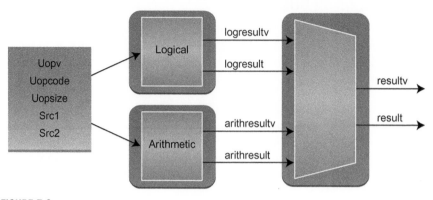

FIGURE 7.9

ALU block-level diagram.

observation, and suspect a logic bug in a particular area of your design. As with any FPV effort, you must now choose a hierarchy level in your RTL at which to run FPV. The usual capacity limitations need to be considered here, such as being unable to run at a full cluster or chip level. Of course, you should employ the standard methods used to make designs more tractable for FPV: blackboxing large memories, reducing parameters, turning off scan modes, and so forth. However, you do have a slight advantage over general FPV runs in this case: you can take into account specific characteristics of the bug you are observing. For example, you might normally be unable to run FPV at a cluster level due to the large amount of logic. But if you know from the bug you are observing that a particular functional block is involved, you may be able to blackbox unrelated blocks.

TIP 7.23

When using FPV for post-silicon debug, in addition to the usual FPV complexity techniques, try to identify units/subunits unlikely to be involved in your particular bug and blackbox them. This may enable you to run FPV on a larger block than you could for general pre-silicon validation.

In the case of our ALU, we are told that our sighting occurs after a series of add operations. Thus, it is likely that we do not need the logical subunit, so we should blackbox this for FPV purposes. So our first step is to blackbox the logical subunit and use FPV to try to cover the point. Here we create a cover point to look for cases where the *result* signal is seen without having resulted from a valid ALU uop:

```
c1: cover property (resultv&& !$past(uopv,ALU_DELAY));
```

When we run this cover point, FPV will quickly come back with a waveform that shows the blackboxed logical subunit generating a *logresultv* value of 1. This is because, as we have seen in previous chapters, when a unit is blackboxed, its outputs are freely generated by the FPV environment. This shows that we need to add an assumption to keep the blackboxed unit quiescent and avoid bogus traces. This is a common situation when we are blackboxing large parts of the logic while chasing a specific bug: rather than a pure blackbox, we need to make sure the ignored parts of the logic are not generating bogus traces that look like our bug but are unrealistic. Just as in regular FPV runs, you should expect a few iterations of wiggling as you fix your assumptions to avoid incorrect traces.

TIP 7.24

Just as in regular FPV, you will need several iterations of wiggling to get the assumptions right for post-silicon debug. Pay special attention to outputs from major parts of logic that you have blackboxed.

Now suppose we have made this fix and are attempting to run our cover point *c1* again, but hit an FPV complexity issue. We should take a closer look at other ways we can narrow the proof space that the FPV tool is examining. In particular, in this case we were told that a series of add operations is triggering the bug. This means that in addition to eliminating the logical subunit, we should also constrain the arithmetic subunit to only consider *OPADD* operations:

```
fv_overconstrain_add:
    assume property (Uopcode == OPADD);
```

While this might be too overconstraining for a general-purpose proof, again we need to keep in mind that we are trying to focus on a particular bug we have observed in the post-silicon lab. In general, we should not be afraid to add very specific assumptions to help narrow down the proof space to correspond to the bug we are chasing.

TIP 7.25

For post-silicon debug, do not be afraid to overconstrain the design to focus on specific values or behaviors related to the bug you are examining.

Once we have added this assumption, we are focusing more directly on our suspected bug. Now when we attempt the FPV proof on our cover point, we are much more likely to be able to see a real waveform that corresponds to our problem from the lab. Once we have reproduced this in an FPV environment, it will probably be very easy to find its root cause in the RTL logic.

THE PARADOX OF TOO MUCH INFORMATION

One tricky issue that is sometimes faced by those performing post-silicon FPV is the paradox of having much more information than is needed. For example, suppose our debug lab has sent us a set of scan traces from our ALU, showing the values of thousands of signals over the course of thousands of cycles. In theory, we could convert these to thousands of assumptions, in line with the principle above of overconstraining our design to focus on the bug. But will this help our FPV run?

Actually, adding large numbers of assumptions can often increase the complexity of the state space, reducing rather than increasing the efficiency of FPV. While a small number of assumptions can help to reduce the problem space, having lots of assumptions can make it a more computationally difficult problem to explore that smaller space. Since we are working with heuristics and provably complex problems, there are no hard-and-fast rules here, but in general, you should avoid converting a full scan dump into FPV assumptions.

Figure 7.10 illustrates this issue in an abstract way. The oval on the left represents the full behavioral space of a design. The one in the middle shows the space with a small, clean set of assumptions: for any given point, it is fairly easy to determine whether it is in the acceptable proof space. The one on the right illustrates the situation with a complex set of assumptions. While the overall legal proof space that must be analyzed may be smaller, it now is very complex to determine whether any given behavior is inside or outside the acceptable space, due to the irregular boundaries created by the large number of assumptions.

Thus, instead of blindly translating all your scan data to assumptions, use your scan dump as a source of information and just choose a handful of significant signals based on your knowledge of the most important parts of the design for your particular bug. For those signals that you have identified as important, use the scan dump values to create assumptions. It can be difficult when you do not know exactly where the bug is, but try to be sparing in your choice of significant signals, to avoid a complexity blowup due to assumption handling.

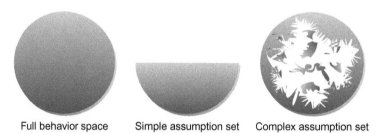

Full behavior space   Simple assumption set   Complex assumption set

FIGURE 7.10

Abstract view of behavior space with simple or complex assumption set.

USING SEMIFORMAL DESIGN EXPLORATION

One other important technique you are likely to make use of in post-silicon analysis is *semiformal* verification. This refers to the idea of running FV starting from a known active state, a "waypoint," rather than starting from a reset point. This makes the verification less general, but when trying to reproduce or hunt for bugs, can enable you to reach a bug much faster if the proper waypoints are chosen.

In the case of our ALU example, suppose we find that FPV always hits complexity issues after reaching a proof bound that encompasses two complete ADD operations. We can set our first waypoint to be a cover point indicating the completion of the first operation:

```
waypoint1: cover property ( resultv &&
    $past(uop,ALU_DELAY)==OP_ADD);
```

When we get a cover trace for this property, we can then save that and use it as the reset phase for our next FPV run. This means we will be doing a less general analysis that full FPV—starting from the trace of one particular completed ADD operation rather than a fully general one—but this may allow the formal engine to reach a depth where it has analyzed three ADD operations instead of just two.

In cases of greater complexity, it is often beneficial to define several waypoints: use FPV to cover the first one, then use the first waypoint to start an FPV run that reaches the second, and so on. For example, perhaps we might need to define a second waypoint, indicating the completion of the next ADD operation, in order to generate a run that reaches the bug on the ALU. On some models, the use of multiple waypoints can enable successful FPV bug hunting at a significantly greater depth than might initially seem feasible.

We will discuss semiformal verification in more detail in Chapter 10, where we describe many techniques for dealing with complexity. But we highlight it here because it is a method that has shown itself to be particularly valuable in the context of using FPV to analyze post-silicon bugs.

PROVING YOUR BUG FIXES CORRECT

Once you have successfully reproduced a post-silicon bug by generating a trace with FPV, you will hopefully be able to examine the RTL operations involved and come up with a bug fix. Then you will face another issue, similar to the diagnosis problem but with some important differences: proving the bug fix correct. This is actually one of the really powerful arguments for using FPV in post-silicon: the ability to not only replicate a bug, but to then prove that a proposed fix really fixes the bug, for traces more general than the particular one that triggered the initial issue. As you have probably seen if you have been involved in real-life post-silicon debug challenges, it is often the case that an initially proposed bug fix for a tough post-silicon issue will overlook some detail and not be a fully general fix.

The most obvious way to check the completeness of a bug fix is to load your modified RTL into the same FPV environment that you used to diagnose the bug and make sure it proves that your bug-related cover point can no longer be reached. This is an important sanity-check, and if the models you are using are very complex for FPV, or required techniques such as semiformal verification to enable a usable run, it may be the best you can do to gain confidence in the fix. But you should not stop at this point if you can avoid it.

Remember that for diagnosing the issue, we stressed the need to overconstrain the design to focus on the particular bug. But when trying to prove the bug fix fully general and correct, you need to reexamine the overconstraints, and make sure they were each truly necessary. For example, in our ALU model, we might ask ourselves:

- Can this only happen with addition ops?
- Does the logical subunit have a similar issue to the arithmetic one?

To answer these questions, we need to either remove some of the assumptions and blackboxes or create special-case FPV environments with a different set of assumptions to check the parts of the logic we skipped: check operations other than *OPADD*, or switch the blackbox to the arithmetic subunit while un-blackboxing the logical one.

> **TIP 7.28**
>
> Once you have a bug fix passing in a post-silicon FPV environment, review the overconstraints and blackboxing you did to get the initial diagnosis running. If possible, remove the extra constraints or add runs for other cases, to check that your bug fix is fully general.

Conceptually, it is often much easier to generalize an FPV environment than it would be to generalize a simulation environment, when trying to provide more complete checking of a proposed bug fix. The challenge is to recognize that you need to pay extra attention to this problem; after a grueling high-pressure post-silicon debug session, there is often an inclination to declare victory as soon as FPV first passes. FPV has a lot of power, but you must remember to use it correctly.

SUMMARY

As you have probably noticed, this chapter was a little different from the past few, in that it provided a grab bag of several different "apps" applicable at various phases of the SOC design and verification flow. We looked at methods that are applicable across the spectrum of SOC design, including:

- Reusable Protocol Verification: Creating a set of FPV-friendly properties for a common protocol that allows you to reuse verification collateral with confidence, and even to explore the protocol independently of any RTL implementation.
- UCE: Using FPV to help rule out impossible cover points in a primarily non-FPV validation environment.
- Connectivity Verification: Using FPV to ensure that the top-level connections, including possible MUXed or conditional connections, in an SOC model are working as intended.
- Control Register Verification: Using FPV to formally check that control registers are properly implemented according to their access specification.
- Post-Silicon Debug: Using FPV to reproduce inherently hard-to-reach bugs that were found in post-silicon, and to prove that proposed fixes are truly comprehensive enough to cover all cases.

As we mentioned at the beginning of the chapter, this is just a sampling, and we could have gone on to describe many more specific FPV applications. However, all these methods are circling around one central theme: you should think about FPV not as a specific point tool, but as a general toolkit for logically analyzing RTL models. This is equally true in block-level design and validation, full-chip SOC integration, or post-silicon debug. Regardless of your project phase or status, if you are in any situation where you need to logically verify or interact with RTL, you should be examining opportunities to use formal methods.

PRACTICAL TIPS FROM THIS CHAPTER

7.1 If using a well-defined protocol, check whether a set of protocol-related properties is available for purchase before investing a lot of effort into manually creating properties.

7.2 When representing aspects of a protocol that are constant for any given implementation, use a SystemVerilog parameter rather than a signal or variable.

7.3 When dealing with a two-way protocol, use parameters and macros to enable your properties to be either assertions or assumptions depending on the configuration.

7.4 When defining a reusable property set for a protocol, a critical step is to run a standalone self-checking environment on your property set, before integrating it with any RTL design models.

7.5 Create a good set of cover points for your reusable property set, just like you would in any FPV effort.

7.6 In any reusable property set, create redundant self-checking properties representing behaviors that should be true of the protocol, and use this to verify the consistency and correctness of the property set.

7.7 Remember that your protocol property set's self-consistency environment can also be a useful tool for experimenting with and learning about the behavior of the protocol, independently of any particular RTL design.

7.8 Define a set of annotations in your protocol specification that enable you to connect rules defined by your specification to assertions in your property module, and use scripts to find any potential holes.

7.9 If you have a project that is stressing simulation-based validation and failing to reach some of its cover points, a lightweight UCE FPV run can help eliminate some of them.

7.10 If doing a UCE FPV run on a model containing simulation-focused assertions, use your FPV tool's commands to convert assertions to assumptions for the FPV run.

7.11 If you are assembling a design that has conditional connections between top-level pins and numerous internal IPs, consider using FPV for connectivity verification.

7.12 When building a model for connectivity FPV, start by building your top-level chip with all submodules blackboxed, then un-blackbox the modules that participate in top-level connectivity selection and MUXing.

7.13 If you are having trouble compiling pad cells or getting reports of unexpected combinational loops during connectivity FPV, you may need to create a logical view of some of your pad cells.

7.14 If your connectivity FPV runs are slowed down by the logic that programs control registers, consider making those registers cut points and assuming them constant so you can focus on just checking the connectivity logic.

7.15 You may need to wiggle your first few attempts at connectivity FPV and add top-level assumptions or modify clock specifications, just like any other FPV effort.

7.16 Consider using FPV to verify that your control registers are all correctly read and written according to their specified access policies.

7.17 If using FPV to verify control registers, first check to see if this feature is offered natively by your FPV tool. If not, examine your company's specification for its control registers, and generate assertions related to each defined operation for each register type. Don't forget to include assertions both that correct operations succeed, and that incorrect operations do not modify the register value.

7.18 Run control register FPV at the level of some block that has a register-oriented interface with address, opcode, and data inputs/outputs, rather than including top-level decode logic.

7.19 Keep the control register FPV environment focused on this local block. Also remove any assumptions that constrained control registers for your full unit verification.

7.20 If registers in your design can be wider than a single address increment, or other forms of register aliasing are possible, be careful to account for this in your assertions.

7.21 If your register block has internal write paths that can modify registers without using the externally specified register interface, add assumptions that turn off these writes for control register FPV, or create reference models of the registers to use with your assertions.

7.22 Consider using FPV in cases where a post-silicon bug sighting is suspected to be a logic bug, especially if pre-silicon validation was simulation based. If your random simulations missed a bug, you probably need FPV's capability to back-solve for a set of inputs leading to a particular behavior.

7.23 When using FPV for post-silicon debug, in addition to the usual FPV complexity techniques, try to identify units/subunits unlikely to be involved in your particular bug and blackbox them. This may enable you to run FPV on a larger block than you could for general pre-silicon validation.

7.24 Just as in regular FPV, you will need several iterations of wiggling to get the assumptions right for post-silicon debug. Pay special attention to outputs from major parts of logic that you have blackboxed.

7.25 For post-silicon debug, do not be afraid to overconstrain the design to focus on specific values or behaviors related to the bug you are examining.

7.26 If you have large amounts of post-silicon data from a scan dump or similar source, choose a small number of significant signals to use for assumption generation, based on your knowledge of the design. Creating too many assumptions, such as by converting the full scan dump into an assumption set, can add rather than reduce FPV complexity.

7.27 If facing a complexity issue that prevents FPV from reaching the bound needed for a post-silicon bug, you should strongly consider defining some waypoints and using semiformal verification to resolve the issue.

7.28 Once you have a bug fix passing in a post-silicon FPV environment, review the overconstraints and blackboxing you did to get the initial diagnosis running. If possible, remove the extra constraints or add runs for other cases, to check that your bug fix is fully general.

FURTHER READING

[Ela14] Abdul Elaydi and Jose Barandiaran, "Leveraging Formal to Verify SoC Register Map," Design and Verification Conference (DVCon) 2014.

[Han13] Mark Handover and Kenny Ranerup, "Using Formal Verification to Exhaustively Verify SoC Assemblies," Design and Verification Conference (DVCon) 2013.

[Hot06] C. Richard Ho, Michael Theobald, Brannon Batson, J. P. Grossman, Stanley C. Wang, Joseph Gagliardo, Martin M. Deneroff, Ron O. Dror, and David E. Shaw, "Post-Silicon Debug Using Formal Verification Waypoints," Design Automation Conference (DAC) 2006.

[IEE09] Institute of Electrical and Electronics Engineers (IEEE), 1685–2009—IEEE Standard for IP-XACT, Standard Structure for Packaging, Integrating, and Reusing IP within Tools Flows.

[Job12] Barbara Jobstmann, "Leveraging Formal Verification Throughout the Entire Design Cycle," Design Verification Club 2012, http://www.testandverification.com/DVClub/21_Nov_2012/12%20-%20Jasper%20-%20Barbara%20Jobstmann%20(Speaker).pdf.

[Par09] S.B. Park, T. Hong, and S. Mitra, Post-Silicon Bug Localization in Processors Using Instruction Footprint Recording and Analysis (IFRA) IEEE Transactions on Computer Aided Design, Vol. 28, No. 10, 1545–1558, October 2009.

[Ray09] S. Ray and W. A. Hunt, Jr. "Connecting Pre-silicon and Post-silicon Verification," Formal Methods in Computer-Aided Design (FMCAD) 2009, Austin, TX, November 2009.

[Roy08] Subir K. Roy, "Top Level SOC Interconnectivity Verification Using Formal Techniques," Eighth International Workshop on Microprocessor Test and Verification, 2008.

[Sel11] E. Seligman, R. Adler, S. Krstic, and J. Yang, "CompMon: Ensuring Rigorous Protocol Specification and IP Compliance," Design and Verification Conference (DVCon) 2011, February 2011.

[Tho07] Gaurav Manoj Thottasseri, Gupta, and Mandar Munishwar, Developing Assertion IP for Formal Verification Design and Reuse, 2007, http://www.design-reuse.com/articles/20327/assertion-ip-formal-verification.html.

Formal equivalence verification

Formal combinational equivalence checking tools have become robust enough to be incorporated routinely into industrial methodologies.
—Randy Bryant and James Kukula

Now that we have explored various property-based formal verification (FV) methodologies, we are ready to discuss the equivalence aspect of FV, termed formal equivalence verification (FEV) or formal equivalence checking (FEC). To simplify the discussions throughout the chapter, we will consistently use FEV to refer to formal equivalence.

FEV can be broadly defined as comparing two models to determine whether they are equivalent. In general, we refer to the two models being compared as the specification (SPEC) model, and the implementation (IMP) model. Typically, the SPEC will be the more abstract model: it may be a register transfer level (RTL) model, an unoptimized schematic netlist, a reference model, or a description in a high-level modeling language. The IMP will usually be an equally or more concrete model for comparison: a more refined model, a new or updated RTL, or an optimized schematic netlist implementation.

The need for FEV can be seen as a natural outgrowth of the increased level of design abstraction as the industry has matured over the past half century. During the initial days of chip design (before 1980), the designers used to draw the circuits by hand and work at the transistor level. In the following decade (1981–1989), the drawing of such circuits was improved with the aid of computer-aided design (CAD), and circuit design became much simpler, but was not yet optimal. In these early days, very few practicing engineers thought about verifying their designs formally; the technology had not yet reached the level where such tools were possible for practical use.

The RTL mode of designing started around the early 1990s and is still the major mode of logic design as of this writing. With the advent of RTL, new tools were introduced to automatically synthesize the coded design into functional schematic netlists. This allowed the generation of much more complex netlists than were possible with previous methods, and necessitated good RTL-versus-netlist FEV tools. In the twenty-first century, the C/C++/SystemC mode of coding the design has begun to emerge, where the design is defined in the high-level language, and a new generation of synthesis tools can convert the high-level language to RTL and even to the netlist. Hence formal equivalence checks have become an even more important requirement to ensure that designs are faithfully translated across the different abstraction levels. Due to these various motivations, FEV is one of the most mature FV techniques; it is now considered a standard requirement to ensure the design intent is maintained as designers refine their abstractions into real designs.

In this chapter we explore the various equivalence techniques, look at their applications in the real world, and show how this requires a different style of interaction with the tools and with your design. In line with the emphasis of this book, we will be primarily discussing usages where at least one of the models is RTL. These are also the usage modes for which the most mature industry tools are available.

TYPES OF EQUIVALENCE TO CHECK

Before we begin a detailed discussion of FEV techniques, it is important to define what we mean by "equivalence." In a general sense, we define equivalence by choosing a set of *key points*, points in the two models being compared that are expected to be logically identical given the same set of input stimuli. FEV then consists of assuming the input key points receive identical values, and verifying that the logic cones driving the internal and output key points will then be equivalent in the two models. Depending on the equivalence checking technique being used, the key points may include:

- Primary inputs
- Primary outputs
- State elements (latches and flip-flops)
- Blackboxes
- Cut points

Figure 8.1 illustrates the general concept of key points and logic cone checking for FEV. The logic cones being compared are circled.

Derived from this basic concept, there are several major notions of equivalence that are commonly used by current EDA tools: combinational equivalence, sequential equivalence, and transactional equivalence.

COMBINATIONAL EQUIVALENCE

Combinational equivalence is the most mature FEV technique in the EDA industry; using this technique to compare RTL and schematic netlists is considered a requirement at most companies doing chip design. This is the primary

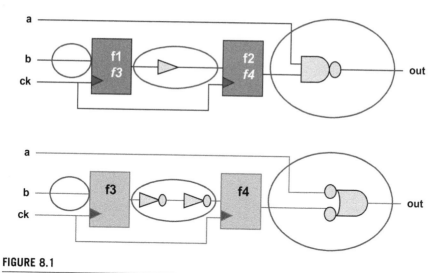

FIGURE 8.1

Key point mapping for FEV. Flop f1 maps to f3, and f2 maps to f4.

FEV technique used for state-matching models, where every state element (latch or flop) in the SPEC corresponds to a specific state element in the IMP. In this mode, two designs are claimed to be equivalent when all combinational logic between any pair of corresponding states are logically equivalent. In other words, there is a 1:1 correspondence between the state elements of the two models. Whenever the equivalence of a pair of state elements in the two models is checked, the tool uses the assumption that corresponding state elements in their fanin cones will contain identical values at all points in time. In effect, every latch or flop in the two designs is being treated as a cut point, with verification only encompassing the logic between the state elements.

This might seem like a huge limitation—but it arose in tandem with logic synthesis technology that has a similar structure. In other words, most EDA tools that synthesize netlists from RTL are also state-matching, guaranteeing (mostly) that each state element in the netlist will correspond to a state element in the RTL. In addition, the state-matching compromise makes the FEV problem much more tractable: FEV tools that use this method just need to analyze Boolean expressions, with no need to account for value changes over time. Thus, combinational FEV is the technique used in most RTL to netlist logic checkers today. If state elements are present, then not only are the outputs compared, but the logic cones driving each pair of corresponding states is checked individually. Since the RTL and netlist state elements directly correspond to each other, this check guarantees that the netlist is truly an implementation of the RTL.

As depicted in Table 8.1, the key points are comprised of the input-output interfaces and the internal state elements. The main points of comparison are the state elements *{F1, F3}* and *{F2, F4}* and the output *out*. As long as each of

Table 8.1 Key Point Mapping Table for Figure 8.1

Circuit A	Circuit B	Type
a, b, Ck	a, b, Ck	Input
F1	F3	Flop
F2	F4	Flop
Out	out	Output

the internal and output key points can be shown to have logically equivalent combinational driving cones in both models, we can confidently say that the models are equivalent.

TIP 8.1

If your design is comprised of simple combinational logic, or if there is a state-matching relation between the flops across two models you want to compare (as is the case when netlists are generated by most synthesis tools), a combinational FEV tool will probably be the most efficient way to prove equivalence.

You can probably think of some major limitations of this type of equivalence. For example, what happens if you want the implementation to recode a finite-state machine (FSM), using a different set of intermediate states to ultimately generate the same output? The application of combinational equivalence to FSMs is limited to comparing models that have equivalent sets of state elements. If this condition is not met, the combinational FEV tool will report the two models as nonequivalent. As we will see later in this chapter, modern RTL-netlist FEV tools do have some clever optimizations for very simple cases of non-state-matching, such as flop replication or constant propagation. But in general, the state-preserving requirement is a stringent one, and there are many FEV scenarios in which it must be relaxed for effective verification.

SEQUENTIAL EQUIVALENCE

Sequential equivalence is also referred to as *cycle-accurate equivalence* by some vendors. With sequential FEV tools, we ask the question of whether two models will ultimately generate the same outputs at the same times based on an equivalent set of inputs, without requiring that internal state elements fully correspond. Thus, sequential FEV tools can handle cases like the recoded FSM described above.

In general terms, sequential FEV can be considered equivalent to the formal property verification (FPV) we discussed in Chapter 6, with the SPEC being equivalent to a large reference model. Instead of asking the question, "Is the property *RTL model output* $==$ *reference model output* always true?" we ask the similar question, "Is the RTL model always equivalent to the reference model?" In fact, because good commercial sequential FEV tools have only appeared on the market very recently, it was common for many years for engineers to use FPV tools as simple sequential FEV tools in this way. They would create an enclosing module with both the SPEC and IMP model inside, create assertions that the outputs are equivalent, and run a standard FPV tool. However, now that there are tools available that specialize in sequential FEV, if you do have a reference model that is complete enough that you can just check equivalence instead of needing to write properties, it is usually better to use sequential FEV. This method can take advantage of engine improvements targeted at equivalence checking.

TIP 8.2

If you have both FPV and sequential FEV tools available, you should usually use the sequential FEV tools when trying to solve a non-state-matching model equivalence problem.

Unlike combinational checkers, sequential equivalence checkers can verify designs with common functionality despite differences in:

- State Representation
- Pipeline depth
- Interface timing and protocols
- Resource scheduling and allocation
- Differences in data types
- Clock gating and other power-saving features

For example, when using sequential FEV, one of the designs under comparison might be a pipelined version of the other. We could prove the equivalence of the pure behavioral model of RTL to the complete pipeline implementation, and satisfy ourselves that they do indeed implement equivalent functionality. One common application of this methodology is during the equivalence check of an unpipelined and pipelined model in RTL. In the simplest case of comparison, one can assume that the same input patterns are applied to the corresponding inputs of both the designs, and the outputs are compared with some known delay after the RTL pipeline is completely filled.

TRANSACTION-BASED EQUIVALENCE

This is another variant of sequential FEV. In some cases, one model will be highly abstract compared to the other, and its outputs will generally not match cycle-by-cycle, except for certain well-defined transactions. This means we need a looser notion of equivalence, based on checking that legal transactions are handled equivalently. The equivalence can be after a fixed number of RTL clock cycles, which could signify the transaction, or a completely unpredictable number based on the transaction completion. Hence, this notion is more generic and is a superset of all the equivalence modes: models that are not combinationally or sequentially equivalent may still be able to demonstrate transaction-based equivalence.

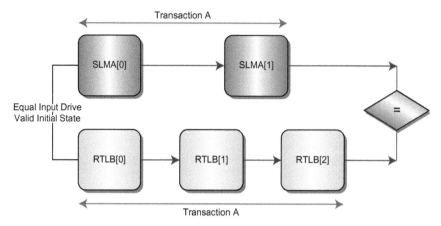

FIGURE 8.2

Transaction-based equivalence check.

Figure 8.2 illustrates a high-level view of a transaction-based equivalence check. To further clarify what FEV is doing, let's examine a conceptual view of the "transaction space" of a typical design.

This notion of equivalence is quite general and encompasses the previous notions of equivalence described in this section. This model of equivalence:

- Does not assume that the amount of time (or the number of state transitions) required to complete one transaction will be the same for the RTL and the system-level design (SLM).
- Denotes the end of a transaction by either a fixed number of RTL cycles or some kind of "data ready" handshaking protocol.
- Assumes the user is able to specify a set of initial states (a partial assignment of values to the state-holding elements) for both the RTL and system-level design, which represents the model state at the start of a valid transaction.
- Assumes the user is able to specify a set of states for both designs that correspond to the end of a transaction.

At the end of a transaction, the outputs of the two designs are compared and a check is made to ensure the ending state of both designs still satisfies the state invariants and constraints. Thus, this form of verification can handle cases where changes in the design abstraction level have only preserved behavior for certain well-defined transactions, rather than following the more stringent matching requirements of sequential FEV.

TIP 8.3

If a design change involves complex sequential changes that are beyond the capability of your sequential FEV tool, you may be able to verify it with transaction-based FEV.

Transaction-based FEV tools are a relatively new style of FV, and not very mature in the EDA marketplace as of this writing, so the usage details discussed in the remainder of the chapter will primarily focus on combinational and sequential FEV.

FEV USE CASES

The two types of FEV flows that currently have the most mature tools available in the EDA industry are RTL to netlist FEV, and RTL to RTL FEV, so we will focus on those.

RTL TO NETLIST FEV

Logic synthesis, a process by which an RTL model of a design is automatically turned into a transistor-level schematic netlist by a standard EDA tool, has been a mature process in the industry for almost two decades. However, logic synthesis as a process is prone to bugs. There are too many transformations happening that can alter the netlist in the wrong manner and make it define functionality other than what was intended in the original RTL. These bugs may be the result of erroneous or incomplete user instructions to the synthesis tools, ambiguities and misunderstandings of SystemVerilog or other RTL languages, wrongly documented design libraries or components, or occasional errors in the synthesis tools themselves. Thus, nearly everyone doing logic synthesis these days uses (or should be using!) a combinational FEV tool to check that their RTL matches their netlist.

Let's look at how this form of equivalence works, looking at the example from Figure 8.1 again, reproduced below for convenience. You can see that both circuits compute the NAND of input a with the value input b had two cycles earlier, though the details of the gates used differ slightly (Figure 8.3).

The first step in establishing equivalence is to map all the key points between the two circuits. The inputs of the two circuits are mapped in such a way that they are driven by the same variables and values for the analysis. The outputs of the two circuits would have to be equal formally. Then, since this is combinational FEV, we need to map all state elements of the design. The total mapping list for this example is shown in Table 8.2.

Most combinational FEV tools have auto-mapping facilities where the key points across two designs are automatically mapped, including the interface signals, internal state elements, and any blackboxes. This is usually based on a combination of matching the names, and heuristics such as looking for internal logic cones with a corresponding set of inputs.

Once the mappings are complete, the FEV tool needs to perform the actual verification. To do this, it computes the Boolean equations describing the values of each noninput key point, and compares to check that corresponding key points

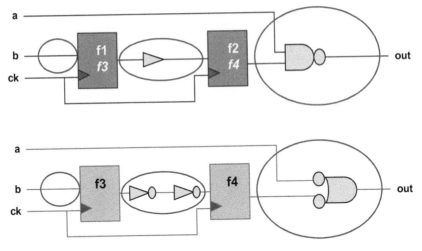

FIGURE 8.3

Reviewing the example in Figure 8.1.

Table 8.2 Mapping List for Example Circuit

Circuit A	Circuit B	Type
a, b, Ck	a, b, Ck	Input
F1	F3	Flop
F2	F4	Flop
Out	out	Output

Table 8.3 Equivalence Results for Example Circuit

Circuit A	Circuit B	Type	Status
a, b, Ck	a, b, Ck	Input	Mapped
F1 = b	F3 = b	Flop	Match
F2 = F1	F4 = F3	Flop	Match
out = !(a & F2)	out = !a || !F4	Output	Match

have equivalent equations. As you can see in Table 8.3, in this example all signals match; even though the equations for the *out* signal look slightly different, they are logically equivalent after substituting the corresponding mapped nodes and expanding using DeMorgan's laws. Of course, most real FEV tools would not put the Boolean value expressions directly in the result table, since on realistic models they are gigantic and ugly. Such expressions can usually be viewed using a user command though.

When doing RTL-netlist FEV, there are a number of basic complications that arise due to the nature of synthesized netlists, which are different from RTL in several subtle ways. They tend to be based on established cell libraries, and contain some non-logic-changing transformations that are perfectly safe, but technically break the state-matching paradigm. Modern FEV tools can handle these complications easily in most cases, but occasionally may require some user guidance or specific directives to look for certain types of optimizations.

RTL TO RTL FEV

There are many cases when it is useful to be able to compare two RTL models. The ability to formally determine functional equivalence between RTL models is a key enabler in physically aware front-end design methodologies that are being practiced in high-performance designs. Cases such as parameterization, timing fixes, pipeline optimizations, clock gating, and "chicken bit" verification can all be checked exhaustively using FEV tools, providing much better overall confidence than older simulation-based methods.

Parameterization

Parameterization is the process of inserting the parameters necessary for a complete or relevant specification of a design. Most legacy designs include RTL that originally hard-codes the parameters such as data widths, maximum message sizes, or number of threads. As new projects plan on the usage of the design in various configurations, the design team needs to insert parameter options in place of the RTL constants; this often makes designers very nervous about maintaining overall correctness, since such a replacement can touch hundreds of individual files. As an example, Figure 8.4 shows the many proliferations of a family of graphic designs targeted at a wide variety of markets. An obvious verification strategy for this kind of problem is to run FEV on the design, with the non-parameterized code as the SPEC and the parameterized code, with the default parameters, as the IMP.

In most cases, this can be handled by a combinational FEV tool, though you may need to use sequential FEV in cases where your parameterization is accompanied by related structural changes in the state elements.

TIP 8.4

If you are replacing constants with parameters in an RTL model, you should make use of a combinational or sequential FEV tool to ensure that you have not altered the logic.

Timing fixes—logic redistribution

Fixing critical timing paths is one of the more time-consuming activities for any synchronous design. One of the regularly used solutions for fixing critical

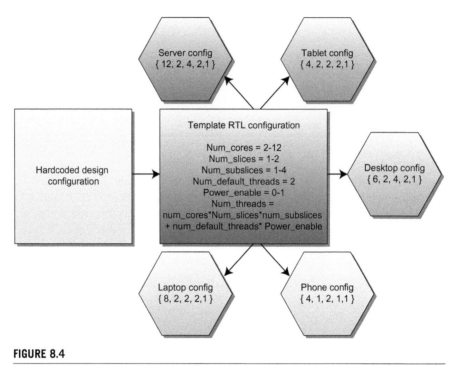

FIGURE 8.4

Parameterization of common code catering to different configurations.

paths is to redistribute the logic across the different pipeline stages. Studies suggest that a significant number of unintentional functional bugs are introduced while fixing timing issues. These kinds of failure scenarios could be easily avoided by running FV, making sure the design retains its sanity irrespective of the logic redistribution across pipelines.

As shown in Figure 8.5, there is a huge combinational path in between the first and second flops that would be redistributed to fix the violation, by moving some of the logic past the second flop. The same outputs would ultimately be generated, but the intermediate value of this internal flop would occur at a different stage of the computation. These two designs would no longer be state-matching: while they might have the same number of flops, the functionality of the flops would differ due to the redistribution of logic in the pipelines. Thus, sequential FEV is the preferred tool for this kind of checking.

TIP 8.5

If redistributing logic across pipe stages in RTL, use a sequential FEV tool to ensure that you have not altered the logic.

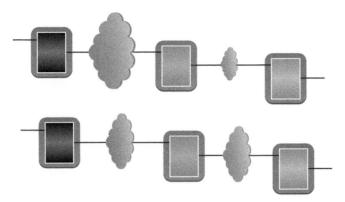

FIGURE 8.5

Timing fixes—redistribution of logic across stages.

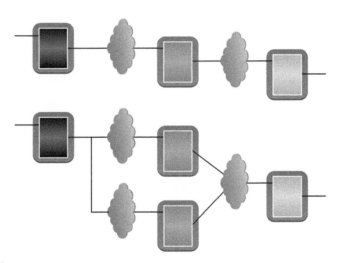

FIGURE 8.6

Timing fixes—critical path reduction.

Timing fixes—critical path reduction

Where modifying pipe stages is not a viable option, designers often bifurcate the computation logic and redirect some of it through a parallel flop path as shown in Figure 8.6.

While some commercial combinational FEV tools can intelligently handle these kinds of cases, sometimes user intervention is required for proper analysis. Sequential FEV tends to perform better in these kinds of scenarios.

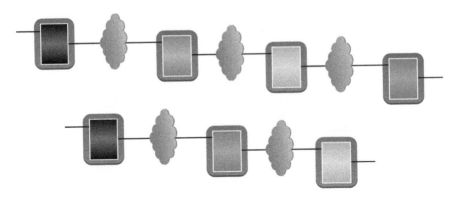

FIGURE 8.7

Re-pipelining optimizations.

> **TIP 8.6**
>
> When splitting a pipeline into parallel paths for timing reasons, use a combinational or sequential FEV tool to ensure you did not alter the logic. Sequential FEV tools are more likely to be able to handle these cases.

Pipeline optimizations

As manufacturing processes, algorithms, and implementation methodologies mature over time, designers often spot opportunities to reduce the depth of a pipeline. However, sometimes timing fixes and other algorithm requirements may require an addition of an extra pipeline stage while retaining the functionality.

Depending on the case of re-pipelining optimization, one of the design portions of Figure 8.7 can be considered as the specification and the other as the implementation. The set of states has changed, but the end-to-end functionality remains unperturbed; hence, some form of FEV should be used to verify this change. The equivalence check would necessitate defining the latency differences between the two models. If it is a simple difference, a sequential FEV tool should be able to verify this change, though if the change is complex a transaction-based FEV tool might be required.

> **TIP 8.7**
>
> If changing the length of a pipeline while preserving functionality, use a sequential or transaction-based FEV tool to verify that you have not altered the logic.

Chicken bit validation

Chicken bits, also known by the less colorful term *defeature bits*, are extra control signals exposed to the driver to disable a feature in silicon. They are used to provide the ability to "chicken out" of design changes made where confidence is not

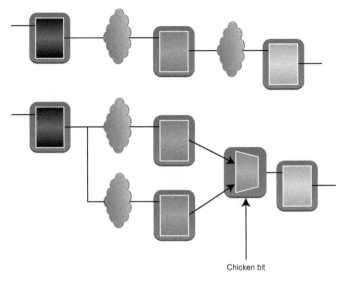

Chicken bit

FIGURE 8.8

Chicken bit verification.

high; this often happens when fixing a bug very late in a project, or when a critical new feature is added at the last minute. Most fixes to stable designs these days do implement chicken bits, and many bugs result when they unintentionally affect other functionality. Validation of a chicken bit can be challenging, because disabling a feature is often as intrusive in the code as the feature itself.

Figure 8.8 illustrates a typical implementation of a chicken bit, where the new bit feeds a MUX that selects between old and new implementations of the logic leading to a particular flop.

One way to guarantee the correctness of the design changes is to run FEV of the earlier design against the current design in question with the new functionality disabled. Sometimes this can be done with a combinational FEV tool, but in cases where the change spans logic across multiple state elements, sequential FEV is often required.

TIP 8.8

If inserting a chicken bit to disable some new functionality, run combinational or sequential FEV of the old logic versus the new logic with the chicken bit turned on, to check that when the new functionality is disabled, the design behavior truly matches the original design.

Clock gating verification

One of the most commonly used low-power techniques in modern designs is clock gating, features that turn off the clock in certain cases to avoid toggling unused logic, thus reducing the overall power consumption. It is critical to implement this feature correctly for data integrity. If the clock is not shut down properly for a piece of logic, improper state signal values and signal glitches can propagate and lead to data corruption. The default simulation-based verification strategy for a clock-gated design is to run the golden regression test suite on both the pre-clock-gated design and the post-clock-gated design, with the assumption that the golden test suite exercises all corner cases when clocks would be gated. However, this assumption is not always true. Coverage of the corner cases is always challenging because the existing suite might not expose all scenarios: if there are k clock domains in a model with clock gating, simulation-based validation could require simulation of 2^k possible gating configurations. The best strategy is to use sequential FEV tools for RTL vs. RTL comparison, with clock gating turned off in one copy of the RTL and turned on in the other: proving the two models equivalent shows that clock gating does not change any design behavior. Due to the heavy interaction of clock gating with the design of the state elements, sequential FEV is usually much more successful than combinational FEV for this type of verification.

TIP 8.9

If inserting clock gating into a design, use sequential FEV to compare the design with clock gating on and off, to ensure that the clock gating has not altered the logic.

RUNNING FEV

There are a number of common aspects of FEV that you will deal with in most combinational or sequential FEV runs. You must start by choosing the models to compare, with your selection of SPEC and IMP models defining your main verification task. You must deal with key point mapping; this is a must for combinational FEV, and can save you significant effort in sequential FEV. You may need to define some assumptions and constraints, though this tends to be less effort in FEV than in FPV. Finally, you must debug any mismatches reported by your FEV tool.

CHOOSING THE MODELS

This may seem like a fairly obvious necessity: before you verify something, you need to know what you are trying to verify. In the case of FEV, you need to choose a SPEC and IMP model to compare. Depending on the phase of your project and your motivation for FEV, however, there may be some factors you should consider before deciding on this.

Which models to verify?

If you are trying to compare two RTL models or two netlist models after an implementation change, bug fix, or insertion of a feature that should not change existing functionality, the choice of SPEC and IMP is fairly clear: the old model should be the SPEC, and the new model should be the IMP.

In the case of verifying the correctness of synthesis, however, you have a wider degree of freedom. Usually the process of synthesizing a netlist from an RTL model proceeds in several stages. For example, your project's synthesis process may look like this:

1. *Original RTL*: The RTL model that your design team has provided.
2. *Pre-Synthesis Elaboration*: A Verilog representation of your elaborated RTL, with modules uniquified and various user synthesis directives applied.
3. *Unoptimized Netlist*: The first netlist representation, logically implementing your RTL but with no backend considerations taken into account.
4. *Timing-Optimized Netlist*: A netlist with optimizations applied to meet timing requirements.
5. *Scan-Inserted Netlist:* A netlist where scan and debug functionality has been inserted.
6. *Power-Optimized Netlist*: A further refinement to add isolation and retention cells, and other power considerations.

At first, it might appear that the simplest process is to just run FEV of your starting RTL against the final power-optimized netlist. This may work fine, but there are many cases where this end-to-end process could run into complexity issues. While these can be addressed using many standard formal complexity techniques, as we will discuss later in this chapter, the simplest choice might be to split the verification: verify the RTL against one of the intermediate netlists, and then verify that netlist against the final one. We have often seen cases where the full end-to-end run creates a major complexity issue, while adding an intermediate stage and splitting the effort into two runs results in very efficient execution.

If running RTL-RTL FEV to verify a bug fix, re-pipelining, clock gating, or similar scenarios, you may have to think about similar considerations. Are you trying to verify a bunch of changes at once, or can you get intermediate versions of the RTL where one major type of change exists in each version? If you can verify your changes in smaller stages instead of doing one full end-to-end run, this may save you from many complexity challenges.

Cell libraries

A cell is a transistor-level design that implements a basic logic function, such as AND gates, flip-flops, or multiplexers. Modern synthesis tools build their netlists from a cell library, rather than directly generating a transistor-level model. Cells hide the transistor-level logic and are delivered with behavioral descriptions and a logical Verilog that can be used when verifying the design in an FEV tool.

The library providers certify the correctness of the cell behavior. To verify this at the library level, they either use specialized FEV tools that can analyze a transistor-level cell model and derive the intended logic (not discussed further in this book due to our RTL focus), or run transistor-level circuit simulations in Spice or a similar tool.

A common mistake made by naive FEV users when comparing RTL to netlists, or when doing netlist-netlist comparisons, is to include the full transistor-level models of the library cells, and try to verify these complete netlist models. This results in a huge complexity blowup, and often creates extra confusing key points based on internal cell implementation details.

TIP 8.10

If doing RTL-netlist FEV, make sure you are using a released cell library with verified behavioral specifications, and loading the behavioral representation of your cell library.

KEY POINT SELECTION AND MAPPING

The next major element of setting up an FEV environment is the idea of key point mapping. As we have discussed in previous sections, an FEV key point is similar to the FPV notion of a *cut point*. It is a point known to correspond in your SPEC and IMP designs, so the FEV tool can optimize by proving that this point is equivalent in the SPEC and IMP logic, and then assume this equivalence is true instead of re-proving it when analyzing downstream logic. By using these key points, an FEV tool can significantly reduce the amount of logic it needs to verify at once. In addition to internal cut points, we usually also label primary inputs and outputs of the model as key points, since establishing the correspondence between the inputs and outputs of both models is critical to defining the equivalence verification task.

The simplest type of key point selection is the use of all latches and flops as key points, a major optimization that has enabled high-confidence combinational FEV of RTL against synthesized netlists. This takes advantage of the expectation that synthesis tools will be largely state-preserving when creating netlists from RTL, so we can confidently expect that state elements in the RTL will have corresponding state elements in the netlist. This then means that only the logic clouds between these key points need to be compared to prove equivalence. Figure 8.9 again reviews the partitioning of logic by key points in a simple pair of designs, with the FEV tool only needing to compare the circled combinational clouds in the SPEC and IMP to prove equivalence.

In a sequential equivalence tool, the only guaranteed key points are the model inputs and outputs. However, providing internal key points can significantly improve the efficiency of such tools, and often make a previously infeasible

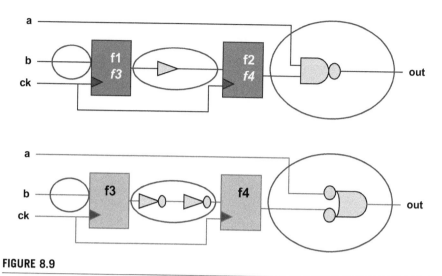

FIGURE 8.9

Key point mapping for FEV. Flop f1 maps to f3, and f2 maps to f4.

equivalence problem solvable. So if you are running sequential equivalence, you should think about potential key points to define, especially if you are trying to verify changes to one small region of a model where the SPEC and IMP are mostly state-matching.

Defining the mappings

In many cases, while a combinational FEV tool does its best to automatically determine all the mapping between corresponding SPEC and IMP key points in a state-matching design, there will still be a few that it misses. Perhaps the naming convention used by your synthesis tool managed to confuse the FEV tool's mapping algorithm, or someone made a hand edit to the netlist and gave arbitrary names to some of the nodes. You may also be working with a sequential FEV tool, where initially it is not mapping internal nodes by default, but you have identified a large class of corresponding points that you want the tool to map.

To handle these situations, FEV tools provide the ability to specify mapping rules, regular expressions that tell the tool how to transform SPEC signal names to match the IMP ones. For example, you might have a synthesis tool that changes array references in brackets to use double underscores to separate the index: *foo[12]* in the RTL might become *foo__12__* in the netlist. To enable mappings between these equivalent nodes with slightly different names, you could provide directives to your FEV tool something like this:

```
add map rule [ __
add map rule ] __
```

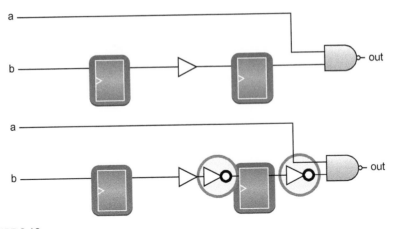

FIGURE 8.10

State negation.

State negation

A common synthesis optimization that can break state-matching is state negation, where a signal is inverted at the inputs and outputs of a flip-flop for timing reasons. Figure 8.10 shows an example of this optimization, where we have two equivalent designs, but added inversions before and after the lower right flop in the second one. This means the value in that flop for the IMP model will be negated with respect to the corresponding SPEC flop above, even though the output *out* will ultimately be the same.

To support this methodology, modern combinational FEV tools are smart enough to accommodate such state negations. This is usually handled with a *negated mapping*, where instead of mapping point A in one model to point B in the other, A is mapped to $\sim B$. Some FEV tools can automatically discover these and create these inverted mappings, but there are cases where the user needs to specify the inversions. You need to look for cases where the FEV proof results include mismatching state elements that seem to have logic off by a single inversion, as viewed in a debugger, and consider these cases as candidates for inversion mapping.

Note that it is safe to mark a state key point as a negated mapping even if you are not sure—any wrong inversion will be detected in the downstream logic, and result in an FEV mismatch that you will need to debug. This does not apply to primary inputs our outputs however; you need to be very careful when selecting these points for negated mappings, since their input cone (for inputs) or output cone (for outputs) is not visible in the current FEV run.

TIP 8.11

If an internal signal mismatches in RTL-netlist FEV and seems to be off by a single inversion, it is a good candidate for negated mapping. Do not put such mappings on primary input our output signals, however, unless you are very sure that the negated mapping is correct.

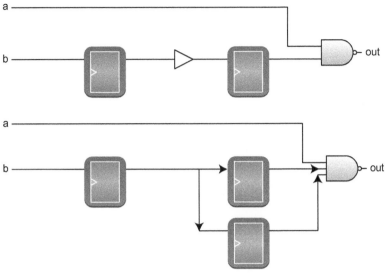

FIGURE 8.11

State replication.

State replication

Certain timing fixes commonly inserted by synthesis tools require *state replication*, where one flip-flop is replaced by a set of equivalent flip-flops. This kind of change may also be manually inserted into netlists during the late phases of design, to fix timing without touching RTL. Figure 8.11 illustrates a typical example.

This is another case that can usually be automatically inferred by a good FEV tool during key point mapping, but may require user directives or hints in some cases. If you see leftover key points in your netlist that are not mapped to anything after the mapping phase, check whether some of them may be due to cases of state replication.

> **TIP 8.12**
>
> If extra netlist flip-flops are left unmapped by the mapping phase of RTL-netlist FEV, check to see if some of them may be cases of state replication.

Unreachable points

One other complication you are likely to encounter when setting up key point mapping is the concept of *unreachable points*. An unreachable point is a state element that cannot logically affect any output of the design. These often appear in an RTL model as a result of disabled or removed features, or parts of reused code that are no longer relevant. They may also appear in netlists as a result of a synthesis tool inserting some standard library component in which only a part of its functionality is used. Since combinational FEV breaks up the logic at all state elements, these unreachable points are identified as key points as in the rest of the design, and may result in reports of unmapped key points. Most modern FEV tools can identify unreachable points, and enable users to exempt them from mapping and verification.

However, there are certain cases where you will want to keep the unreachable points in your design and ensure that their equivalence is verified. Before blindly turning on tool options to ignore unreachable points, check that you are not dealing with any of the following cases:

- *Bonus logic.* These are extra logic cells that are not currently used, but are expected to be included in the design in case they are needed for last-minute or post-silicon logic fixes.
- *Scan, power, or other special-purpose functionality.* You may have pieces of RTL that appear to be disconnected from the rest of the logic, but will become connected after some later step like scan or power feature insertion. You need to make sure to include such logic in FEV, so it is not lost from your design.

TIP 8.13

Review the set of unreachable points reported by your RTL-netlist FEV tool, and make sure they are included in your key point mappings and verified if they represent logic you want to see in the netlist, such as bonus cells, scan, or power.

Delayed and conditional mappings

Most of the mapping complications we have discussed above are primarily issues in combinational FEV runs, when doing a state-matching comparison between RTL and netlists. But if performing sequential FEV, you need to think about a somewhat different set of mapping complications. Most commonly, an output key point of your IMP model may not always be expected to precisely match the corresponding output of your SPEC model.

There is often some delay between the outputs of the models. This will happen, for example, if comparing a non-pipelined and a pipelined model, or two pipelined models with different sets of stages. Your FEV tool will probably provide a way for you to specify some kind of delayed mapping, where outputs are supposed to correspond after some delay determined by the pipeline depth.

Similarly, there may also be a need for conditional mapping. For example, it may be the case that when there is a valid operation, the outputs of your SPEC and IMP correspond; but when the operation is not valid, there is no need to enforce equivalence. Again, your FEV tool should provide a way to incorporate this issue into your mappings.

> ### TIP 8.14
>
> If running sequential FEV in cases where pipeline depth or other delays or qualifying conditions may vary between the SPEC and the IMP, be sure to think about using delayed or conditional mappings on your outputs.

Debugging mapping failures

It may often be the case that after you have done your best to account for all the issues described above in an RTL-netlist FEV run, you may still have a handful of unmapped points in the SPEC and the IMP with no obvious name correspondence to something in the other model. If you are stumped about the proper mappings for some internal points, try verifying the equivalence of some of the points that are successfully mapped. When looking at the counterexamples your FEV tool generates for the failures, examine any differences in the input cones on the two sides carefully. You may see failures that result from a small set of unmapped points in each of the input cones of the mapped points—which might be a good hint as to the mappings needed.

> ### TIP 8.15
>
> If having trouble mapping all your key points, first look for root causes related to typical synthesis netlist optimizations or unreachable points. Then look for name-based correspondence, and consider running partial verification on nearby points that are mapped to get some better hints.

ASSUMPTIONS AND CONSTRAINTS

In general, assumptions and constraints are not nearly as much of a challenge in an FEV context as they are in FPV. This is because a very large and important class of starting assumptions is implicitly created by the key point mapping process: the assumption that corresponding key points at the inputs of any logic cone are equivalent in the SPEC and IMP models. Often these will be all the assumptions you need in order to prove equivalence. However, there are a few cases where other assumptions or constraints will likely be necessary.

Removing some functionality

As we saw in our discussion of chicken bit verification and clock gating verification above, there are often cases where the main point of the FEV run is to check that when some piece of new or modified functionality is removed, the two models are otherwise equivalent. To perform the desired removal within one of the models, you can usually use an SVA assumption, or a tool directive. For example, if a pin called

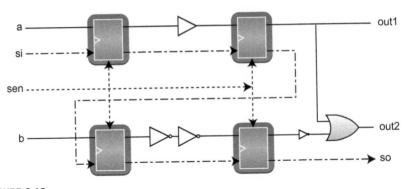

FIGURE 8.12

Scan insertion. Scan (si/sen/so) paths are not represented in RTL.

defeature controls whether some new feature is active, you may need to add an assumption like

```
fev_feature_off: assume property (defeature == 1);
```

Scan (and other netlist-only feature) insertion

A common feature of modern hardware designs is implementation of scan chains during synthesis. This is sometimes also referred to as *design for testability*, or DFT. A scan chain, a long serial path to enable the export of arbitrary internal states to a small set of pins, is needed to enable observation of internal states of the design and is very critical for post-silicon debug. Due to the nature of scan chains, the order of the states is highly dependent on the ultimate layout of the design, independent of the logical RTL hierarchy. Thus, scan chains would be difficult to represent in RTL, and most synthesis tools automatically insert the scan chains during synthesis. Figure 8.12 illustrates a typical scenario of scan chain insertion.

Since scan logic is not represented in the RTL but is present in the netlist, it must be disabled when checking RTL-netlist equivalence. Usually there is a simple top-level mechanism to disable scan, such as the *sen* signal in the example in Figure 8.12; most likely, telling your FEV tool to hold this at a constant 0 will shut off scan.

```
fev_scan_off: assume property (sen == 0);
```

If you see lots of logic mismatches that involve signals with scan-related or DFT-related names in your first FEV attempt, you probably forgot to do this. You need to identify the scan condition and give the proper assumption or directive to your FEV tool to disable it. You then also need to be careful that your scan chain is verified through other means, since it cannot be properly handled by RTL-netlist FEV.

TIP 8.16

If you see lots of mismatches in RTL-netlist FEV that involve signals with scan or DFT-related names, check that you properly disabled scan for your model.

We should also point out that the scan issue can be seen as a specific case of a more general issue, the use of aspect-oriented programming (AOP) with RTL. AOP is the general concept, originally from the software world, of having an external specification of some "aspect" of the RTL, such as scan, power, or debug, which is not directly represented in the logic. These aspect-based behaviors are expected to be part of the final design, often through automatic insertion into the RTL or netlist during some stage of synthesis. In any such case, you need to be careful that you exercise available mechanisms to inform your tools when such aspects are or are not included, and find a way to turn them off when comparing aspect-inserted and non-aspect-inserted models, or to insert them equivalently. Some current FEV tools have features to directly support various AOP cases, such as the insertion of power-related features through Universal Power Format (UPF) files, and verify that models with and without the aspect insertion are equivalent. In general, you should carefully look at any design flows that insert logic at the netlist level, and consider whether they represent AOP cases similar to scan that require special FEV handling.

DEBUGGING MISMATCHES

As you probably expect, most engineering time you will spend on FEV is to debug cases where the tool reports that your two models are mismatching; the logic driving a particular pair of mapped flip-flops or outputs differs between the SPEC and IMP. Most tools provide schematic or waveform views for debug, and naive FEVers often make the mistake of quickly getting lost staring at these views and tracing logic differences. When beginning to debug your FEV mismatches, you should start by looking at the following:

- *Sort by cone size.* The logic cones of your failing compare points can significantly vary by complexity: there may be some very simple ones where you can fully comprehend the logic view at a glance, and complex ones that have hundreds of nodes. Your FEV tool should enable you to sort the failures by cone size. Your debug will usually be much more productive if you start with the smallest.
- *Check the fanin cone differences.* Most tools provide a way to get a list of the key points in the fanin cones. If a pair of corresponding nodes differ, and have different key points in their fanins, that is an important hint about the root cause of the difference. There may be mapping issues at some of those fanin points—perhaps a poorly written regular expression in your mapping rules has set the wrong pairs as corresponding. Or the key point difference may indicate

a crucial piece of missing logic, such as scan, that either needs to be ignored (as discussed above), or was incorrectly synthesized and indicates a real bug.

- *Look for common themes.* If you have a lot of failures, and are not able to find any obvious problems when looking at the fanin of the first one, look at several of them and see if there is a pattern: for example, do all the failures happen to have some small set of signals in the fanin cones? Again, this may indicate a handful of signals that were incorrectly mapped, or a crucial piece of noncorresponding functionality that you should have been ignoring.
- *Check for inverse mappings.* If you have pairs of nodes with identical fanin cones and similar logic, but precisely opposite values, consider whether this may be a case of state negation, where you need to specify an inverse mapping.

Once you have tried all the above methods, you are probably ready to start looking at the more detailed debug views from your FEV tool. Remember to start by looking at the mismatches with the smallest cones first.

TIP 8.17

When debugging FEV mismatches, first sort them by the cone size, and start with the simplest. Then check for fanin cone differences, look for common themes, and check for inverse mappings. After this, start using your FEV tool's more advanced debug features, but be sure to look at the smallest cones first.

We should also point out that debugging will change depending on the type of formal equivalence you are checking. The above issues apply in general to both combinational and sequential FEV. When using a sequential FEV tool, however, there are a few other issues to consider, such as being sure you have checked the possible need for delayed or conditional mappings, as described in the key point mapping subsection above. In addition, sequential FEV runs will often encounter failures that relate to multicycle behaviors. You should still start by looking at the issues above, but in most cases, the debug techniques you use for the trickiest differences will be similar to the FPV debug discussed in previous chapters.

ADDITIONAL FEV CHALLENGES

Aside from the basic issues in setting up and running FEV described above, there are a few additional wrinkles that you may face when trying to run FEV on your designs in practice.

LATCH/FLOP OPTIMIZATIONS

One complication that often occurs when verifying RTL models against synthesized netlists is that the tools could optimize some of the designs during the synthesis, breaking the strictly state-matching paradigm. Fortunately, many of

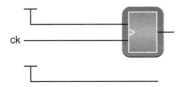

FIGURE 8.13

A constant-driven state element equivalent to direct connection.

these common optimizations can be handled in combinational FEV tools through simple "remodeling" heuristics, essentially hacking the internal representation in a logically sound way to restore the state-matching. Figure 8.13 shows a simple example of a constant propagation, where a flop with a constant driver is replaced with a simple constant, which reduces the gate count without altering functionality.

Most combinational FEV tools can automatically detect and handle this kind of simple optimization. Some other examples of such optimized comparisons are

1. Latch folding: combining two adjacent latches into an equivalent flip-flop.
2. Exploiting transparency: if a latch is clocked with a constant 1, treat as a buffer.
3. Feedback loops: Treating a flop as a latch in some cases, if its data feeds back directly to its input.

In general, if your synthesis flow performed these optimizations but you did not provide directives to your FEV tool to handle them, you will see mismatched state key points on the RTL or netlist side of your verification, which could not be mapped to a corresponding point.

TIP 8.18

If you still have unmapped key points in RTL-netlist FEV after applying the various techniques above, check to see if some of these are due to cases of latch/flop optimizations, such as constant propagation, latch folding, latch transparency, or feedback loop replacement.

CONDITIONAL EQUIVALENCE

At some point, you are likely to attempt to run FEV on a pair of models that are only equivalent under certain conditions. For example, maybe one model contains an RTL feature that is no longer used, and thus needs to be turned off. Or perhaps your synthesis tool took advantage of a user hint and generated a netlist that logically differs from your RTL under certain invalid input conditions. One example of such a circuit optimization is depicted in Figure 8.14, showing two pieces of logic that are equivalent under the assumption that a must always equal 1.

We will not spend too much time on this issue, since it is essentially the same issue we faced with assumptions for FPV in earlier chapters. You may need to do

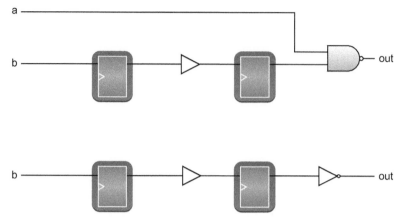

FIGURE 8.14

Conditional equivalence: if (a == 1), the logic matches.

some wiggling: examine the initial counterexamples generated by your FEV tool, and identify assumptions you might need in order to define equivalence.

TIP 8.19

In early phases of FEV, you may need to do some wiggling, examining the initial counterexamples, identifying missing assumptions, and generating needed assumptions, just like in FPV.

The main complication here is that if you are doing combinational FEV, assumptions may be added at each layer of state elements, rather than just on the inputs.

TIP 8.20

Be careful if adding assumptions for combinational FEV: assumptions specified on inputs are not automatically propagated to the next layer of flip-flops by most combinational FEV tools, so you may need to add them at each pipe stage.

You also should pay attention to the specifications you gave to your synthesis tool: if you provided synthesis constraints, such as particular sets of signals being constant, equivalent, or mutually exclusive, you should provide similar assumptions to your FEV tool.

TIP 8.21

When running RTL-netlist FEV, check that any input constraints you gave to your synthesis tool are replicated in your FEV environment.

DON'T CARE SPACE

The Don't Care space (DC space) is the part of your problem space for which you do not have a defined behavior. For example, suppose you have this code fragment in your RTL:

```
case (myvec)
  2'b00: out = 0
  2'b01: out = 1
  2'b10: out = 1
Endcase
```

What is the expected behavior in the case where the *myvec* signal has the value 2'b11? It is not defined in the code. How should this be handled for use with an FEV tool?

To answer this question, it is critical that we look at the difference between the SPEC and IMP models. In the case of RTL-netlist FEV, it is usually fairly obvious that the RTL is the specification, and the netlist is the implementation. When doing RTL-RTL FEV, you need to be careful that the model you label as the SPEC is truly the definition of the correct behavior, such that the IMP is considered correct if and only if it generates the same output as the SPEC in all legal cases. How we treat DC space forms a fundamental asymmetry between the two designs:

- SPEC: DC space in the specification provides an implementation choice: it basically indicates that we do not care about the results in those cases. Anything the implementation does for those cases is considered correct.
- IMP: If there is DC space in the implementation model, this can be very dangerous, indicating implemented logic that does not provide a deterministic result. If the implementation defines DC space that is not a subset of the specification DC space, FEV tools will report a mismatch.

This fundamental asymmetry can be surprising to some users: it is possible to successfully prove model A matches model B in an FEV tool, then reverse the two models and prove that model B mismatches model A, due to DC space! A related, and even more confusing, situation that we have seen on several actual projects is the following: two netlists synthesized from the same RTL, and each formally verified as equivalent to that RTL, are proven nonequivalent to each other by FEV. This situation is illustrated in Figure 8.15.

Looking at the example case statement again, it is easy to see how this might happen. When *myvec* is 2'b11, the first synthesis run might choose to set *out* to 1 for timing/area reasons, while the second synthesis, under different timing/area constraints, sets *out* to 0. Both are perfectly legal implementations of the RTL, since that case was in the DC space, and thus had no particular value specified. But since the two IMP models generate different values for this specific case, they will not match when compared to each other.

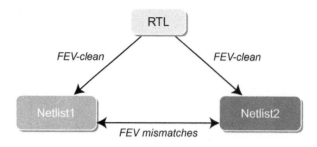

FIGURE 8.15

Two netlists match the same RTL, but not each other.

Most FEV tools have directives that allow you to report on and examine the DC space; be sure to look at this if you unexpectedly see an FEV mismatch between two derived or synthesized models that were FEVed in the past against a common source.

> **TIP 8.22**
>
> If two models that were derived from (and FEVed against) a common model mismatch in FEV, take a close look at the DC space. This is especially likely to be an issue if comparing two different netlists synthesized from the same RTL model.

COMPLEXITY

As with any FV process, FEV is solving problems that are known to take exponential time in the worst case, and thus prone to complexity issues: you may see the tool run forever, time out, or run out of memory on your system. In combinational FEV, the state-matching requirement reduces complexity in the majority of cases, but it is still possible for the tools to have trouble verifying large logic cones. In sequential FEV, we largely face the same types of complexity issues that we do in FPV models, though there are still some ways to take advantage of the fact that we are working in an equivalence context.

Chapter 10 gives a detailed set of techniques for covering hard complexity cases in FV. Here we summarize some basic techniques for dealing with complexity, which are particularly applicable in an FEV context, and should be the first things you think about when facing FEV complexity issues.

- *Adding Verification Stages.* As we discussed in earlier subsections, your synthesis process likely contains a number of distinct stages, such as an unoptimized netlist, a timing-optimized netlist, and a scan-inserted netlist. If you are attempting an end-to-end FEV run, you may find that using intermediate stages and breaking it into a set of smaller FEV runs completely eliminates the complexity issues.

> **TIP 8.23**
>
> When dealing with FEV complexity issues, see if you can identify intermediate models and split an end-to-end FEV run into a set of smaller runs.

- *Blackboxes:* In FEV, there are several obvious cases where you can blackbox logic instead of including it in your checking. Just as with FPV, blackboxing a module means that its internals are ignored by the tool, and its outputs are considered free inputs to the rest of the model. However, there is a key difference that makes blackboxing much easier to use in FEV than FPV: for FEV, outputs of corresponding blackboxes are mapped during the key point mapping phase, just like primary inputs. This means that as long as you choose blackboxes with corresponding outputs in both designs, the necessary assumptions on the blackbox outputs are automatic, inherently assuming that corresponding outputs in the two models are equal.
  - *Memories and caches.* Memory and caches are some of the hard nuts to crack; these tend to cause complexity blowup for FV tools. If you are FEVing models containing memories and caches, usually it makes the most sense to blackbox them. Most memories are checked for RTL-netlist equivalence at the transistor level, using specialized flows beyond the scope of this book, anyway.
  - *Trusted IP.* Blocks supplied by third parties, which are pre-verified and your team is not touching, should be safe by definition to ignore for FEV.
  - *Known unchanged blocks.* Similarly, if you are verifying a design change and know that some portion of the design has not changed, it should be safe to blackbox.

> **TIP 8.24**
>
> When running FEV, look for blackboxing opportunities to reduce complexity. If there are known unchanged blocks, trusted IP, or standard substructures such as memories or caches that have their own specialized verification flows, blackbox these in your FEV runs.

- *Hierarchical FEV:* To overcome capacity issues, FEV can often be handled using a "divide-and-conquer" approach. The idea here is to start by proving FEV on some lower-level modules, and then prove equivalence at the top level with these sub-blocks blackboxed. For example, suppose we run into a complexity issue when verifying the design in Figure 8.16.

  In this design, there are five major blocks (A, B, C, D, and E) and surrounding control logic interacting with these blocks. We can verify that block A is equivalent in both models first, then block B, and so on. After we have verified each of the blocks individually, we can then verify the top-level

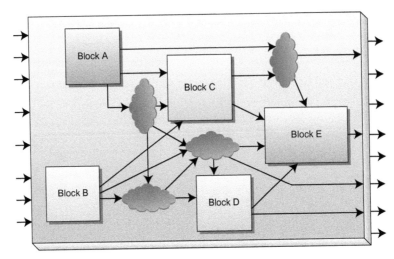

FIGURE 8.16

Hierarchical design that has five blocks.

model, with the submodules blackboxed. Be careful though: this only works if we guarantee that no cross-hierarchy optimizations have been performed, such as moving logic from the top level to block D. Most synthesis tools allow us to specify hard boundaries over which such optimizations are not permitted.

TIP 8.25

If facing FEV complexity issues on a design where the SPEC and IMP have equivalent sets of submodules, consider using a hierarchical approach: verify each submodule equivalence first, then blackbox the submodules and do top-level FEV. For this to work, you may need to constrain a synthesis tool to prevent optimizations across certain hierarchies.

- *Additional key points (cut points):* Remember that by default, combinational FEV identifies primary inputs, primary outputs, and state elements as key points. Sequential FEV usually only identifies inputs and outputs as key points initially, though can perform better if some internal state elements are identified as key points as well. In either case, you can also divide the logic at points other than the states, commonly referred to as *cut points*. In simpler terms, a cut point is a non-state point that is treated as a key point, which could be mapped and verified across two models just like flops and latches are handled for combinational FEV. Identifying the critical cut points can drastically reduce the logic that needs to be verified. Be careful though: in some cases, by hiding logic that is needed for a proof of the next downstream key point, adding a poorly chosen cut point can result in a false negative, and create more debugging work.

> **TIP 8.26**
>
> When running FEV, look for opportunities to provide additional internal key points to reduce complexity: add state key points if running sequential FPV, and non-state cut points in either combinational or sequential FPV.

- *Case-splitting:* As we have discussed in an FPV context, restricting the verification to certain modes or cases using assumptions can significantly reduce the complexity. For example, if verifying a design that can support multiple message widths depending on a control register programmed during reset, execute multiple FEV runs, each using assumptions to enforce a particular message width.

> **TIP 8.27**
>
> If facing FEV complexity problems, look for opportunities to case-split, restricting the model to certain subsets of its functionality for each of multiple FEV runs.

- *Don't Care Assignments:* This is an issue unique to FEV. As discussed in the previous section, DC space usually results from RTL ambiguity. A large DC space can complicate the verification problem, and may result in a significant increase in complexity. Thus, by replacing ambiguous RTL containing DC space with a model that has definite results prescribed for each operation, you can sometimes gain significant FEV complexity reduction. Your FEV tool may provide options to directly fix the DC space, for example by always choosing 0 for any ambiguous RTL assignment. Be careful though: if doing RTL-netlist FEV, you need to rerun synthesis with the same constraints when removing DC space, or else you risk introducing a real mismatch. If running RTL-RTL FEV, you need to be careful to remove DC space equivalently in both models.

> **TIP 8.28**
>
> If facing FEV complexity problems, and your FEV tool reports that there is nontrivial DC space in your specification model, consider removing the DC space and replacing it with concrete requirements.

Disabling Synthesis Optimizations: In RTL-netlist FEV, many complexities result from synthesis tools doing aggressive optimization, which can significantly rewrite a combinational logic cone. As a last resort, if you have a model where FEV does not converge and cannot resolve it by any of the other methods above, you might want to tell your synthesis tool not to optimize the logic in question. Most synthesis tools that provide complex optimizations also provide a way to turn them off in selected regions of your model.

TIP 8.29

If your other attempts to solve an RTL-netlist FEV complexity issue have failed, consider rerunning synthesis with optimizations turned off in the complex region.

SUMMARY

In this chapter, we have introduced you to the concept of FEV, a powerful general technique for determining the equivalence between two different models. The models can be high-level models, RTL, or netlists, though as in most of this book, we focus on cases where RTL is involved. We discussed various ways to define equivalence: combinational equivalence, where models need to match at all state elements; sequential equivalence, where the models just need to ultimately generate the same results; and transactional equivalence, where the behaviors need to correspond for certain well-defined transactions.

We then discussed two major cases of FEV flows that are used with RTL: RTL-netlist FEV, and RTL-RTL FEV. RTL-netlist FEV is the most mature formal flow in the EDA industry and is considered essential for verifying synthesis of schematic netlists from RTL. RTL-RTL FEV is useful in a number of common scenarios, such as parameterization, timing fixes, pipeline optimizations, chicken bit validation, and clock gating validation.

We then described the basic elements needed to set up an FEV run:

- Choosing the models: You need to decide what your SPEC and IMP will be, and include a logical representation of your cell library if needed.
- Key point selection and mapping: Mapping the key points is a critical element of FEV, enabling the proof engines to take advantage of similarity between the models.
- Assumptions and constraints: While key point mappings provide the majority of starting assumptions, you may still need constraints to focus on desired functionality.
- Debugging failures: Be sure to take advantage of the unique characteristics of FEV, such as the ability to compare corresponding logic cones, when first debugging FEV failures.

We concluded this chapter with a description of some additional challenges that you may face when running FEV, including latch and flop optimizations, conditional equivalence, DC space, and formal complexity issues.

PRACTICAL TIPS FROM THIS CHAPTER

8.1 If your design is comprised of simple combinational logic, or if there is a state-matching relation between the flops across two models you want to compare (as is the case when netlists are generated by most synthesis tools), a combinational FEV tool will probably be the most efficient way to prove equivalence.

8.2   If you have both FPV and sequential FEV tools available, you should usually use the sequential FEV tools when trying to solve a non-state-matching model equivalence problem.

8.3   If a design change involves complex sequential changes that are beyond the capability of your sequential FEV tool, you may be able to verify it with transaction-based FEV.

8.4   If you are replacing constants with parameters in an RTL model, you should make use of a combinational or sequential FEV tool to ensure that you have not altered the logic.

8.5   If redistributing logic across pipe stages in RTL, use a sequential FEV tool to ensure that you have not altered the logic.

8.6   When splitting a pipeline into parallel paths for timing reasons, use a combinational or sequential FEV tool to ensure you did not alter the logic. Sequential FEV tools are more likely to be able to handle these cases.

8.7   If changing the length of a pipeline while preserving functionality, use a sequential or transaction-based FEV tool to verify that you have not altered the logic.

8.8   If inserting a chicken bit to disable some new functionality, run combinational or sequential FEV of the old logic vs. the new logic with the chicken bit turned on, to check that when the new functionality is disabled, the design behavior truly matches the original design.

8.9   If inserting clock gating into a design, use sequential FEV to compare the design with clock gating on and off, to ensure that the clock gating has not altered the logic.

8.10   If doing RTL-netlist FEV, make sure you are using a released cell library with verified behavioral specifications, and loading the behavioral representation of your cell library.

8.11   If an internal signal mismatches in RTL-netlist FEV and seems to be off by a single inversion, it is a good candidate for negated mapping. Do not put such mappings on primary input our output signals, however, unless you are very sure that the negated mapping is correct.

8.12   If extra netlist flip-flops are left unmapped by the mapping phase of RTL-netlist FEV, check to see if some of them may be cases of state replication.

8.13   Review the set of unreachable points reported by your RTL-netlist FEV tool, and make sure they are included in your key point mappings and verified if they represent logic you want to see in the netlist, such as bonus cells, scan, or power.

8.14   If running sequential FEV in cases where pipeline depth or other delays or qualifying conditions may vary between the SPEC and the IMP, be sure to think about using delayed or conditional mappings on your outputs.

8.15 If having trouble mapping all your key points, first look for root causes related to typical synthesis netlist optimizations or unreachable points. Then look for name-based correspondence, and also consider running partial verification on nearby points that are mapped to get some better hints.

8.16 If you see lots of mismatches in RTL-netlist FEV that involve signals with scan or DFT-related names, check that you properly disabled scan for your model.

8.17 When debugging FEV mismatches, first sort them by the cone size, and start with the simplest. Then check for fanin cone differences, look for common themes, and check for inverse mappings. After this, start using your FEV tool's more advanced debug features, but be sure to look at the smallest cones first.

8.18 If you still have unmapped key points in RTL-netlist FEV after applying the various techniques above, check to see if some of these are due to cases of latch/flop optimizations, such as constant propagation, latch folding, latch transparency, or feedback loop replacement.

8.19 In early phases of FEV, you may need to do some wiggling, examining the initial counterexamples, identifying missing assumptions, and generating needed assumptions, just like in FPV.

8.20 Be careful if adding assumptions for combinational FEV: assumptions specified on inputs are not automatically propagated to the next layer of flip-flops by most combinational FEV tools, so you may need to add them at each pipe stage.

8.21 When running RTL-netlist FEV, check that any input constraints you gave to your synthesis tool are replicated in your FEV environment.

8.22 If two models that were derived from (and FEVed against) a common model mismatch in FEV, take a close look at the DC space. This is especially likely to be an issue if comparing two different netlists synthesized from the same RTL model.

8.23 When dealing with FEV complexity issues, see if you can identify intermediate models and split an end-to-end FEV run into a set of smaller runs.

8.24 When running FEV, look for blackboxing opportunities to reduce complexity. If there are known unchanged blocks, trusted IP, or standard substructures such as memories or caches that have their own specialized verification flows, blackbox these in your FEV runs.

8.25 If facing FEV complexity issues on a design where the SPEC and IMP have equivalent sets of submodules, consider using a hierarchical approach: verify each submodule equivalence first, then blackbox the submodules and do top-level FEV. For this to work, you may need to constrain a synthesis tool to prevent optimizations across certain hierarchies.

8.26 When running FEV, look for opportunities to provide additional internal key points to reduce complexity: add state key points if running sequential FPV, and non-state cut points in either combinational or sequential FPV.

8.27 If facing FEV complexity problems, look for opportunities to case-split, restricting the model to certain subsets of its functionality for each of multiple FEV runs.

8.28 If facing FEV complexity problems, and your FEV tool reports that there is nontrivial DC space in your specification model, consider removing the DC space and replacing it with concrete requirements.

8.29 If your other attempts to solve an RTL-netlist FEV complexity issue have failed, consider rerunning synthesis with optimizations turned off in the complex region.

FURTHER READING

[Abr10] J. A. Abraham, "Formal Equivalence Checking," University of Texas at Austin EE-382M Lecture Notes, February 2010, http://www.cerc.utexas.edu/~jaa/ee382m-verif/lectures/5-2.pdf.

[Bau06] J. Baumgartner, H. Mony, V. Paruthi, R. Kanzelman, and G. Janssen, "Scalable Sequential Equivalence Checking Across Arbitrary Design Transformations," International Conference on Computer Design (ICCD) 2006.

[Bry02] Randal E. Bryant and James H. Kukula, "Formal Methods for Functional Verification," International Conference on Computer Aided Design (ICCAD) 2002.

[Cha09] Pankaj Chauhan, Deepak Goyal, Gagan Hasteer, Anmol Mathur, and Nikhil Sharma, "Non-Cycle-Accurate Sequential Equivalence Checking," Design Automation Conference (DAC) 2009.

[Cha14] Prosenjit Chatterjee, Scott Fields, and Syed Suhaib, "A Formal Verification App Towards Efficient, Chip-Wide Clock Gating Verification," Design and Verification Conference (DVCon) 2014.

[Coh08] Orly Cohen, Moran Gordon, Michael Lifshits, Alexander Nadel, and Vadim Ryvchin, "Designers Work Less with Quality Formal Equivalence Checking," Design and Verification Conference (DVCon) 2010.

[Koe05] Alfred Koelbl, Yuan Lu, and Anmol Mathur, "Formal Equivalence Checking Between System-Level Models and RTL," International Conference in Computer Aided Design (ICCAD) 2005.

[Koe07] Alfred Koelbl, Jerry Burch, and Carl Pixley, "Memory Modeling in ESL-RTL Equivalence Checking," Design Automation Conference (DAC) 2007.

[Kir14] M. V. Achutha KiranKumar, Aarti Gupta, S. S. Bindumadhava "RTL2RTL Formal Equivalence: Boosting the Design Confidence," Formal Methods Singapore, 2014.

[Mis06] A. Mishchenko, S. Chatterjee, R. Brayton, and N. Een, "Improvements to Combinational Equivalence Checking," International Conference in Computer Aided Design (ICCAD) 2006.

[Pix92] Carl Pixley, A Theory and Implementation of Sequential Hardware Equivalence IEEE Trans. Computer-Aided Design, 1469−1478December 1992.

[Ros14] Wolfgang Roesner, "Aspect Oriented Design-Optimizing SOC Verification via Separation of Concerns," Design Automation Conference (DAC) 2014.

[Sav10] H. Savoj, D. Berthelot, A. Mishchenko, and R. Brayton, "Combinational Techniques for Sequential Equivalence Checking," Formal Methods in Computer Aided Design (FMCAD) 2010.

Formal verification's greatest bloopers: the danger of false positives

Beware of bugs in the above code; I have only proved it correct, not tried it.
—**Donald Knuth**

By this point in the book, you are probably convinced that formal verification (FV) provides us a set of powerful techniques for analyzing and verifying today's modern VLSI and SOC designs. Because FV does not rely on specific test vectors, but mathematically proves results based on all possible test vectors, it can provide a degree of confidence that is simply not possible using simulation, emulation, or similar methods.

We have also seen, however, that there tends to be a significant amount of user input and guidance required to operate FV tools. Among the many factors that are dependent on user input are:

- *Selecting/partitioning the design:* Since most forms of FV usually require running at some unit or cluster level below the full-chip, or running at full-chip with blackboxing of many units below, the user is always making important decisions about where to actually target the FV effort.
- *Register transfer level (RTL) (and/or schematic) models:* The user must choose the correct design files to compile as the main input to the verification effort and chose a correct set of compile settings like parameters or `define flags. This usually includes both core files that the user wrote and library files provided by another department or company to define standard reusable functionality.
- *Properties:* Another key input to FV is the set of properties the user is verifying. For formal property verification (FPV) and related methods, the assertion properties are the key verification target, and the assumptions provide the major constraints. In the case of formal equivalence verification (FEV), there are also mapping properties that connect signals from one model to the other.

- *Abstractions*: As we have seen in our complexity discussions, there are many cases where FV initially performs poorly on a design, and users must abstract or simplify parts of the design to make them more tractable.
- *Tool knobs*: We should not forget that, like any EDA tool, FV tools have many settings that must be chosen by the user, such as the types of engines to use, proof bounds for bounded runs, and the version of the IEEE SystemVerilog Assertions (SVA) standards in effect.

Thus we see that while FV engines are providing mathematical certainty in the domain of their analysis, there are many opportunities for users to provide erroneous input or specifications to the tools. This is not unique to formal methods, of course—this is true of nearly any type of verification method. The danger, however, is that the expectations are higher for FV: many managers know very little of the technical details, but have absorbed the meme that *FV means mathematical certainty*, as illustrated in Figure 9.1.

To clarify, we are not retreating from the main point of this book: FV methods are a very powerful and accurate means of design verification, and in many cases exponentially more effective and cost-efficient than simulation-based approaches. But we need to be careful to realize that FV is run by actual human beings, and thus is not exempt from the fact that it is possible to make mistakes. The most dangerous types of mistakes are what is known as *false positives*, where a design is reported correct but later found to contain a bug. When managers who expect that their design has been mathematically proven with formal certainty suddenly get reports of a bug in the "proven" products, they tend to be extremely unhappy.

FIGURE 9.1

Naive attitudes about simulation versus FV.

These are often a consequence of *overconstraint*, where user assumptions or directives prevent the tool from considering all legal behaviors.

We should also mention that another class of errors, *false negatives*, is common with FV tools. As we have seen many times in previous chapters, false negatives are an expected part of the verification process. Initial FV runs almost never include all the assumptions needed, so most FV engineers spend a large proportion of their time examining waveforms resulting from false negatives, figuring out why they are not really errors, and adding the proper assumptions or tool constraints. False negatives are significantly less dangerous than false positives, since they may result in extra engineering time, but will not lead to a buggy design being labeled correct. They are most often the result of *underconstraint*, where the tool is considering behaviors that should not be in the verification space.

Thus, false positives are the more critical concern when talking about ways FV might go wrong. We need to be careful to understand potential causes of these false positives and understand what we can do to prevent them. The best way to illustrate this is by looking at a set of real-life cases. So in this chapter, our discussion will focus on a number of examples where we or our colleagues have seen false positives: cases where a design was considered formally proven or "clean" at some point, and later found to contain a bug that was missed in the initial verification effort. Naturally, we have had to abstract many details of these examples, for space, simplicity, and readability, but you can be confident that anything you read in this chapter was based on actual FV work that took place at Intel. Based on these observations of real cases, we will then discuss what actions should be taken to prevent many classes of false positives.

MISUSE OF THE SVA LANGUAGE

One simple type of false positive can arise from the misunderstanding of SystemVerilog or the SVA assertion language. Some of these examples will likely seem silly or trivial on first reading, but remember that these are all based on real cases we have seen in practice.

THE MISSING SEMICOLON

Yes, you read that section title correctly: the first case we discuss is that simple, just *one* missing semicolon. Most people would probably think that missing semicolons would always be caught by the compiler, so why even worry about such cases? But in fact, the SVA language does provide the ability for a subtle case of a missing semicolon to effectively negate an assertion, causing an FPV proof to be skipped on a real design project.

To see how this happened, look at this code fragment:

```
assert property (foo)
assert property (bar) else $error("Bar problem.");
```

You have probably spotted a few oddities of the code above. First, the assertions are not labeled: remember that an SVA assertion starts with a *label:* before the *assert* keyword. However, labels are optional in SVA, so that alone is not technically a problem.

The real issue is: how is an SVA assertion terminated? The full SVA assertion syntax looks basically like this:

```
[<label>:]  assert  property  (<prop>)  [<pass_action>]  [else
<fail_action>];
```

In other words, after the assertion's property expression, there are two optional action blocks: the *pass_action*, a SystemVerilog command to execute when the assertion passes, and a *fail action*, which is executed when the assertion fails. The semicolon marks the end of all action blocks.

This means that if an assertion is missing a semicolon, the next SystemVerilog statement to appear is considered its pass action—even if that statement is another assertion. So, for the first assertion above, we have:

- Assertion condition = foo
- Pass action = assert property (bar) else $error ("Bar problem.");

The second assertion has become the pass action of the first one! In simulation, this might be okay, since whenever the first assertion passes, the next assertion is checked as its pass action. But FPV tools typically ignore the action blocks, which were mainly designed for use in simulation. This led to a real issue on a major design project at Intel, where a validation engineer discovered at a late stage that an assertion was being ignored in FV. It took some staring at the code with language experts to finally identify the issue.

ASSERTION AT BOTH CLOCK EDGES

An even more subtle case than an assertion being ignored is the case when an assertion exists, but is timed differently than the user expects. Look at the following assertion, intended to indicate that whenever a request signal rises, it is held for at least six cycles:

```
hold_request: assert property (@(clk1))
        $rose(req) |=> ##6 (!$fell(req));
```

Have you spotted the subtle error here? Rather than specifying an edge of the clock, the clocking argument to the assertion just specifies a plain clock signal. Instead of @(clk1), the assertion should have used @(posedge clk1). As we saw in Chapter 3, in such a case the assertion is sensitive to both positive and negative edges of the clock. For simple Boolean assertions, being sensitive to both edges just results in extra checking, so is ultimately harmless, other than a slight performance cost. However, when there are repetitions or delays, as in the ##6 delay operator, this is much more serious: the count is effectively half of what the user intended, counting six phases, which are equivalent to three cycles.

This type of issue is especially insidious because the assertion will still be actively checked, and might even catch some real bugs. For example, if the request falls after only one cycle, or two phases, the assertion above will successfully catch the issue. In the real-life case where we encountered this situation, the user was especially confused because he had caught real errors when running FPV with this assertion, yet a simulation run late in the project reported that they had found an error, using an independent checker, where a request disappeared after five instead of six cycles. Again, it took a careful review of the code to properly identify this issue.

SHORT-CIRCUITED FUNCTION WITH ASSERTION

Another subtle case involves assertions that may actually never get checked at all. It can occur when an assertion is placed inside a function, and some calls to that function are inside complex logic expressions. Look at this example code fragment:

```
function bit legal_state(
    bit [0:3] current, bit valid;
    bit_ok: assert #0 (!valid || (current != '0));
    legal_state = valid && $onehot(current);
endfunction
. . .
always_comb begin
if (status || legal_state(valid, state)) . . .
```

Since a procedural `if` inside an `always_comb` is executed every cycle by definition, the author of this code thought he could be confident that the assertion `bit_ok` would always be checked. But this was incorrect, due to a clever feature of the SystemVerilog language known as *short-circuiting*.

The idea of short-circuiting is to leverage the fact that in certain types of logical expressions, you can figure out the ultimate result without examining all the terms. In particular, anything ANDed with a 0 will result in a 0, and anything ORed with a 1 will result in a 1. Thus, if you are analyzing an OR expression, you can finish as soon as you have determined that some term is a 1. Like the C programming language, SystemVerilog explicitly specifies this in the Language Reference Manual (LRM), stating that if the first term of an OR is 1 or the first term of an AND is 0, the remaining terms of the expression should not be evaluated.

In the example above, we see that `status` is ORed with the call to `legal_state`. This means that if `status == 1`, tools are not expected to evaluate the function call—and as a result, assertions inside that function are not evaluated in such cases. This is another issue that may be deceptive to users, because they will likely see some cases, cases where status == 0, in which the assertion is functioning correctly and can even detect bugs. But, as some unfortunate Intel users discovered the hard way through bug escapes, the assertion is effectively ignored by EDA tools when status == 1.

Once understood, this issue can be resolved fairly easily. The simplest method is to place the function-containing argument first in the expression. Be careful if using this solution though: if you have multiple function-containing terms, you may need to break down the expression into several intermediate subexpression assignments to ensure all terms are evaluated every cycle.

SUBTLE EFFECTS OF SIGNAL SAMPLING

This is another very tricky SVA issue, a case where an assertion was apparently generating an incorrect result that took many hours of debug to finally understand. This issue results from the sampling behavior defined for assertion variables. In the following code fragment, look closely at the signals passed in to the assertion:

```
input logic[31:0] index;
. . .
current_pos_stable: assert property ($stable(req[index]));
```

At first glance, this seems like a relatively simple property. We have some vector req, and wish to ensure that whichever position in the vector is currently selected by index has been stable for at least one cycle. But what values are being used for req and index?

Remember that concurrent assertions and sampled value functions like $stable always use the sampled value of each variable, in effect the final value of the variable from the end of the previous time step. The trick here is to recognize that there are two sampled values in the property expression above: req and index. The $stable function uses the last value of each of them for its check: so if index just changed, it will actually compare the current value in the current position of req to the last cycle's value in a different position! The waveform in Figure 9.2 illustrates an example of this situation causing a false

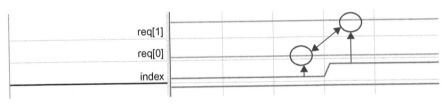

FIGURE 9.2

Sampling a moving index.

negative, where each element of the vector is stable, but a moving index causes the expression `$stable(req[index])` to be unstable.

In real life, this situation is dangerous, in that it can generate both unexpected false negatives and unexpected false positives. And once again, this is an example where in many cases, those where the index is not moving, the assertion can seem to be working fine, and successfully help to detect many real RTL bugs. The fact that some subset of cases is not being correctly checked may easily be missed.

This one is also a little trickier to solve than some of the other cases we have mentioned. When we faced this issue, our key insight was to realize that we really want the index to be constant for each comparison, even though we wanted the `req` vector to be sampled as normal. We were then able to solve it by using a `generate` loop to define the index as a compile-time constant, creating a family of assertions checking that for each constant index, if it happens to be currently active, the stability condition is met.

```
generate for (genvar i = min; i < max; i++) begin
  current_pos_stable: assert property ( (i == index) | ->
      $stable(req[i]));
end
```

LIVENESS PROPERTIES THAT ARE NOT ALIVE

The final SVA issue we describe relates to an advanced feature of FPV, the ability to analyze "liveness" properties on traces of potentially unbounded length. For example, as we have seen in earlier chapters, this assertion states that a request will eventually get a response:

```
response_good: assert property (
              request | -> s_eventually(response));
```

The *s_* before the eventually indicates that it is a *strong* property: even if it has no finite counterexamples, it can be falsified by an infinite trace that enters a loop in which the awaited condition never happens. This contrasts with *weak* properties, which can only be falsified by a finite counterexample, and are considered true if no such finite counterexample exists.

In SVA, properties are weak by default, unless an explicitly strong operator is used. This means that the property below, even though it might seem conceptually similar to the one above, can never fail in FPV; when looking at any finite "counterexample," you cannot be sure whether the response would have arrived a few cycles after it ended:

```
response_weak: assert property (
              request | -> ##[1:$](response));
```

Unfortunately, the concept of strong and weak properties was not clearly defined in the 2005 LRM. These ideas and related operators such as *s_eventually* were introduced in the 2009 revision. Before that, properties like *response_weak* above were the only practical way to express liveness, so most FPV tools built for SVA 2005 were designed to treat *##[1:$]* properties as implicitly strong.

This created some pain when some Intel projects upgraded from SVA-2005-compliant to SVA-2009-compliant tools. When initially ported, all of the liveness properties written in the *##[1:$]* form seemed fine—they had passed on the existing (already verified) models before and after the upgrade, so initially we thought that our FPV runs were properly checking them, and happily moved forward with the changes.

It was only after a user made a change that they knew should invalidate some liveness properties, and became confused when they all still passed, that we realized something incorrect was happening. In effect, all our liveness properties were unfalsifiable, since they were considered weak by default under the new standard. Thus, ever since the upgrade, none of the liveness proofs on properties written in the old 2005 style were valid. We had to modify our code to fix all such cases, or get our tool vendors to slightly violate the LRM and treat 2005-style liveness assertions as strong.

PREVENTING SVA-RELATED FALSE POSITIVES

Our best advice for preventing these kinds of issues is probably something you have heard in other contexts as well: run good lint checks on your RTL. *Linting*, the process of running a software tool that does structural checking on a piece of RTL to find common cases of legal code with unintended behavior, has become very standard and mature in the industry. If you are a serious, well-disciplined designer (very likely, given that you had the wisdom to decide to read this book), you need to be running regular lint checks on any RTL code you develop.

> **TIP 9.1**
>
> Always run lint checks on any RTL code you develop.

If you are relying on other team members or many layers of scripts to get your RTL lint checks done, be careful to double-check that your assertion code is included in the linting. Due to early lint tools that generated some bogus warnings on SVA assertions, we have seen many cases of projects that show excellent discipline in RTL linting, but exclude SVA code from the process completely. If your coworkers are nervous about enabling linting for SVAs, just show them the examples above in this section, and there is a good chance they will reconsider.

> **TIP 9.2**
>
> Double-check that SVA assertion code is included in your project's lint processes.

One other critical factor in linting is to make sure you have a good set of lint rules implemented. The cases we have discussed in this section inspire rules like the following:

- Flag any assertion that exists entirely inside another assertion's action block.
- Flag any assertion that is active at both clock edges.
- Flag any assertion-containing function that is invoked in a short-circuitable position of a logical expression.
- Flag any case where a sampled variable is used as a vector index in an assertion or sampled value function.
- Flag any properties that seem to be aimed at liveness and are weak due to being written in the SVA 2005 style.

Keep in mind that, due to lack of space, the cases in this section were just a few examples; for a more complete set of SVA-related lint rules, see [Bis12] and talk to your EDA vendor to make sure a good set of SVA lint rules are implemented.

TIP 9.3

Make sure that your project's linting program includes a good set of SVA-related lint rules.

We should also mention, however, that manual review is always a good supplement to lint checks. While linting can detect a wide variety of issues as we mention above, we have seen that the SVA language does contain many pitfalls and opportunities to write assertions that do not say exactly what the author intended. Thus, we suggest that every unit also plan assertion reviews with an SVA expert before the RTL design is closed.

TIP 9.4

Review each unit's assertions with an SVA expert before tapeout, to help identify cases where the assertion doesn't quite say what the author intended.

VACUITY ISSUES

As we have discussed throughout this book, one important consideration when doing FV is vacuity: the idea that you may have unintentionally overconstrained the environment. This would mean that important behaviors in the verification space are ruled out by your assumptions or other parameters of your proof setup. In the worst case, if you create an assumption that defines a globally false condition, such as $(1 == 0)$, all possible inputs may be ruled out, and all assertions are trivially considered true due to the absence of any legal inputs at all. When this happens, your FV proofs will be reported as passing—but will potentially be overlooking key bugs.

MISLEADING COVER POINT WITH BAD RESET

The next case we discuss is another seemingly trivial error, but one that can have consequences that are a bit subtle if you are not careful. Remember that one important technique we use to sanity-check our formal environments is proving cover points. These show that under our current set of assumptions and settings, we are able to replicate interesting behaviors in our design.

An important aspect of cover points that requires extra care is the reset condition. Remember that during the reset stage of a design, it is often possible for many internal elements to attain transitory "garbage" values that do not represent actual computation. This is why the SVA language provides the reset feature (`disable iff`) for assertion statements, to shut them off during reset. For an ordinary assertion, if you accidentally provide the wrong reset argument, you will quickly catch this during simulation or formal analysis, as bogus failures are reported during reset. But what happens if the reset argument to a cover point is wrong?

A cover point with an incorrect reset may be reported as covered, due to the garbage values see during reset—but it is entirely possible that the cover point is not reachable outside reset, and this coverage report is hiding a real vacuity issue. Here is an example cover point, based on a real case from an Intel design:

```
c1: cover property (disable iff (interface_active_nn)
    (data_bus != 64'b0));
```

This cover point is checking that a data bus is capable of attaining a nonzero value, a good type of check to include in any formal environment. The reset signal name `interface_active_nn` on this design follows a convention that signals ending in *nn* are active on 0 values instead of 1, but this slipped the mind of the cover point author: the disable term should really be based on `!interface_active_nn`. As a result, instead of being shut off when the interface was inactive, this cover property checked the data bus only when the interface was inactive. This resulted in an incorrect report that the condition was covered, when in fact some bad FPV tool directives were preventing any nonzero data in cases where the interface was active. The issue was discovered when bugs in the "proven" part of the design were later reported from simulation.

The reset conditions are a fertile ground for generating broken verification environments. The above example is just one of many cases we have observed where some portion of a design was deactivated due to expecting a reset of opposite polarity. This can be especially dangerous in designs with multiple reset signals, where it is possible that some subset are correct, creating the illusion of some nontrivial activity, while others are wrong.

Another critical thing to watch for is cases where an FPV environment "cheats" to simplify the reset process. Many tools have an option available to look for any flops that do not have a determined value after reset, and automatically set such flops to 0 (or to 1). This can often save time in early stages of setting up FPV on blocks with complex reset. But this can also hide a class of bugs, since if you have flops with an indeterminate starting state, you need to make sure that your model behaves correctly regardless of what values they assume. This has also happened to us in real examples.

PROVEN MEMORY CONTROLLER THAT FAILED SIMULATION

The next example we discuss shows a case where the set of assumptions and cover points provided an interesting and powerful FPV environment—but one crucial requirement was not properly communicated from a neighboring unit.

In one of our chipset designs, we verified a number of properties of a memory controller block. This was a block that received requests, related to performing some operation at a particular memory address, and processed them according to the opcode passed in, as illustrated in Figure 9.3.

When initially proving the assertions on this design, the validation engineers encountered a number of counterexamples with a common cause: an opcode and address would specify a multicycle operation, but before the operation would complete, the address on the address bus would change. After finding this situation and discussing over the course of several meetings, the engineers involved in this effort agreed that changing the address of a pending request would be an absurd way to use the memory controller, and thus could be ruled out by an assumption. Once this assumption was added, the properties were fully verified, finding a few RTL bugs along the way and resulting in completing the FPV effort with high confidence.

However, as it turned out, the assumption that the address bus would not change during an operation was incorrect. This requirement had not been clearly communicated to all designers, and some of the RTL had been written with the implicit idea that after the cycle when a request was made, the controller would have already captured the address in local memory, and thus not care if garbage values appeared on the address bus while the operation was in progress. Thus, the unit supplying the inputs to this model really would change the address of pending requests, rendering some of the initial FPV proofs invalid. In this case, the

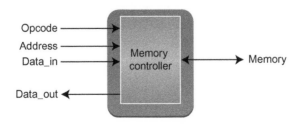

FIGURE 9.3

Memory controller design.

assumptions ruling out these inputs had actually ruled out a part of the real problem space, as currently understood by the neighboring unit's designer.

Fortunately, this was discovered before tapeout: the FPV assumptions were included in the full-chip simulation regressions, and these regressions detected the failing assumptions, alerting the validation team of this disconnect in requirements. This also uncovered a real RTL bug where if the address bus changed when a request was pending, the design would behave incorrectly. Both the RTL code and FPV environment needed to be fixed after this failure was observed.

In general, this issue points to the importance of the *assume-guarantee* philosophy behind FV. Whenever using assumptions in FV, you should always have a good understanding of how their correctness is verified, whether through FV on an adjacent unit, extensive simulation, or careful manual review.

CONTRADICTION BETWEEN ASSUMPTION AND CONSTRAINT

The next case we discuss was one of the most disastrous ones in this chapter: it is a case where an Intel validation team, including one of the authors, reported that a design was FEV-clean for tapeout, indicating that we were confident that we had formally proven the RTL design was equivalent to the schematic netlist. However, when the chip came back from the fab and we began testing it, we discovered that the first stepping was totally dead—and this was due to a bug that should have been found by FEV.

After many weeks of intense debugging, we figured out that the FEV environment was vacuous: the proof space contained inherent contradictions. Remember that any formal tool is analyzing the space of legal signal values, under the current set of assumptions and tool constraints. If this space is completely empty—that is, there are no legal sets of inputs to the current design—then the formal tool can report a trivial "success," since no set of inputs can violate the conditions being checked. Most modern formal tools report an error if the proof space is null, but this feature had not yet been implemented in the generation of FEV tools we were using on that project.

However, there was still a bit of a mystery: how could this happen when we were running nightly simulations? All our assumptions were being checked in simulation as well as FV, so shouldn't some of the contradicting assumptions have generated simulation errors? The subtlety here was that there are various kinds of tool directives that implicitly create assumptions. In particular, as we discussed in Chapter 8, FEV environments use key point mappings to show how the two models are connected. Many of these mappings can create implicit assumptions as well. For example, look at the one-many mapping:

```
sig -> sig_dup_1 sig_dup_2
```

This represents a case where a single flop in the RTL design, `sig`, was replicated twice in the schematics. This is a common situation for timing reasons; while it makes sense logically to think of a single signal `sig` in the RTL, physically it needs two replicated versions to drive different parts of the die. In this case, we are also implicitly creating an assumption equivalent to

```
implicit_assume: assume property (sig_dup_1 == sig_dup_2);
```

In other words, any time we have a one-many mapping, we are implicitly telling the tool to assume that all the signals on the right-hand side have the same value.

In the FEV failure we are currently discussing, one mapping looked like this:

```
myflop -> myflop_dup_1 myflop_inv_1
```

This represents a case where a single flop in the RTL design, `myflop`, was replicated twice in the schematics. This is a common situation for timing reasons; often a high-speed circuit can be implemented more efficiently if a flop is replicated twice to drive it signal to diverse locations on the die. In this case, one of the replicated flops is logically inverted, as indicated by the _inv_ in its name. Usually in such cases we expect an inverse mapping:

```
myflop -> myflop_dup_1 ~myflop_inv_1
```

The FEV owner happened to omit the $\sim$ sign before the inverted flop. This created a major issue because without the inversion, this mapping was creating an implicit equivalence between `myflop_dup_1` and `myflop_inv_1`. But elsewhere in the design, there was a direct assumption that the two signals `myflop_dup_1` and `myflop_inv_1` were inverse of each other:

```
a1: assume property (myflop_dup_1 == ~myflop_inv_1);
```

Together, the broken mapping and the assumption above told the FEV tool that the only legal cases were ones where `myflop_dup_1` was both equal to and the inverse of `myflop_inv_1`—so the set of legal inputs became the null set. The verification was then reported as passing, because no set of legal inputs could violate the equivalence property. This passing status was vacuous, actually checking nothing, but at the time we did not have an FEV tool version that automatically reported vacuousness. A last-minute manual RTL change had been made, so there really were nonequivalent key points, which went undetected before tapeout.

Most modern FEV tools have features to automatically report this kind of totally vacuous proof, but we still need to be careful of the dangers of partially vacuous proofs, where accidental overconstraints rule out large parts of the desired behavior space.

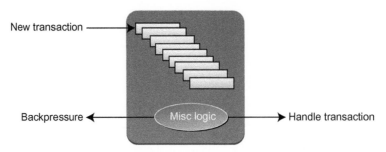

FIGURE 9.4

Transaction queue with backpressure.

THE QUEUE THAT NEVER FILLS, BECAUSE IT NEVER STARTS

Our next example comes from a chipset interface design where a set of incoming transaction requests is placed in a queue, which has a limited size. Periodically the control logic removes the next transaction from the queue for processing. However, the time taken per transaction can vary, so there is a danger of the queue overflowing when too many messages arrive at the wrong time. When the queue is almost full, it sends a backpressure signal to indicate that no more transactions should be sent.

The design constraints for this interface were very tight: the designer wanted to ensure that the queue would never overflow, but also did not want to send out an overly cautious backpressure signal that would stop traffic too early and reduce effective bandwidth. She implemented some backpressure functionality that seemed to work correctly in all the simulation tests she tried, but was still nervous that the design might be failing to send backpressure in some rare cases that could generate an overflow. Thus, she asked for help from the FPV team. Figure 9.4 illustrates the verification challenge at a high level.

When setting up the design for FPV, the validator created a good set of assertions to prevent queue overflow and added numerous assumptions related to the legal opcodes and other control signals for the transactions. After debugging some initial problems with verification environment and some other constraints, the assertions were all proven true in FPV.

However, the designer was initially skeptical based on how (apparently) easy the process had been and requested some more solid evidence that the FPV environment was working properly. The validator responded by adding various cover points, including ones to observe completed transactions. It was a good thing they did this—because it turned out that no completed transactions were possible! Due to a simple flaw in an assumption, requiring that an opcode be illegal instead of requiring that an opcode be legal, all ordinary transactions were ruled out. The flaw was similar to the following:

```
// Variable transaction_check is 1 if transaction is BAD
assign transaction_check =
```

```
   ((opcode != LEGAL1) && (opcode == LEGAL2) ...)
// Assertion missing a ~
a1: assert property (transaction_check);
```

Fortunately, once the cover point failure was discovered, the designer and validator were able to identify the flawed assumption and fix it. After this was done, a rare overflow condition was discovered, and the designer realized that the backpressure signal needed to be generated with slightly more pessimism. After this RTL fix, she was able to prove the design correct with confidence, observing that all the cover points were covered and the assertion proofs passed.

As you have read in earlier chapters, we always recommend that you include a good set of cover points in your FPV efforts, just as the designer and validator did in this example, to help detect and correct overconstraint.

PREVENTING VACUITY: TOOL AND USER RESPONSIBILITY

As we have seen in the examples in this section, we must constantly think about potential vacuity issues when doing FV. A naïve view of FV is that it is solely about proving that incorrect behaviors never occur, and once you have done that, you have full confidence in your verification. However, an equally important part of the process is to verify that, in your current FV environment, typical correct behaviors are included in the analysis.

The techniques that we mentioned in the previous section—linting and manual reviews—are a good start. They can detect a wide variety of situations where an incorrectly written assertion is leaving a hole in the verification. The case of the cover point with bad reset polarity could have been discovered earlier if these methods had been used correctly. But these are just a beginning; there are several more powerful methods that should also be used to prevent vacuity.

The most commonly used vacuity prevention method is to include FV assertions and assumptions in a simulation environment. We are not suggesting that you do full simulation-based verification on each unit that replicates your FPV effort. But in most real-life cases, full-chip simulation needs to be run anyway, to get a basic confidence in full-chip integration and flows, while FV is run at lower levels or on partial models. While it covers a much smaller space than FV, simulation tends to actively drive values based on real expected execution flows, and so it can often uncover flawed assumptions. Such a simulation revealed the bad memory controller assumption in our second example above. Thus, you should include your FV assertions and assumptions in simulation environments whenever possible.

TIP 9.5

Always include your FV assertions and assumptions in any available simulation environments.

Due to increasing awareness of vacuity issues, many EDA FV tools include built-in vacuity detection. Tools can now detect cases where a set of contradicting assumptions rules out the entire verification space, as in the example above where we had a contradiction between an assumption and an FEV mapping constraint. Most FPV tools also offer "trigger checks," automatic cover points to detect at the individual assertion level when an assertion precondition is not met. Some formal tools also offer coverage checking features, where they can try to identify lines, branch points, or other important parts of RTL code that are and are not covered in the current FV environment. You should be sure to turn on these features if available in your current tools.

TIP 9.6

Turn on any vacuity checking, trigger checking, and coverage check offered by your EDA tools, and look carefully at the results.

You need to be careful, however, not to be overly confident in the automated checks of your tools. For example, automated vacuity checking may report that the proof space is not empty, while large classes of interesting traffic are being ruled out. This is what happened in our example above with the queue that could never fill. The proof space was not fully vacuous, since the design could participate in scan protocols, power down, and other secondary tasks. Yet the most important part of the design, the processing of transactions, was effectively disabled by broken assumptions.

The best way to discover this kind of situation is by adding cover points: try to think of typical good traffic for a design, and cover examples of each common flow. When these are reported as covered, you can look at the resulting waveforms and gain confidence that your expected behaviors really are possible under your current formal constraints. You may be getting a sense of déjà vu by now, since we have emphasized this point at so many places in the book—but that is because it is so important. In any FV effort, creating a good set of cover points is critical.

TIP 9.7

Always create a good set of cover points representing typical behaviors of your design, to help sanity-check the proof space of your FV environment.

A final piece of advice for preventing vacuity is to always be conscious of the reset sequence you are using. Start by reviewing the polarity of every reset signal you use, and make sure they are correct. You should also try to make your reset as general as possible: do not force starting values of 0 or 1 on nodes that are truly not reset or you may risk hiding some real issues.

TIP 9.8

Double-check the polarity of all reset signals and make sure that their values in the FV environment match the design intent.

TIP 9.9

Make your reset sequences for FV as general as possible, not setting any signals that do not need to be set for correct FV proofs. Be especially careful of tool options that allow global setting of 0/1 on nonreset nodes.

This advice may seem like somewhat of a contradiction from some earlier chapters, where we suggested the use of intentional overconstraint to reduce complexity or stage the verification process. Those suggestions still apply though; here we are pointing out the potential dangers that can result if you do not follow them carefully. Make sure you are fully aware of any intentional overconstraints, or reset and initialization conditions that are not fully general, and can justify and document why these do not create a gap in your verification process.

TIP 9.10

Make sure you are fully aware of any intentional overconstraints, or reset and initialization conditions that are not fully general, and are used to stage the verification process or reduce complexity. Justify and document why these do not create a gap in your verification process.

IMPLICIT OR UNSTATED ASSUMPTIONS

When thinking about vacuity issues, as we discussed in the previous section, each user tends to focus on the set of assumptions and tool constraints that they created as part of their formal environment. But what if something inherent to the environment is quietly creating assumptions or constraints on its own? Often it is possible that tools or libraries come with their own set of implicit constraints, and the user needs to be careful that they are using the tools properly in their current context. We have seen some situations where these implicit assumptions have caused problems that were caught very late in a project.

LIBRARIES WITH SCHEMATIC ASSUMPTIONS

As we mentioned in Chapter 8, schematic netlists are often built based on standard cells, basic logic elements such as AND gates, OR gates, and muxes, that have been pre-designed at the transistor level and can be instantiated to implement the desired logic. These libraries are pre-verified: if a cell claims to be an AND gate, an FEV tool can accept that as an axiom, rather than having to go through the compute-intensive process of doing every proof at the transistor level. Thus, they are a key factor in making FEV practical and commonplace.

However, in some cases a library cell may include optimization that depends on some assumptions on their inputs. Figure 9.5 shows an example of such a case.

This is a simple selector that drives the upper value to *out* iff signal *b* is high, and drives the lower signal to *out* iff signal *a* is high. But if you remember your introductory electrical engineering class, you can probably spot a few problems in this design. What if neither *a* nor *b* is high? In that case, *out* is a floating node, very undesirable in most cases. And even worse, if both are high, then the two input wires are shorted together. On the other hand, this cell is much better for area and performance than the "safe" version would be, since that would require many more transistors. If we can guarantee at all times that precisely one of these values is 1 and the other is 0, this cell should be acceptable in practice.

Thus, a library may be delivered with some required assumptions for certain cells. Users of such a library are required to guarantee that these assumptions will be met if these cells are used. Thus, in the FEV process for designs containing such libraries, an extra step is needed: *schematic assumption verification*. This is essentially a miniature FPV run focused on the set of properties in the library. If this is omitted, the library cannot be trusted to deliver the claimed functionality.

The lack of understanding of this requirement is what led to another case of dead silicon on an Intel design. An engineer responsible for a late change on a project reran the FEV flow to check his edits. He did not understand the purpose of the schematic assumption verification step, and looking up the documentation, he read that it was a form of FPV. Since FPV was not listed in the required tape-out checklist for this particular block (the main validation strategy was simulation), he marked his FEV run as clean with that step disabled.

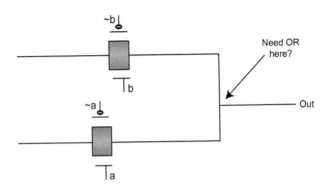

FIGURE 9.5

Design cell requiring schematic assumption.

As a result, the design was not using its library cells safely, and the initial silicon came back dead. The omitted schematic assumption step was discovered when FEV experts re-examined all the tapeout flows as part of the debug process.

EXPECTATIONS FOR MULTIPLY-DRIVEN SIGNALS

Another common case that can create confusion is when the tool makes some implicit assumption common to the industry and misinterprets the intention of a design. An example of this situation is the case of RTL signals with more than one driver. How should such a signal be handled? It turns out that there is a common convention, used by many industry synthesis and FEV tools, that a multiply-driven RTL signal should be handled as a "wired AND." The result should be interpreted as the AND of all the drivers, and the synthesis tool should generate a circuit where the multiple drivers are combined with an AND to generate the overall value. This interpretation is the default in many tools.

On one recent Intel design, a late stage inspection of the schematic revealed that a connection at the top level was different than what the designer expected. On closer examination, we discovered that one of the wires involved had been declared as an "inout" at a cluster interface where logically it should have been an input. This meant that the top-level net that was driving it became multiply-driven, as it could get values from either its true driver or the inout signal. The synthesis tool had then synthesized AND logic for this net. The design had passed FEV, despite this difference between the RTL and netlist, because our FEV tool defaulted to treating multiply-driven signals as wired AND gates.

Once the issue was discovered, we were able to fix the problem in the netlist. We also changed the settings of our FEV tool to treat multiple driver situations more conservatively: it would examine every driver and make sure that for each node, the precise set of drivers matched between the RTL and netlist. This would automatically uncover cases where such a net is synthesized into a wired gate by the synthesis tool. We were then able to rerun FEV and prove that, under our now-stronger definition of equivalence, there were no further errors.

UNREACHABLE LOGIC ELEMENTS: NEEDED OR NOT?

Another area where many FEV tools have a default view that can cause problems is in the issue of "unreachable" logic elements. Remember that, as we discussed in Chapter 8, many FEV tools simplify the equivalence problem by breaking up the designs at internal flops and verifying the equivalence of each of those flops between the designs. If a subset of flops targeted for verification in one design do not have a corresponding element in the other, it is reported as a mismatch in most cases.

However, a common exception to this methodology is what is known as an unreachable point. An *unreachable point* is a node in the design that cannot affect any output. These are most often due to some subset of the logic functionality that has been logically tied off, perhaps the implementation of some mode from a previous design that no longer exists. Another case is totally disconnected logic elements. These may arise from the insertion of "bonus cells," extra logic that does nothing in the current design, but is placed on the chip in areas with extra open space, in case a late logic fix is needed and the design team does not want to redo the entire layout. Figure 9.6 illustrates the concept of reachable and unreachable points.

How should FEV tools handle unreachable points? Intuitively, we might expect that all such points should be reported, and the users could double-check to make sure the list is reasonable, identifying any that look suspicious. If comparing RTL to schematics, and some known modes were tied off or disabled in the design, some unreachable points could be very reasonable. But if comparing a schematic design before and after a small change, we would expect unreachable points to be very rare, and each one should be scrutinized very carefully.

However, as it turned out, one of our FEV tools had a default setting that would report unreachable points due to tied-off logic, but silently ignore completely disconnected nodes. In one of our chipset designs a few years ago, the schematics had been fully designed, gone through several validation flows, and was in a stage where backend designers were making minor schematic changes to optimize timing and area. Each designer who had touched the schematics had diligently run FEV to compare the models before and after their changes and make sure their edits were safe. But one of them carefully did a last-minute visual inspection of the layout, and discovered a surprising open area with no bonus cells.

It turned out that one of the late edits had been done with a script that accidentally deleted a large class of bonus cells. All the FEV flows had passed, because (at the time) none of the team was aware that the tool's default setting ignored disconnected cells when checking equivalence. This was a lucky find: some later post-silicon fixes would have been significantly more expensive if the team had

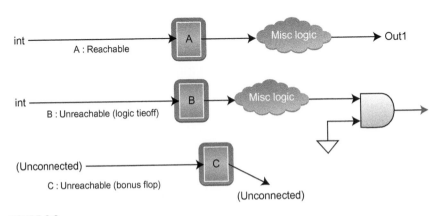

FIGURE 9.6

Reachable and unreachable points.

taped out without these bonus cells. Once the team determined the root cause of the issue and realized the mistake in the FEV settings, they were able to fix them so future edits would not face this risk.

PREVENTING MISUNDERSTANDINGS

The kind of issues we discuss in this section, where a user misunderstands the underlying behavior of formal tools and libraries, are among the hardest ones to detect and prevent. However, there are a few good strategies that can be utilized to minimize these issues.

You should be sure to understand the validation expectations of any external components or IP used in your design and delivered by another team. If someone else is providing a library of cells used in your RTL-netlist FEV runs, make sure to check for any requirements related to schematic assumption checking. Similarly, if integrating an externally provided IP or similar module and trusting its functionality rather than re-verifying it, make sure you verify that your design complies with its interface requirements.

> ### TIP 9.11
>
> Review the interface expectations of any externally provided libraries or IPs whose functionality you are trusting rather than re-verifying. Make sure your verification plan includes checks that you are complying with any documented requirements.

In addition, review all tool control files with an expert in the relevant tool. This is a little different from our suggestion a few sections back about assertion reviews: here the required expertise is not in the content of the design itself, but in the tools used with the design. In all of the examples above, an expert with a proper understanding of the tools could have spotted and prevented the issues. Review by an expert can often help reveal potential issues and unexpected implicit requirements.

> ### TIP 9.12
>
> Before completing a project, review your FV environments and tool control files with an expert on the tools and libraries involved.

One other strategy is to be careful about the settings in any tool you use. There are usually a variety of options to control how the verification environment will behave, and often there are more forgiving and more conservative ways to set the options. If you do not fully understand some verification step, like the schematic assumption step in one of the cases above, the conservative choice is to turn it on by default unless you are sure it can be safely turned off. As another example, options that allow weaker checking of some design construct, such as treating multiply-driven nets as wired AND gates, or ignoring some classes of unreachable cells, are inherently dangerous and you should be careful about them. Where you have a choice, try to choose the more conservative option, so you do not gloss over any real errors. You need to be careful here, as in some cases your tool may have a weaker default that matches common industry practice.

TIP 9.13

Review options that your FV tool provides, and try to choose more conservative checks in preference to weaker ones, unless you have a strong understanding of why the weaker options are acceptable for your particular case.

DIVISION OF LABOR

The final class of false positive issues we discuss relates to cases where we divide a problem into subproblems. It is often the case that we cannot run our FV task on a large design all at once; as we have seen in our discussions of case-splitting strategies in earlier chapters, subdividing the problem is often a critical enabler for FV. We also have cases where a portion of a design, such as an analog block or a complex floating point operation, is beyond the domain of our current tools and must be verified separately through other means. But whenever we subdivide the problem, we need to make sure that the sum total of our verification processes verifies all parts of the design.

LOSS OF GLUE LOGIC

As we have mentioned above, it is very common for an analog block to be black-boxed for the purpose of FV. In one of our test-chip designs, we had such a case, where the FEV owner was responsible for verifying that the RTL and schematics matched from the top level down to the boundary of an analog block, while the analog block owner was responsible for a separate (simulation-based) verification process to ensure the correctness of that block's schematic netlist.

The actual instantiation of the analog block was similar to the illustration in Figure 9.7, with a small amount of glue logic connecting the true analog logic to the design.

This raises an interesting question: which team is responsible for verifying the RTL-schematic equivalence of the glue logic? In this case, there was a bit of miscommunication. The analog design owner thought it was outside his domain of responsibility, since the glue logic looked like any other synthesizable block, just a small set of gates easily analyzable by a standard FEV tool. But from the point of view of the synthesis FEV owner, the glue logic was part of the analog block, so his verification blackboxed at the level of the outer boundary in Figure 9.7. As

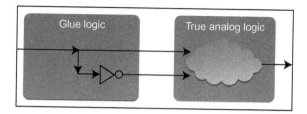

FIGURE 9.7

Analog block with glue logic.

a result, nobody considered themselves responsible for verifying the glue logic. Despite the fact that it was a relatively trivial handful of gates, it was off by one inversion, causing incorrect functionality for the first stepping.

This is an error that could have been easily detected during pre-silicon FEV, if only the glue logic had been correctly included.

CASE-SPLITTING WITH MISSING CASES

Another common way that a FV task can be subdivided for complexity is through case-splitting. It is often convenient to subdivide for different modes, especially in a model that can be used in several different modes that are not expected to change dynamically. One example of this is in a chipset design where we were supporting the PCI Express (PCIE) protocol, a popular bus interface protocol that has several modes that support varying degrees of parallel traffic, known as *x4*, *x8*, and *x16* mode.

In the PCIE block of one chipset design a few years ago, the designer was worried that some complex changes that had recently been made to improve timing and area might have caused bugs in the functionality. Thus, he asked an FPV expert to help set up a verification environment and check that the block would still work as expected. When the validation requirements were originally described, once again there was a slight miscommunication issue: "We changed functionality for the *x8* mode" was interpreted to mean, "We only need to verify the *x8* mode." The FPV expert set up the initial verification environment, helped prove and debug numerous assertions about the design's functionality, and even found some very interesting RTL bugs along the way. Eventually he reported that the verification was complete, as all the assertions were proven.

During a review of the "complete" verification, it was discovered that the FPV environment only covered the *x8* mode. The designer then explained that while this was where the most interesting changes were, the logic for all the modes was intertwined in many places, and verification was still required for the *x4* and *x16* modes in addition. Thus, the verification run was not as complete as originally thought and required several more weeks of work, during which one additional bug was found, before being truly finished.

Another very similar example came from a case where we were verifying an arithmetic block, with a 6-bit exponent. To simplify the problem, it was split into two cases: one where the value of the exponent ranged between 0 and 31, and the other where it ranged from 33 to 64. As the astute reader may have already noticed, the validator forgot the critical value of 32, which turned out to be especially risky (being a power of 2) and was the one case with an implementation bug. The bug was discovered much later than desired.

UNDOING TEMPORARY HACKS

An additional hazard related to division of labor can occur when one part of the team believes they own a piece of validation collateral, and thus can freely hack it to make things convenient for various EDA tools. By a "hack," we mean a change to the collateral files that may be logically unsound, but due to tool quirks or bugs, makes some part of the verification process more convenient. In an ideal world, we would never have to do such things to make our tools happy. But sadly, most VLSI design today occurs in the real world rather than an ideal one.

In one of our chipset designs, some team members used a new timing tool and found that it had a problem with a bunch of our library cells. We had some cells in our library that consisted of a pair of back-to-back flops, a common situation for clock domain crossing synchronization. This new timing tool, due to a software bug, had a problem handling these cases. The timing engineers noticed that the library cells were available in two formats: one was a proprietary format, intended mainly for timing tools, and the other was in standard Verilog. Thinking that they were the only users of the proprietary format, they hacked the files so each pair of flops was replaced by a single one. The modified files were then checked in to the repository for future use.

Unfortunately, the timing engineers' assumption that the proprietary format was used only for timing was not quite correct. These files actually could optionally be used instead of Verilog by both synthesis and FEV tools, and the presence of the corrupted files led to numerous two-flop synchronizers throughout the design being quietly replaced with single flops during design and verification flows. Because synthesis and FEV both used the corrupted files, the problem was not detected until very late in the project. Fortunately, a manager questioned the use of the proprietary format for FEV, and the team decided that it was safest to base the equivalence checking on the Verilog representation. Once this was done, the true issue was discovered, and the design could be corrected before tapeout.

SAFE DIVISION OF LABOR

The issues discussed in this section are another set of cases where the human factor becomes critical. In most cases, there is no way a single person can fully verify a modern VLSI design; the verification problem must always be broken down into many subproblems, with the proper specialists and tools taking care of each part. However, we must always keep in mind that there should be someone on the team with a global view, someone who understands how the problem has been divided and is capable of spotting cases of a disconnect between owners of different portions of the verification. There should always be validation reviews at each major hierarchy and at the full-chip, including both the owners of the subproblems and a global validation owner who understands the big picture.

TIP 9.14

Whenever a validation problem is subdivided among several owners, somebody should be responsible for understanding the global picture and should conduct reviews to make sure all the pieces fit together and every part of the divided problem is covered.

Aside from the understanding of the overall validation process, understanding the tools involved remains important for this set of issues as well. As we discussed in the previous section, tools have many individual quirks and hidden assumptions, and it is best to have someone with a good understanding of the tools involved participate in the reviews. The discovery of the issue of hacked cells that were fooling FEV and synthesis, for example, stemmed from a tool expert questioning the slightly dangerous use of poorly understood proprietary formats when running FEV. Thus, these issues provide yet another reason to pay attention to the tip in the previous subsection and try to always include a tool expert in validation reviews.

SUMMARY

In this chapter we have explored various types of issues that have led to false positives in FV: cases where some type of FV flow was run, and at some point in the project, the design was labeled "proven" when there was actually something logically unsound about the verification. The worst cases of false positives led to the manufacturing of faulty chips, resulting in massive expense and costly delays to fix the designs and create new steppings.

The major classes of mistakes we observed that led to false positives included:

- *Misuse of the SVA language.* As we saw, there are numerous cases in which the details of SVA can be tricky. Issues ranging from a simple missing semicolon to complex sampling behavior can cause an SVA assertion check to differ in practice from the user intent. Any code where nontrivial SVA assertions are used should be subject to good linting and manual reviews.
- *Vacuity issues.* There are many ways that a significant part of the verification space may be eliminated from an FV process. It is critical to think about both cases of full vacuity, where the verification space is the null set, and partial vacuity, where there is an interesting verification space but important cases are ruled out. Tool features can be used to detect a subset of these problems, but these should

always be supplemented with manual cover points, and with inclusion of FV assertions and assumptions in available simulation environments.

- *Implicit or unstated tool assumptions.* Many EDA tools have implicit defaults or assumptions based on the most common usage patterns in the industry, which may or may not apply to your particular case. You should carefully review your settings and run scripts with a tool expert, trying to err on the side of choosing more conservative options whenever you lack a detailed understanding of some part of the process.
- *Division of labor.* Due to the complexity of modern designs and the variety of validation problems, division of labor among teams and processes is usually unavoidable. But this type of division also creates the danger that some portion of the design or validation problem remains uncovered, because of miscommunication or misunderstandings among the subteams involved. You need to make sure someone on the team has a global view and is helping to review the various pieces of the validation process and to ensure that they all fit together correctly.

Again, while the discussions in this chapter reveal some subtle dangers where misuse of FV led to expensive rework, we do not want to scare you away from FV! Most of the false positive situations above actually have analogs in the simulation world; and in simulation, the problems are compounded by the fact that coverage of the validation space is so limited to start with. As you have learned by this point in the book, FV is a very powerful technique that leads to true coverage of your mathematical design space at levels that simulation engineers can only dream of. But with this great power comes great responsibility: to understand the limits of the FV process and to take whatever action we can to reduce the danger of missing potential issues. By understanding the cases discussed in this chapter and using them to inform your FV flows, you can formally verify your designs with even greater confidence.

PRACTICAL TIPS FROM THIS CHAPTER

9.1 Always run lint checks on any RTL code you develop.

9.2 Double-check that SVA assertion code is included in your project's lint processes.

9.3 Make sure that your project's linting program includes a good set of SVA-related lint rules.

9.4 Review each unit's assertions with an SVA expert before tapeout, to help identify cases where the assertion doesn't quite say what the author intended.

9.5 Always include your FV assertions and assumptions in any available simulation environments.

9.6 Turn on any vacuity checking, trigger checking, and coverage check offered by your EDA tools, and look carefully at the results.

9.7 Always create a good set of cover points representing typical behaviors of your design, to help sanity-check the proof space of your FV environment.

9.8 Review the interface expectations of any externally provided libraries or IPs whose functionality you are trusting rather than re-verifying. Make sure your verification plan includes checks that you are complying with any documented requirements.

9.9 Before completing a project, review your FV environments and tool control files with an expert on the tools and libraries involved.

9.10 Double-check the polarity of all reset signals and make sure that their values in the FV environment match the design intent.

9.11 Make your reset sequences for FV as general as possible, not setting any signals that do not need to be set for correct FV proofs. Be especially careful of tool options that allow global setting of 0/1 on nonreset nodes.

9.12 Make sure you are fully aware of any intentional overconstraints, or reset and initialization conditions that are not fully general, and are used to stage the verification process or reduce complexity. Justify and document why these do not create a gap in your verification process.

9.13 Review options that your FV tool provides, and try to choose more conservative checks in preference to weaker ones, unless you have a strong understanding of why the weaker options are acceptable for your particular case.

9.14 Whenever a validation problem is subdivided among several owners, somebody should be responsible for understanding the global picture and should conduct reviews to make sure all the pieces fit together and every part of the divided problem is covered.

FURTHER READING

[Bis12] Laurence S. Bisht, Dmitry Korchemny, and Erik Seligman, "SystemVerilog Assertion Linting: Closing Potentially Critical Verification Holes," Design and Verification Conference (DVCon) 2012.

[Fen10] Xiushan Feng, Joseph Gutierrez, Mel Pratt, Mark Eslinger, and Noam Farkash, "Using Model Checking to Prove Constraints of Combinational Equivalence Checking," Design and Verification Conference (DVCon) 2010.

[Knu77] Donald Knuth, "Notes on the van Emde Boas Construction of Priority Deques: An Instructive Use of Recursion," March 1977, http://www-cs-faculty.stanford.edu/~uno/faq.html.

[Kup06] Orna Kupferman, "Sanity Checks in Formal Verification," Proceedings of the 17th international conference on Concurrency Theory (CONCUR) 2006.

[Sel07] Erik Seligman and Joonyoung Kim, "FEV's Greatest Bloopers: False Positives in Formal Equivalence," Design and Verification Conference (DVCon) 2007.

[Tah02] S. Tahar, E. Cerny, and X. Song, "Formal Verification of Systems," *Class Lecture Notes*, May 2002, http://users.encs.concordia.ca/~tahar/coen7501/notes/1-intro-02.06-4p.pdf.

Dealing with complexity

Designs are tuned to the extent that they are almost wrong.
—Roope Kaivola

Formal verification (FV) engines have made amazing progress over the past three decades, in terms of the sizes and types of models they can handle. As we have seen in the previous chapters, FV can now be used to address a wide variety of problems, ranging from targeted validation at the unit level to solving certain types of connectivity or control register problems on a full-chip design. But we still need to remember one of the basic limitations we described back in Chapter 1: FV tools are inherently solving NP-complete (or harder) problems, so we constantly need to think about potential compromises and tricks to handle complexity.

How will you know if you are facing complexity issues in your FV tasks? The complexity problem can manifest itself as memory blowups, where memory consumption increases until your machine capacity is exhausted, or as cases where some proofs never complete. You may also see a tool crash or timeout related to these causes. Solving complexity in the FV domain requires some clever techniques, very different from the solutions deployed in simulation.

In this chapter, we start by discussing state space and how it is related to design complexity. We then move on to some more detailed discussion of some of the techniques discussed in our earlier chapters, such as blackboxing, cut points, driving constants, and decomposing properties. Then we introduce some fancier techniques that can result in significant increases to the capabilities of your FV runs.

In this chapter, we focus on an example using formal property verification (FPV), but most of the general principles we describe will apply to other forms of FV as well. Whether you are hitting complexity issues in FPV, formal equivalence verification (FEV), or one of the more specific FPV-based flows, you should think about how each of these methods might apply to your design.

DESIGN STATE AND ASSOCIATED COMPLEXITY

The design state consists of the values of each input and state element at a particular moment in time. The state elements include flops, latches, and memory elements. If we consider a simple design with n state elements, theoretically, we would have 2^n

possible configurations. These state elements in conjunction with the number of inputs (m) and their combinations (2^m) would form the full design state that could be conceived. The total number of such conceivable states for a design would be $2^{(n+m)}$. Simple math would reveal that the number of possible states in a trivial design with 10 inputs and 10 flip-flops to be 2^{20}, or 1,048,576. We can now imagine the number of states that would be possible for realistic designs and the number needed to analyze state changes over time. Given this inherently huge state space, it is somewhat amazing that with current EDA tools, we can often run FV on designs with around 40,000 flops, analyzing behavior spanning hundreds or thousands of time steps, and not experience noticeable complexity issues.

As we have seen in the discussions in earlier chapters, after reset, a design will be in one of the states, termed "reset state" of the design. Normally, only a small subset of the state elements is initialized by reset, with the rest left unconstrained and treated by FV tools as if they could assume any arbitrary value, as long as it does not violate any assumptions. Thus, the number of possible valid reset states is generally more than one and they form a small region in the state space rather than a single unique state. FV effectively analyzes all reset states in parallel.

The real-life operation or simulation of a register transfer level (RTL) design can be seen as a meandering path through the state space starting at reset. As a design operates, it transitions from a reset state to other states at each subsequent clock tick. Thus, it traverses one point in the state space to another, forming a trajectory. Simulation or emulation tools examine one trajectory at a time, while formal tools analyze all such trajectories in parallel. This concept can be well understood by the state space diagram in Figure 10.1.

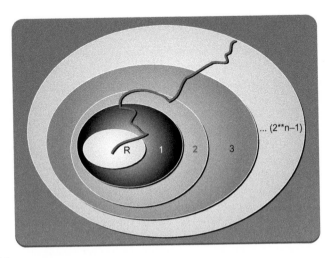

FIGURE 10.1

State space diagram and state space traversal.

As can be observed from the diagram in Figure 10.1, the design starts with the reset state (the oval labeled R). The possible states during the first cycle are depicted by oval {1}. Similarly, states possible in the second cycle are shown by oval {2}, and so on. The design would start its traversal from the {R} state and work through the next set of states until it reaches the final state. A typical simulation test would explore one trajectory at a time as depicted in the illustration. FV would explore all states possible in each clock cycle, as represented by the growing series of ellipses in the diagram.

If the FV tool reaches a full proof, it has effectively explored all these ellipses out to include all possible states reachable by the design. If it does a bounded proof, it is still covering a very large region of the space in comparison to simulation; the outer circle in Figure 10.1 represents a proof to a bound indicated by the outermost ellipse, which represents some specific number of cycles. It would guarantee that there is no failure possible within that bound, but the design might fail outside that range. All the regions in the diagram are not equal, due to varying complexity of the logic: small increments in the depth achieved can be hugely significant depending on the property being checked. For example, a design may spend 256 cycles waiting for a startup counter to complete, and then start a very complex operation when the count is done. In that case, analyzing each of those first 256 cycles may be easy, while the cycle after the counter completes may expose the full logic of the design.

This exponentially growing state space is a major source of complexity issues for FV. This difficulty, known as *state space explosion*, is a typical culprit preventing us from achieving the full convergence on the design.

We should point out, however, that the above discussion pertains to types of FV that analyze behavior over time: FPV, or sequential FEV. Combinational FEV, since it breaks up models at state elements, allows a much simpler analysis by formal tools: they just need to comprehend the Boolean logic that describes the next state at each latch, flop, and output for a single cycle. But remember that even analyzing correctness of a single state is an NP-complete problem (equivalent to the SAT problem), so it is possible that complicated RTL logic can cause a complexity blowup even in combinational FEV. Although the focus of this chapter is on the more difficult complexity problems encountered in sequential FV techniques, many of the methods described in this chapter can be useful with combinational FEV as well.

EXAMPLE FOR THIS CHAPTER: MEMORY CONTROLLER

To make the examples in the chapter more concrete, we will consider a memory controller interface, with the basic structure shown in Figure 10.2.

The block here contains two memory protocol engines (MPEs) and two memory read/write arbiters (MRA). The protocol engines and the arbiters are tightly

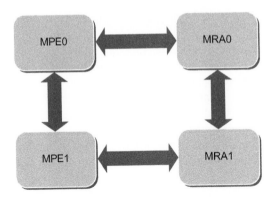

FIGURE 10.2

Sample memory interface logic.

connected to each other to work in tandem to access the memory locations from various memory modules and serve a range of requestors.

The memory arbiter selects between several requestors vying to send a memory address and request using the following priority scheme:

```
Refresh > Read > Write
```

One other important function of the MRA is to check and avoid hazards like read after write (RAW), where a read in the pipeline may return a value that predates a recent write. This hazard check requires an address compare operation. The controller is a fully contained block that makes sure the memory access functions are hazard free and guarantees correct data storage and retrieval.

The MPEs contain a wide variety of decision finite-state machines (FSMs) and implement a multitude of deep queues to store the in-flight content and perform some on-the-fly operations. The MPEs enforce protocol adherence and maintain many data structures to ensure consistency.

Some of the properties that are hard to converge for this controller are:

- Fair arbitration across all read and write requests
- Faithful data transfer through the controller
- Priority preserved across all requestors
- Conformation to protocol requirements
- Avoid RAW hazards
- Eventually every request is granted

In the remainder of this chapter, we will often refer to this example as we discuss how we might use various techniques to handle potential complexity issues during its FV.

OBSERVING COMPLEXITY ISSUES

Complexity issues in FV manifest themselves as:

- Memory blowups—Caused by the state explosion problem and resulting in insufficient resources. Sometimes it also results in system crashing or angry emails from your network administrator.
- Indefinite runtime —While the tool works on the problem within a defined set of resources, it is continually exploring more states and never completes within a stipulated time period.
- A low bound on the bounded proof—Bounded proofs are often okay if the bounds are reasonable, but a low bound that fails to match cover point requirements or that fails to exercise interesting logic is not acceptable.
- Tool crashes—When system capacity is stressed for any of the above reasons, tools sometimes fail to report this cleanly and crash instead.

As you saw in Chapter 6, we advise that you begin FV efforts with an attempt to estimate complexity issues in advance, by planning your verification with the aid of a block diagram and your knowledge of major submodules. The design itself could be too huge to be handled by typical FV tools, and you may need to focus on lower levels or find major blackboxing opportunities. The design might also contain many memory elements that are wide and deep, a large set of counters, or logic styles (such as floating point arithmetic) that do not cooperate well with your tool set.

The first general estimate can be obtained from the number of flops in the module that is under test. A finer estimate would be to assess the number of flops in the logic cone of each assertion; this information can often be reported by your FPV tools. A number of flops might also be added to the cone of logic for proving the assertion because of the constraints that are coded. As we have mentioned, a rule of thumb we use is that your tool should not need to analyze more than 40,000 state elements. You can try with more than this and may find that your tools continue to work reasonably well, but as you grow the number of state elements, expect to spend more time dealing with complexity.

Also, do not forget that model-checking engines used in typical FPV tools are getting smarter day by day, which means that even though we suggested a rule of thumb of aiming for less than 40,000 state elements, they can sometimes converge on bigger design sizes (that rule of thumb may be outdated by the time you read this book!). Designs that were deemed not fit for convergence through FV a couple of years ago are easily going through the latest engines. The EDA industry and academia are actively working and collaborating on improving engines. There is somewhat of an arms race going on here though; while the engines further their convergence capabilities, designs also continue to grow in complexity.

> **TIP 10.1**
>
> It is recommended to first analyze your design for complexity before you begin an FPV effort. Look at the total number of state elements at the top level and in each major submodule, and try to aim for a size with fewer than 40K state elements.

As we mentioned in Chapter 6, we also suggest initially targeting bounded proofs rather than full proofs, since these are often much less expensive to obtain. Use your knowledge of the design and a good set of cover points to try to estimate a reasonable bound. Most projects we have worked with at Intel were comfortable with accepting a bounded proof in place of a full proof as a signoff criterion, as long as the bound was well justified. Thus, before making major efforts to deal with complexity, because your proofs are bounded rather than full, be sure to consider whether the bounded proofs are good enough for your current problem.

> **TIP 10.2**
>
> Don't panic if you have a bounded proof rather than a full proof. Make sure that the expected deep design behaviors are covered by proving a good set of cover points. A bounded proof may be fully acceptable as a signoff criterion.

SIMPLE TECHNIQUES FOR CONVERGENCE

Before we start describing more advanced complexity techniques, we should review and expand upon the basic methods that were discussed in earlier chapters. If you do encounter a complexity issue, be sure you attempt to make full use of each of these suggestions.

CHOOSING THE RIGHT BATTLE

When we choose the design hierarchy level for formal proof development, we need to make sure that we are not biting off more than we can chew. We need to identify the right set of logic where our tools are likely to converge, but where our analysis region is large enough to encompass an interesting set of proofs without requiring massive development of assumptions on the interface.

Let's look again at our memory controller example. When we look at the number of state elements in the memory interface block as a whole, we might find that the amount of logic is too large, on the order of 100K state elements after blackboxing embedded memories. Thus, we are unlikely to get full convergence on the properties. If this is the case, it might be a good idea to verify the

MPE and MRA blocks separately. Because there are two instances of each of these submodules (identical aside from instance names), in effect we would only have to verify 1/4 as much logic in each FPV run, which is a powerful argument in favor of this method. On the negative side, this would create a need for us to write assumptions that model the inter-unit interfaces between the MPEs and MRAs, which we would not have to do if verifying the top-level unit.

We also need to consider the issue of locality of the property logic. Most FPV tools have intelligent engines that try to minimize the amount of logic they are using in each assertion proof, only bringing in the relevant logic affecting that assertion. Even though the full model may have 100K flops, if we expect that each of our assertion proofs will be almost entirely local to one of the MPE or MRA submodules, it may be that we do not pay much of a complexity penalty for loading the full model.

One issue to be cautious of when deciding to run on the lower-level models is that we may initially underestimate the level of assumption writing that needs to be done. If during our initial wiggling stages, where we are looking at counterexamples and developing additional assumptions, we find that our set of assumptions grows too large or unwieldy, we may want to consider backing off our approach of verifying the subunits. We would then verify the full unit, with the logic of all four major submodules combined, and be prepared to look at other techniques for reducing complexity.

TIP 10.3

Partition a large component into smaller, independently verifiable components to control the state explosion problem through compositional reasoning. But if you find during wiggling that this causes a need for too much assumption creation, consider verifying the larger model and using other complexity techniques.

ENGINE TUNING

Before trying any fancier complexity techniques, make sure you are taking full advantage of the engine features offered by your FV tool. Most current-generation FV tools contain multiple engines, implementing different heuristics for solving FV problems. These engines are often tuned to optimize for certain design structures and it is highly recommended that you choose the right set of the engines to solve the problem you are trying to verify. Information about the engines is typically available from the user guide or the data sheets of vendor provided tools. Some engines are good at bug hunting, so are the best choice when you are in early design or validation stages and are expecting many property failures. Others are optimized for safety properties and some at converging liveness properties. Some engines are programmed to function by iteratively adding logic to the analysis region to achieve convergence, while others search deep in the state space to hit hard cover points.

> **TIP 10.4**
>
> Experiment with the engines offered by the tool, before you start resolving the convergence of hard properties. Many engines are optimized to work on a subset of design styles or property types; choose the right engine for the property under consideration.

In many cases, individual engines provide certain "knobs," additional optional parameters for controlling their behavior more directly. Look for the following opportunities for finer-grained control over your engine behavior:

- *Start:* You may be able to control how deep in the state space the engine should start looking for counterexamples: perhaps you suspect an error when a 64-deep queue is full, for example, so you might tell the engine to start searching at depth 64. This may hurt performance if there was a much shorter failure to find, however. You also have to be careful to check whether this option will cause your engine to assume there are no earlier failures, in which case the proofs may be logically incomplete in cases without a failure. We have also experimented with a "swarm" strategy where a user runs many copies of the FV run in parallel on a pool of machines, each with a different start depth, to try to maximize the speed at which they find the first failure, at the expense of spending significantly more compute resources.
- *Step:* Similarly, for engines that incrementally move more deeply into the verification space, you might be able to tell them to check for failures every n cycles, for some n, rather than at every possible depth. Again, this is more appropriate when you expect failures, since depending on your tool, it may cause some to potentially be missed, or hurt performance if it causes the engine to skip over easy failures.
- *Waypoints:* Some engines, also known as "semiformal" engines, try to start by finding interesting individual traces deep in your design space, and then explore the complete space from there. In such engines, specifying a *waypoint*, or interesting cover point that you think might result in potential failures soon afterwards, can help direct the search. This technique actually can be implemented manually, as we discuss in a later section below, but we mention it here since some FPV tools have lightweight semiformal capabilities built into their engines. Your tool may also contain some nonsemiformal FPV engines that can use waypoint information in clever ways to guide the search process.

> **TIP 10.5**
>
> If you are focusing on bug hunting or are in early stages of FPV, and expect many failures, take advantage of tool settings such as *start*, *step*, and *waypoints* to enable more efficient bug hunting runs.

BLACKBOXING

Blackboxing, or marking submodules to be ignored for FV purposes, is one of the major techniques for reducing complexity of a design. When a module is blackboxed, its outputs are treated as primary inputs to the design: they can take on any value at any time, since their logic is not modeled. Because it is relatively easy to do with most tools and can have huge effects on FV performance, you should think about opportunities for blackboxing at the beginning of any FV effort.

One nice aspect of this technique is that it is guaranteed to never create a false positive (aside from the lack of verification of the blackbox itself). This is because blackboxing a module makes its outputs more general: the FV tool may produce additional false negatives, spurious counterexamples that the user must debug and use to suggest new assumptions, but will never report an assertion passing if it is possible that some actions of the blackboxed module could have caused it to fail. Thus, it is safe to blackbox too much logic, and later un-blackbox if too many incorrect counterexamples result.

There are many common types of logic that should almost always be blackboxed for FV purposes, since they either contain styles of logic for which common FV tools are not well suited, or are known to be verified elsewhere. For example, caches and memories are really hard to analyze, due to their gigantic state space, and the functionality of data storage and retrieval is usually not very interesting. There are alternate methods of proving the functional correctness of the memory elements and caches, using specialized formal or simulation tools.

In general, if you see any of these in a unit on which you are planning to run FV tools, strongly consider blackboxing them:

- Memories and caches
- Complex arithmetic or data transformation blocks like multipliers, dividers, complex functions, or floating point logic
- Analog circuitry
- Externally supplied (pre-verified) IPs
- Blocks known to be FVed at a lower level
- Specialized functions unrelated to your FV focus (power, scan, and so on)

TIP 10.6

To address FV complexity, blackbox memories/caches, complex arithmetic or data transformation blocks, analog circuitry, externally verified IPs, blocks known to be separately verified, or specialized function blocks unrelated to your FV focus.

PARAMETERS AND SIZE REDUCTION

Be sure to look in your model for opportunities to reduce the size of a large data path or large structure. For example, if our MRA contains an N-bit wide data path in which essentially the same logic is used for every bit, do you really need to represent the full width of the data path? Often you can reduce it to a handful of bits, or even a single bit, and still have confidence that your FV proofs ultimately apply to all bits of the bus.

To better enable this method, you should work with your design team to make sure that your RTL is well parameterized. If every submodule of the MRA has a *DATA_WIDTH* parameter they inherit from the next higher level, making this size reduction in the MRA FPV environment could be a one-line change; but if there are a dozen submodules that each have the *N* hardcoded to some number, say 32, this edit would be painful.

In other cases, you may have several instances of a block, but be able to essentially run your verification with only a single instance active. In our memory controller, is there significant interaction between the two MPEs, or can the majority of our properties be sensibly proven with one of the two identical MPEs blackboxed, or with a top-level parameter modified so there is only one MPE?

> **TIP 10.7**
>
> Look for opportunities to take advantage of symmetry and reduce the sizes of regular data structures or occurrences of repeated modules.

> **TIP 10.8**
>
> Make sure parameters are used whenever possible to specify the sizes of repeated or symmetric structures in RTL, so you can easily modify those sizes when useful for FPV.

CASE-SPLITTING

When we have large parts of the logic operating separately and we try to verify a very general property, we often end up effectively verifying multiple submachines all at once. This can add a lot of logic to the cone of influence. In our memory controller example, if you have chosen to run your proofs at the top level, do operations tend to exercise all four major submodules (MPEs and MRAs) at the same time, or do different types of accesses essentially exercise subsets of them independently? In the arithmetic logic unit (ALU) example we discussed in Chapter 6, where there are two sets of operations (adder and logic ops) that go to completely different subunits, do we really need to verify all operations at once? Trying to do unnecessarily general property checking that encompasses large portions of the logic all at once can result in significant complexity issues.

You should be sure to examine your design's *care set* (set of input conditions you *care* about-- as opposed to *don't care* about-- to verify) and identify opportunities for *case-splitting*, adding temporary constraints to restrict each proof

Table 10.1 Example Case-Split of Care Set

Case	Opcode Range	Scan Mode
Case 1	8'h00-8'h7f	OFF
Case 2	8'h80	OFF
Case 3	8'h81-8'hff	OFF
Case 4	All	ON

attempt to a subset of the design logic. This may also create an opportunity to perform independent runs on a network of workstations, so the subproblems can be verified in parallel.

Table 10.1 depicts how the case-splitting might be done on an example care set. Case-splitting would decompose the care set into multiple slices that could be effectively handled by the tools. The cases may be symmetric, or some may encompass more data than others: in the example in Table 10.1, the validator suspects that boundary opcode value 8'h80 will have unique difficulties, so that case has been separated out, while the other cases cover wider ranges. In addition, there may be special modes to handle; the split in this table also has one case for scan mode, in which all opcode values (for that mode) are handled. For each case, you need to add assumptions that set relevant inputs to restricted or constant values, which only exercise the chosen case.

TIP 10.9

Decompose the input care set into simple cases to assist convergence on your design.

Be careful, however, to ensure that you have proven that the sum total of all your cases truly covers all possible operations of your design. As we saw in Chapter 9, if you are not careful, you can end up ignoring parts of your design space while splitting up cases. Unlike techniques such as blackboxing, case-splitting can be unsafe and lead to false positives, since you are introducing assumptions that restrict the verification space for each case. If aiming for full proof FPV or FEV, you need to have a strong argument or formal proof that the sum total of your cases covers all activity of your design.

You also need to think about whether the different cases are truly independent, or can interact with each other: think about cross-products. For example, in our memory controller, while we might be able to create independent proofs that individual memory read operations on MRA0 and MRA1 are correct in the absence of external activity, do we need to worry about cases where the two MRAs are acting at once or quickly in succession, and their operations may interfere with each other? If so, after we complete our initial proofs for the split cases, we may still need to run proofs on the full model without case restrictions. This does not mean our case-split was a bad idea however: it is very likely needed to enable us to more quickly find and debug an initial set of issues in bug hunting FPV, even though it leaves some gaps if our goal is full proofs.

One other point you should keep in mind is that sometimes one level of case-splits might not be sufficient, and we might need secondary case-splits to bring complexity under control. For example, if we find that we still have a complexity issue in the ALU from Chapter 6 after restricting the opcode to arithmetic operation, we may need to further split down to create individual proof environments for ADD, SUB, and CMP operations.

PROPERTY SIMPLIFICATION

There are numerous cases where you might be able to make your assertions much simpler for the formal tools to analyze, by rewriting them in a simpler form or splitting a complex assertion into multiple smaller assertions.

Boolean simplifications

If you have a property with an OR on the left side of an implication or an AND on the right side, it can easily be split into multiple smaller properties. Of course you can probably come up with other simple transformations, based on principles such as the Boolean laws we discussed in Chapter 2. Smaller and simpler properties are likely to be much better handled by the FPV tools and ease convergence, which also provide significant debug advantages.

The simplest examples of this kind of transformation are replacing

```
p1: assert property ((a || b) |-> c);
p2: assert property (d |-> (e && f));
```

with

```
p1_1: assert property (a |-> c);
p1_2: assert property (b |-> c);
p2_1: assert property (d |-> e);
p2_2: assert property (d |-> f);
```

If you think about it a little, there are many opportunities for similar transformations of more complex properties, since a sequence may often represent an implicit AND or OR operation. For example, we could replace

```
p3: assert property (A ##1 B |-> C ##4 D);
```

with two simple properties

```
p3_1: assert property (A ##1 B |-> C);
p4_1: assert property (A ##1 B |-> ##4 D);
```

This technique can be generally applied on protocol assertions like req-ack handshakes. Instead of writing a complete assertion for the whole behavior, we can break down the property into its component elements, based on the arcs of its timing diagram. Be careful, though, that you have a strong logical argument that the sum total of your decomposed properties is equivalent to your original property.

> **TIP 10.10**
>
> When possible, split complex assertions into simpler atomic assertions, whose union would imply the original check intended.

Making liveness properties finite

One other type of property simplification we should discuss relates to *liveness* properties, assertions that describe behavior that may extend infinitely into the future. These are generally harder for formal tools to fully analyze, so sometimes limiting the unbounded nature of liveness can help in convergence. The new limit defined should have a large enough number to mimic a large bound that it seemingly appears as a liveness condition.

For example,

```
will_respond: assert property {req |-> s_eventually(rsp)}
```

might be replaced by

```
will_respond50: assert property { req |-> ##[1:50] rsp }
```

Here we are assuming that you have a model with a logical depth significantly smaller than 50, and a good set of cover points showing that a reasonable set of operations of your model could occur within that time limit. Some model-checking engines work much better with a defined bound and could converge faster.

While this technique creates a stronger assertion, and is thus technically safe from false positives, you will often find that it causes a bogus proof failure due to external inputs not responding within the specified time. Thus, when using this technique, you may also need to add companion assumptions that force external readiness conditions to be met within a related time boundary. For example, if in our design there is a backpressure signal that may prevent a response, we would need to make sure that signal changes within 50 cycles:

```
bp_fair50: assume property (req|->
        ##[1:50] !backpressure);
```

Similarly, limiting the bound of potentially infinite-time assumptions is sometimes helpful to verify design properties. For example, the above *bp_fair50* assumption might be an appropriate bounded replacement for a more general liveness assumption like:

```
bp_fair: assume property (req|->
        s_eventually(!backpressure));
```

Putting a finite bound on assumptions, using *bp_fair50* rather than *bp_fair*, is also often helpful in reaching interesting states in the formal analysis. However, keep in mind that such simplifications are technically a form of overconstraint and thus can be potentially dangerous. It is always advisable to constrain the design under test (DUT) as loosely as possible. Removing these delay constraints would give the engines higher freedom to explore deeper state space. If you use these techniques to address convergence issues, we would advise extra review, and consider relaxing them after your initial round of FV is complete.

CUT POINTS

As we have mentioned in earlier chapters, a cut point is a location in the model where you "cut" a node away from its input logic cone, allowing it to freely take on any value. When a node is cut, the FV tool can then remove the node's input logic from formal analysis. It is a similar concept to a blackbox: you can think of a blackbox as a case where every output of a submodule has become a cut point. Using cut points is a more fine-grained technique, targeting individual nodes in a design. As we discussed in Chapter 8, the key points used by FEV can also be thought of as a type of cut point.

Like a blackbox, applying a cut point is always a logically safe transformation, possibly introducing false negatives, but never risking a false positive. Cut points increase the space of legal behaviors, since the cut point's fanin logic is treated as returning a fully general arbitrary value, but often with the benefit of a decrease in the complexity of the remaining logic. If the removed logic truly was irrelevant to the proof, you should see correct results after adding a cut point. If you made a mistake and the logic you removed was relevant, this should be apparent when debugging the false negatives, and you see the cut point value affecting your result. You may need to add related assumptions to model the missing logic, or choose a different cut point.

To see an example of where you might find a good cut point, let's look again at the memory controller example. You may recall that the MRA arbiter checks for a RAW hazard and performs certain actions as a result. Suppose we trust the logic that computes whether we have a RAW hazard (perhaps it was reused from a previous successful project), and are not worried about verifying that calculation. The intent of the property being checked is to verify that the read is properly delayed when we have a RAW hazard; for the purposes of this check, it does not really matter whether there was a real RAW hazard embedded in the operations performed. Hence, we can safely place a cut point at the output of the RAW computation as depicted in Figure 10.3. The RAW bit is then a free variable and can take any value for the verification.

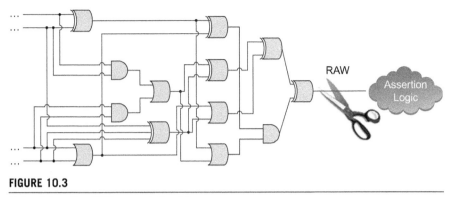

FIGURE 10.3

Cut point on the RAW computation bit.

Now the complexity of the logic being checked is drastically reduced, since we are skipping all the logic that computed whether we had a RAW hazard. Since the RAW bit is free to take any value, we might hit false negatives and have to add some assumptions on the bit to make it realistic. For example, maybe the nonsensical case where a RAW hazard is flagged during a nonread operation would cause strange behavior.

If you are having trouble identifying cut points for a difficult property, one method that can be helpful is to generate a *variables file*. This is a file listing all the RTL signals in the fanin cone of your property. Most FPV tools either have a way to generate this directly, or enable you to easily get this with a script. There may be hundreds of variables, but the key is to look for sets of signal names that suggest that irrelevant parts of the logic are causing your property fanin to appear complex. For example, you may spot large numbers of nodes with "scan" in the name, and this would indicate that one of them is probably a good cut point to remove scan-related logic.

TIP 10.11

Use cut points to free design logic and reduce complexity, in cases where you can identify large blocks of logic that are not in a blackboxable standalone module but are irrelevant to your verification. If you are having trouble identifying good cut points, generate a variables file and review the nodes involved in your property's fanin cone.

In combinational FEV, you can think of the combinational method as having predefined all state elements as cut points to optimize the comparison. Adding additional non-state cut points for combinational FEV, or adding state or non-state cut points for sequential FEV, can significantly improve performance. Just as in FPV, though, you need to be careful if you are removing critical logic, and may need to compensate by adding assumptions.

We should also mention here that in some cases, we have found that we can successfully run a script to find good FEV cut points through a brute-force method: look for intermediate nodes in the logic of a hard-to-prove key point with similar names or fanin cones in both models, and try to prove the intermediate nodes are equivalent. If the proof succeeds, that node is likely a good cut point. This can be time consuming, but running a script over the weekend that focuses on a particular logic cone of interest can sometimes be successful in finding useful cut points.

Blackboxes with holes

One specific application of cut points that you may sometimes find very useful is the idea of creating a blackbox with "holes"—that is, where a submodule is almost completely blackboxed, but some small portion of the logic is still exposed to the FV engine. This is often needed when some type of interesting global functionality, such as clocking or power, is routed through a module that is otherwise blackboxed for FV. This situation is illustrated in Figure 10.4.

In Figure 10.4, we want to blackbox the block on our left while running FPV at the *TOP* level, but this causes our proofs to fail in the target block on the right, due to a dependence on some clocking logic that is inside the blackbox. To fix this, instead of declaring the module as a blackbox, we can write a script to add cut points for all outputs of the module except the outputs we want to preserve. In our example, we would want to preserve the input logic for output *ck*, and the script should find and cut the other module outputs (points *a*, *b*, *c*). Utilizing the script, we effectively create a blackbox with a hole to preserve the one piece of logic we need.

TIP 10.12
If one of your proposed blackboxes needs a "hole" to allow a small piece of FV-critical logic to be visible, use cut points instead of blackboxing. You can declare each of the module's outputs a cut point, except for the one whose logic you need.

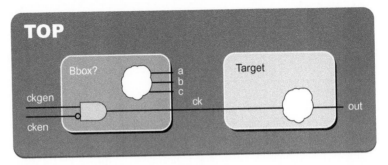

FIGURE 10.4

Example where we need a "hole" in a blackbox.

SEMIFORMAL VERIFICATION

In the section on engine parameters above, we introduced the concept of "semiformal" verification. This is worth more discussion here, because even when your tool has a built-in semiformal engine, understanding details about the underlying method can enable you to use it much more effectively. Suppose you are in a bug hunting FPV environment, and you find that your tool is getting stuck attempting to hit a deep cover point. For example, you might run your tool for a week, getting to bound 1,000 in your proofs, but find that one of your cover points still has not been hit. In our memory controller example, suppose we have a refresh counter that initiates a special action every 2^{13}, or 9,192 cycles. It is likely that our tool will never be able to reach such a depth, due to exponential growth of the state space. But we might be very concerned about checking for potential errors that can occur when the refresh condition is hit. Is there any way we can search for such a bug?

A simple solution is to think about *semiformal* verification. Instead of starting from a true reset state, we will provide an example execution trace to the tool as a starting point. Most FPV tools allow you to import a reset sequence from simulation, so we could just harvest a simulation trace that ran to 9,000 cycles and got close to a refresh point. Alternatively, you can try to get an efficient cover trace (500 cycles, for example) from your FPV tool, feed that "waypoint" back in as the reset sequence, and iteratively repeat the process until you have built up a series of cover traces that covers a 9,000-cycle execution. Once you have reached a waypoint that you think is close to a potential source of error, then have the formal engine explore exhaustively for assertion failures, using that waypoint as the reset point to start its exploration.

Since you are starting with one particular deep trace, rather than a truly general reset state, this method is only for bug hunting, rather than full proof FPV: many valid execution paths are not checked. However, it is an excellent method for discovering tricky corner-case bugs triggered by deep design states, since you still gain FPV's distinct benefit of exhaustively exploring the design space starting from a particular point. This method is illustrated in Figure 10.5.

In Figure 10.5, each star represents an intermediate waypoint, a cover point fed iteratively to the tool by the user, with the red path marking the execution trace that is generated as a pseudo-reset for FPV. The black circle represents the subspace that is exhaustively searched for assertion failures by the FPV tool, showing that error condition *ERR* will be found, even though it is much deeper than the tool was able to explore by default. However, since the other error condition *ERR2* is reachable only by a very different execution path than the user focused on, it will not be discovered by this method.

While semiformal verification sacrifices the fully exhaustive search of full proof FPV, it is still a very powerful validation method: it is equivalent to running an exponential number of random tests in a small region of the state space. Thus, if you suspect deep bugs that are triggered by a condition that you cannot exercise with your current proof bounds, you should strongly consider using this method.

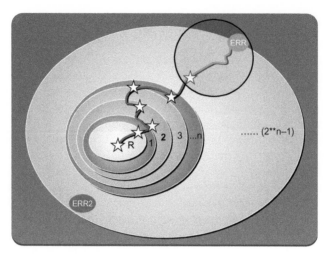

FIGURE 10.5

Semiformal FPV. Error ERR will be found, but ERR2 will be missed.

TIP 10.13

If you suspect potential issues triggered by a design state that cannot be reached within your current proof bound (as detected by failed cover points), consider enhancing your bug hunting with semiformal verification.

In addition, be sure to examine the features offered by your verification tool; many modern FPV tools offer some degree of automation for semiformal verification. Your tool may allow you to directly specify a series of waypoints, without having to manually extract each trace and convert it to a reset sequence.

INCREMENTAL FEV

Suppose you have successfully run full proof FPV on a complex design and have been continually running regressions on it, but the regressions are very time consuming. In some cases, we have seen at Intel, we have been able to use advanced complexity techniques to successfully verify a unit, but the FPV ultimately takes several weeks to run, due to high complexity and a large number of cases that have been split.

Then a new customer request comes in and you need to modify your RTL. Do you need to rerun your full set of FPV regressions? What happens if your new change further increased the design complexity and your original FPV regressions now crash or fail to complete after several weeks?

In cases where you have changed a design that had a difficult or complex FPV run, you should consider doing an incremental RTL-RTL FEV run instead of rerunning your FPV regression. Assuming you insert your change carefully and include a "chicken bit," a way to shut off the new features, you do not really need to re-verify your entire design. Just verify that the new design matches the old one when the new features are turned off; if you were confident in your original verification of the old model, this should be sufficient. Then you only need to write and prove assertions specifying the newly added features, which might take up significantly less time and effort than rerunning your full proof set on the entire model. We have seen cases at Intel where a formal regression that took several weeks could be replaced with a day or two of FEV runs.

TIP 10.14

If you have made changes to a stable design that had a time-consuming and complex FPV run, consider replacing FPV regressions with an FEV equivalence proof that your changes did not modify existing functionality.

HELPER ASSUMPTIONS ... AND NOT-SO-HELPFUL ASSUMPTIONS

Now that we have reviewed the basic complexity techniques that should be in your toolkit, it is time to look at a few more advanced ones. One idea you should consider when running into complexity issues is the concept of *helper assumptions*: assumptions that rule out a large part of the problem space, hopefully reducing the complexity and enabling model convergence. This is illustrated in Figure 10.6.

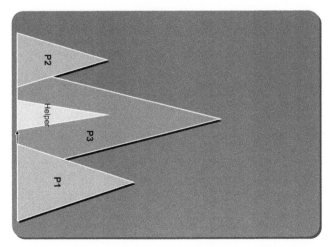

FIGURE 10.6

Helper assumptions for faster convergence.

In Figure 10.6, the yellow part of the cone of influence of a property has been ruled out by helper assumptions, reducing the logic that must be analyzed by the formal engines.

WRITING CUSTOM HELPER ASSUMPTIONS

As with many aspects of FV, the most powerful aid you can give to the tools comes from your insight into your particular design. Are you aware of parts of the functional behavior space that do not need to be analyzed in order to prove your design is correct? Do implicit design or input requirements theoretically eliminate some part of the problem space? If so, write some assumptions to help rule out these cases.

Some of the starting assumptions we have created in previous chapters, such as restricting the opcodes of our ALU or setting scan signals to 0, can be seen as simple examples of helper assumptions. Looking at our memory controller example, let's suppose we have added our cut point at the RAW hazard computation. We know the RAW hazard can only logically be true when a read operation is in progress, but there is nothing enforcing that condition once the cut point is there—it is possible that our FPV engine is wasting a lot of time analyzing cases where a non-read operation triggers a RAW hazard. Thus, an assumption that a RAW hazard only occurs on a read operation might be a useful helper assumption.

If you are facing a complexity issue, you should think about the space of behaviors of your design, and try to find opportunities to create helper assumptions that would rule out large classes of irrelevant states.

> ### TIP 10.15
>
> If dealing with complexity issues, think about opportunities for "helper assumptions" that would rule out large parts of the problem space, and add some of these to your design.

LEVERAGING PROVEN ASSERTIONS

If you are working on a design where you have already proven a bunch of assertions, and only some small subset is failing to converge, this may provide a nice opportunity to grab a bunch of "free" helper assumptions. Most modern FPV tools have a way to convert assertions to assumptions. Use these tool features to convert all the proven assertions to assumptions—you can then leverage them as helper assumptions for the remainder of the proofs. Some tools will do something like this automatically, but even if your tool claims to have this feature, don't take it for granted—it may be that some of your "hard" proofs started before all your "easy" proofs were completed, so many complex proofs may not be taking advantage of all your proven assertions. Thus, starting a new run with all your proven assertions converted to assumptions may provide a significant advantage.

TIP 10.16

If some of your assertions are passing, but others are facing complexity issues, convert your passing assertions to helper assumptions for the next run.

If you are using one of the modern *assertion synthesis* tools, which can auto-generate some set of assertions, this may provide additional easily proven properties that you can use as helper assumptions. But avoid going overboard and creating too many assumptions or you may face the problem mentioned in the next subsection.

DO YOU HAVE TOO MANY ASSUMPTIONS?

Paradoxically, although assumptions help to fight complexity by ruling out a portion of the problem space, they can also *add* complexity, by making it more compute-intensive for the FV engines to figure out if a particular set of behaviors is legal. You may recall that we made the same point in the context of FPV for post-silicon in Chapter 7, since it is common for post-silicon teams to have too many assumptions available due to scanout data. Figure 10.7 provides a conceptual illustration of why adding assumptions can either add or remove complexity. While a good set of assumptions will reduce the problem space, large sets of assumptions might make it computationally complex to determine whether any particular behavior is legal.

Thus, you need to carefully observe the effects as you add helper assumptions, to determine whether they are really helping. Add them in small groups and remove the "helpers" if it turns out that they make performance worse.

TIP 10.17

Monitor the changes in proof performance after adding helper assumptions, and remove them if they turn out not to help.

Full behavior space   Simple assumption set   Complex assumption set

FIGURE 10.7

Adding assumptions can make FPV easier or harder.

In addition, you may want to look at your overall set of assumptions, and think about whether they are all truly necessary: were they added in response to debugging counterexamples during wiggling, in which case they probably are essential, or were they just general properties you thought would be true of your interface? For example, one of our colleagues reported a case where he removed an assumption in the form "*request* |- > *##[0:N] response*", a perfectly logical assumption for an interface—and a formerly complex proof was then able to converge. Even though he was now running proofs on a more general problem space, where time for responses is unbounded, this more general space was easier for the FPV engines to handle.

TIP 10.18

If you have a large number of assumptions and are facing complexity issues, examine your assumption set for ones that may not truly be necessary. Sometimes removing unneeded assumptions, even though it widens the problem space covered by FV, can actually improve performance.

GENERALIZING ANALYSIS USING FREE VARIABLES

The concept of a *free variable* is actually nothing new: it is quite similar to a primary input, just a value coming into your design that the FV engine can freely assign any value not prohibited by assumptions. A free variable is different in that it is added as an extra input by an FPV user, rather than already existing as an actual input to the model. Usually you would create a free variable by either adding it as a new top-level input to your model, or declaring it as a variable inside your model and then using commands in your FPV tool to make it a cut point.

Free variables provide a way to generalize the formal analysis, considering cases involving each possible value of the variable at once. When the model contains some level of symmetry to be exploited, these variables can significantly increase the efficiency of formal analysis.

EXPLOITING SYMMETRY WITH RIGID FREE VARIABLES

Let us consider a variation of our MRA unit where it maintains tokens for various requestors and grants them according to the priority. We want to prove one property for each requestor if the tokens are granted to them based on the requirement.

```
parameter TOKEN_CONTROL = 64;
generate for (i = 0; i < TOKEN_CONTROL; i++) begin
  ctrl_ring(clk,grant_vec[i], stuff)
```

```
    a1: assert property (p1(clk,grant_vec[i],stuff))
  end
endgenerate
```

Since we placed the assertion inside the generate loop, we would end up proving slightly different versions of the assertion 64 times, which is not an optimal solution. This may result in significant costs within our FPV tool, in terms of time and memory. Is there a better way to do this? This is where a free variable can make a huge difference. We can remove assertion a1 from the generate loop and instead prove the property generally with a single assertion:

```
int test_bit; // free variable
test_bit_legal: assume property
    (test_bit> =0 && test_bit<64);
test_bit_stable: assume property (##1 $stable(test_bit));
a1: assert property (p1(clk,grant_vec[test_bit],stuff));
```

As you can see above, using the free variable *test_bit* makes the assertion general: instead of analyzing each of the 64 cases separately, we are telling the FPV tool to complete a general analysis, proving the assertion for all 64 possible values of *test_bit* at once. Many FPV engines work very well on such generalized properties. If there is symmetry to exploit, with all 64 cases involving very similar logic, the FPV tools can take advantage of that fact and cleanly prove the assertion for all bits at once.

We need to be careful when using free variables, however. In the above example, we added two basic assumptions: that the free variable takes on legal values, and that it is a stable constant for the proof. You will usually need such assumptions when using free variables to replace generate loops or similar regular patterns.

TIP 10.19

Use rigid free variables to replace large numbers of assertion instances in generate loops with a single nonloop assertion.

OTHER USES OF FREE VARIABLES

The example above is one of the simpler cases of using free variables, to generalize analysis of each iteration in a large loop. Another common usage of free variables is to represent a generalized behavior, where some decision is made about which of several nondeterministic actions is taken during each cycle of execution. For example, a free variable can be used to represent indeterminate jitter at a clock domain crossing boundary, or the identity of a matching tag returned in the cache for a memory controller. Again, look for cases where multiple behaviors are handled by the same or symmetric logic, which can be exploited by FPV engines.

When using a free variable in one of these cases, you will probably not want to assume that it is permanently constant as in the rigid example above. Instead, you need to add assumptions that define when changes may occur.

In some cases, free variables can also be tough for convergence, even with similar pieces of logic applied across the bus width. It might be imperative to use case-splitting across the free variables for better convergence, while not compromising on the exhaustiveness. In the above defined logic if adding a free variable to replace 64 bits results in greater complexity, perhaps we can split the data bus into four 16-bit representations and allow the FV tool to run parallel sessions on these four care sets.

```
(top_freevar == 0) |-> (freevar >= 0 && freevar <= 15)
(top_freevar == 1) |-> (freevar >= 16 && freevar <= 31)
(top_freevar == 2) |-> (freevar >= 32 && freevar <= 47)
(top_freevar == 3) |-> (freevar >= 48 && freevar <= 63)
```

This method of splitting the cases, along with the free variable technique to exploit symmetry, can greatly simplify proving properties on complex logic.

TIP 10.20

Consider adding free variables when you need to represent one of several behaviors that will be chosen each cycle based on analog factors or other information unavailable during formal analysis, such as clock domain crossing jitter or tag hits in a blackboxed cache.

DOWNSIDES OF FREE VARIABLES

Although adding a free variable can often improve efficiency, remember that like assumptions, free variables can be a double-edged sword. When there is symmetry to exploit, this technique is a very powerful way to exploit it. But if you have an example where generalizing the analysis causes FPV tools to try to swallow multiple dissimilar pieces of logic all at once, the free variable is probably the wrong choice. You may want to choose case-splitting, running truly separate proofs for the different parts of the design space, instead.

TIP 10.21

If you add a free variable and find that it hurts FPV performance rather than helping it, you are likely working on an example where case-splitting is a better option.

Also, keep in mind that free variables will make your assertions and assumptions less useful in simulation or emulation. If you are planning to reuse your FV collateral in these environments, you will need to carefully add simulation-friendly directives to randomize your free variables, and even then will only get a small fraction of the dynamic coverage you would get from other properties. This is because the random values chosen for free variables will only rarely coincide with those driven by simulation.

ABSTRACTION MODELS FOR COMPLEXITY REDUCTION

Abstraction is one of the most important techniques for scaling the capacity of FPV. In this context, abstraction is a process to simplify the DUT or its input data while retaining enough of the significant logic to have full confidence in our proofs. Many of the previous techniques we have discussed, such as blackboxing, cut points, and free variables, can be considered lightweight abstractions. Most abstraction models make use of free variables. However, now we are discussing more complex abstractions, where we remodel more of the logic to simpler versions that can help us overcome complexity barriers.

There are many ways of abstracting a design. Some of the most common types of abstractions are:

- *Localization*: Eliminate logic that is probably irrelevant to your proofs, such as by adding cut points or blackboxes.
- *Counter abstraction*: Instead of accurately representing a counter, create a reduced representation of its interesting states.
- *Sequence abstraction*: Represent an infinite traffic sequence by analyzing behavior for a small set of generalized packets.
- *Memory abstraction*: Represent a memory with a partial model that only accurately tracks certain elements.
- *Shadow models*: Choose a subset of some block's logic to model, and allow arbitrary behavior for the unmodeled regions.

Because most abstractions significantly simplify the model, you need to keep the issue of false negatives in mind: any bug found may or may not apply to the real model, so you need to double-check potential bug finds against the actual design. You also need to be careful of false positives: as you will see below, while the majority of abstractions are generalizing the model and thus safe in the same way as cut points or blackboxes, some are naturally coupled with assumptions that limit behavior and can hide bugs.

Now we will look at examples of some of the basic types of abstractions.

COUNTER ABSTRACTION

One common cause for complexity is because of the large sequential depths owing to counters. The state space diameter of the design is large in the presence of deep counters, and even worse when there are multiple counters whose outputs can interact: formal analysis may have to reach depths proportional to the product of the counter sizes to handle all possible combinations. As a result, FV of designs with counters can be complex, and is very likely to contain cover points (and thus potential assertion failures) that are not reachable by any feasible bounded proof. Moreover, the scenarios or counterexamples generated by the FV tool tend to be very long and difficult to understand.

One simple way to deal with counters in the verification process is to ignore how the counter should count and simply assign arbitrary values to the counter; this can be easily done by blackboxing the counter or making its output a cut point. In many cases, however, specific values for the counters and the relationships among multiple counters are vital to the design. Therefore, assigning arbitrary values to counters during the verification process may result in unreliable verification. So, we need to see the effect of counter values on the downstream logic before abstracting them out.

Many useful checks can be proved by replacing the counter with a simple state machine model, abstracting the state graph of an N-bit counter to a few states such as: 0, 1, at-least-one, at-least-zero. If you can identify particular values where the counter performs interesting actions, you may find that creating specific states for these makes it easier for the formal tool to quickly reach interesting model states. An example of a counter abstraction is depicted in Figure 10.8.

In Figure 10.8, when in the reset state, the model nondeterministically (based on whether a free variable is 0 or 1) decides each cycle whether to stay in that state or transition to the next state. The simplest types of counter abstractions might only represent the reset state, indicating a noncritical value of the counter,

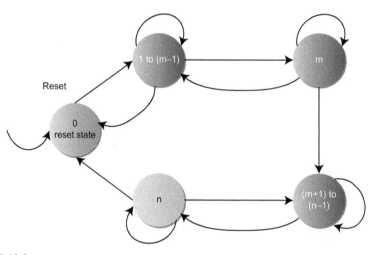

FIGURE 10.8

Abstracted counter model.

and one critical state, representing a counter value that triggers some action by a design.

Figure 10.8 depicts a counter abstraction model where several critical states are determined by the downstream logic. There are two critical states in the figure, n and m. To use this kind of abstraction, you basically need to make the original counter output a cut point, model your abstract state machine and your free variable, and then add assumptions that the original counter output always matches the output of your state machine.

The abstraction model of the counter has significantly fewer states than the counter itself, thereby simplifying the counter for the verification process. Some commercial tools now support built-in counter abstraction as a part of their offerings, making this method much easier to use than in the past.

TIP 10.22

If you are facing complexity issues on a design with one or more counters, consider using a counter abstraction. Be sure to check for automated counter abstraction options in your FPV tool before doing this manually.

SEQUENCE ABSTRACTION

In case of data transport modules, the prime responsibility of the design is to faithfully transfer the data. Sequence abstraction aims at replacing an infinite set of possible data sequences by a small set of generic representatives. The complexity for this kind of transporter arises from the properties written to check that the sequence of the incoming packets is maintained at the output.

Figure 10.9 demonstrates a mechanism to verify a design by replacing all possible packets with three distinct, but otherwise unspecified, packets, C, B, and A. We use a set of rigid free variables to define these generic arbitrary packets, constrain the inputs with assumptions stating that sequences may consist only of these packets, and then check that all possible input sequences are replicated at the output. Using this method, we can check for cases where a packet is dropped, replicated, reordered, or corrupted.

Since we are using free variables to allow arbitrary contents of our three target packets in each run, our proofs are very general, covering any kind of behavior that can be generated by continuous traffic consisting of three arbitrary (but constant) packets. Note, however, that this simplification can hide some potential bugs. For example, suppose a sequence of six distinct packet values, with no two being equal, causes some internal state machine to get into a bad state. This case will be missed, since we are only allowing a total of three distinct packet values.

This abstract model is capable of representing a large class of potential behaviors, and is likely to enable verification of a data transport model with high confidence. You do need to keep the limitations in mind, however, when deciding

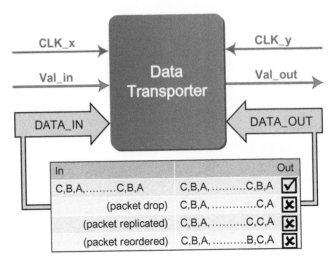

FIGURE 10.9

Sequence abstraction methodology.

whether you can consider such a proof sufficient if your requirement was for full proof FPV; you should have a strong argument for why your limited number of packets should be sufficient to explore the behaviors of your design.

We should also mention that there are some other related forms of sequence abstraction (see [Kom13], for example) where rather than limiting the data that is allowed to arrive, you allow all possible data, but carefully set up your assertions to only track data that matches a small set of tags. This enables a more general analysis, sometimes with the expense of higher verification complexity.

> **TIP 10.23**
>
> If you are facing complexity issues on a data transport design, consider using a sequence abstraction, representing or checking a small set of possible data items instead of fully general sequences of data.

Sequence abstractions are strong enough to represent a wide gamut of sequences and are very useful on data transport designs. Some commercial tools include the sequence abstraction mechanisms as a part of their offerings, thereby allowing the users converge faster on their data transfer designs.

MEMORY ABSTRACTION

Memories, caches, or deep queues are virtually guaranteed to create complexity for FV tools, since they are basically gigantic collections of state elements. For example, a small register file with 16 entries of 64 bits each would roll out to

1,024 state elements, each of which could potentially take on new values during any clock cycle. On the other hand, memories are very regular structures, and we can usually trust that the memory itself is verified separately through specialized techniques. Thus, it is often pragmatic to blackbox memories for FV purposes, and trust that they will be verified elsewhere.

However, we cannot always safely blackbox a memory and still obtain FV proofs. Some of our properties may depend on seeing a value written to memory and then having the same value retrieved; if we completely blackbox the memory, wrong values will potentially be seen for every memory read. Thus, we need some way to functionally represent the memory in our FV environment.

A simple solution is to use parameters to reduce the memory size, as discussed in the section on parameters and size reduction earlier in this chapter. If the memory is read-only, as in a store for preprogrammed microcode, an alternative solution is to replace it with a simple module containing a large set of constant assignments rather than true state elements. Sometimes these solutions will not be sufficient, however, and a more powerful abstraction method must be used to provide a simpler representation of the memory that does not cause complexity for formal engines.

One useful way of abstracting memory is by replacing it with a new version that has a small set of "interesting" locations. For example, suppose we know that even though we have a large memory in our model, our assertions only related to operations using four memory elements at a time. Instead of worrying about all the memory entries, we define a memory that is only concerned about four entries, Entry_1 through Entry_4, as shown in Figure 10.10.

The basic interfaces for the memory would still be maintained, but we only accurately represent the memory for four particular arbitrary locations, to be represented by free variables. Our abstracted module might contain code something like this:

```
// free variables, will define as cut points in FV tool commands
logic [11:0] fv_active_addr[3:0]; // rigid vars for active address
logic [63:0] fv_garbage_data;     // supplies random data
```

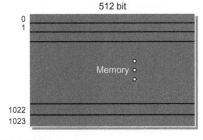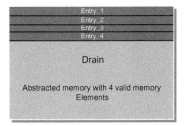

FIGURE 10.10

Memory abstraction.

```
logic [63:0] ABSTRACT_MEM[3:0];  // The abstracted memory
logic garbage;        // 1 if outputting garbage
// Keep active_addrs constant during any given run
active_addr_rigid: assume property (##1 !$changed(fv_active_addr));
always @(posedge clk) begin
  for (int i = 0; i < 4; i++) begin
    if ((op == WRITE) && (addr == fv_active_addr[i]))
      ABSTRACT_MEM[i] <= din;
    if ((op == READ) && (addr == fv_active_addr[i]))
      dout <= ABSTRACT_MEM[i];
  end
  if ((op == READ) && (addr != fv_active_addr[0])
    && (addr != fv_active_addr[1])
    && (addr != fv_active_addr[2])
    && (addr != fv_active_addr[3])
  ) begin
    dout <= fv_garbage_data;
    garbage <= 1;
  end else begin
    garbage <= 0;
  end
end
```

Now, instead of tracking all the entries, our accesses are limited to just four interesting entries. The abstraction is independent of the memory size and we can achieve a huge memory reduction. The complexity of the memory accesses is limited to just tracking four entries. Since these are arbitrary entries, addressed by free variables that can take on any legal value, this does not hurt the generality of any proofs that only involve four memory locations. Any accesses to other locations will return arbitrary "garbage" values.

Once we have modeled the memory, we may also need to make sure our assertions will only make use of the selected addresses, either by adding new assumptions or by adding assertion preconditions. These assumptions are not strictly required, but may be needed to avoid debugging many assertion failures due to memory reads to nonmodeled addresses that return garbage values. If we have created a signal to indicate when a nontracked memory address was accessed, like *garbage* in the code example above, this is fairly simple:

```
// Make sure address used matches a modeled address
no_garbage: assume property (garbage == 0);
```

In some cases, you also might want to return a standard error value for such garbage values, say 32'hDEAD_BEEF, so that you can always check for the error condition with a standard signature. When we try to create such a standard garbage value, we would have to add a constraint on the input not to feed in such a value.

Be careful when using this type of abstraction. If you do have properties which depend on more active memory elements in play than you have allowed for in your abstractions, you might find that your new assumptions or preconditions have overconstrained the environment and hidden important behaviors, creating a risk of false positives. Always be careful to combine this type of abstraction with a good set of cover points.

We should also mention here that some vendors have provided toolkits for automatic memory abstraction, so be sure to look into this possibility before implementing such an abstraction from scratch. This may save you significant effort.

TIP 10.24

If blackboxing or reducing a large memory does not work well for your design, consider implementing a memory abstraction. Also, check to see if your FPV tool vendor has built such a capability directly into the tool, before implementing the abstraction by hand.

SHADOW MODELS

The final form of abstraction we want to discuss is really a catchall for a large class of design abstractions not otherwise covered in this chapter. If you have a particular submodule that is causing complexity issues, you might want to think seriously about replacing it with a *shadow model*, an abstract replacement model that encompasses some but not all of the functionality, using free variables to replace real and complex behaviors with arbitrary simple ones. The counter and memory abstractions we have discussed above can be considered special cases of this: the counter models an abstract state instead of keeping the count, and the memory only keeps track of a subset of its actual information.

Shadow models are not limited to these cases, however. Some other examples where FV users have seen this type of abstraction to be useful include:

- Arithmetic blocks: recognize that an operation has been requested and set output valid at the right time, but return arbitrary results.
- Packet processing: acknowledge completion of a packet and check for errors, but ignore decode logic and other handling.
- Control registers: ignore register programming logic, but preset standard register values, and enable the block to act like a normal Control Register (CR) block for read requests.

Overall, you should consider shadow models a very general technique. Any time you are facing a complexity issue, look at the major submodules of your design, and ask yourself whether you really need to represent the full extent of the logic. Chances are that you will find many opportunities to simplify and make FV more likely to succeed.

> **TIP 10.25**
>
> If you are facing complexity issues on a design with many submodules that cannot be blackboxed, examine the hierarchy for areas where complex logic can be abstracted to a shadow model, while still enabling the proofs of your important assertions.

SUMMARY

Complexity issues are an inherent challenge in FV, because the underlying problems that must be solved by FV engines are NP-complete. Thus, in this chapter we have explored a number of techniques for dealing with complexity and enabling your FV tools to succeed despite initial problems with runtime or memory consumption.

We began by reviewing our cookbook of simple techniques, most of which have been discussed to some degree in earlier chapters.

- Start by choosing the right battle, selecting a good hierarchy on which to run FV.
- Use the right options with your tool's engines.
- Consider blackboxing or parameter reduction to directly reduce the model size.
- Look at opportunities for case-splitting, property simplification, and cut points.
- If focusing on bug hunting, also consider semiformal verification to reach deep states more easily.
- If verifying small changes to a model that has been mostly verified before, consider replacing FPV with incremental FEV.

Once you have gotten as far as you can with these simple techniques, it is time to consider some powerful but more effort-intensive methods.

- Helper assumptions can enable you to significantly reduce the problem space for FV engines. You also need to look at the converse problem, whether too many assumptions are actually adding rather than reducing complexity.
- Generalize analysis using free variables, which can often enable FV engines to solve your problems much more cleanly and quickly.
- Consider developing abstraction models, which can massively reduce complexity by looking at more general versions of your RTL or its input data.

By carefully using a combination of the above methods, we have found that many models that initially appear to be insurmountable challenges for FV can actually be verified successfully.

PRACTICAL TIPS FROM THIS CHAPTER: SUMMARY

10.1 It is recommended to first analyze your design for complexity before you begin an FPV effort. Look at the total number of state elements at the top level and in each major submodule, and try to aim for a size with fewer than 40K state elements.

10.2 Don't panic if you have a bounded proof rather than a full proof. Make sure that the expected deep design behaviors are covered by proving a good set of cover points. A bounded proof may be fully acceptable as a signoff criterion.

10.3 Partition a large component into smaller, independently verifiable components to control the state explosion problem through compositional reasoning. But if you find during wiggling that this causes a need for too much assumption creation, consider verifying the larger model and using other complexity techniques.

10.4 Experiment with the engines offered by the tool, before you start resolving the convergence of hard properties. Many engines are optimized to work on a subset of design styles or property types; choose the right engine for the property under consideration.

10.5 If you are focusing on bug hunting or are in early stages of FPV, and expect many failures, take advantage of tool settings such as start, step, and waypoints to enable more efficient bug hunting runs.

10.6 Blackbox memories/caches, complex arithmetic or data transformation blocks, analog circuitry, externally verified IPs, blocks known to be separately verified, or specialized function blocks unrelated to your FV focus.

10.7 Look for opportunities to take advantage of symmetry and reduce the sizes of regular data structures or occurrences of repeated modules.

10.8 Make sure parameters are used whenever possible to specify the sizes of repeated or symmetric structures in RTL, so you can easily modify those sizes when useful for FPV.

10.9 Decompose the input care set into simple cases to assist convergence on your design.

10.10 When possible, split complex assertions into simpler atomic assertions, whose union would imply the original check intended.

10.11 Use cut points to free design logic and reduce complexity, in cases where you can identify large blocks of logic that are not in a blackboxable standalone module but are irrelevant to your verification. If you are having trouble identifying good cut points, generate a variables file and review the nodes involved in your property's fanin cone.

10.12 If one of your proposed blackboxes needs a "hole" to allow a small piece of FV-critical logic to be visible, use cut points instead of blackboxing. You can declare each of the module's outputs a cut point, except for the one whose logic you need.

10.13 If you suspect potential issues triggered by a design state that cannot be reached within your current proof bound (as detected by failed cover points), consider enhancing your bug hunting with semiformal verification.

10.14 If you have made changes to a stable design that had a time-consuming and complex FPV run, consider replacing FPV regressions with an FEV equivalence proof that your changes did not modify existing functionality.

10.15 If dealing with complexity issues, think about opportunities for "helper assumptions" that would rule out large parts of the problem space, and add some of these to your design.

10.16 If some of your assertions are passing, but others are facing complexity issues, convert your passing assertions to helper assumptions for the next run.

10.17 Monitor the changes in proof performance after adding helper assumptions, and remove them if they turn out not to help.

10.18 If you have a large number of assumptions and are facing complexity issues, examine your assumption set for ones that may not truly be necessary. Sometimes removing unneeded assumptions, even though it widens the problem space covered by FV, can actually improve performance.

10.19 Use rigid free variables to replace large numbers of assertion instances in generate loops with a single nonloop assertion.

10.20 Consider adding free variables when you need to represent one of several behaviors that will be chosen each cycle based on analog factors or other information unavailable during formal analysis, such as clock domain crossing jitter or tag hits in a blackboxed cache.

10.21 If you add a free variable and find that it hurts FPV performance rather than helping it, you are likely working on an example where case-splitting is a better option.

10.22 If you are facing complexity issues on a design with one or more counters, consider using a counter abstraction. Be sure to check for automated counter abstraction options in your FPV tool before doing this manually.

10.23 If you are facing complexity issues on a data transport design, consider using a sequence abstraction, representing or checking a small set of possible data items instead of fully general sequences of data.

10.24 If blackboxing or reducing a large memory does not work well for your design, consider implementing a memory abstraction. Also check to see if your FPV tool vendor has built such a capability directly into the tool, before implementing the abstraction by hand.

10.25 If you are facing complexity issues on a design with many submodules that cannot be blackboxed, examine the hierarchy for areas where complex logic can be abstracted to a shadow model, while still enabling the proofs of your important assertions.

FURTHER READING

[Agg11] Prashant Aggarwal, Darrow Chu, Vijay Kadamby, and Vigyan Singhal, "End-to-End Formal Using Abstractions to Maximize Coverage," Formal Methods in Computer Aided Design (FMCAD) 2011.

[Cla00] E. Clarke, O. Grumberg, S. Jha, Y. Lu, and H. Veith, "Counterexample-Guided Abstraction Refinement," Computer Aided Verification Conference (CAV) 2000.

[Cha13] Lukas Charvat, Ales Smrcka, and Tomas Vojnar, "An Abstraction of Multi-Port Memories with Arbitrary Addressable Units," Fourteenth International Conference on Computer Aided Systems Theory, 2013.

[Dat08] Abhishek Datta and Vigyan Singhal, "Formal Verification of a Public Domain DDR2 Controller Design," VLSI Design 2008.

[Eme05] E. Allen Emerson and Thomas Wahl, "Efficient Reduction Techniques for Systems with Many Components," 2005, http://www.cs.ox.ac.uk/people/thomas.wahl/Publications/ew05a.pdf.

[Gan04] Malay K. Ganai, Aarti Gupta, and Pranav Ashar, "Efficient Modeling of Embedded Memories in Bounded Model Checking," Computer Aided Verification Conference (CAV) 2004.

[Goe11] Richard Goering, "Archived Webinar: Using Scoreboards with Formal Verification," 2011, http://community.cadence.com/cadence_blogs_8/b/ii/archive/2011/12/07/archived-webinar-using-scoreboards-with-formal-verification.

[Jas14] Jasper Design Automation, Jasper Proof Accelerators Data Sheet, http://jasper-da.com/products/proof-accelerators.

[Jon00] Robert Jones, Carl Seger, John O. Leary, Mark Aagard, and Thomas Melham, "A Methodology for Large Scale Hardware Verification," Formal Methods in Computer Aided Design (FMCAD) 2000.

[Kim08] Moonzoo Kim, Yunja Choi, Yunho Kim, and Hotae Kim, "Formal Verification of a Flash Memory Device Driver—An Experience Report," SPIN 2008.

[Kom13] Chris Komar, Bochra Elmeray, and Joerg Mueller, "Overcoming AXI Asynchronous Bridge Verification Challenges with AXI Assertion-Based Verification IP (ABVIP) and Formal Datapath Scoreboards," Design and Verification Conference (DVCon) 2013.

[Kun11] Wolfgang Kunz, "Formal Verification of SystemsonChip—Industrial Experiences and Scientific Perspectives," European Test Symposium (ETS) 2011.

[Log00] G. Logothetis and K. Schneider, "Abstraction from Counters: An Application on Real-Time Systems," Design Automation and Test in Europe (DATE) 2000.

[Loh14] Laurence Loh, "Raising the Bar in Generating High-Quality Configurable IP," Jasper User Group (JUG) 2014.

[Mgu14] M. Achutha KiranKumar, V. Aarti Gupta, and S. S. Bindumadhava, "RTL2RTL Formal Equivalence: Boosting the Design Confidence," Design and Verification Conference (DVCON) Europe 2014.

[Ver98] Miroslav Verev and Randy Bryant, "Efficient Modeling of Memory Arrays in Symbolic Ternary Simulation," Carnegie Mellon University Research Showcase, 1998.

[Wan01] D. Wang, P.-H. Ho, J. Long, J. Kukula, Y. Zhu, T. Ma, and R. Damiano, "Formal Property Verification by Abstraction Refinement with Formal, Simulation and Hybrid Engines," Design Automation Conference (DAC) 2001.

Your new FV-aware lifestyle 11

The presence of microprocessors and ASICs to improve and enrich our lives is pervasive. Advances in manufacturing technology continue to accelerate, which enables creation of exciting, previously unattainable products. There is also a general optimism surrounding the arrival of new *Internet of Things* devices. Many factors are critical in the successful development of new designs. Bob Colwell (former Chief Architect at Intel and former Director, Microsystems Technology Office, DARPA), during a keynote talk at HotChips in August 2013, described the chip designer's task using the algorithm in Figure 11.1.

This algorithm highlights that many interconnected factors are at play in developing a commercially successful product. Industry estimates suggest more than half the effort to create a new design is spent on design verification and validation. Pulling in completion of functional verification tasks and reducing the risk of late surprises can help improve the overall time to market or provide more time for other critical tasks. In this book we've espoused formal verification (FV) as a terrific method to check correctness for an astronomical number of design behavior possibilities. We hope you too are now also an FV technology enthusiast!

When considering how to deploy FV as part of a design verification strategy, start out as a problem solver. By first understanding what issues are troublesome for design and validation, FV capabilities will be better applied and lead to a strong ROI. The historical design verification viewpoint has often been to apply FV as "something extra" that is added to a standard process as an additional form of insurance. Instead, when focus is placed on how to complete design and validation tasks most efficiently, the FV techniques we've described can solve a variety of problems. As we have repeatedly stressed throughout this book, you

```
Given constraints {area,schedule,team,tools,power}
            How can I best design a chip to
                sell huge unit volumes
                     at high yields
                     and high profits?
```

FIGURE 11.1

The canonical "Moore's Law" chip designer's algorithm.

should be thinking of FV as a general toolkit for interacting with and understanding your register transfer level (RTL), rather than as a set of specific point flows. Depending on the challenges encountered by a product development team, there are many ways FV can be beneficially utilized.

USES OF FV

As you have seen in this book, there are many phases of your design and validation flows where FV is likely to enable better results at less cost than alternative methods.

DESIGN EXERCISE

As RTL is being developed, formal property verification (FPV) can provide a key capability to enable early confidence in correct behaviors: an "instant testbench" capability that allows observation of a unit in action without the burden of developing a complex simulation environment. In the earliest stages, particularly when design features are being implemented for the first time, there may be very limited or no validation infrastructure available to exercise the design.

FPV tools can search for valid stimulus sequences that drive the design to targeted conditions and states pertinent to the new code. As the design evolves further, often with little maintenance, FPV will automatically search for new scenarios to reach the desired result. This is a key advantage of FPV that enables early bug hunting: expressing the destination is far easier than describing the journey. You don't need to specify specific inputs at every cycle to lead the design to a particular state.

Design exercise using FPV can be much faster to bring online than development of new testbench collateral and, when successful, can motivate further use of FPV for general bug hunting, or even as the primary unit-level verification technique. Even when simulation is planned for the bulk of the verification effort, the increase in RTL quality due to early FPV can reduce the effort needed to fully develop the testbench. This is because the accelerated discovery of flow-impacting bugs in local designs helps to increase the likelihood that your RTL will behave well when first integrated into larger simulation environments.

BUG HUNTING FPV

Using a bug hunting FPV strategy can be a beneficial complement to a simulation-based validation approach and can lead to discovery of complex bugs missed in simulation tests. The goal for FPV here is to target complex scenarios and discover subtle corner cases that are unlikely to be hit with simulation. This can also apply to late design changes when there isn't adequate time to achieve desired coverage levels using simulation prior to design tapeout.

During verification plan development for FPV bug hunting, the most important design requirements need to be identified and then written as assertions to be checked. FPV can then be used to discover how such requirements may be violated. Alternatively, bug hunting using FPV can be in response to results from simulation-based verification where coverage is not adequate or large numbers of late bug finds lead to a desire for greater validation confidence.

FULL PROOF FPV

Full proof FPV is the most powerful use of FPV, seeking to demonstrate that a design adheres to its specification for all possible behaviors. When successful, full proof FPV leads to extremely high confidence in a design, arguably equivalent to having run all possible simulation tests. Earlier stages of design exercise and bug hunting provide verification feedback while developing an FPV environment that addresses any design complexity issues and ensures checking will cover the design space. Staging the objective incrementally in this fashion also facilitates learning the nuances of the specification and design.

When shifting to full proof FPV, you need to pay significant attention to building a robust environment. The process of wiggling the design to identify the necessary interface assumptions can be time consuming, but needs to be completed for there to be confidence in the proofs. While it is very tempting to direct attention to adding new assertions, it is vital that assumption checking and cover point checking are not delayed until after assertions are proven. Once proofs are completed, make sure to review assertions, assumptions, and cover points with architects and design experts.

You can use full proof FPV to verify complex or risky designs and completely replace simulation testing. This can be especially beneficial in situations where the design behavior is hard to cover through simulation. Full proof FPV typically requires high effort for the high return provided. The completeness of the endeavor is dependent on the definition of a solid set of assertions that fully define the behavior of the design, a solid set of cover points, and a well-checked (minimal) set of assumptions that characterize all possible inputs. All of these together comprise the specification and need to be appropriately reviewed.

SPECIALIZED FPV USING APPS

There has been a significant growth in the creation of prepackaged domain-specific FPV applications or "apps" that can greatly accelerate the use of FPV. The packages cover a wide set of applications and are accessible to less experienced FPV users. In this book, we have focused on five of the most commonly used FPV apps:

- *Reusable Protocol Verification*: Create a set of well-defined properties that describe a commonly used protocol, enabling consistent reuse in formal and simulation-based validation environments.
- *Unreachable Coverage Elimination (UCE)*: Use FPV tools to detect and eliminate cover points that are theoretically impossible to exercise, reducing wasted time in simulation.
- *Connectivity Verification*: In a complex SOC, use FPV to ensure that top-level pins are properly connected to the specified IP blocks under each possible setting.
- *Control Register Verification:* Check that in control register blocks, each register correctly implements its specified access policies.
- *Post-Silicon Debug:* Use the power of FV to isolate and reproduce complex bugs that were missed in previous simulation environments.

While each of these applications is very powerful on its own, the key point here is to think of FPV as a general tool for interacting with your RTL. Whenever embarking upon any kind of RTL-based design or validation process, you should examine the opportunities for FV. Do not limit yourself to the particular applications we described here—these are just a small example of the many possibilities for leveraging formal technologies in your RTL development.

FORMAL EQUIVALENCE VERIFICATION

Most likely, you already had some degree of familiarity with combinational RTL-netlist formal equivalence verification (FEV) before reading this book. Due to the maturity and effectiveness of these tools, this form of FEV is now a standard requirement for checking the synthesis of schematic netlists at nearly every major design company. This method does have some complexities for numerous corner cases, though, and a deeper understanding can definitely increase your effectiveness as a design and validation engineer.

However, a powerful recent development has been the growth of sequential FEV tools, tools that can check the equivalence between two RTL designs, or between a high-level model and an RTL design, without needing to meet the strict state-matching requirements of combinational FEV. This means that in addition to checking netlist implementations, you can effectively use FEV to address a wide variety of challenging problems, including

- *Parameterization*: Checking that RTL functionality has not changed after parameter insertion.

- *Timing Fixes:* Checking that RTL functionality remains identical after a change inserted to fix timing.
- *Pipeline Optimizations*: Checking for identical RTL functionality after a change to the stages of a pipeline.
- *Chicken Bit Validation*: Proving the correctness of a "chicken bit" used to enable backoff of a late or complex design feature.
- *Clock Gating Verification*: Proving that insertion of clock gating has not introduced functional error.

As with FPV, the key here is not to focus on the individual applications—the above are just a small sample—but to clearly understand the type of new capabilities that modern FEV tools provide. We now have effective tools for functionally comparing two RTL (or higher-level) models, even if they are not state-matching, so we should be sure to leverage them effectively in any situation where such comparisons would be useful.

GETTING STARTED

How can you introduce your team to FV? Promising the moon and failing to deliver can leave a negative impression that may require considerable time from which to recover. We encourage you to set ambitious long-term goals, but for the first step, expectations need to be appropriately grounded and achievable. It does help to have someone with experience to smooth out the process of applying FV to a real design. This support might come from the EDA tool vendor or from within your company. In some circumstances, good or even impressive results may come early. In others, it may take some time. Though saving just one re-spin or preventing a recall every few years is probably a more than adequate return for an investment in FV, such success isn't guaranteed, and goals should be set such that desirable results are delivered on a regular cadence.

Begin by looking at the most important problems faced by your design or validation team and try to connect them with the opportunities offered by formal technologies. For example:

- Have your projects been plagued by poor RTL quality during the first cluster and chip level simulations? If so, you may have a strong need for design exercise FPV.
- Do you have a small number of high-risk blocks that resulted in silicon escapes on similar projects? This probably means you should aim for bug hunting FPV.
- Have you had problems with wrong top-level connections discovered at late stages in your designs? In this case, you may want to explore the connectivity FPV application.

- Are you spending too much time in the silicon lab trying to understand logic errors that escaped your other validation environments? This might be effectively addressed by the post-silicon FPV application.
- Has your team failed to correctly implement "chicken bit" features during late bug fixes? If so, it may be the right time to introduce sequential FEV.

If FV is a new technique for your team, the right preparation for both your team and infrastructure is the key to success. Make sure you manage expectations and communicate regularly with all stakeholders. Before beginning preparations, we recommend you identify a design exercise or bug hunting objective on an FV-friendly component where there are correctness concerns.

An FV-friendly component has a well-defined, stable interface and can be evaluated by the FV tool chain fairly quickly. An FV-friendly component is also one where stakeholders are truly committed to supporting the effort (better yet, if they are FV enthusiasts!). Larger designs with significant complexity can be deferred to a later stage after your initial success.

We do encourage full proof FPV use to provide complete unit-level design verification in the long term, but as a first step, targeting discovery of local flaws on a small design can be more tractable. While design verification seeks to ensure the absence of bugs, operationally, success is often subjectively assessed using the rate and number of bugs discovered in a design. A component with flaws can provide the opportunity to demonstrate an immediate impact. While we are recommending the target design component be modest in size, completing the task must be meaningfully motivational—not just "nice to have."

In many work environments, the first step to adopting a new technique is to pilot its use on a previously verified design. Such a pilot is essential to ensure the tools and flows work and also for validators to gain experience be successful on a live project.

ENGINEER PREPARATION TO USE FV

To be successful, engineers need a basic understanding of what FV is, especially the differences from simulation as described in Chapter 4. A basic familiarity with SVA or another assertion language is also critical, and to be effective, a new FVer should understand the architecture and design of the module being verified. Application of FV techniques is a bit of a cultural shift from simulation, so start by building confidence using small examples.

During your ramp-up or pilot, we recommend using a stable component from your target design that has already been validated. You might choose to plant a few simple bugs (crossed wires, replacing XOR gate with an OR gate, or the like) or try to discover already-known bugs in the design to create a challenge. While you may not find real bugs, applying FV techniques will reinforce the ideas presented in this book and accelerate the understanding of the benefits of the shift in validation perspective.

More broadly, design and architecture stakeholders should become familiar with the process required to complete FV proofs, especially how FV environments are built incrementally and what assistance may be required to debug counterexamples that often seem short and unnatural because the system is under-constrained.

TOOL PREPARATION

Prior to working on a "live" design, both the tools and team need to be ready. In addition to tool flows working with your design, start thinking about how your FV runs might be incorporated into regular regressions, just like other forms of validation, to ensure the continued health of your models. As the design evolves, automation of both regressions and FV status tracking can save overhead and accelerate the discovery of newly introduced bugs and environment issues. When the amount of FV collateral increases, automation can help reduce overhead, allowing validators to focus on the verification task. Different FV tool suites provide some functionality to support validation methodology, but such capabilities need to be integrated into your flows. Also, like most other EDA tools, support for tool use and maintenance should be factored in to resource requirements.

MAKING YOUR MANAGER HAPPY

One of the tough challenges that needs to be addressed by FV engineers is to translate the benefits of using formal into a language understandable by management. The most common term used to measure the benefits of a technology is by estimating the ROI, the Return On Investment. We have seen significant ROI resulting from introducing the various FV techniques described in this book—but because they often do not lend themselves to the same metrics that are typically used to measure other validation methods, such as simulation, it is often difficult to understand and communicate this ROI effectively.

Whatever may be the form of FV you deploy on your design, it is always advisable to have some measure of your efforts. Quantification of your investment and results will help the management understand the effectiveness of FV and help to document your work. There are two different schools of thought in defining the ROI of FV. One option is to estimate the absolute ROI to quantify its objective effectiveness, while another school of thought is to compare these numbers to dynamic simulation, the primary competing technology.

The investments in any project for validation would be measured with respect to the engineering costs. These include the human and machine costs incurred to develop the validation environment, run the specific test suite, and validate the design under test (DUT). The returns obtained can be quantified as the number of bugs found and the coverage achieved. ROI would then be a ratio of the returns on the investment made for verifying the design. The cost of exposing and fixing a bug varies drastically based on the phase of the project at which it is exposed. You may also want to take the complexity of each bug into account in your calculations. Considering various such concepts, we present here a proposed method to calculate the ROI of formal for your project.

ROI CALCULATION

We recommend tabulating all the details by closely tracking your time spent since the inception of the activity until you get a logical conclusion. Some of the parameters that can be of help to you are depicted in Table 11.1.

Absolute ROI can be derived from the parameters defined in Table 11.1. The set of derived parameters are detailed in Table 11.2.

Often, it would make sense to compare the ROI derived from FV to similar efforts of running dynamic simulations (or similar technologies such as emulation). We indicate the simulation with the suffix "_D". Though it is not an apples-to-apples comparison, examining these numbers side-by-side can provide additional insights into design and verification processes.

To create a practical set of comparative ROI calculations, we recommend using the same parameters as above, except the number of bugs found should be replaced with the percentage of bugs found by different methodologies. The relative ROI list should look like the one depicted in Table 11.3.

Table 11.1 Parameter Definitions

Parameter	Depiction
Number of engineers worked on the problem	N_{E_F}
Average bandwidth/engineer	B_{w_F}
Number of weeks spent on effort	W_{w_F}
Total time spent in hours	$T_{s\_F} = B_{w\_F}{}^a W_{w\_F}{}^a 40^b$
Project schedule in weeks	P_{w_F}
Scaled engineering costs	$C_{E\_F} = T_{s\_F}/(P_{w\_F}{}^a 40)$
Machines used for computations	M_{c_F}
Runs/week	R_{w_F}
Number of days of run	D_{w_F}
Total machine-days/week	$T_{m\_F} = M_{c\_F}{}^a R_{w\_F}{}^a D_{w\_F}$
Project machine-days/week	P_{m_F}
Scaled machine costs	$C_{m\_F} = T_{m\_F}/P_{m\_F}$
Coverage (% cover points hit)	Cov_{tot_F}
Bugs found by the method	N_{B_F}

[a] Assuming eight hours/day for a five-day work week = 40 hours/week.
[b] Machine runs are not limited to a working day but for the whole week = seven days/week.

Table 11.2 Derived ROI Parameters

ROI parameter	Depiction
Bugs found by FV	N_{B_F}
Total coverage achieved by FV	Cov_{tot_F}
Bug–engineering cost ROI	N_{B_F}/C_{E_F}
Bug–machine cost ROI	N_{B_F}/C_{m_F}
Coverage–engineering cost ROI	Cov_{tot_F}/C_{E_F}
Coverage–machine cost ROI	Cov_{tot_F}/C_{m_F}

Table 11.3 Basic Comparisons of Formal and Dynamic Verification ROI

ROI parameter	Formal	Dynamic	Relative
Bugs% found by FV	$N_{B\_F}/(N_{B\_F}+N_{B\_D})$	$N_{B\_D}/(N_{B\_F}+N_{B\_D})$	N_{B_F}/N_{B_D}
Total coverage achieved	Cov_{tot_F}	Cov_{tot_D}	
Bug–engineering cost ROI	$B_{EC\_F}=N_{B\_F}/C_{E\_F}$	$B_{EC\_D}=N_{B\_D}/C_{E\_D}$	B_{EC_F}/B_{EC_D}
Bug–machine cost ROI	$B_{MC\_F}=N_{B\_F}/C_{m\_F}$	$B_{MC\_D}=N_{B\_D}/C_{m\_D}$	B_{MC_F}/B_{MC_D}
Coverage–engineering cost ROI	$C_{EC\_F}=Cov_{tot\_F}/C_{E\_F}$	$C_{EC\_D}=Cov_{tot\_D}/C_{E\_D}$	C_{EC_F}/C_{EC_D}
Coverage–machine cost ROI	$C_{mC\_F}=Cov_{tot\_F}/C_{m\_F}$	$C_{mC\_D}=Cov_{tot\_D}/C_{m\_D}$	C_{mC_F}/C_{mC_D}

A few elements are not accounted for in these formulas: licensing costs, machine procurement costs, and license utilization numbers. We omit these here, since they involve many business issues beyond the technical focus of this book, though you may wish to consider these aspects when analyzing the usage at your company.

The ROI numbers can give a decent picture of the effectiveness of one methodology compared to the other. This may be a bit tricky though, as one might argue that the FV and simulation portions of the team are given fundamentally different validation problems, and finding bugs might be inherently easier or harder for the blocks given to one team rather than another. Regardless of this issue, calculations using these factors can result in interesting numbers to examine and discuss.

In an ideal world, a scientifically controlled comparison experiment would start both the simulation (DV) and FV activities at the same time, by separate, equally talented teams trying to complete identical projects without talking to each other, and compare the time taken by the methodologies to achieve full convergence and verification closure. Unfortunately, we find it hard to imagine any company agreeing to spend the budget or manpower needed for such an elaborate controlled experiment.

Table 11.4 shows the ROI results based on a recent Intel project, where the FV and DV teams were working together on validating parts of the design.

These ROI numbers do vary, but they consistently show that for this project, formal methods were very competitive.

It has been our experience that these numbers are typically lower as we delay the deployment of FV to later phases of a project. Since the health of the model continually increases, as engineers find and fix bugs discovered in simulation, we have even experienced cases where FV introduced too late in a project merely reproduced known issues and did not find any new bugs. In such a case, however, FV still provided full coverage of interesting scenarios and gave a much higher level of confidence to the designers. While this aspect is hard to measure, you do need to keep this qualitative benefit in mind: even when not finding new bugs, FV can result in a positive contribution to the project.

Table 11.4 A Real Intel Example of ROI Tracking

ROI parameter	FV	DV
Engineers worked on the problem	2	4
Average bandwidth/engineer	75%	75%
# WWs spent on effort	32	40
# hrs/WW	40	40
Total engineer time in hours	1920	4800
Project schedule in weeks	84	84
Scaled engineering costs	0.57	1.43
Machines used for computations	8	30
Runs/week	1	4
# days of run	3	0.75
Total machine-days/week	24	90
Project machine-days/week	157	157
Scaled machine costs	0.15	0.57
Coverage (% cover points hit)	28%	25%
Bugs (%)	71.5	28.5

	Item	FV	DV	ROI (FV advantage)
1	Engineering Costs	0.57	1.43	
2	Machine Costs	0.15	0.57	
ROI#1	Bugs/Eng Costs	125.13	19.95	6.3X
ROI#2	Bugs/Machine Costs	467.73	49.72	9.4X
ROI#3	Coverage/Eng Costs	0.25	0.09	2.8X
ROI#4	Coverage/Machine costs	0.92	0.22	4.2X

BUG COMPLEXITY RANKING

You may have noticed one critical flaw in the above calculations: we cannot attach the same weight for all the bugs. The kind of issues found early in a typical design would be very straightforward and can be easily found through directed tests. In later stages, there may be very subtle bugs lurking, even ones that might lead to expensive silicon recalls if not discovered through FV. Thus, you may want to come up with some kind of weighting for your bug finds, as in the example in Table 11.5. The numbers may seem somewhat arbitrary, but they are based on estimates by project experts of the relative risk that those bugs would have escaped to a late project phase or to silicon, and the level of extra project costs that would have resulted.

The depiction in Table 11.5 is for a design where we were running DV and FV in parallel. The issues were placed in different categories after discussions with the designers and microarchitects. The power of FV can be easily seen from the number and the kind of bugs found by different methods as depicted in the table. The value of high-quality or critically complex bugs, often bugs that could only be found in practice by formal methods, can be thousands of times greater than the value of a simple bug.

PROGRESS TRACKING

Another important factor to keep in mind is that during the course of design and validation, you need ways to report FV progress to your management. This can

Table 11.5 Modified Bug Calculation Using Complexity Ratings

Bug complexity calculator	Equation	Weight	Number of bugs		Weighted #	
			FV	DV	FV	DV
Simple bug	FV = DV	1	20	2	20	2
Could have been found after longer DV runs	FV = 100 DV	100	6	1	600	100
Moderate corner case, maybe possible in DV	FV = 500 DV	500	1	1	500	500
FV quality bug; Would be extremely lucky to catch in pre-silicon	FV = 1000 DV	1000	5		5000	
Critically complex bug	FV = 5000 DV	5000	1		5000	
		Total	33	4	11120	602
		%	89	11	95	5

be challenging when first introducing these methods: in the context of simulation, many managers are used to seeing a set of standard coverage metrics gradually ramp up over the course of a project, and not having a similar measure for FV can make them very nervous. This issue is aggravated by the fact that FV efforts can be "lumpy," with sudden increases in proof completion at points where you successfully overcome some complexity obstacle, such as introducing a new abstraction model, or add a good assumption that enables correct behavior. In fact, there are several ways of tracking the progress on formal front, and by combining these you can increase the likelihood that you continually have reasonable data to enable reporting FV progress.

In cases where you have a large set of discrete proof targets, either properties for FPV or key points for FEV, a simple tracking of the total set of targeted points and their proof status can often be very useful, as in the example illustrated in Figure 11.2. This table shows the proof status of all properties during each work week (WW) of a project.

Using this measurement can be tricky though, especially if additional assertions and cover points are being continually created (a good practice we recommend) based on observed failure traces and interesting hypotheses that arise during debug. This might cause relatively long periods during which the growth in the proportion of successful proofs is relatively small.

Thus a complementary measure, *assertion density*, can be an excellent supplement, showing how the set of assertions, assumptions, and cover points is growing throughout the verification process, increasing the confidence and functional coverage of the model. Typically you might measure the average assertion statements (including assumptions and covers) per line of code or per module. Growth

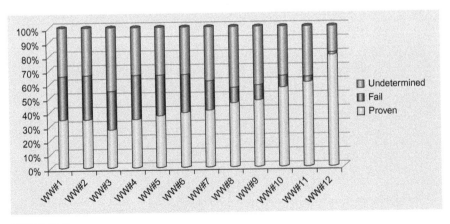

FIGURE 11.2

FPV tracking chart.

in this graph can be used to show clear progress during early wiggling, when the overall growth in successful proofs is temporarily stalled while needed interface constraints are being discovered (see Figure 11.3).

Another important mode of tracking the formal progress is looking at the bug trend throughout the design cycle. Depicted in Figure 11.4 is an example project timeline through which the number of bugs found during each WW is closely monitored. As the design nears freeze, we would hope to see a decline in the bug trend. If the growth in successful proof count is slowed due to finding numerous

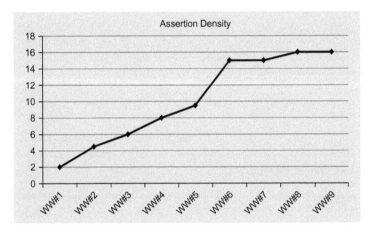

FIGURE 11.3

Tracking assertion density improvement.

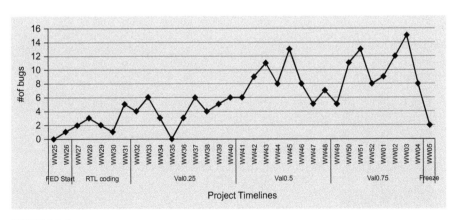

FIGURE 11.4

Trends in bug discovery over the course of a project.

bugs, this measure is a good way to show this alternative form of progress. It might also be good to use the weighted bug count, as described in the previous section, rather than the absolute number of bugs, to properly capture the importance of subtle high-quality bugs that can be found only with formal methods. Figure 11.4 shows an example of a project's bug trend graph.

You should also keep in mind that versions of some conventional measures of validation progress can also be reported in an FV context. You can report the number of SVA cover points successfully hit, though you need to make it clear that this means something different for formal and simulation contexts. If a cover point is hit in FV, this usually means a large class of cases related to that cover point is being analyzed by the formal environment, rather than the simulation interpretation that this just shows a hit on a single test. Depending on the functionality offered by the FV tools you are using, you may also be able to report code, block, or expression coverage, though these similarly have more expansive interpretations for FV than simulation. Thus, you should report these when available, but avoid directly comparing them side-by-side with simulation numbers.

WHAT DO FVers REALLY DO?

For a long time the tasks, results, and needs of engineers who were responsible for verifying designs or design engineers who took advantage of FV tools were not well understood by the authors' peer groups. In your case, we hope this book has helped to demystify the process for you. You still may face challenges, however, in enabling others to understand this new mode of interaction with your RTL models.

In discussions with customers, tool suppliers, management, and other stakeholders, we used the following lighthearted descriptions to help clarify FV responsibilities throughout the product development lifecycle and clarify how partnership with them could improve the impact of FV and accelerate the broader project objectives.

FVers are like:

Astronomers: FV work requires creating upfront abstract theories (assertions) about how the universe (design) behaves based on partial information and then refining our understanding through additional observations that are inconsistent with the original specification (counterexamples). While verifying a design, many discoveries are made about how the design actually works that are frequently undocumented. FV tools explore the universe of all possible stimulus variable values unless constraints are introduced.

Wine makers: Pruning, grafting, and genetic engineering of the RTL is often needed to complete complex proofs. Proof development can require building special models of the RTL that are tailored to specific proofs. Automated pruning by an FV tool greatly reduces checking complexity, but still may not be enough, so users can further prune a design. Auxiliary proofs grafted onto the process, to show simpler logic is functionally equivalent to the real RTL, allow FPV tools to replace the more complex RTL and end up with less overall complexity.

Quilt makers: Complex properties or designs can require a divide-and-conquer approach. In these circumstances, the assumptions on each block must be proved as assertions elsewhere, and may themselves require new assumptions. The final proof is stitched together with many specifications and proofs to verify the larger objective. Infrastructure support that tracks the status and dependency relationship of the individual specification proofs is essential for success.

Environmentalist: Reduce, reuse, recycle. Continuous process improvement is a goal of all engineering work. From one project to the next, proof development infrastructure can be highly reusable. Interface protocol specifications can often be reused, but where logic changed significantly, parts of the proof decomposition strategies could often be recycled. Another form of reuse is through close collaboration with other FV teams. We have found it very beneficial to bring colleagues together to share ideas and challenges and work on unified, common approaches that would improve verification quality and reduce effort.

Dentists: Regular checkups of the RTL (regression) are essential to avoid "proof decay." With daily design changes, the logic must be re-verified to ensure no new errors have been introduced. Some proofs may be developed for a one time purpose (design exploration or designer exercise), but the vast majority of proofs developed are intended for reuse. Effort put into making proofs robust and reusable quickly pays off.

Inventors: Solving hard problems often requires experimentation and innovation, coming up with creative compromises or abstractions to counter the challenges of FV on large or complex designs. It is also impressive to see how designers can find new opportunities to utilize this new mode of RTL interaction to build apps or other solutions to design challenges.

Bungee jumpers: Quick dives (searches) into the behavior space of a design can be achieved with a formal model. "What if" inquiries enable a validator to quickly observe new behaviors and waveforms. Interactive proof systems that incrementally add or remove behavioral constraints provide a very efficient means to reverse engineer a design and to find the root cause of a failure.

Judge: Verification engineers need to act as impartial reviewers of whether or not a design satisfies its specification. The ultimate goal is not to find bugs, but to affirm the functional correctness of the design. In doing so, it is important to assess the internal design correctness and also view the design from the broader perspective of how the design will be utilized.

SUMMARY

We hope this book has imparted new skills and energized your enthusiasm to apply FV. The application of FV provides a game-changing technique to vastly improve the modern digital design development process. Using a design and verification strategy that includes FV technology can greatly increase confidence in a design's correctness, accelerate bug discovery, and reduce schedule uncertainty. FV can enable creation of more robust designs and a reduced likelihood that a "diving save" will be needed to address late discoveries.

The strategies discussed in this book evolved over time in response to opportunities identified to positively impact project demands: schedule, quality, and resources. Perhaps the most significant development over the last decade has been the improved maturity of tools, along with continued advances in the capabilities of the underlying checking algorithms and supporting methodology. The arrival of reusable libraries and FV proof lifecycle infrastructure, such as debuggers, databases, and regression tools, have all contributed to transitioning FV from an art toward a rigorous engineering practice. Commercially available tool kits that package domain-specific expertise also have lowered the startup costs. A decade or so ago you would have needed an FPV expert for every verification step, to tweak the underlying formal engine and enable FPV execution to reach your objectives. Now, advances and standardization of practices have reduced this effort to the point where a user's time is almost entirely focused on driving actual verification of the design.

In the past, the possibility of finding rare corner-case bugs was seen as the chief selling point of FV. Discovering subtle corner-case bugs and latent bugs won't happen every day, but the satisfaction of finding such bugs or being able to provide assurance a design is sound never grows old. We hope, however, that we have convinced you that FV is more than just a last-mile strategy for finding rare bugs.

Use of FV is more than a convenience, it is mind-expanding—a tool that enables creativity to flourish. Modern designs are extremely complex with many concurrent actions. FV tools enable interaction with RTL in fundamentally new ways, allowing evaluation of and experimentation with possibilities that cannot be calculated in one's mind. We can explore the "billions and billions" of possible design behaviors and guide the chip development process toward producing a robust part. Through traditional verification, equivalence checking, or specialized apps, we can use FV to influence and improve all aspects of our design process, from front-end architecture down to post-silicon debug.

Now that you have reached the end of this book, it is time for you to stop reading about FV and start practicing it. Grab a small RTL model and fire up your company's favorite FPV or FEV tool. Whether you think of yourself as an astronomer, a wine maker, a dentist, an inventor, or just a regular engineer trying to do your job more efficiently, you will find that this new form of RTL analysis will expand your horizons and open new possibilities in your design and verification flows. Once you get started, also be sure to visit http://formalverificationbook.com and share your experiences. We hope to hear from you soon!

FURTHER READING

[Bau13] Jason Baumgartner, Viresh Paruthi, Ambar Gadkari, Pradeep Nalla, and Sivan Rabinovich, "Formal Verification at IBM-Applications and Algorithms," Workshop on Making Formal Verification Scalable and Useable, Chennai Mathematical Institute, 2013.

[Col13] Robert Colwell, The Chip Design Game at the End of Moore's Law *Hot Chips*, August 2013.

[Kas09] Jim Kasak, Ross Weber, and Holly Stump, "Formal Verification Deployment Reveals Return on Investment," Chip Design Magazine, http://chipdesignmag.com/display.php?articleId=3398.

[Par11] Viresh Paruthi, "Large-Scale Application of Formal Verification: From Fiction to Fact," Formal Methods in Computer Aided Design, 2011.

[Sin11] Vigyan Singhal, "Deploying Formal in a Simulation World," International Conference on Computer-Aided Verification, 2011.

Index

Note: Page numbers followed by "*f*" and "*t*" refer to figures and tables, respectively.